Image © David Lambroughton

Contents

Southeastern BC
Regions 4: Kootenay
Region 8: Okanagan

Testimonials

"Tells you anything and everything you could possibly want to know about fishing…"

~ *Vancouver Sun*

"What a goldmine of information!!! Just what I was looking for!"

~ *Gerry Moore*

"With their guides you will be an expert on the lake even before you get there."

~ *Fishing4Fools.com*

British Columbia

Total Area... 944 735 km²
Population...4 113 487
Capital...Victoria
Largest City...Vancouver
Highest Point...Mount Fairweather
4 663 meters (15 299 ft)
Tourism info...1.800.HELLO.BC
www.hellobc.com

1

#106- 1500 Hartley Ave,
Coquitlam, BC, V3K 7A1
Toll Free: 1-877-520-5670
E-mail: info@backroadmapbooks.com

Backroad Mapbooks

DIRECTORS
Russell Mussio
Wesley Mussio

VICE PRESIDENT
Chris Taylor

COVER DESIGN & LAYOUT
Farnaz Faghihi

COVER PHOTO
David Lambroughton

CREATIVE CONTENT
Russell Mussio
Wesley Mussio

PROJECT MANAGER
Andrew Allen

PRODUCTION
Farah Aghdam, Joana Maki,
Shaun Filipenko, Oliver Herz,
David Mancini, Matthew Steblyna,
AJ Strawson, Dale Tober

SALES / MARKETING
Chris Taylor / Nazli Faghihi / Basilio Bagnato

EDITOR
Russell Mussio

Library and Archives Canada Cataloguing in Publication
Ernst, Trent
Southeastern BC fishing mapbook [cartographic material] : region 4:Okanagan, region 8: Kootenay : BC's most complete lake & stream guide / Trent Ernst. -- 1st ed.

(Fishing mapbooks)
Includes index.
ISBN 978-1-897225-32-5

1. Fishing--British Columbia--Okanagan Valley (Region)--Maps. 2. Fishing--British Columbia--Kootenay Region--Maps. 3. Fishing--British Columbia--Okanagan Valley (Region)--Guidebooks. 4. Fishing--British Columbia--Kootenay Region--Guidebooks. 5. Okanagan Valley (B.C. : Region)--Bathymetric maps. 6. Kootenay Region (B.C.)--Bathymetric maps. 7. Okanagan Valley (B.C. : Region)--Guidebooks. 8. Kootenay Region (B.C.)--Guidebooks. I. Title. II. Title: Fishing mapbook, southeastern BC. III. Series.

G1172.S625E63E75 2008   799.109711'5   C2008-902316-1

Copyright © 2014 Mussio Ventures Ltd.

Acknowledgements

We would like to thank everyone for their support and encouragement to resurrect the Fishing Mapbook series. This book is a collaboration of many organizations and people, and is intended to be a resource that can and will be used by all anglers on southern BC. First off, this is a big thank you to the Freshwater Fisheries Society of BC, in particular Brian Chan. They helped us refine our lake list and gave us many helpful pointers along the way. Then there is Trent Ernst. He took over the writing and research of the lakes and streams and has really learned to fish out impressive information. Of course we cannot forget the helpful team of mappers, editors and graphics people at Backroad Mapbooks. These are the people who pieced everything together in such a convenient, yet comprehensive package. Thank you Farah Aghdam, Andrew Allen, Basilio Bagnato, Farnaz Faghihi, Nazli Faghihi, Shaun Filipenko, Oliver Herz, Joana Maki, David Mancini, Matthew Steblyna, AJ Strawson, Chris Taylor, and Dale Tober.

When doing our research, we had to consult numerous people who live and play in the Okanagan and Kootenays. Again, we would like to thank the fine folks at the Freshwater Fisheries Society of BC. The fisheries biologists in the Kootenays and Okanagan, specifically Brian Jantz in the Okanagan and John Bell in the Kootenays, were also great helps, and added tremendously to the quality of the information.

We would like to thank Savas, Nick and Matt at Trout Water Fly & Tackle who reviewed and updated many of the Okanagan area lakes. They really know their stuff. Some other people who went above the call of duty include Gordon at Barren Fly and Tackle, Rob at Castlegar Sport and Fly Shop and Gord at the Kootenay Fly shop. And a special thanks to Len at Vernon Outdoors, Sandy at Kencraft and Ellery at Oliver Home Hardware who all provided a lot of information for lakes in the book. Also, club contacts like Ruben with the Kalamalka Fly Fishers provided a fair bit of information.Finally, to all those people we talked to and forgot to mention, thank you. It is our forgetfulness, not our ingratitude that precludes us mentioning you specifically.

The maps and charts are courtesy of Backroad Mapbooks. However, they had to source Fisheries for the templates for the Lake Depth Chart Maps as well as Geogratis and the Ministry of Sustainable Resources for the source data for the overview maps.

Finally we would like to thank Allison, Devon, Jasper, Nancy, Madison and Penny Mussio for their continued support of the Backroad Mapbook Series. As our family grows, it is becoming more and more challenging to break away from it all to explore our beautiful country.

Sincerely,

Russell and Wesley Mussio

Disclaimer

Help Us Help You

A comprehensive resource such as Fishing Mapbooks for Southeastern BC could not be put together without a great deal of help and support. Despite our best efforts to ensure that everything is accurate, errors do occur. If you see any errors or omissions, please continue to let us know.

All updates will be posted on our web site: www.backroadmapbooks.com

Please contact us at:
Mussio Ventures Ltd.
Unit 106- 1500 Hartley Ave
Coquitlam, BC, V3K 7A1

Email: updates@backroadmapbooks.com
P: 604-521-6277 toll free 1-877-520-5670
F: 604-521-6260 , www.backroadmapbooks.com

Introduction
Fishing Southeastern BC

Welcome to the Second Edition of the Fishing Mapbook for Southeastern BC!

The Okanagan and Kootenay regions together make up Southeastern BC; boasting some of the most stunning landscapes and scenery in Canada. With its majestic mountains, towering peaks, awe inspiring waterfalls and electric-blue lakes, Southeastern British Columbia is a land of pure and awesome beauty.

This guidebook features many of your favourite lakes and streams found in the Okanagan and Kootenay regions of British Columbia. Our Fishing Mapbooks are designed to take the guesswork out of your fishing experience. Spend less time traveling the waterways and more time reeling in the prize, by using our depth charts and river maps to pin down fishing hot spots. Add in our helpful fishing tips, access details and information on facilities, and you have all that you need to fish with confidence.

With some of the warmest lakes and rivers in the province as well as streams that flow directly from glaciers, you can expect to find warm and cold water species coexisting, sometimes in the same body of water. Perhaps one of the best kept secrets amongst the locals is what lurks in the depths of these valley lakes and rivers. Start your own epic tale by hooking into a variety of sportfish species including trout, char, kokanee, bass and even Chinook salmon on lakes like Arrow, Kootenay, Mara and Okanagan or rivers like the Columbia and Shuswap.

Not to be overlooked are the many lakes that lie within the magnificent hills surrounding these valleys. These hidden backcountry gems offer incredible angling opportunities. The prolific fly hatches, nutrient rich environment and crisp waters make the high country of this region a fantastic lake fishing destination. The incredible fishing, serenity and stunning scenery of these mountain lakes make for the ideal getaway. From remote, 4wd access lakes, to even more remote, hike-in lakes that see only a handful of anglers a year, there is a destination for everyone in Southeastern BC.

Home to the world famous Gerrard trout and the Elk River, arguably, one of the finest cutthroat rivers in the world, the BC interior holds epic legends for its fishing adventures. The big lakes, small streams, high and low elevation lakes make this region an ideal playground for anglers.

You will need to weave your way through a maze of winding backroads through this adventurer's paradise to reach many of these fishing hotspots. We recommend you equip yourself with a copy of our comprehensive regional Backroad Mapbooks (Thompson Okanagan and/or the Kootenay Rockies BC) as well as our Backroad GPS Map for BC. In addition to the detailed backcountry maps, our Mapbooks and Backroad GPS Maps provide descriptions on everything from camping areas to other fishing opportunities and are the perfect accompaniment to the Fishing Mapbook Series.

We certainly hope you enjoy using this guidebook as much as we did making it. Rest assure the detailed combination on how and where to fish in Southeastern British Columbia within this fishing guidebook is the most comprehensive source you will ever need to enjoy your fishing adventures on this magnificent land.

BACKROAD HISTORY

The Fishing Mapbook Series evolved from research done when creating the Backroad Mapbooks. Russell and Wesley Mussio, as well as their team of researchers, really enjoy exploring and fishing new lakes but would get frustrated trying guess where to fish. After stumbling across the depth charts for a few lakes, they learned how to read a lake a lot quicker and start working the right areas much sooner.

Although there were a few other companies producing individual lake charts and selling them for a premium, in typical entrepreneurial fashion the brothers decided to take it one step further. Rather than selling individual charts, they put several lakes in a single reasonably priced book and added valuable information on everything from directions and facilities to fishing tips and stocking information.

Today, the series have evolved into even bigger books and now cover the popular streams in the area. We also work with key people in the industry to help gain valuable insight into each lake, river and region we cover.

Regional Boundaries

Lake Chart Classifications

✛✛	Rocks		Sandbar
🦅	Swamp / Marsh		Provincial Park
→	Stream		Lake
▬▬	Highway	──	Side Road
═══	Main Road	----	Old Road/Trail
═══	Railways	━━━	Management Zones

Recreational Activities and Miscellaneous

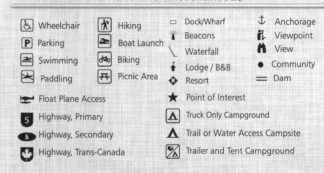

♿	Wheelchair	🚶	Hiking		Dock/Wharf	⚓	Anchorage
P	Parking	🏊	Boat Launch		Beacons		Viewpoint
	Swimming	🚴	Biking		Waterfall		View
	Paddling	🛝	Picnic Area		Lodge / B&B	●	Community
	Float Plane Access				Resort	═	Dam
5	Highway, Primary			★	Point of Interest		
5	Highway, Secondary			△	Truck Only Campground		
	Highway, Trans-Canada			▲	Trail or Water Access Campsite		
					Trailer and Tent Campground		

Conservation Officer Service District Offices

Castlegar..250-365-8611
Cranbrook 250-489-8537
Creston 250-428-3220
Fernie..250-423-7551
Invermere..250-342-4266
Nelson...250-354-6397
Revelstoke...250-837-9683
Grand Forks...250-442-4350
Kelowna, Penticton, Princeton & Vernon.....................
....1-877-356-2029

Regions 4 & 8: Kootenays & Okanagan

Fish and Wildlife Regional Office Kootenays
Cranbrook: 205 Industrial Rd. G, V1C 7G5, 250-489-8540

Kootenay Trout Hatchery
Fort Steele: 4522 Fenwick Rd, V0B 1N0, 250-429-3214

Fish and Wildlife Regional Office Okanagan
Penticton: 102 Industrial Place, V2A 7C8, 250-490-8200

Summerland Trout Hatchery
Summerland: 13405 Lakeshore Drive S, V0H 1Z1, 250-494-0491

Map Key
Southeastern BC

River Hot Spots

1. Columbia River
2. Elk River
3. Kettle River
4. Shuswap River
5. St Mary River
6. Wigwam River

Backroad Mapbooks
BRMB
backroadmapbooks.com

Lake Hot Spot - Region 4 (Kootenay)

1. Arrow Lake
2. Box Lake
3. Cartwright Lake
4. Champion Lakes (1,2 & 3)
5. Christina Lake
6. Cleland Lake
7. Duck Lake
8. Kootenay Lake - North
9. Monroe Lake
10. North Star Lake
11. Premier Lake
12. Slocan Lake
13. Summit Lake (Nakusp)
14. Whiteswan Lake
15. Whitetail Lake

Lake Hot Spot - Region 8 (Okanagan)

16. Arlington Lakes
17. Beaver (Swalwell) Lake
18. Davis Lake
19. Dee Lake Chain (Dee, Island, Deer, Crooked)
20. Hidden Lake
21. Jackpine Lake
22. Jewel Lake
23. Kentucky & Alleyne Lakes
24. Mabel Lake
25. Osprey Lake
26. Oyama Lake
27. Pinaus Lake Chain
28. Sugar Lake
29. Vaseaux Lake
30. Wood Lake

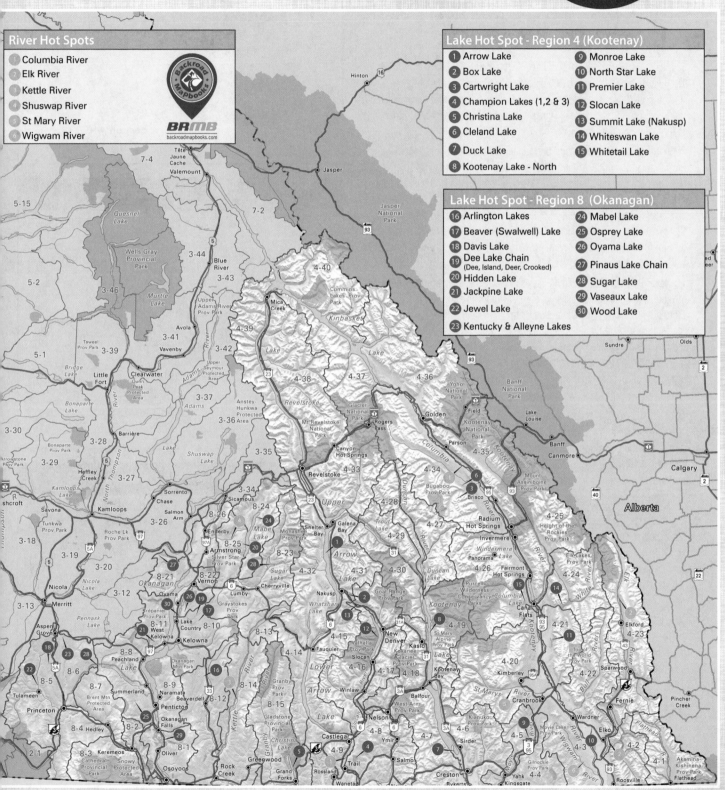

Navigating

Fish Species

The book begins with a rather elaborate section on the main sportfish species in the region. In it we give pointers on how to identify and fish for these
sometimes elusive fish. These tips should not be overlooked, as they are an
accumulation of many years of personal experience and research. Of course
there are many anglers out there that know a lot more than we do, but few
sources put it all together in such a convenient, compact package. Whether
you are new to the area or new to fishing or have fished these holes for years,
we guarantee that following these tips will help you find more fish.

The Lakes (Bathymetric Charts)

The lake fishing section of this book features all of the favourites as well
as some of those lesser know lakes that can produce that lifetime fishing
memory. With so many lakes to choose from, the task was indeed a challenge
to try to get that right mix in our book.

Similar to this book's predecessors, Fishing BC Okanagan and Kootenays, we
have highlighted many of the better lakes with depth charts. These charts, if
read properly will help you pinpoint the likely areas on a lake to start fishing.
These charts show the contours of the lake and help readers figure out where
the shoals, drop-offs, hidden islands or basically any sort of water structure
that will likely hold fish is located. Reviewing these charts before visiting the
lake for the first time could reveal where to find the fish. At the very least, they
will help you know where to start fishing.

We have also included the fish species and whether they are stocked or not
for each listing. In some cases we even tell you how and what to fish with. If
there are no fishing tips included under the individual listing, you can refer to
the front or back of the book to refresh yourself on tactics and fly patterns of
the prominent species in that lake. Of course, when you get to the lake and
there are other anglers there do not be shy to ask where to fish and what to
use. Most people are more than willing to help out.

Rivers & Streams

The river or streams section is new to the series, but follows the similar pattern of including fish tips, access and facilities for each stream that is highlighted. Of course, the river maps are a popular feature that include fishing
pools and popular access points where possible.

Fishing Tips & Techniques

Near the back of the book this is another excellent resource to refer to. In this
section, we give pointers on how to fish using the various lake and stream
fishing techniques, as well as some useful fishing tips. Constant referral to
this section will help anglers new and old to the sport.

Map Key & Index

There are also handy planning tools such as the Overview Map and an Index.
If you know the waterbody you are planning on visiting, you simply turn to the
lakes or river section and find the listing you are interested in. Alternatively,
you can look it up in the index to see what page it is listed on.

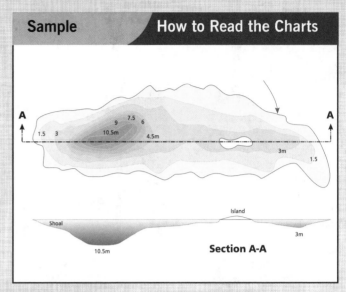

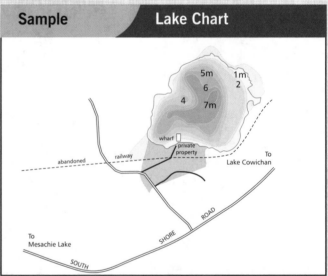

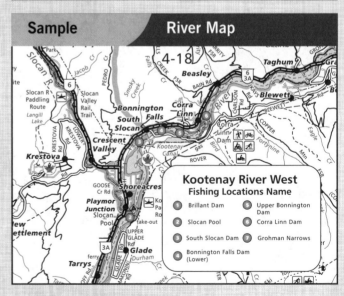

Southeastern BC Fish Species

Southeast BC has a good variety of species of fish. Because most of the rivers flow into the Columbia, and a series of hydroelectric projects have stopped the migration of salmon upstream, there are a very few anadromous species in the region. The two exceptions are the Okanagan River, which sports a fair return of sockeye, and the Shuswap, which features fairly strong returns of Chinook and Coho. The occasional steelhead will find its way up the Okanagan, but not enough to call it a fishery.

Brown Trout were originally introductions into Canada from Scotland, and is considered one of the most difficult trout to catch; it is wily and suspicious of anything that isn't presented perfectly. However, a well presented fly has been known to capture their attention. Brown trout were introduced into the Kettle River system, and can still be found in the West Kettle and Similkameen Rivers, although they are taken only very rarely. They are more adaptable to warmer water than other trout and can be seen cruising shorelines near stream mouths. Brown Trout can be identified by the presence of large, dark brown or black spots, surrounded by pigmented halos of blue and red colouration. Brown trout spawn in the fall and early winter.

Bull Trout are actually char that are often confused with Dolly Varden. Recognized by their pinkish spots on the body, bull trout are also noted for having a large head. These fish spawn in the fall and are not known for their great fighting ability. The fish are found in larger lakes and a few streams feeding primarily on insects, eggs and small fish. They prefer cold water and grow slowly.

Bull trout can reach up to 9 kg (20 lbs) but 2-5 kg (5-10 lb) fish are more common in larger lakes. Try trolling a green or orange Flat Fish or a Krocodile, or fishing the creek mouths with bait balls (a large cluster of worms and hook). Also, jigging with a bucktail and flasher in the winter or spring near a large creek mouth can be very successful. Fly fishers should try a larger leech pattern. In rivers, these fish rarely get over 1 kg (2 lbs) in size. Fly anglers will find streamer patterns effective, while spincasters can try silver coloured spoons. Due to significant declines in their population, tough regulations have been imposed in an effort to maintain the resource.

Burbot (Ling Cod) are a large bottom feeder that used to be a common sportfish. Over fishing has drastically affected the numbers and size and many lakes are now catch and release only for this tasty fish. Ling cod are an ugly fish that is easily recognized by their large mouth and long brown body with sharp fins. Jigging near creek mouths can produce the odd cod to 4 kg (10 lbs) in the larger water bodies.

Chinook are the largest of the Pacific Salmon. They can reach an impressive 27 kg (60 lbs) on occasion. Salmon are not common in Southeastern BC, as the historical runs though the Columbia River system are now blocked by a series of hydroelectric dams. However, there is a fair run of Chinook in the Shuswap River, which drains into the South Thompson, and then into the Fraser. Casting or drift fishing with cured roe into deep holes seems to be the most effective method. If trout are cleaning the hook of bait, switch to lures, wool (white, red or pink) or flies. Lures of choice include a Kitimat spoon or Spin-N-Glos.

The fly angler will need heavy gear and fast sinking lines with short strong tippet to get down to the deep holes. Shooting heads allow increased line control and help maintain a drag-free drift. Patterns mixing bright and dark colours seem to be most effective. Woolly Buggers, Egg Sucking Leeches or Marabou Eggs dead drifted are equally good.

Cutthroat Trout (Westslope) are native to the upper Kootenay River watershed in the East Kootenays. You will find stocked cutthroat (both Westslope and Yellowstone) in mountain lakes and streams since they prefer colder water than rainbow trout. Cutthroat spawn in the spring, which may be as late as early July in the high mountain streams. Cutthroat are long and slender with a red slash under their jaw. The Westslope strain do not have as many spots as coastal cutthroat and males keep some of their red colour after spawning.

BROWN TROUT

Black or brown spots, many with light halos

Adipose fin with spots

Tail with few or no spots

BULL TROUT

Large, broad, flattened head

No worm-like markings on dorsal fin

Whitish to pinkish spots, largest spots smaller than pupil

Upper jaw curves down

Body flattened on underside

White leading edges on lower fins

BURBOT

Two dorsal fins

Single barbel

Single anal fin

CHINOOK

Black mouth, black gums

Round spots on both lobes of tail

CUTTHROAT TROUT

Teeth in throat at back of tongue

Spots more numerous on posterior half of body

Large mouth (extends well past eye)

Red slash under lower jaw

Westslope Cutthroat are usually caught on artificial flies, small spoons and small spinners. You will find them in great numbers in many streams, most notably the Elk River and its tributaries. They are usually found in the 25-50 cm (10-20 in) range, but there are a few lakes in the region where they can get to 50-75 cm (20-30 in). The larger fish can be over eight years old since cutthroat live much longer than other fish species. Since the cutthroat are predatory fish, they feed extensively on kokanee, sculpins and sticklebacks, but if baitfish aren't present, they will survive quite nicely on insects. A fly imitating a baitfish is a good choice when baitfish are present. Muddler Minnow or Wool Head Sculpin are two such patterns to try. Cast around the drop-off areas as the cutthroat tend to cruise the near shore area in search of baitfish.

In the high mountain rivers, like the Elk, cutthroat generally feed on insects, and the region is famous for its great top-water cutthroat fishing. A box full of different colour and sizes of Tom Thumbs can go a long way towards imitating many of the hatches, but some people prefer specific flies, like an Elk Haired Caddis or a Green Drake Dun.

EASTERN BROOK TROUT

Red spots with blue halos

Worm-like markings on back and dorsal fin

Pinkish-orange paired fins edged in white

KOKANEE

No distinct black spots on sides

Long anal fin (13 or more rays)

LAKE TROUT

Worm-like markings on back and dorsal fin

Tail deeply forked

LARGEMOUTH BASS

Large wide lower jaw slightly
longer than the upper jaw

The anal and pelvic fins are green
to olive with some white

RAINBOW TROUT

Small black spots mostly restricted
to above the lateral line

Radiating rows of spots on tail

No teeth in throat at back of tongue

Eastern Brook Trout are actually char that were first introduced into BC in the early 1900s. The species is now found in many of the cooler streams and smaller mountain lakes in the province, where there is low concentration of oxygen that does not favor other species of trout. Easily identified by the large number of speckles, they are good fighters and very tasty. They spawn in October and have been known to reach 1 kg (2 lbs) in size in lakes, while stream brook trout are generally smaller.

Brookies feed on insects and shrimp. Although any number of spinners and lures can be effective, the most proven combination for spincasters is a small Deadly Dick with a worm, cast from shore or from a boat towards shore. Fly anglers, on the other hand, endlessly debate what the most effective way to catch this prized fish is. Every lake seems to have its own preference. Depending on the time and season, the type of fly to use varies. During spawning season, large, attractor type flies can be very effective. They are also a popular fish for ice fishing, as they typically remain quite active through the winter.

Kokanee (a word that means 'red fish') belong to the same species as sockeye salmon but instead of swimming to the ocean, they remain in freshwater their entire life. They are found in many lakes and rivers throughout Southeastern BC, and are easily recognizable by their slim silver bodies and forked tail. Kokanee turn a brilliant red when they spawn in the late summer. In the plankton-rich interior lakes, they can reach 3 kg (5 lbs) but 25–30 cm (10–12 in) fish are more common. Local anglers call them by a variety of nicknames: kickininee, little redfish, landlocked salmon, Kennerly's salmon, silver trout and yanks.

Okanagan Lake supports two types of Kokanee salmon—ones that spawn in streams, and ones that spawn along the lakeshore. During their entire feeding life the two types mix in the lake. At sexual maturity, usually at age three, they spawn and die. In streams they usually spawn from early September through to mid-October, while shore spawners spawn from mid-October to mid-November.

Kokanee are best caught on a Willow Leaf with a short leader and a Wedding Band and maggot. Troll as slow as possible and in an "S" pattern so your line, will speed up or slow down and change depths as you round the bend. This entices the fish to bite. Trolling with one ounce of weight or less, which takes the lure to 5-15 m (15 to 45 ft), is the most productive. An exciting alternative is to try to catch kokanee on a fly. In the spring, chironomids and mayflies can yield surprising results.

Lake Trout are another mis-named char, and are slowly becoming known by their proper name: Lake Char. They are only found in large, deep and cold lakes. They grow very slowly but often reaches sizes in excess of 10 kg (25 lbs), since they live longer than most other fish species. Fish to 3 kg (5 lb) are quite common. Lakers are a fall spawning fish and are recognized by their forked tail, long head and large snout as well as an abundance of spots. These fish stay near the surface during the early spring and late fall when the water temperatures are cold. In the summer, the fish retreat to the depths of the lake so it is best to troll deep during summer months.

Lake trout are not great fighters, and are often spurned by anglers who prefer more acrobatic fish. However, they do have a lot of mass, and there's something special about catching a fish that big. Down rigging equipment must be used to have any significant success when fishing for summer lake trout. The best lures to find lakers are silver spoons or spinners, which imitate the fish's main food source, the minnow. The most effective method used with these lures is trolling. Trolling presents the lure effectively and covers a lot of territory, which is an asset when trying to find lake trout. For fly anglers, the best opportunity to have good success for lake trout is during the spring. Trolling minnow imitation flies on a sinking line can produce well. Ice fishing for the big fish can be quite effective, although the big lakes rarely freeze. During winter, lakers can be found closer to the surface and they readily hit small spoons tipped with minnows.

Largemouth Bass are found in the shallow, low lying lakes and streams of Southeastern BC, mostly tucked up against the US border. These waterbodies are often too warm to support extensive trout populations, and have been stocked (usually illegally) to provide an alternative fishery. In lakes with largemouth bass, top water lures and flies can create a frenzy of action. Plastic jigs or any minnow imitation lure or fly can also be productive. Largemouth bass generally grow larger than its cousin, the smallmouth bass.

Rainbow Trout are native to many streams and lakes in British Columbia. Due to their hardy nature and the fact they are an excellent sportfish, they are stocked throughout the province. Rainbow get their name from the colourful strip they get when spawning in the spring. Like other forms of trout, rainbow will eat whatever they can get. The mainstay of their diet in many lakes and rivers are small shrimp (scuds), leeches and insects, but they will also eat small baitfish if given the opportunity. During spawning season, they are quite fond of free-floating eggs.

The fish varies in size depending on the waterbody and strain you catch. The Kootenay Region is home to the Gerrard strain of rainbow trout. These monsters are the world's largest strain of rainbow trout, and are mostly found in the larger lakes of the Kootenays. They reach 9 kg (20 lbs) at full maturity, but can grow to an amazing 16 kg (40 lbs). The best way to catch these big trout is to troll a polar bear or bucktail fly on the surface in the fall or winter at a speed of 4-5 kmh (2-3 mph). As the season progresses into the late spring or summer, you must use a planer board or downrigger in order to get to the depth that the fish inhabit. Try an Apex, Lyman plug or flasher with a hoochie at the 30-90 ft (10 to 30 m) level. A float with a grasshopper at a creek mouth or off a rock wall is also very effective in the summer.

There are other strains of rainbow in the Kootenays, mostly found in the smaller lakes. The unproductive lakes can have small trout that average under 30 cm (12 in), while it is not uncommon to land a trophy-sized trout on a lake like Premier or Whiteswan. Even on smaller lakes trolling for rainbow is usually the most popular way to catch the fish. Lake trolls, spinners, spoons and plugs have all been known to produce, especially tipped with powerbait or a worm. Even fly anglers have taken to dragging around a leech or nymph pattern in order to cover more water. But on many lakes, a simple hook with bait and bobber can work just as well as any other method.

However, trolling is not the only way to catch rainbow. Southeastern BC is home to some rather large insect hatches and matching the hatch will go a long ways towards success. Chironomids are popular early in the season, but are replaced by caddis flies, mayflies, damsel flies and dragonflies later in the season. Trout tend to stay hidden in the depths during the day, and you will have to fish deeper with a leech or a nymph pattern. In the late evenings, though, top water fishing with dry flies offers great excitement. While there are specialty flies to imitate most every insect, a box full of Tom Thumbs tied with various colours at a variety of sizes will often suffice.

Smallmouth Bass are the close cousin of the largemouth bass (although technically, neither is a bass: both are members of the sunfish family) and are found in many of the low elevation lakes and streams. They spawn in May to June, at which time they become an aggressive fish that is very easy to catch. Bass hang around cover such as a sunken log, lily pad or weed bed or even man-made structures such as docks. Unlike largemouth, smallmouth do not move much from their hiding place so you have to get you plug or fly right in close to these types of cover. Larger fish tend to hold in deeper water and rarely come out during the day. Smallmouth bass will strike most well presented bait that resembles the chironomids, small baitfish, leeches and tadpoles that they feed on. Fly fishers should use attractor type patterns such as a Woolly Bugger or Werner shrimp. If spincasting, there are many different plugs such as Rapalas. Other tackle to try includes spinner blades, buzzy baits, orange Flatfish or plastic worms.

Walleye (Pickerel) are a prized sportfish that is mainly found in the Columbia River in June, but can also be found on some Columbia tributaries, including the Kettle. They feed mainly on baitfish, although they do take leeches. Jigs are the lure of choice. Walleye travel in loose schools and once you find one you should be able to catch more. They are most active during the darker times of the day, especially early morning and evening.

Whitefish are a silvery fish with large scales. They spawn in the fall and give a good fight even in the winter. They can reach 50 cm (20 in) but average 30 cm (12 in). They are not a popular fish, because they are quite boney, and they don't offer the same acrobatics as trout. Nonetheless, they are a great game fish since they are much more aggressive and less spooky than trout. They feed mainly on insects and will readily strike spinners, spoons or other shinny lures. Fly-fishing can also be effective, especially in the spring during the mayfly hatch. The presence of whitefish in a lake is usually a sign that the other sportfish (like lake trout and rainbow) are going to be bigger since the other species like to feed on the smaller whitefish.

Yellow Perch are an invasive species that have been illegally introduced into many of the smaller, warmer lakes of Southeastern BC. They are active throughout the year, especially during ice fishing season. They are also quite prolific, and where there is one perch, there is usually a ton of them. They are small (rarely more that 0.5 kg/1 lb), but feisty and are a great starter for kids. In addition to worms with a float, perch love small minnows, which are particularly effective when ice fishing. Small jigs and bodies will also work quite well.

Before fishing any lake or stream in British Columbia, it is essential to read the Freshwater Fishing Regulations. For in-season regulation changes go to: www.env.gov.bc.ca/fw/fish. There are also separate regulations and licenses for all salmon bearing streams. Be sure to visit www.pac.dfo-mpo.gc.ca/rec-fish for more information.

SMALLMOUTH BASS

Jaw extends to about middle of eye

Three short spines on anal fin

WALLEYE

Spiny anterior dorsal fin

Sharp, fang-like teeth

White corner on lower half of tail

WHITEFISH

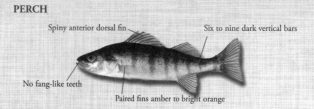

Large scales

Adipose fin

Teeth weakly developed or absent

PERCH

Spiny anterior dorsal fin

Six to nine dark vertical bars

No fang-like teeth

Paired fins amber to bright orange

A Message from the Freshwater Fisheries Society of BC

Welcome to the Southwestern BC edition of the Fishing Mapbook - your indispensable guide to a vast region that offers the most diverse fishing opportunities in the province. Whether first-timer or lifelong angler, this guide provides a wealth of information, from basic techniques to lake-specific tips.

The FFSBC is very pleased to once again partner with Backroads Mapbooks on the entire Fishing Mapbook series. Established in in 2003, the Society's mandate is "to conserve and enhance the freshwater fisheries of BC for the benefit of the public". Funded largely by fishing licence revenues, one of our responsibilities is to deliver the provincial fish stocking program. We stock close to 1,000 lakes and streams around BC every year, including many of the lakes featured in this guide. We also conduct research to continually improve the health and sustainability of BC's freshwater fisheries, while increasing the efficiency and reducing the environmental impact of our hatchery operations.

The Society's work, however, goes beyond fish hatcheries and stocking programs. We're also assisting with the recovery of endangered white sturgeon on the Kootenay, Columbia and Nechacko rivers. And all around the province, with help from partners such as the Habitat Conservation Trust Foundation and Columbia Basin Trust, we're making it easier and more enjoyable for people to go fishing.

One of our most successful programs is Learn to Fish — a two to four-hour introduction to responsible fishing — designed especially for youngsters. Close to 30,000 kids and their parents take part annually in the sessions held at our hatcheries and at parks and campgrounds, and with help from our partners we're working to expand the program to even more places around BC.

Another popular initiative is our Rod Loan program. Lack of gear can be a real barrier for potential anglers, but thanks to support from our partners, the Society is able to provide more than 5,000 free starter sets every year.

With so many BC residents concentrated in urban and suburban areas, access to good fishing is a challenge. For that reason, the Society has pioneered Fishing in the City programs, in which we work with local municipalities to create well-stocked, easily accessible fishing waters close to (and in some cases within) BC's major cities.

To find out more about programs in your region, to get the latest stocking reports, or to buy a fishing licence, just visit the Society's website at www.gofishbc.com. We also encourage you to sign up for our monthly e-newsletter, featuring tips from our angling advisor Brian Chan and other experts. You can follow us on Facebook or Twitter for even more current news, and we welcome your questions and comments at fish@gofishbc.com

The Freshwater Fisheries Society exists for and because of you — the anglers of BC. When you purchase your fishing licence each year you're helping to fund our work - and that work is creating the best freshwater fisheries in North America. We thank you for your support, and wish you and your family great fishing.

Don Peterson
President

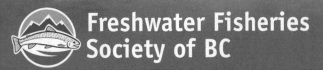

Freshwater Fisheries Society of BC

Aberdeen (Heart) Lake

Location: 23 km (14 mi) southeast of Vernon
Elevation: 1,278 m (4,193 ft)
Surface Area: 241 ha (595 ac)
Mean Depth: 9 m (30 ft)
Max Depth: 18 m (59 ft)
Way Point: 50° 07′ 00″ Lat - N   119° 03′ 00″ Lon - W

Fishing

The dam between Aberdeen and Haddo Lake has helped create a series of decent fishing lakes southeast of Vernon. Aberdeen is one of the biggest lakes in the area and is fed by Heart Creek. Anglers will find wild rainbow trout that can reach 1 kg (2 lbs) in size. However, summer drawdown can affect this fishery later in the summer and into early fall, and as a result, it is best to fish here in the spring.

The lake offers a wide array of areas to concentrate on. In particular, the many islands provide nice shoals where foraging trout often collect. There are also several points along the lakeshore that can be very productive. Similar to most lakes in this region, Aberdeen Lake is tea coloured even after the spring runoff. Normal fly patterns are productive, although it is recommended to tie all patterns with some attractant like crystal flash or flashabou.

The size and depth of the lake makes this an ideal trolling lake. Trollers should concentrate near drop offs along the larger holes in the lake. A willow leaf with wedding ring or small lure will work the best, but you can try small, flashy spoons or even a streamer-type fly.

When the trout are feeding in the shallows on insects, it is a prime time for fly fishers who will do well using dragonfly or damselfly nymph patterns. However spin fishermen need not be left out, as small lures like a Flatfish or Hotshot and tiny jigs can often fake it as nymphs or even scuds.

Directions

To find the lake, follow Highway 6 east from Vernon to Learmouth Road. Turn south on Learmouth and follow this windy backroad east to Reid Road, which will take you south to Bluenose Road and eventually the Aberdeen Lake Forest Service Road. The Forest Service Road marks the beginning of the gravel road that is signed with kilometre markings as well a resort signs. Keep left at the 11 km mark and continue straight at the 14 km mark. Just before the 17 km mark on what is known as Haddo (signed Hadow) Main, a side road branches to the right. The series of old roads in this network can be confusing but if you stay right and then take the next two lefts you should reach the shoreline. This is a former recreation site and there is ample space to camp and a place to launch the boat.

A good map such as those in the *Thompson Okanagan Backroad Mapbook* will help you find this and the many other lakes in the area. It is also recommended to have a 4wd vehicle, especially during wet weather.

Other Options

If you continue southwest along the rough side road, which is actually the old Haddo Main, you will reach the north end of **Haddo Lake**. Another rough side road leads to the recreation site, while the 'main' road accesses the dam area. The lake offers fishing for rainbow trout that are rumoured to reach 2 kg (4.5 lbs) in size.

Facilities

A former recreation site is found near the southern shore of the lake. You can still camp and launch a boat here, but the rough access limits trailers.

Species
Rainbow Trout

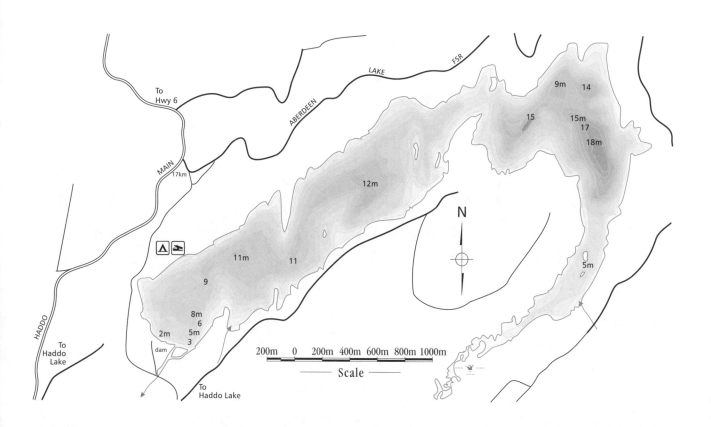

Location: 20 km (12 mi) east of Canal Flats
Elevation: 1,167 m (3,829 ft)
Surface Area: 25 ha (62 ac)
Mean Depth: 6.7 m (22 ft)
Max Depth: 14.8 m (49 ft)
Way Point: 115° 32' 00" Lat - N   50° 07' 00" Lon - W

Area Indicator

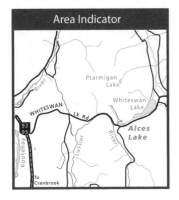

Species

Rainbow Trout

Alces Lake Fish Stocking Data			
Year	Species	Number	Life Stage
2008	Rainbow Trout	1,000	Yearling
2007	Rainbow Trout	1,000	Yearling
2006	Rainbow Trout	1,000	Yearling

Fishing

Alces Lake is often overlooked by anglers due to its close proximity to the much more popular Whiteswan Lake. However, the small lake does provide great fishing for stocked rainbow trout that are rumoured to reach 5 kg (11 lbs). Trout average around 30-35 cm (12-14 in) in size, but the fish do grow larger, partly due to the strong fishing restrictions on the lake.

Trolling a wet fly such as a leech or larger nymph pattern can produce results throughout the year. There are also periods of excellent top water action on this lake. In spring, it is best to focus efforts along shoal areas such as the large shoal found near the north middle portion of the lake. Another high priority area should be in the west end of the lake where the north and south shoals squeeze off the depths of the lake. In this region, trout tend to concentrate during low light periods when they cruise for food. During summer, the deep hole in the eastern end of the lake is a good bet to find holding trout.

Shore fishing is quite possible from the south shore of the lake off of the Whiteswan Lake Forest Service Road. There are open areas at the east and west ends, too, that will make shore casting possible. The north shore of the lake is accessible by a trail, but finding an area that is clear enough to cast a fly from is a bit more difficult; there is a point near the east end of the lake that might be your best bet.

To maintain the quality fishery, there is an artificial fly only, bait ban and electric motors only restriction on this lake. Be sure to check the regulations for the specific closure dates on Alces Lake.

Directions

Alces Lake is found in Whiteswan Lake Provincial Park. The small lake can be reached by taking Highway 93/95 to the Whiteswan Lake Forest Service Road south of Canal Flats. The forest road is well maintained and can be travelled by cars and/or RV's. The first lake you will see is Alces Lake. Parking is available at the campsite found at the west end of the lake.

Facilities

As a part of **Whiteswan Lake Provincial Park**, Alces Lake is home to a campground area complete with a boat launch. To the east, there are three other campgrounds available at Whiteswan Lake. In total there are 88 campsites between the two lakes. Camping is open from May 1 to September 30. Call 1-800-689-9025 (or 604-689-9025 in Greater Vancouver) or visit www.discovercamping.ca for reservations. For more information on specific parks visit www.bcparks.ca

Other Options

The closest angling alternative to Alces Lake in the area is obviously **Whiteswan Lake**.

The bigger lake lies just to the east of Alces Lake and offers good fishing for the stocked Gerrard rainbow trout species. These large growing trout have been known to reach the 5 kg (11 lb) range. Regardless of their size they put up a great fight when hooked. Camping opportunities also exist at Whiteswan.

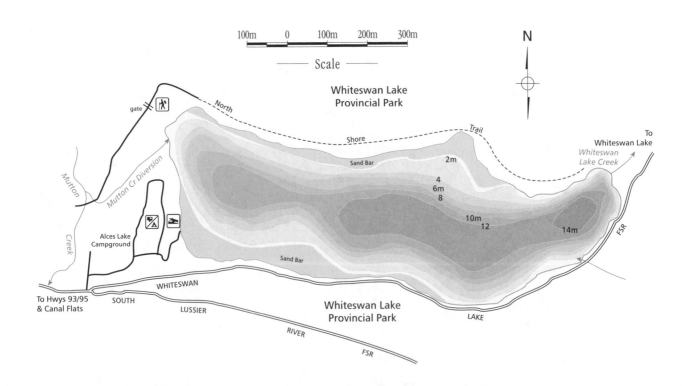

Allendale Lake

Location: 28 km (17 mi) southeast of Penticton
Elevation: 1,550 m (5,085 ft)
Surface Area: 21 ha (51 ac)
Mean Depth: 4.2 m (14 ft)
Max Depth: 11 m (36 ft)
Way Point: 49° 23' 00" Lat - N   119° 20' 00" Lon - W

Fishing

Allendale Lake is a remote lake found high in the hills above Penticton. The small lake is stocked annually with rainbow trout by the Freshwater Fisheries Society of BC and offers some decent fishing for generally small rainbow.

The lake is a high elevation lake, and the angling season begins later than at many other lakes in the area. The lake isn't usually completely free of ice until late spring. As a result, the hatches start later on the lake, and often overlap. This means that fly fishers can have a great time when the fish are biting at anything. Of course, there are days when multiple hatches mean that the fish are only eating one source of food, and it's up to you to figure out what it is.

The shoal area along the southeast side of the lake is a prime hatch area, especially in spring. The small inflowing creek is also a prime holding area for cruising rainbows.

As a general rule, fishing a chironomid pattern is never a bad thing early in the season. Chironomids can vary in colour from lake to lake, and even from hatch to hatch. A small dip net will help you scoop out some of the critters to check the size and colour. Fishing a pupa imitation on a floating line with a long leader and a strike indicator will work well. Allow the fly to sink down to the bottom and retrieve it very slowly. Another option, especially in deeper water, is to use a full sinking line and allow the fly to sink straight down to the bottom, and then retrieve very, very slowly.

In the evening, when the chironomids begin to emerge from the lake, it is possible to use a dry fly using a long leader 3-4 m (10-12 ft) together with a 1 m (3-4 ft) tippet in size 4X-6X. Using a size 14-16 Lady McConnell, cast the fly out to cruising fish.

Nymph patterns and attractors like a Carey Special or a Woolly Bugger can also work well, especially in the fall.

Facilities

Allendale Lake is home to a small recreation site complete with an outhouse and a few picnic tables. There is space for 6 groups and a cartop boat launch. The access road is fairly rough limiting trailers. Along with the recreation site, there is private property around the lake. Please respect the private property and be sure to pack out what you pack in at this user maintained recreation site.

Other Options

A good area alternative to Allendale Lake is **Solco Lake**, which can be found be following either the Ripperto or Tuzo Forest Service Roads east to the Solco Lake Branch Road. Also known as Fish Lake, this is considered one of the better fly-fishing destinations in the area. The high elevation ensures the rainbow trout remain active throughout the year and the scenery is simply outstanding.

Directions

This fantastic lake can be found only an hour from Penticton by first travelling south along Highway 97 to Okanagan Falls. At Okanagan Falls, look for the Okanagan Falls Forest Service Road, which starts at the edge of town and follows the south side of Shuttleworth Creek. You eventually pass Ripperto, then Tuzo Forest Service Roads before crossing the creek. Take the next right, which should be the Allendale Lake Road, and follow this road to the southern end of Allendale Lake.

Allendale Lake Fish Stocking Data			
Year	Species	Number	Life Stage
2013	Rainbow Trout	3,500	Yearling
2012	Rainbow Trout	1,500	Yearling
2011	Rainbow Trout	1,500	Yearling

Area Indicator

Species

Rainbow Trout

Allendale Lake Rec Site

Kilmer Cr

N

100m   0   100m   200m

Scale

Location: 28 km (17 mi) north of Princeton
Elevation: 853 m (2,799 ft)
Surface area: 62 ha (153 ac)
Mean depth: 14.9 m (49 ft)
Max depth: 39 m (128 ft)
GPS Waypoint: 49° 41′ 00″ Lat - N   120° 36′ 00″ Lon - W

Allison Lake

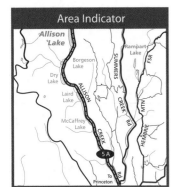

Area Indicator

Directions

You can find Allison Lake about 28 km (17 mi) north of Princeton off the west side of Highway 5A. The main access to the lake is via the boat launch and picnic area in the park at the south end of the lake.

Other Options

In the hills above Allison Lake, **Stringer Lake** can be found by following a steep 4wd access road off the east side of Highway 5A. The small, high elevation lake is stocked regularly with rainbow trout.

Fishing

Allison Lake is one of those beautiful highway side lakes designed to entice people to stop and cast a line. It has prominent shoals and is known to be quite productive despite the ease of access. To help offset the steady fishing pressure, the Freshwater Fisheries Society of BC stocks the lake annually with over 10,000 rainbow trout. These trout average 0.5 kg (1 lb) in size, although have been known to reach 1.5 kg (3.5 lbs) in size. The freshwater shrimp found in the lake help plump up the trout. The odd kokanee is also found in Allison Lake.

The narrow lake is found beside Highway 5A. It is made up of two distinct sections, north and south. The southern sections is generally shallow and has a maximum depth of 5 m (16 ft) and is usually the slowest part of the lake, especially through the summer months. The northern half of the lake can reach depths of 9 m (29 ft) and is blessed with several prime shoal areas that make for quality fishing opportunities, especially during the spring and fall periods.

Look for drop off areas with weed growth for prime locations for cruising trout. There is a pair of prominent points along the eastern shore, and a small stream flows in between the two. Try fishing around here, as well as at the prominent shoal area at the north end of the lake. Summer draw down on the creek can result in low water levels, which adversely affects the fishing later in the year.

During summer, troll leeches and dragonfly nymphs deep during the day when hatch activity is limited and watch for hatches to emerge. A lake troll with a Wedding ring and worm or bait is a popular option for non-fly anglers. Spincasting with spoons and small spinners can work from a small boat or tube. Lures such as a silver Dick Nite, Flatfish, Kamlooper, Mepps or Panther Martin can all entice the rainbow to bite.

The lake has a relatively open shoreline, especially around the eastern side. Shore casting is feasible, although getting out onto the water will improve your coverage. As a general rule, trout look for food at the top of the lake or at the bottom, and most of the time, it is at the bottom. They will rise on still summer evenings to take midges, caddisflies and even dragon and damselflies off the surface, but most of the time they will be found feeding near the bottom.

Facilities

Allison Lake Provincial Park is a small park located on the south end of the lake. The rustic campground offers a total of 22 campsites found above the highway, while a boat launch and picnic facilities are found next to the lake. The park can be busy during the summer months, although it is often one of the lesser-utilized parks in the area.

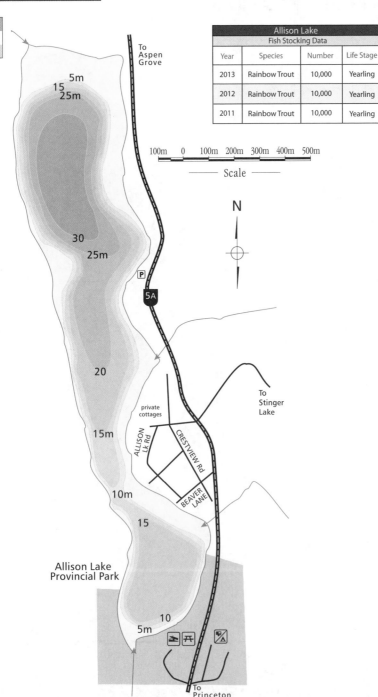

Allison Lake Fish Stocking Data			
Year	Species	Number	Life Stage
2013	Rainbow Trout	10,000	Yearling
2012	Rainbow Trout	10,000	Yearling
2011	Rainbow Trout	10,000	Yearling

Species
Rainbow Trout
Kokanee

Arlington Lakes

Fishing

The Arlington Lakes are a trio of lakes located just west of Highway 33. Their easy access, nice setting and the fact that the fishing can remain constant throughout the open water season makes these higher elevation lakes a popular destination for area anglers. In addition to rainbow, perch provide a good alternative, especially through the ice in winter.

The deepest of the three lakes is the First Arlington Lake, while the other two lakes average approximately 6 m (13 ft) in depth. Trolling is the most common way of fishing these lakes, although people are known to fish from shore where ever they can find a hole in the bushes large enough to cast from. For the kids, the worm and bobber can provide a good day's worth of fun on all three lakes.

Fly-fishing is also a productive method of angling on the lakes, as the small nature of the trout respond well to a variety of flies. For added fun, try using small top water or dry fly patterns.

The lakes hold plenty of redside shiners, which the trout will eat. A minnow pattern will work for fly anglers, while spincasters can use a variety of small spoons and other lures that resemble these minnows. The lakes are also unique in the fact they hold crayfish and patterns that resemble these creatures can do well.

A common problem for beginning anglers is that they don't let their fly or lure get down deep enough. A fly on a slow sinking line can sometimes take a couple minutes to sink down to the bottom. Even fishing a lure needs a degree of patience until it sinks down to where the fish are. Try counting to five before you retrieve. If your lure hasn't hit bottom, count to ten on the next cast, then 15, then 20, until you lure finally hits bottom. Once it is there, subtract five seconds on the next retrieve until you find where the fish are holding.

Facilities

Found a mere 3 km from the highway, the **Arlington Lakes Recreation Site** is a popular camping spot. So popular that the recreation site actually has a full-time attendant on duty from the middle of May until the end of October. It isn't just anglers here, though. The site is just off the highway, and it's right on the Kettle Valley Railway section of the Trans Canada Trail. It is a pretty spot, with 23 campsites that are beautifully set on either side of the southern lake. A boat launch is available.

Other Options

A fantastic angling alternative to the Arlington Lakes can be found just to the north in the Hydraulic/McCulloch Lakes area. Within a small area, you can find over ten productive lakes. Some of the more popular lakes that should be visited in the area are **Barge Lake, Ern Lake** and **Hydraulic (McCulloch Lake)**. All the lakes in the area offer stocked and/or natural trout fishing for rainbow and/or brook trout.

Directions

Travelling east along Highway 33 from the city of Kelowna, the Arlington Lakes lie off the west side of the highway down a gravel forest access road. As of 2011 there still was a small sign posted off the side of the highway marking the road to the lakes. Begin looking for the access road about 24 km south of the cut off to the Big White Ski Area or 25 km north of Beaverdell. The access road is approximately 3.5 km long and travels between the second and third Arlington Lake.

Species
Rainbow Trout
Yellow Perch

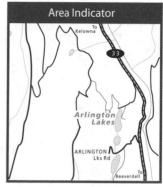
Area Indicator

1st Lake

Elevation: 1,052 m (3,451 ft)
Surface area: 17 ha (43 ac)
Mean depth: 3.5 m (11 ft)
Max depth: 8 m (26 ft)
GPS Waypoint: 119°4′00″ Lon - W 49° 37′ 00″ Lat - N

2nd Lake

Elevation: 1,052 m (3,451 ft)
Surface area: 5.2 ha (13 ac)
Mean depth: 2 m (7 ft)
Max depth: 6 m (20 ft)
GPS Waypoint: 119° 05′00″ Lon - W 49° 37′ 00″ Lat - N

3rd Lake

Elevation: 1,052 m (3,451 ft)
Surface area: 18 ha (43 ac)
Mean depth: 9 m (29 ft)
Max depth: 26 m (84 ft)
GPS Waypoint: 119° 05′00″ Lon - W 49° 36′ 00″ Lat - N

Map labels:

To Kelowna

1st Lake

24
21m
18
15m
12
9m
6
3m

2nd Lake

1m
3
5m
6

Arlington Lakes Rec Site

1m
3

3rd Lake

5m
6
8m

(Trans Canada Trail) Valley

Railway

ARLINGTON

LAKES Rd

VALLEY

KETTLE

WEST

Kettle

Hall Cr

To Beaverdell

N

100m 0 100m 200m 300m 400m 500m
Scale

Location: Nakusp
Elevation: 441 m (1,447 ft)
Surface Area: 22,947 ha (56,682 ac)
Max Depth: 308 m (1,010 ft)
Way Point: 117° 55'00" Lon - W 50° 26'00" Lat - N

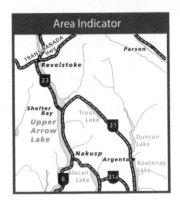

Area Indicator

Species
Bull Trout
Burbot
Kokanee
Rainbow Trout
Whitefish

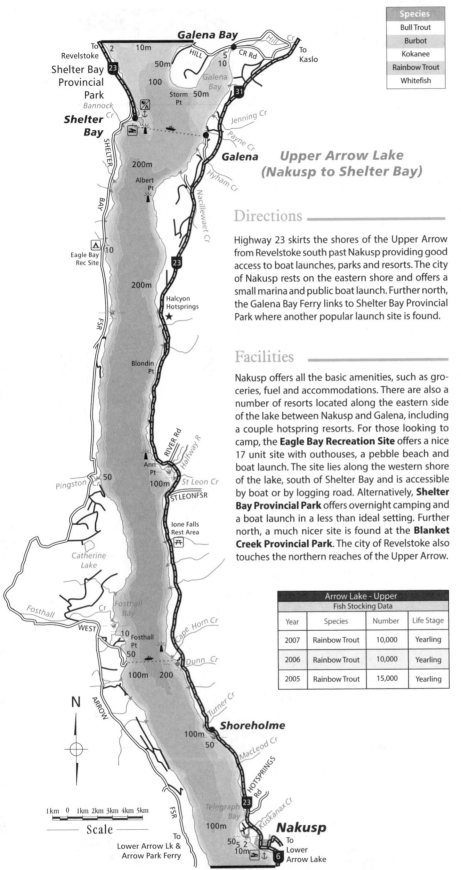

Upper Arrow Lake
(Nakusp to Shelter Bay)

Directions

Highway 23 skirts the shores of the Upper Arrow from Revelstoke south past Nakusp providing good access to boat launches, parks and resorts. The city of Nakusp rests on the eastern shore and offers a small marina and public boat launch. Further north, the Galena Bay Ferry links to Shelter Bay Provincial Park where another popular launch site is found.

Facilities

Nakusp offers all the basic amenities, such as groceries, fuel and accommodations. There are also a number of resorts located along the eastern side of the lake between Nakusp and Galena, including a couple hotspring resorts. For those looking to camp, the **Eagle Bay Recreation Site** offers a nice 17 unit site with outhouses, a pebble beach and boat launch. The site lies along the western shore of the lake, south of Shelter Bay and is accessible by boat or by logging road. Alternatively, **Shelter Bay Provincial Park** offers overnight camping and a boat launch in a less than ideal setting. Further north, a much nicer site is found at the **Blanket Creek Provincial Park**. The city of Revelstoke also touches the northern reaches of the Upper Arrow.

Arrow Lake - Upper Fish Stocking Data			
Year	Species	Number	Life Stage
2007	Rainbow Trout	10,000	Yearling
2006	Rainbow Trout	10,000	Yearling
2005	Rainbow Trout	15,000	Yearling

Fishing

Before the construction of the Hugh Keenleyside Dam, Upper Arrow Lake was actually a separate lake. But once the area was flooded, the two lakes became one big one. Still, it seems, the fish seem to think that there are two lakes. The kokanee prefer the Lower and the trout prefer Upper Arrow Lake. It is rumoured that the best fishing on the lake is found between Nakusp and Shelter Bay offering the best fishing of the lake. This is probably due mainly to the greater depths found in this portion of the lake.

The big lake is home to a variety of sport fish species. Rainbow trout and kokanee make up the bulk of the action in both Arrow Lakes, although there are some very big bull trout known to inhabit the lakes. Whitefish and burbot are also found in the Arrow Lakes in decent numbers, although they receive little attention by anglers.

Although trolling is the proven method, shore fishing is certainly an exciting alternative. The best period for success in these areas is during the spring, when runoff brings nutrients and oxygen into the lake. Rainbow and other species tend to congregate near these inflows, increasing your rate of success. Try working a small spinner or lure along creek mouths or even a bobber with a worm can work. Fly anglers can find success with a bead head nymph drift fished or even chironomid patters. Stripping the odd streamer or Woolly Bugger can sometimes create a stir in the pools and result in a big strike.

The famous Gerrard trout has also been stocked in the lake and there have been recent reports of some large rainbow being caught. Bull trout are being caught in the 3–4 kg (6.5–9 lb) range with some reaching up to 6 kg (13 lbs). The best method for finding rainbow and bull trout is to use a fast troll in the 10-30 m (30-100 ft) depth range. Try a plug that will imitate a minnow or even a silver or bronze coloured spoon, such as an Apex, Gibbs Hockey Stick or Coyote spoon. The best times to fish are in the late fall or early spring, with some success found in winter as well.

Anglers and boaters on Arrow Lake should be aware that the lake experiences dramatic draw downs of water levels at times during the year. These draw downs can dramatically alter depth chart information, boating safety and fishing quality. Be sure to consult locally for current conditions and check the fishing regulations before heading out on the lakes.

Arrow Lake - Lower

Location: 15 km (9 mi) west of Castlegar
Elevation: 457 m (1,499 ft)
Surface Area: 16,390 ha (40,483 ac)
Max Depth: 180 m (590 ft)
Way Point: 118°04 00" Lon - W 49° 51' 00" Lat - N

4 Region

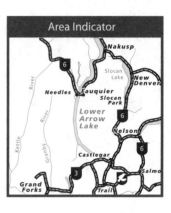

Area Indicator

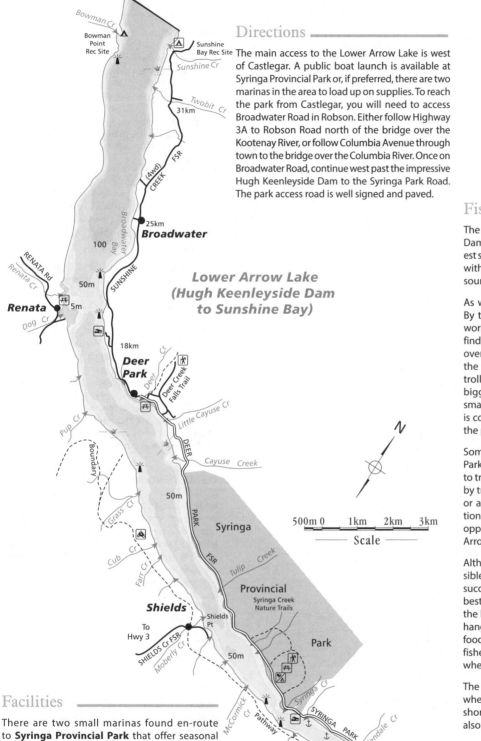

Directions

The main access to the Lower Arrow Lake is west of Castlegar. A public boat launch is available at Syringa Provincial Park or, if preferred, there are two marinas in the area to load up on supplies. To reach the park from Castlegar, you will need to access Broadwater Road in Robson. Either follow Highway 3A to Robson Road north of the bridge over the Kootenay River, or follow Columbia Avenue through town to the bridge over the Columbia River. Once on Broadwater Road, continue west past the impressive Hugh Keenleyside Dam to the Syringa Park Road. The park access road is well signed and paved.

Fishing

The Lower Arrow Lake between Hugh Keenleyside Dam and Deer Park makes up some of the shallowest sections along the Arrow Lakes. When combined with the drastic fluctuations in water level, a depth sounder is highly recommended.

As with all big lakes, fishing is best from a boat. By trolling, you are able to cover more area and work different depths easier. This will allow you to find those big rainbow trout and bull trout (trout over 5 kg/10 lbs are caught annually) as well as the numerous kokanee that inhabit the lake. Try trolling a streamer fly, Apex lure or plug for the bigger fish. The smaller kokanee tend to go for small, flashy lures with red or pink. The Lower Arrow is considered one of the best kokanee fisheries in the province.

Some anglers say the best fishing is north of Deer Park, while others will argue that it is not necessary to travel that far up the lake. Most success is found by trolling around creek mouths near the drop off or along steep rock cliffs. The fishing in this portion of the lake can be hit and miss but with the opportunity to hook into some big trout, the Lower Arrow continues to draw trout hunters.

Although shore fishing is quite limited, it is possible to shore cast near creek mouths with some success for rainbow and bull trout or whitefish. The best time to fish these areas is in September, when the kokanee spawn, as the bull and rainbow trout hang around the mouth of the creeks waiting for food (in the form of kokanee or kokanee eggs). Flyfishermen can also have some luck in the evenings when the fish start to rise for insects.

The best time to fish here is in fall and early winter when the big Gerrard rainbow move in closer to shore. During this time, some big bull trout can also be lured.

Species
Bull Trout
Burbot
Kokanee
Rainbow Trout
Whitefish

Facilities

There are two small marinas found en-route to **Syringa Provincial Park** that offer seasonal mooring, fuel and supplies as well as access to the lake. The park itself is open for camping from May through September; it also offers a separate day-use area with a beautiful sandy beach and a paved boat launch. For more rustic facilities, there are recreation sites available for boaters to explore along the more northern reaches of the Lower Arrow. Two such sites are the **Bowman Point Recreation Site** and the **Sunshine Bay Recreation Site**. Both sites are equipped with mooring buoys for boaters and have limited space for tents.

Location: 12 km (7.5 mi) southwest of Elko
Elevation: 795 m (2,608 ft)
Surface Area: 23 ha (58 ac)
Mean Depth: 7.3 m (24 ft)
Max Depth: 15.2 m (50 ft)
Way Point: 115° 13′ 00″ Lon - W 49° 14′ 00″ Lat - N

Baynes Lake

Directions

You can find Baynes Lake near Kikomun Creek Provincial Park southeast of the city of Cranbrook. The lake is accessible off the west side of the Jaffray-Baynes Lake Road, which is found off the south side of Highway 3/93 south of Jaffray. The lake is home to a number of private cabins and can be accessed by all vehicles.

Fishing

Baynes Lake is stocked annually with rainbow trout, which provide for good fishing at times for decent sized rainbow. The lake is also inhabited by brook trout, which were stocked in the past. However, in the past decade, largemouth bass have found their way into the lake, most likely through bait buckets during ice fishing. Today, the bass have established themselves in the lake and while the lake is still stocked with trout, many prefer to chase after the bass.

Rainbow trout and brook trout anglers will find better success in the spring just after ice off. Chironomid fly patterns can work well during this time as well as other nymph patterns such as a damselfly or dragonfly nymphs. As the lake begins to warm up in the late spring, trout anglers will need to fish deeper.

Late spring is also when anglers can find good success for largemouth bass. During this time bass can be quite aggressive to anything that looks like food. Largemouth are a predatory fish that like to feed on other fish smaller than themselves. The trouble with the largemouth bass population is that there are lots of fish, but very few that are of a size worth catching. Or at least, that's what we've heard. There's a chance that there are some monsters lurking in the deep that haven't been caught yet, but the average catch here is quite small (less than 30 cm/12 inches and often half that). Streamers can work well for fly anglers while spincasters should use spinners. As the heat of summer sets in, bass seekers should try slowing presentations down using a leech type pattern or a tube jig.

The lake is a popular ice fishing lake. Rainbow tend to stay just below the ice; the water might be coldest in this layer, but it also has the most oxygen. However, they can be at most any depth, based on a variety of factors. Try dangling a minnow or worm or salmon egg a few inches under the ice, slowly dropping it down until you start to have results. When the water stratifies in the winter, so do the fish, and once you've figured out how deep one fish is, you've found the depth that most of them are at. During winter, ice fishers can have good success using bait.

There is an electric motor only restriction on this Baynes Lake.

Facilities

The closest overnight facility to Baynes Lake is **Kikomun Creek Provincial Park**. The park is home to a good variety of campsites next to the man-made Lake Koocanusa. Alternatively, there are a few forest recreation sites found in the area around Baynes Lake.

Other Options

The much larger Lake Koocanusa lies to the west of Baynes Lake. **Lake Koocanusa** is best fished via a boat and can be accessed from Kikomun Creek Park. The large man-made lake offers fishing for bull trout, kokanee and the odd cutthroat trout.

Baynes Lake Fish Stocking Data			
Year	Species	Number	Life Stage
2013	Rainbow Trout	9,625	Fall Catchable
2012	Rainbow Trout	1,050	Catchable
2011	Rainbow Trout	8,060	Fall Catchable

Species
Brook Trout
Largemouth Bass
Rainbow Trout

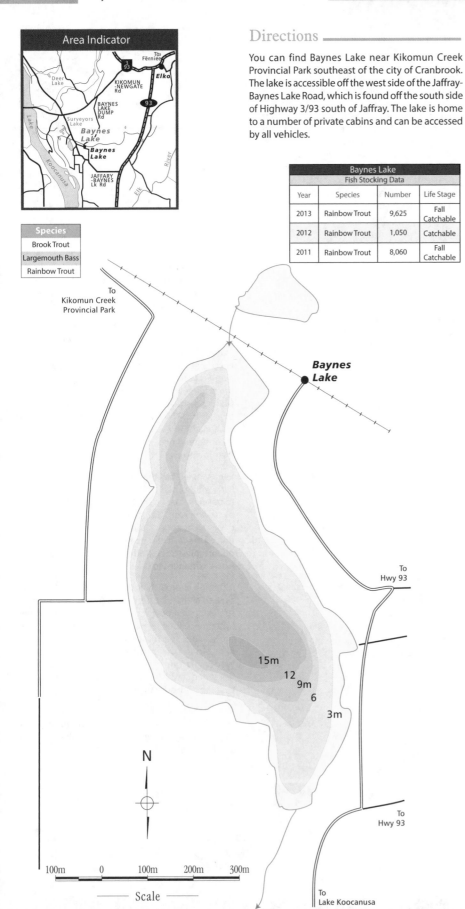

Area Indicator

Bear & Fish Lakes

Fish Lake

Elevation: 1,073 m (3,520 ft)
Surface Area: 7 ha (17 ac)
Mean Depth: 3 m (10 ft)
Max Depth: 5.8 m (19 ft)
Way Point: 117° 10'00" Lon - W 50° 02'00" Lat - N

Directions

You can find both Bear Lake and Fish Lake almost half way between the small towns of Kaslo and New Denver. The lakes sit side by side and are easily accessible off Highway 31A. Parking is available at the Fish Lake Rest Area or just off the side of the highway.

Facilities

While both lakes have small pull out areas off the highway for access, **Fish Lake** also offers a small highway rest area. It is also possible to launch a boat into both lakes, although the launching facilities are rudimentary at best. The odd traveller has been known to camp alongside these lakes, although there are no established facilities.

Other Options

The **Kaslo River** drains the lake and accompanies Highway 31A as it dips down towards Kaslo and the Kootenay Lake. The fast flowing stream offers some good fly-fishing for small rainbow and bull trout. It is a fly only, catch and release stream above its confluence with Keen Creek and closed to fishing below the creek.

Fish Lake Fish Stocking Data			
Year	Species	Number	Life Stage
2013	Rainbow Trout	1,500	Yearling
2012	Rainbow Trout	1,500	Yearling
2011	Rainbow Trout	1,500	Yearling

Species
Rainbow Trout

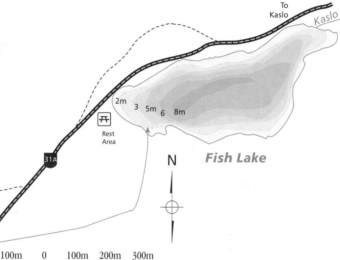

Bear Lake

Elevation: 1,085 m (3,560 ft)
Surface Area: 10 ha (26 ac)
Mean Depth: 3.5 m (11 ft)
Max Depth: 8.8 m (29 ft)
Way Point: 117° 11'00" Lon - W 50° 02'00" Lat - N

Bear Lake Fish Stocking Data			
Year	Species	Number	Life Stage
2007	Rainbow Trout	1,500	Yearling
2006	Rainbow Trout	1,500	Yearling
2005	Rainbow Trout	1,500	Yearling

Fishing

Bear and Fish Lakes are two small Kootenay Lakes that sit near the highest point that Highway 31A hits as it makes its way between Kaslo and New Denver. The lakes lie on either side of the highway, a few hundred metres apart from each other below the alpine peaks of the Goat Range Provincial Park. The beautiful scenery, good fishing for stocked rainbow trout and the easy access make these lovely lakes a fantastic place to spend an afternoon.

Figuring out which lake is which can be a bit of a problem. Originally, Bear Lake was the lake furthest to the east, while Fish Lake was the lake furthest to the west. Due to a clerical error, their names were transposed in 1893, and the wrong names became official. This wouldn't be a problem, except for the residents of the area, particularly old-timers, who still use the original names.

We've gone with the official names, with Bear Lake being the westernmost of the two. The lake's shoreline is almost completely open, with Highway 31A passing on the south and the Bear Lake Road passing by on the north, both close enough (usually), that there are no trees between the road and the lake. Fishing from the shoreline is easy. Two creeks flow into the lake from the north, one at each end of the lake, and the outflow creek to Fish Lake leaves the lake in the southeastern corner. Try working these spots from the shore or from a float tube.

Fish Lake is accessed from a series of pull offs. Like Bear Lake, the highway passes close enough to the lake that there are no trees between the lake and the highway, making casting from this shore very easy. Try working the inflow or outflow of the Kaslo River at either end of the lake.

Both lakes are stocked annually with rainbow trout, which provide for good fishing success throughout the open water season. The small rainbow in the lakes will readily strike well presented nymphs and on occasion top water flies. Both of these lakes are inundated with caddisfly and other larvae during the spring and if you can match the right hatch, consistency will definitely not be a problem.

Spincasters can do well, although the success rate is not the same as with fly angling. Trolling the lake with a small streamer fly or spoon can also be productive. During winter, ice fishing is commonplace on both lakes with local anglers.

Region 4

Location: 15 km (9 mi) northwest of Slocan
Elevation: 1,457 m (4,780 ft)
Surface Area: 205 ha (506 ac)
Mean Depth: 41 m (135 ft)
Max Depth: 95 m (312 ft)
Way Point: 117° 36′ 00″ Lon - W 49° 52′ 00″ Lat - N

Beatrice Lake

Area Indicator

Species
Rainbow Trout

Fishing

Beatrice Lake is a remote lake that lies in the heart of the majestic Valhalla Provincial Park. To get to the lake, you either have to fly in, or hike a 12 km (7.5 mile) trail that rises steeply from the western shores of Slocan Lake. Because it is so remote, Beatrice Lake does not receive a lot of angling pressure throughout the year. Therefore, fishing can be quite good for small rainbow trout.

Larger rainbow do inhabit the lake but they are much more challenging to catch, especially if you are fishing from shore. Due to the long trek into the lake, it is quite difficult to take in a floatation device or canoe. Those that take the extra effort will be rewarded with some fine fishing.

If you aren't willing to lug a kick boat all that way, don't worry; the shoreline is quite open. Although trout can be found almost anywhere in this lake, the two steep drop offs found along the north and south shore of this lake are some of the best areas to try for larger rainbow. Other places to try are around the two small islands at the east end of the lake, as well as around the inflow and outflow of Beatrice Creek.

Fly anglers can entice strikes with bead head nymphs and even larger patterns such as a Carey Special, Woolly Bugger or other leech pattern. Surface action can be spotty at times, with most trout sipping mayflies or other hatching insects off the surface. However, at certain times of the year, using a flying ant or other terrestrial pattern on the surface can prove to be very effective. Dry flies work better in the early morning or late evening or any time the surface of the lake is calm.

While hike-in alpine lakes are usually the domain of fly angles, spincasters will not be disappointed, as these rainbow are often mesmerized by the fluttering action of a small silver spinner or spoon. If preferred, the good ol' worm and bobber often does the trick.

Caution needs to be taken when fishing here, as this is Grizzly bear country.

Directions

The lake can only be accessed by floatplane or by the 12 km (7.5 mi) trail from the western shore of Slocan Lake. The Beatrice Lake Trail can be reached by the Evans Creek Trail from Slocan City or by boat from Slocan Lake. Taking the Evans Creek Trail, though, will add on another 7.5 km (4.6 miles). The Beatrice Lake Trail ascends through a lush forest valley passing Cahill Lake before reaching Beatrice Lake. It is a difficult trail, with an elevation gain just shy of 1,000 m (3,280 ft).

Facilities

Beatrice Lake offers a few rustic campsites near the eastern shore of the lake. It is also possible to camp at Cahill Lake or areas south of Beatrice if you wish to split the trek into a few days or more.

Other Options

The Beatrice Lake Trail skirts the southern shoreline of **Cahill Lake** en route to Beatrice Lake. Cahill Lake is inhabit by a healthy rainbow trout population and fishing success from shore is often quite good, especially during the early summer period. Rustic camping opportunities are also available at Cahill Lake.

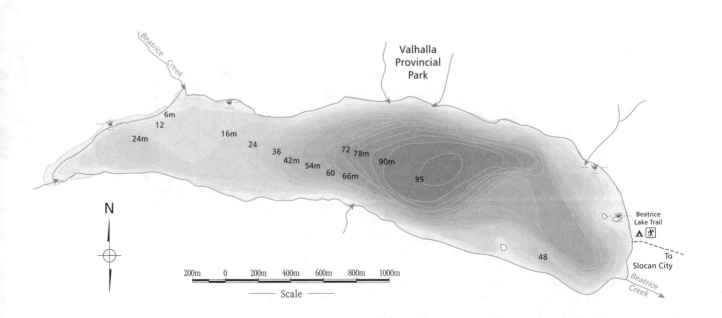

Beaver (Swalwell) Lake

Location: 26 km (16 mi) northeast of Kelowna
Elevation: 1,348 m (4,423 ft)
Surface Area: 306 ha (756 ac)
Mean Depth: 15 m (49 ft)
Max Depth: 30 m (100 ft)
Way Point: 119° 13′ 00″ Lon - W 50° 03′ 00″ Lat - N

Fishing

Also known as Swalwell Lake, Beaver Lake, is one the Okanagan's most popular fishing destinations. Its natural beauty, high catch rate of quality rainbow trout and ease of access, attract anglers of all ages.

The best time to fish the lake is at the end of May through to mid-July and then again in fall. The heavy stocking of the Freshwater Fisheries Society of BC and natural spawning provides great fishing around the many islands and sheltered bays. Visitors will be pleasantly surprised to find fish the average 30 cm (12 in) in size but can reach up to 50 cm (20 in).

Commonly, the use of wedding bands, Flatfish and trolling a Willow Leaf in the deeper areas of the lake and amongst the islands yields good catches. Red, silver and black are productive colours used throughout the year. On overcast days use the darker colours to attract the fish.

Early in the year, fly anglers will find a good chironomid hatch followed by mayflies. If no hatch is noticeable, troll a black or red Doc Spratley, leech and '52 Buick patterns throughout the lake concentrating around the islands and rock outcroppings. Alternatively, casting to rising fish with dry flies such as a Tom Thumb or Humpy around the log debris and shallows can reward you with an explosive strike.

Ice fishing is also very popular due to the good, maintained road access. There are many places on the lake that will be productive, but concentrating near the recreation site or around on of the many islands is recommended. Using a ¼ ounce jig tipped with powerbait or maggots is often used with good success. Don't hesitate to jig a leech or shrimp fly pattern.

Directions

Being a resort destination, this lake is quite easy to find and most vehicles should have no trouble driving up. From Highway 97, look for the Beaver Lake Road at the south end of Lake Country, just as you enter town from Kelowna. Follow this road east, up and out of the valley. The pavement ends soon after you leave the valley floor and you will need to be careful on the steep, windy gravel road. It is about 17 km to the resort at the south end, while the recreation site is found a few kilometres further along, on the way to Dee Lake.

Facilities

The main facility found on Beaver Lake is the **Beaver Lake Mountain Resort** located at the southwest shore of the lake. The resort is a full service facility offering log cottages and boat rentals along with guided outdoor recreation. Those looking to camp in the area will find a nice recreation site near the northeast end of the lake. The **Swalwell Lake Recreation Site** is well maintained, offering about 10 campsites with picnic tables and a decent boat launch. The short access road is a bit rough and not recommended for larger trailers.

Other Options

Beaver Lake is the first of many good fishing lakes in the area. The **Dee Lake Chain**, which includes Dee, Island, Deer and Crooked Lakes, is easily accessed off of the road to Dee Lake. These lakes offer both stocked and natural trout that can reach some nice sizes. Be sure to see the detailed description later in this book for some helpful hints on fishing these lakes.

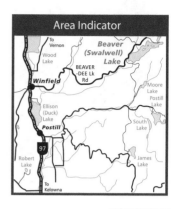

Area Indicator

Species

Rainbow Trout

Beaver (Swalwell) Lake Fish Stocking Data			
Year	Species	Number	Life Stage
2013	Rainbow Trout	35,000	Yearling
2012	Rainbow Trout	35,000	Yearling
2011	Rainbow Trout	35,000	Yearling

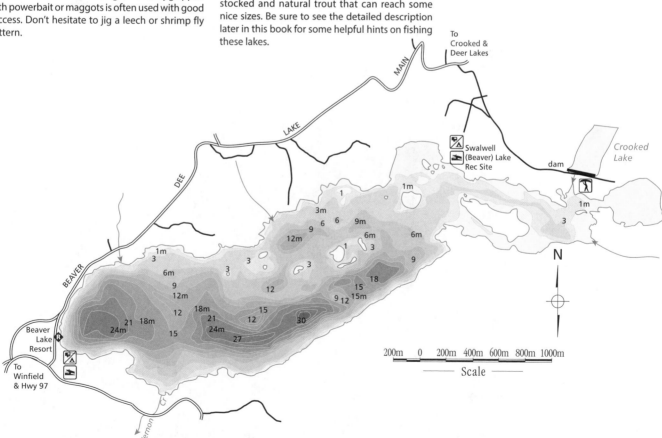

Region 4

Location: 26 km (16 mi) east of Nakusp
Elevator: 866 m (2,841 ft)
Surface Area: 11 ha (27 ac)
Mean Depth: 4 m (13 ft)
Max Depth: 7 m (23 ft)
Way Point: 117° 27' 00" Lon - W 50° 10' 00" Lat - N

Beaver Lake - Nakusp

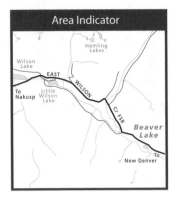

Area Indicator

Species
Bull Trout
Kokanee
Rainbow Trout

Fishing

East of Nakusp, is a handful of great fishing lakes. One of the best is Beaver Lake. It a great place to escape during a weekend and offers good fishing opportunities for small kokanee and stocked rainbow trout. The best time to try the lake is during the spring since the summer heat can slow success somewhat. The fall period marks the resurgence of active rainbow trout and the odd kokanee. Bull trout have also been known to inhabit the lake and there are reports of 3 kg (7 lb) char being caught here.

Fly anglers should try matching the spring chironomid hatch for consistent action for rainbow that average between 25–35 cm (10–14 inches), though have been known to get to 50 cm (20 inches). Kokanee are best caught on small streamers or bucktail flies, while later in the spring and into the early summer, damsel and dragonfly nymphs can work, too. Spincasters should troll a small lake troll with bait (maggots or worms) for kokanee, while small spoons or spinners can hook the odd frustrated rainbow trout.

Bull trout, on the other hand, are predators, and like to feed on the smaller kokanee and rainbow. Try using a small spoon or spinner that imitates a small fish, or even a minnow or worm.

The small, shallow lake is a great lake to fish with a tube or hand launched boat. The thick forest that surrounds the lake makes it hard to fish from shore, but keeps the wind off the lake, too. When other lakes are too choppy to float, Beaver Lake might be a good alternative.

There is an electric motor only restriction on Beaver Lake.

Directions

This small lake can be found east of the town of Nakusp via the East Wilson Creek Forest Service Road. The dusty forestry road is well maintained and can be picked up off Highway 6 north of New Denver or from the west near Nakusp. If you decide to access the road from the Nakusp side, look for the Wilson Lake Road, which eventually changes into the East Wilson Creek Forest Service Road. At the 22 km mark there will be a sign heralding Beaver Lake. Follow this narrow road down to the forest recreation site that provides access to the lake.

Facilities

Beaver Lake Recreation Site is a small, seven unit campsite nestled amidst a grove of western red cedar, hemlock, and grand fir. Anglers will also find a small area where it is possible to hand launch small boats (remember there is an electric motors only restriction on the lake).

Other Options

A nearby angling option to Beaver Lake is **Fitzstubbs Creek**, which flows into and out of Beaver Lake. The small creek holds a population of small rainbow trout and is accessible via the East Wilson Creek Forest Service Road. For a lake fishing alternative, Wilson Lake and Little Wilson Lake are found nearby, west of Beaver Lake. These two lakes are known for great fishing for stocked rainbow trout and offer forest recreation campsites for overnight camping. Look for more details on these lakes later in the book.

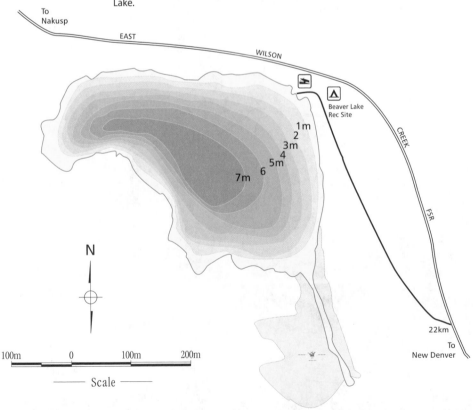

Becker Lake

Location: 9 km (5.5 mi) east of Vernon
Elevation: 1,215 m (3,986 ft)
Surface Area: 8.5 ha (21 ac)
Mean Depth: 5 m (16 ft)
Max Depth: 10.7 m (35 ft)
Way Point: 119° 09'00" Lon - W 50° 15'00" Lat - N

8 Region

Fishing

Becker Lake is a small fishing lake that rests in the popular off-road riding area around Vernon Hill. Stocked annually with brook trout, fishing can be fairly good here, during the spring, fall or through the ice in winter. The brookies can be a real treat to catch, with fish that can be over 1 kg (2 lbs) in size.

Like most small lakes, bringing a float tube or pontoon boat is a real advantage to working the prominent shoal areas. However, there is ample opportunity to cast from shore, including a few rickety looking 'dock' structures. Although imitation flies that match the hatch will regularly take brookies in Becker Lake, big brookies have often been known to hit minnow streamers. There are a lot of bait fish in the lake and imitating these minnows with flies or a spinner could reward the angler with a nice size brook trout. In the slower summer months, try searching patterns, leeches or dragonfly nymphs. If you are trolling with spincasting gear, we recommend using a willow leaf and Wedding Band or other small lure to find those lethargic brookies.

With such nice shoals, this lake is best visited during the cooler periods when the brook trout prefer to cruise the shallower areas looking for food. The lake is known to open up as early as late April. Brookies are also a prime target during the winter through the ice. They are often a little more active than their rainbow counterparts and usually come readily to small jigs or glo hooks with powerbait.

Other Options

A few alternative fishing lakes in the area are **Bardolph Lake** to the east or **King Edward Lake** to the south. You pass by the Bardolph Lake turnoff on the way to Becker, while King Edward Lake lies to the south of Highway 6 off King Edward Lake Road. Both lakes offer fishing for rainbow trout.

Directions

Becker Lake is found in the scenic hills east of the city of Vernon. About 17 km east from the city centre along Highway 6, look for the Nobel Canyon Road sign leading north. This road quickly turns into the Coldstream Creek Forest Service Road. Continue on this road to the Becker Lake Forest Service Road, which turns west at about the 4.5 km mark. Stay on the main road until the 13 km marking where the road is signed the John Park Way. The next left leads to the small recreation site on the north end of the lake.

Due to the many crossroads in the area, a good map such as those found in the Backroad Mapbook for the Thompson Okanagan is recommended. It is also a good idea (although not essential) to have a 4wd vehicle since there a few rough sections in the area.

Facilities

Becker Lake Recreation Site is comprised of two separate sites found at the north end of the lake. Between the sites, there is space for 7 groups. It is possible to launch small boats at both sites, while the eastern site also has a rickety old dock that people use on occasion. The area surround the lake is part of the Vernon Interpretive Forest and is used by everyone from hikers and mountain bikers to ATVers and dirt bikers. The main road beyond the lake also leads to a fantastic viewpoint over the valley.

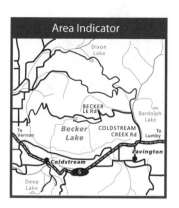

Area Indicator

Species

Brook Trout

Becker Lake			
Fish Stocking Data			
Year	Species	Number	Life Stage
2013	Brook Trout	2,000	Fingerling
2012	Brook Trout	2,000	Fingerling
2011	Brook Trout	2,000	Fingerling

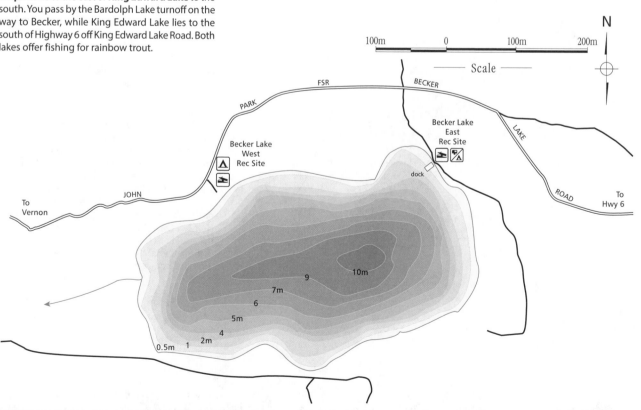

Location: 42 km (26 mi) northwest of Invermere
Elevation: 1,118 m (3,668 ft)
Surface Area: 20 ha (51ac)
Mean Depth: 8 m (26 ft)
Max Depth: 21 m (69 ft)
Way Point: 116° 23′00″ Lon - W 50°47′00″ Lat - N

Big Fish (Dunbar) Lake

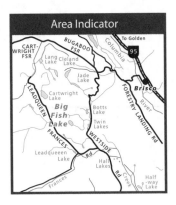

Area Indicator

Species

Cutthroat Trout

Fishing

The last time Big Fish lake was stocked with cutthroat was nearly 20 years ago. But the fish have survived and thrived. In fact, there are reports of 2.5 kg (5.5 lb) trout caught annually.

However, these cutthroat can be finicky at times; and fishing can be hit and miss. Also, most of the fish caught here average only 20-30 cm (8-12 in) in size. But anglers keep coming back in search of those big fish.

To find those larger trout, try working a bead head leech pattern or sculpin type streamer. Larger cutthroat are often aggressive towards baitfish and you may just get lucky and land one of those chunky trout. Trolling along the drop off area along the west side of the lake with a wedding band can be effective. Fly anglers and spincasters should work either of the larger shoal areas on the north or south end. Cutthroat can be suckers for anything bright and shiny, so if you're not having much luck, don't be afraid to tie on your most gaudy lure.

There is a good shoal area at the south end of the lake, which drops off quickly into the deepest section of the lake. Try focusing on this area. Another area that can produce well is near the inflow of a stream along the western shores of the lake.

If you plan to use a boat on Big Fish Lake, be sure to note the engine power restriction. However, many anglers simply cast from the dock at the recreation site. This can be effective earlier in the year when the waters are cooler and the trout are more apt to cruise the shallows in search of food.

Directions

Northwest of Invermere, Big Fish Lake can be reached off Westside Road. Westside Road travels parallel to Highway 95 between the tiny community of Brisco and Radium Hot Springs. From either location, travel west to Westside Road and follow it to the 44 km mark where a left (west) takes you past the Twin Lakes Recreation Site on the Bugaboo-Cartwright Forest Road. Two kilometres later, you will come to Big Fish or Dunbar Lake. The access road is generally drivable by most 2wd vehicles, but can be rutted and wet

Facilities

The **Bigfish (Dunbar) Lake Recreation Site** provides space for about 4 campers next to the lake. The recreation site is set next to the scenic lake and is equipped with a dock and cartop boat launch. If this site is too busy, there are a number of other recreation sites in the immediate area.

Other Options

There are a number of great fishing lakes found within minutes of Big Fish Lake. So if the fishing is a little slow on Big Fish or you would like to try another lake, there are plenty to choose from. The two closest lakes are the **Twin Lakes** to the east. These small, shallow lakes offer fishing opportunities for rainbow trout. **Botts Lake** is found further north than the Twin Lakes on Westside Road, while **Halfway Lake** lies to the south and is a little out of the way. Both lakes offer fishing opportunities for cutthroat trout. All lakes are home to scenic lakeside forest recreation campsites.

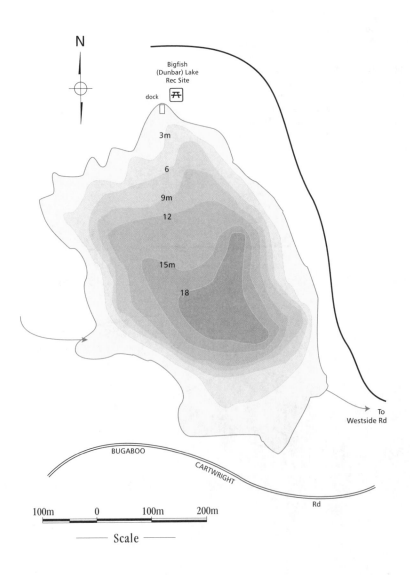

N

Bigfish (Dunbar) Lake Rec Site

dock

3m
6
9m
12
15m
18

To Westside Rd

BUGABOO

CARTWRIGHT

Rd

100m   0   100m   200m

Scale

Bittern Lake

Location: 64 km (40 mi) northwest of Invermere
Elevation: 1,007 m (3,304 ft)
Surface Area: 17 ha (42 ac)
Mean Depth: 4 m (13 ft)
Max Depth: 12 m (39 ft)
Way Point: 116° 35' 00" Lon - W 50° 58' 00" Lat - N

Fishing

Bittern Lake is a deceptive lake. Once people get out onto the lake, they quickly realize that the lake is quite shallow in most places. As a result, the lake is difficult to fish from shore. It is recommended to use a float tube or canoe to access the deeper portions of the lake.

If you are going to try fishing from shore, your best bet is fishing off the dock at the recreation site. This will extend your reach out into the deeper water.

Still, getting out onto the water will vastly improve your success. However, trolling is not your best bet, as the fish can see as well as you can in the clear, shallow water, and they are easily spooked. Instead, head out towards the deep water located just out from the boat launch. Because the water is so clear, it is easy to see the transition zones, as well as the weed beds where the trout like to hide out. Much of the time, it is easy to see the fish, too.

Trout are generally found at the top or bottom of the lake. However, by bottom, we don't mean the deepest point in the lake. Rather, they tend to be found in a layer of water that is a comfortable temperature, usually around 5–7 m (16–22 ft) down, making furtive dashes into shallower water for food, and diving into the relative safety of the deeper water when frightened. Find these transition zones that meet the trout's need for relative safety, comfort and access to food, and you will most likely find fish.

In the spring, try working a chironomid just off the weed beds. Trout also cruise the reed areas looking for damselflies that fall into the lake. If you can watch and learn the trout habits, this type of sight fishing can be a lot of fun at this lake.

Spincasters can try a variety of small spoons or spinners. Another option is to use a float and a worm, dangling the worm just off the bottom.

Directions

Bittern Lake is located south of the small town of Parson and can be reached by taking the Crestbrook Main Road southwest from town. This road crosses the Columbia River before rising to the benchlands to the west. At about the 6 km mark, turn south on the Mitten Lake Road. Follow this rough spur road for another 8 km or so and turn right to find the recreation site and access to the lake.

Anglers visiting this area are well advised to pick up a copy of the *Backroad Mapbook for the Kootenay Rockies BC* along with the *BC GPS Maps*. In addition to a series of detailed maps, they offer write-ups on other fishing opportunities, campsites, trails and much more.

Facilities

Upgraded in 2013 after the fire in the area in 2010, the **Bittern Lake Recreation Site** rests next to the small lake providing a picnic table, outhouse and dock. The open area provides space for at least 2 groups. There is also a rustic boat launch available.

Other Options

Along the Crestbrook Main, if you pass the junction to Bittern Lake, you will pass by the access to a small lake named **Wilbur Lake**. Wilbur Lake is home to a forest recreation campsite and offers fishing opportunities for stocked rainbow trout. The trout can be finicky at times, although some big rainbow are caught in the lake each year.

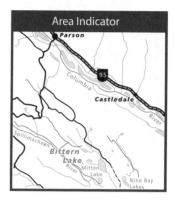

Area Indicator

Species

Rainbow Trout

Bittern Lake Fish Stocking Data			
Year	Species	Number	Life Stage
2013	Rainbow Trout	4,000	Yearling
2012	Rainbow Trout	4,000	Yearling
2011	Rainbow Trout	4,000	Yearling

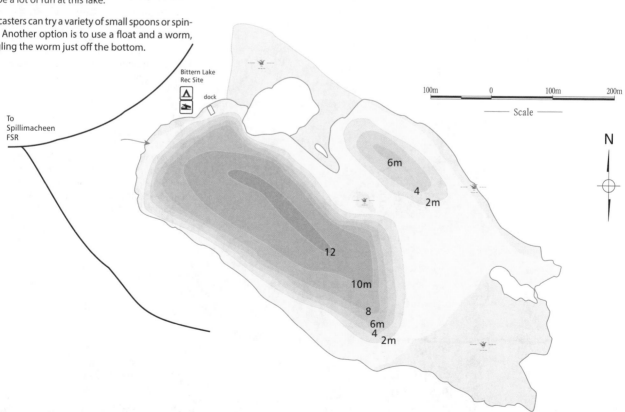

Location: 52 km (32 mi) northeast of Golden
Elevation: 975 m (3,199 ft)
Surface Area: 15 ha (37 ac)
Mean Depth: 2.5 m (8 ft)
Max Depth: 5.1 m (17 ft)
Way Point: 117° 24'00" Lon - W 51° 37'00" Lat - N

Blackwater Lake

Area Indicator

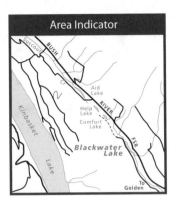

Species
Rainbow Trout

Fishing

Blackwater Lake is a long, thin lake found north of Golden, the first in a chain of lakes stretched out along the Bush River Road. The lake is stocked annually with rainbow trout, which provide for consistent action for most of the year. The trout are generally small but they can be quite aggressive, striking at most well presented lures or flies.

Blackwater Lake is generally shallow, but there is a deep hole almost right in the middle, and is sandwiched between the east and west shorelines. This creates two good drop off areas to focus angling attention on. The western shore of the lake is a jumble of fallen down trees and quite messy. However, these trees do provide shelter for the fish, and should not be overlooked, especially in spring and fall.

During summer, the top layer of water gets too warm for the rainbow trout, and they will retreat to the deeper water. This is because the lake is shallow, with little shade to block the sun.

Bush River Road runs alongside the lake's eastern shore, providing good access to the shoreline, and casting from shore to work the transition zone is possible. However, there is a boat launch at the south end of the lake, and many people who fish here bring a boat, or at least a float tube, to get to the deeper section of the lake.

Either troll along the drop off area with a spoon or fly, or try working the drop offs by casting towards shore from the middle. Spincasters should try a small spinner, such as a Panther Martin or Mepps Black Fury. Alternatively, a small bead head nymph fly pattern can work well at imitating a natural food source for these rainbow. If a nymph pattern doesn't work, try a Doc Spratley or Carey Special, which imitate no specific food source, but seem to produce well most of the time.

Blackwater Lake Fish Stocking Data			
Year	Species	Number	Life Stage
2013	Rainbow Trout	2,000	Yearling
2012	Rainbow Trout	2,200	Yearling
2011	Rainbow Trout	2,000	Yearling

Directions

To find Blackwater Lake, follow the Trans Canada Highway north of Golden to the Big Bend Road. The Big Bend Road soon changes into the Bush River Forest Service Road, which travels northeast past the eastern shore of Blackwater Lake. You can park your vehicle at the recreation site. Anglers with cars and RV's should have no trouble accessing the lake.

Facilities

The **Blackwater Lake Recreation Site** is equipped with four picnic tables, a wheelchair accessible fishing ramp and outhouses. The site also has a cartop boat launch for canoes and small boats. The site can be busy during the summer months, while during the week the logging truck traffic on the Bush River Forest Service Road is heavy at times.

Other Options

Blackwater is the first in a chain of lakes laying alongside Bush Lake Road. Continuing north on the road will bring you past **Comfort, Help** and **Aid Lakes**. The latter lake is still stocked with rainbow, while Comfort and Help are no longer stocked. They still hold some wild brook trout, though. All three lakes have small forest recreation campsites.

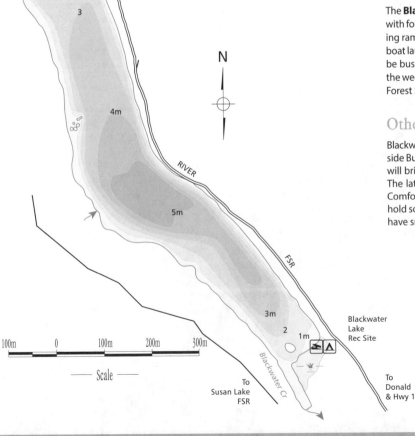

Bluey Lake

Location: 38 km (23.5 mi) southeast of Merritt
Elevation: 999 m (3,278 ft)
Surface Area: 28 ha (69 ac)
Mean Depth: 12 m (39 ft)
Max Depth: 19 m (62 ft)
Way Point: 120° 34' 00" Lon - W   49° 52' 00" Lat - N

Fishing

Bluey Lake is a small but well stocked lake found near Kentucky-Alleyne Provincial Park. The roads in to the lake are rough and difficult to drive, even with a 4wd vehicle when it is wet. Because of this poor access, Bluey Lake does not receive the same fishing pressure as other lakes in the area. But the poor access and intensive stocking has lead to some good fishing for the folks who do make it to the lake.

Most of the rainbow are small, but occasionally, some lucky angler pulls out a fish in the 2.5 kg (5 lb) range. The clear lake has several deeper holes surrounded by nice looking shoals. Try fly-fishing or spincasting near these shoals for best results.

Trolling is seldom tried at the lake because of the poor access and difficulty getting a decent boat into the lake. Also, the lake has limited deep areas so trollers often hang-up, making trolling a rather frustrating experience. A belly boat, however, is wonderful to have.

Spinners and lures like the Mepps, Blue Fox and Flatfish are worth trying with a worm. The preferred patterns at the lake include chironomids, sedges and leeches if fishing deeper. The trout can also be enticed to dry flies like mosquito or Royal Coachman.

Fishing is best after ice-off (mid-May) and late in the fall, as the shallow water tends to get too warm in the summer. Although the fish become sedate and disinterested in food during most of the day, there are some early and late rises. Unfortunately the lack of fight in the usually spunky rainbows during summer days can lead to some uninspired fishing.

Facilities

Bluey Lake has a seven unit recreation site on its shores. It is a rustic, user maintained site that also offers a place to launch small boats. The nearby **Kentucky Alleyne Provincial Park** has 58 camping sites, including a bunch for bigger trailers.

Other Options

There are several different lakes to choose from in the area. The two most popular lakes are **Alleyne** and **Kentucky Lakes**, which receive most of the fishing activity for small trout. Look for details on these lakes later in this book.

Directions

Bluey Lakes is found just south of the beautiful Kentucky-Alleyne Provincial Park. The popular recreation area is highlighted by open range land with encroaching forests. Several small, good fishing lakes dot the landscape.

To reach Bluey Lake, take the Bates Road, a good 2wd road. Bates Road can either be accessed by heading southwest from the Loon Lake exit on the Okanagan Connector or by heading south on Highway 5 from the Aspen Grove Exit and taking a left once you reach the Bates Road turn-off. Once on Bates Road, you will soon reach the north end of Kentucky Lake. Bluey Lake is located south of Kentucky Lake on a rough 4wd road which is probably best left to hiking especially in wetter conditions. The road leads from Bates Road a few hundred meters to the west of Kentucky Lake.

Bluey Lake also can be accessed off of the Dillard Creek Forest Service Road off Highway 5A. An old 4wd road reaches the south end of Bluey Lake from that road.

Species
Rainbow Trout

Bluey Lake			
Fish Stocking Data			
Year	Species	Number	Life Stage
2013	Rainbow Trout	10,000	Fry
2012	Rainbow Trout	10,000	Fry
2011	Rainbow Trout	10,000	Fry

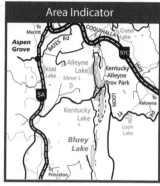

Area Indicator

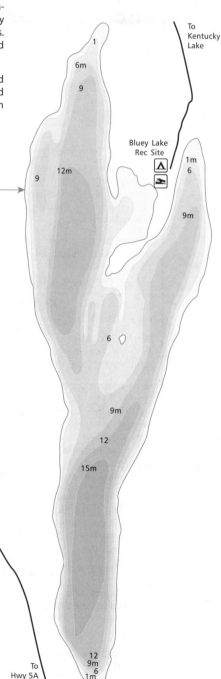

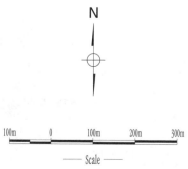

N

100m   0   100m   200m   300m

— Scale —

Boss & Tahla Lakes

Boss Lake

Elevation: 1,022 m (3,350 ft)
Surface Area: 20 ha (49 ac)
Mean Depth: 6 m (19 ft)
Max Depth: 11 m (33 ft)
Way Point: 120° 44' 00" Lon - W 49° 52' 00" Lat - N

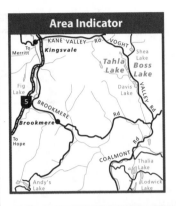

Area Indicator

Tahla Lake			
Fish Stocking Data			
Year	Species	Number	Life Stage
2013	Rainbow Trout	1,000	Yearling
2012	Rainbow Trout	1,000	Yearling
2011	Rainbow Trout	1,000	Yearling

Tahla Lake

Elevation: 1,022 m (3,350 ft)
Surface Area: 12 ha (30 ac)
Mean Depth: 4.5 m (15 ft)
Max Depth: 8 m (26 ft)
Way Point: 120° 44' 00" Lon - W 49° 52' 00" Lat - N

Directions

Southeast of Merritt, you can find a popular chain of lakes including Boss, Davis and Tahla Lakes. The lakes can be found by following the Coquihalla Connector (Hwy 97C) east from Merritt towards Kelowna. About 14 km east of Merritt, the signed Kane Valley Road takes off to the south. Follow this road for about 21 km to the Voght Valley Road. The Voght Valley Road continues south leading by Tahla and Boss Lake about 10 km later. Both roads are gravel, but most cars and larger trailers should have no trouble negotiating them.

Tahla Lake

To Hwy 5 via Kane Valley Rd

Tahla Lake Rec Site

Species
Rainbow Trout

N

Scale
100m   0   100m   200m

Boss Lake

Boss Lake Rec Site

To Davis Lake & Otter Valley Rd

Fishing

These small and easily accessed lakes offer up a fisherman's dream of nice fighting rainbow trout. They are located in the beautiful Voght Valley, which is sandwiched between the Coquihalla Highway and Highway 5A south of Aspen Grove, and are popular destinations for campers and anglers alike.

To help offset the fishing pressure and to help control the red sided shiners that are also present, the Freshwater Fisheries Society of B.C. stocks the lakes annually with rainbow. The best times to fish for the abundant trout are June, July and autumn. Unfortunately, this is also the busiest time of the year and the campsites are often filled and fishing derbies regularly take place during the long weekends. Wise anglers prefer to visit this area in the early spring or on a week day to avoid the crowds.

Many shoals and sunken islands allow a variety of fishing methods. But anglers should note that both lakes are quite shallow and there is an abundance of insect life to replicate.

Fly anglers can have a lot of success on these lakes. In the early summer months, dry fly-fishing while anchored on the shoals can be a lot of fun. Mikulak Sedges, Tom Thumbs and Elk Hair Caddis will coax the trout to the surface, especially in the evening. Other patterns to bring along include chironomids or blood worms (worked deeper), damsel or dragonfly nymph patterns (off the shoals) earlier in the year, while sedges like to emerge around the shoals throughout the summer months. Boss Lake also offers great fly-fishing in the northern section when using leeches.

Trolling a Panther Martin or Flatfish near the drop offs at the south end, particularly on the road side, works well on both lakes. Ice fishing is also popular in the area due to the good road access. Anglers usually set up near the boat launches and use traditional ice fishing lures and bait.

Facilities

Boss Lake Recreation Site is an enhanced site. The busy, semi-open site offers 26 campsites along with a boat launch near the north end of the lake. There is a fee to camp here, while day visitors can use the launch at the southeast corner of the lake.

Visitors to **Tahla** will find a much quieter and smaller campsite along with a launching site at the south end of the lake. There is a fee to camp here, but only room for three or so units. Regardless of which lake you want to visit, come early as they almost always fill up early on weekends.

Boss Lake			
Fish Stocking Data			
Year	Species	Number	Life Stage
2013	Rainbow Trout	6,000	Yearling
2012	Rainbow Trout	6,000	Yearling
2011	Rainbow Trout	6,000	Yearling

Bouleau Lake

Location: 26 km (16 mi) west of Vernon
Elevation: 1,383 m (4,537 ft)
Surface Area: 48 ha (119 ac)
Mean Depth: 8 m (26 ft)
Max Depth: 19.5 m (64 ft)
Way Point: 119° 39' 00" Lon - W   50° 17' 00" Lat - N

8 Region

Fishing

Also known as Beulah Lake, this medium-sized lake is located in the hills west of Vernon. The area around the lake has been heavily logged, so it isn't the prettiest lake in the area, but scenic value is a secondary concern to the quality of fishing. And the fishing at Bouleau Lake is fairly good for generally small, wild rainbow trout.

Because the lake is relatively easy to get to from Vernon, it sees moderate to heavy fishing pressure throughout the spring to fall season. Thankfully the fishing has remained consistent regardless of the pressure. The lake is also at a quite high elevation, which means that, while it is one of the later lakes in the region to be completely ice free, the fishing remains consistent through summer.

The odd rainbow reaches the 0.5 kg (1 lb) range, but most are generally smaller. Although the middle elongated part of the lake would seem to be initially a poor fishing area, the 9 m (30 ft) depth of this stretch of water, with the large shoal areas make for prime fishing in the spring and fall periods, especially for trolling. This part of the lake has a number of points and bays that creates structure for the fish to hold around, especially in spring and fall. During the summer, the hole on the eastern side of the lake makes a prime holding area.

It is a popular family fishing destination, and many people come up here to teach their kids how to fly-fish. And fly-fishing is one of the most popular methods of fishing the lake (though trolling certainly has its supporters). Work a pattern like a beadhead nymph, a leech or even a Woolly Bugger by casting from the deep water into the shallows. Retrieving towards the drop off is one of the most dependable means of finding fish.

Directions

Bouleau Lake is located at the foot of Bouleau and Tahaetkun Mountains west of Vernon. To find the lake, follow Highway 97 north from Vernon and take the turn-off to Kamloops. A few kilometres later, Westside Road branches south and follows the shores of Okanagan Lake to Parker Cove. Look for the Whiteman Creek Forest Service Road, a main logging road heading west that eventually links to Bouleau Main. Both logging roads are in fairly decent shape and most vehicles can make their way up to the recreation site that provides the best access to the lake.

Facilities

The **Bouleau Lake Recreation Site** provides space for a couple groups along the northern shore of the lake. Along with the basic campsite, there is a car top boat launch. If this site is busy, a good alternative is the small recreation campsite area found to the west at Little Bouleau Lake

Other Options

Just to the west of Bouleau Lake lies the much smaller **Little Bouleau Lake**. The smaller has been stocked in the past with rainbow trout and provides for fair to good fishing throughout the season. The lake can be accessed by following the Granite Road branching off Bouleau Main at the southern end of Bouleau Lake. The road may require a 4wd vehicle depending on the current conditions.

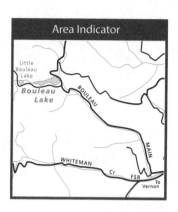

Area Indicator

Species
Rainbow Trout

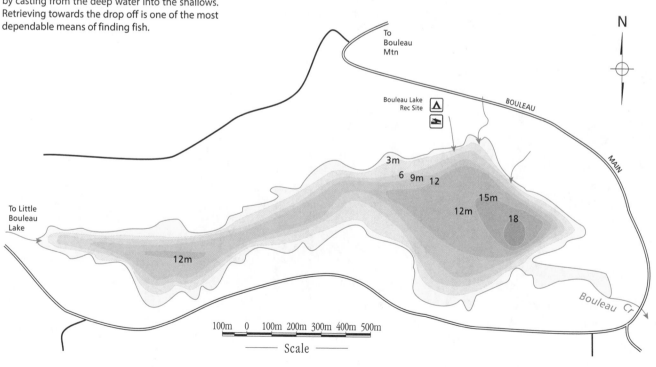

Location: 30 km (18.5 mi) southwest of Creston
Elevation: 1,283 m (4,209 ft)
Surface Area: 28 ha (69 ac)
Mean Depth: 4.5 m (15 ft)
Max Depth: 12.5 m (41 ft)
Way Point: 116° 51′ 00″ Lon - W 49° 00′ 00″ Lat - N

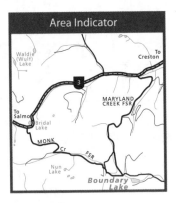

Area Indicator

Species
Brook Trout
Bull Trout
Cutthroat Trout
Rainbow Trout

Facilities

The **Boundary Lake Recreation Site** offers a decent sized campsite for visitors to enjoy. The high elevation, 11 unit recreation site includes a small wharf, cartop boat launch and a beach area and receives significant use during summer weekends. To find some seclusion, it is best visited during the weekdays or in the spring or fall.

Fishing

Boundary Lake is a small, high elevation lake southeast of Kootenay Summit, just a hop, skip and short bushwhack from the US Border. Despite its small size, it is quite deep, with only small shoal areas around the fringe of the lake.

The high elevation limits the fishing season, with ice-off usually occurring in late June. Rainbow trout were stocked for a few years, but the program ended in 2002. The rainbow can still be found occasionally, but the typical catch here is brook trout. The lake still holds the odd cutthroat trout while there are reports that bull trout also inhabit the lake.

One of the recommended areas to focus your angling attention is on the area around the northwest end of the lake. Even during the late summer there is usually a small trickle of water coming into the lake from this side. Coupled with the relatively large shoal area, the angling can get fast and furious in this region.

Many anglers also find that the area right in from of the recreation site can produce well. This is due to the quick drop off that allows fly-fishers and spincasters to work from shore. In fact, most of the shoreline is open, although there are a number of marshy areas.

For even better results, paddle your float tube or canoe out from the drop off and cast towards shore. By working the various depth points along the drop off, you will find where the trout are holding.

Due to the limited open water season, there are usually crossover hatches that make selecting the right fly a challenge. However, the fish are not usually that selective and can also be caught on small spinners or lake trolls.

Directions

This high elevation lake sits just southeast of the Kootenay Summit between Salmo and Creston, the highest highway pass in the country. The lake can be reached by taking Highway 3 west of Creston for about 30 km to the Maryland Creek Forest Service Road. Follow this main road south past all side roads for about 14 km to the first main road junction. Turn east or left on what should still be the Maryland Creek Road. Continue on the main road, avoiding the road junction at 3 km, for another 4.5 km where a sharp right leads down to the recreation site. Although people with cars and small RV's can make it into the lake, a 4wd vehicle with good clearance is recommended. Parking is available at the recreation site.

Other Options

If you plan to spend some time in the Boundary Lake area, two small lakes that often go unnoticed are **Nun** and **Monk Lakes.** These two sub-alpine lakes are found west of Boundary Lake and can only be accessed by trail from the Monk Creek Forest Service Road. The trail is a 3 km (1.9 mi) one-way hike, but the trek is rewarding. Cutthroat Trout inhabit the lakes in good numbers and are usually not that selective. As an added bonus, the scenery is spectacular.

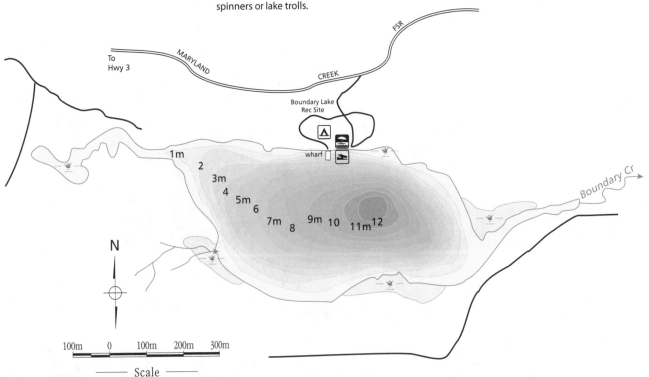

Box Lake

Location: 8 km (5 mi) southeast of Nakusp
Elevation: 584 m (1,916 ft)
Surface Area: 71 ha (175 ac)
Mean Depth: 4.5 m (15 ft)
Max Depth: 7.3 m (24 ft)
Way Point: 117° 43' 00" Lon - W 50° 12' 00" Lat - N

Fishing

The main thing that draws people to Box Lake is the fact that the lake is one of the first lakes in the region that thaws in the spring. In fact, it is not uncommon to be able to wet a line as early as March. With other lakes not being ice free until weeks later, it is one of the most popular early season fisheries in the Nakusp area.

Of course, it's low elevation plays against it, too, as it is one of the first lakes to be struck by the summer doldrums, with fishing slowing down by late spring, only to pick up again in fall. The lake is stocked annually by the Freshwater Fisheries Society of BC with rainbow trout and holds naturally reproducing brook trout. Brook trout were introduced a number of years ago and have had success spawning.

Fly anglers in particular will find they have great success on the lake. During the spring, shortly after ice off, the action on Box Lake can be very steady, especially during chironomid hatches. Look for underwater weed growth and present your fly nearby the structure. Often, the heat of the day will speed up the action significantly as trout cruise the shore areas picking off chironomids by the hundreds. The east and west ends of the lake seem to provide the best results. The drop off region along the north side of the lake is another prime location, especially during the summer months when the fishing in the shoals has slowed down.

Other than chironomids, fly anglers should try a dragonfly or damselfly nymph. Brookies seem to be attracted to bead head patterns of nymphs or small leeches. Spincasters should try a small spinner or spoon for rainbow, while a Deadly Dick tipped with a worm usually works well for brook trout. The brook trout are found more frequently in the shallows around the recreation site, while the rainbow tend to be found a little further offshore.

There are private residents on the north shore as well as an electric motor only restriction on the lake.

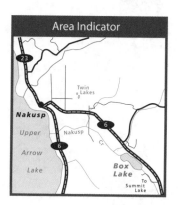

Area Indicator

Species
Rainbow Trout
Brook Trout

Directions

Box Lake lies just south of the town of Nakusp and is accessible via a steep, narrow access road off the west side of Highway 6. Due to its close proximity to Highway 6, anglers often overlook this scenic, roadside lake. When approaching the lake from the south, keep your eyes peeled for the small sign that marks the road to the recreation site. The sign is found south of the lake.

Facilities

The **Box Lake Recreation Site** is a quaint camping area set in the towering cedar and hemlock forest at the south end of the lake. There is space for about 8 groups of campers as well as a small dock with space to launch small watercraft. Note the electric motor only restriction on the lake. Vehicles with trailers will have a difficult time negotiating the steep narrow road down to the lake.

Other Options

Box Lake lies alongside Highway 6 south of Nakusp. Further along the road is **Summit Lake**, off the east side of the highway. There is a small parking area off the highway with a car top boat launch. The lake is stocked regularly with acrobatic, aggressive rainbow trout that can get to good sizes. Look for more details on this lake later in the book.

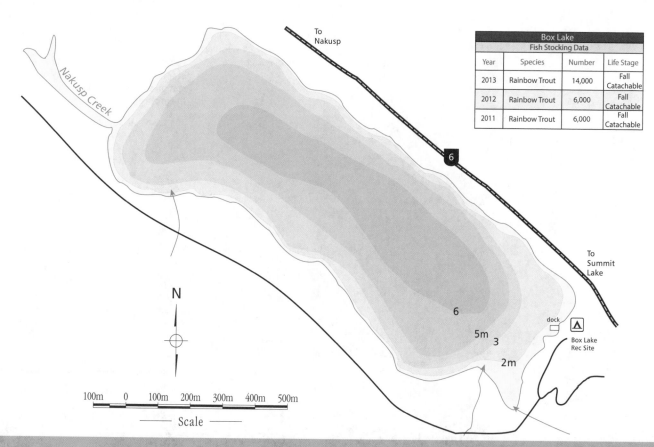

Box Lake			
Fish Stocking Data			
Year	Species	Number	Life Stage
2013	Rainbow Trout	14,000	Fall Catachable
2012	Rainbow Trout	6,000	Fall Catachable
2011	Rainbow Trout	6,000	Fall Catachable

100m 0 100m 200m 300m 400m 500m

Scale

Location: 42 km (26 mi) west of Kelowna
Elevation: 1,707 m (5,600 ft)
Surface Area: 9.2 ha (23 ac)
Mean Depth: 2 m (6 ft)
Max Depth: 6.3 m (12 ft)
Way Point: 120° 02′ 00″ Lon - W 49° 53′ 00″ Lat - N

Brenda Lake

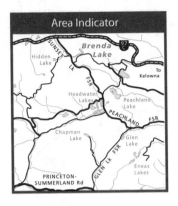

Area Indicator

Species

Rainbow Trout

Brenda Lake Fish Stocking Data			
Year	Species	Number	Life Stage
2013	Rainbow Trout	2,000	Fry
2012	Rainbow Trout	2,000	Fry
2011	Rainbow Trout	2,000	Fry

Directions

This beautiful mountain lake is located west of the city of Kelowna not far off the Okanagan Connector (Hwy 97C). Travel west to the Sunset Exit and follow Sunset Main back to the Sunset Lake Forest Service Road. About 4 km along the Sunset Lake Forest Service Road, you will find the Brenda Forest Service Road off the east side of the road. Follow the Brenda Forest Service Road east to the lake. All of these forest service roads are suitable for a 2wd vehicle but a higher clearance vehicle is an asset during wet periods.

Alternatively, Brenda Lake can be found northwest of Peachland off the Brenda Mines Road. The mine road starts at the end Princeton Avenue in town and continues up to the old mine site. Just before the old mine site, a sign indicates Brenda & MacDonald Lakes. Follow this road, the Brenda Forest Service Road, another 5 km where another left leads a kilometre to Brenda Lake.

Facilities

The **Brenda Lake Recreation Site** rests along the south shore of the lake and is fairly easily accessed, allowing for bigger units to make it in. The camping area is quite a scenic site as it sits amid a treed area along the shore of the lake and is equipped with four sites, outhouses and picnic tables. There is also a rustic boat launch to help get smaller watercraft onto the lake.

Other Options

Only minutes away from Brenda Lake, you can find **McDonald Lake** to the east. McDonald Lake provides a fairly big recreation site as well as fishing opportunities for stocked rainbow trout.

Fishing

Brenda Lake is a beautiful high elevation lake set in a pine forest to the west of Kelowna. Its close proximity to such a large population centre and its easy access off the highway make it a popular spot throughout the summer months, especially on weekends. However, the lake continues to provide fair fishing, partially due to the annual stocking of 2,000 rainbow trout. As an added bonus, the lake is also home to a large population of freshwater shrimp, which provide a steady source of food for the fish that allows the fish to grow quickly.

Because the lake is found at such a high elevation, it is usually not ice free until late spring (May). And, because the lake is so shallow, it does tend to warm up more than deeper lakes at the same elevation. This means that timing is everything here. Although fishing remains consistent in the summer, there are some great periods when the waters are cooler in spring or fall.

The lake is not a deep lake with an average depth of about 3 m (9 ft); therefore, it is essential to locate the drop off areas to find cruising trout. During the spring and fall period you may find rainbows in the shallower sections of the lake, especially near the creek inlet. Although weed growth is not abundant in this lake, look for vegetation near drop offs. These provide at least some shelter for the trout in the shallow lake. However, the lake is stained the colour of a weak tea from the tannins in the water, making it a little harder to see the bottom.

Trolling along the deeper areas can work well using a small spoon or a spinner. However, it is easy enough to cast a lure or, for fly anglers, a leech or Woolly Bugger, and retrieve slowly along the edge of the weed beds.

Fishing from the shore is possible, especially early in spring. Try working your way west from the recreation site, or access the lake from the road near the north end.

There is a fish ladder at the lake's outflow.

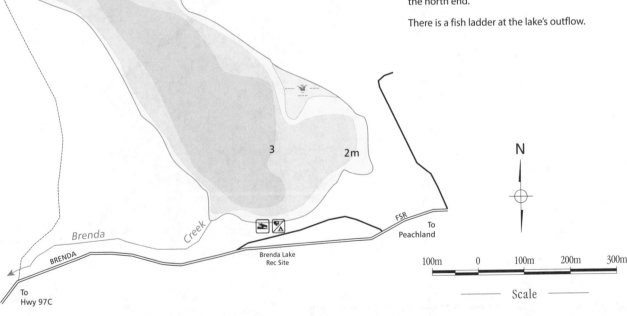

Bull River

Fishing

The Bull River is a popular alternative to folks looking to get away from the Elk River, which in turn is one of the most popular rivers in the region. It is a classic Kootenay freestone stream, with cutthroat and bull trout as well as rainbow and even a few kokanee. The trout can get up to 1 kg (2 lbs). Unlike most of the Class II waters in the Kootenays, the Bull River is actually open to spincasting, and not regulated fly-fishing only.

Bull trout will occasionally take dry flies, but most people who are targeting them specifically usually use something more minnow-like. Fly anglers use things like a Muddler Minnow, while spincasters can use any of a variety of small, silver spoons that imitate a variety of small baitfish.

The cutthroat and rainbow will also chase spoons and spinners, especially small ones on light gear. However, like most of the region's rivers, the Bull is a fly angler's dream as it features prolific hatches.

Rivers in the Kootenays open June 14, and by that time, the hatches have already begun. Salmon flies are among the earliest hatches. By mid-July, the Salmon fly hatch has died down, to be replaced by Golden Stoneflies, Pale Morning Duns and Western Green Drakes. Fishing a stonefly hatch can be a lot of fun, as the trout tend to hit these patterns hard. Fly anglers can also fall back on caddis and chironomid hatches, which occur throughout the open season.

By August, the river gets quite warm, and fishing is not great. However, you can still find sheltered pools in places along the river that offer respectable, if not outstanding, fishing. Try working a terrestrial, like a #8 Foam Hopper.

In the fall, after the heat of summer passes, the river begins to cool down, and the fishing begins to pick up. Terrestrials continue to produce well, as do caddis flies. There are also occasional hatches of other insects, such as Blue Wing Olives.

Be sure to check the regulations before heading out. Like most streams there are catch restrictions and a bait ban from June 15 through October 31. Also, since it is a Class II trout stream, a Classified Waters License is required before fishing the Bull.

Directions

The Bull River is paralleled for nearly all of its length by the Bull River Forest Service Road. This road can be accessed from the south off Highway 3/93 near Galloway, about 14 km (9 miles) west of Elko. Only for a short section near the bottom of the river does the Bull River Forest Service Road not follow the river; instead, this section is best accessed from the Wardner-Fort Steele Road.

The river can also be accessed from the north, but not as easily. If venturing in from that end, be sure to bring along a copy of the Backroad Mapbook for the Kootenay Rockies BC. This book provides detailed roads along with a whole host of other helpful information when exploring the area.

Facilities

There are recreation sites along the river at Norboe Creek, which has space for two units and Forty Mile, with has space five. These rustic sites are user maintained, so please help keep the area as clean as or cleaner than when you arrived.

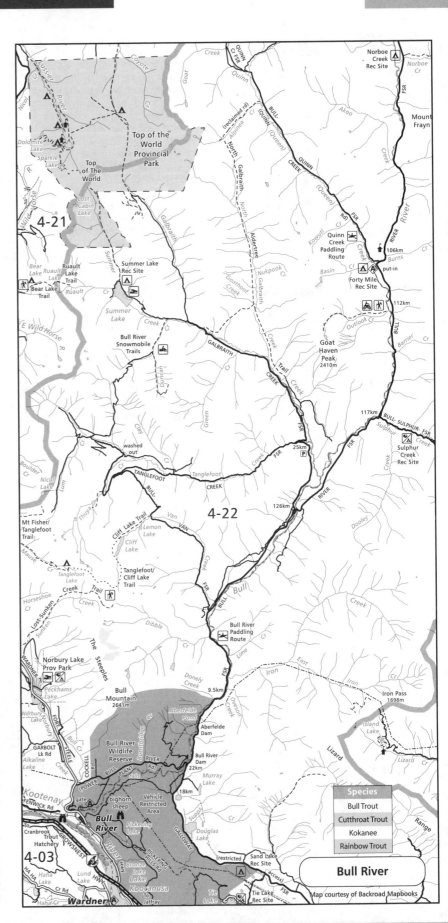

Region 4

Location: 20 km (12.4 mi) northeast of Cranbrook
Elevation: 820 m (2,690 ft)
Surface Area: 7.7 ha (14 ac)
Mean Depth: 3 m (9.8 ft)
Max Depth: 7.2 m (23.4 ft)
Way Point: 115° 38" 50" Lon - W 49° 38' 50" Lat - N

Campbell Lake

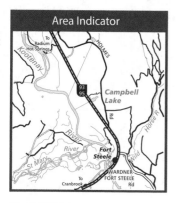

Area Indicator

Species

| Rainbow Trout |
| Brook Trout |

Campbell Lake			
Fish Stocking Data			
Year	Species	Number	Life Stage
2014	Rainbow Trout	1,500	Spring Catchable
2013	Rainbow Trout	1,500	Spring Catchable
2012	Rainbow Trout	1,500	Spring Catchable

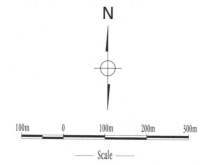

N

100m   0   100m   200m   300m

— Scale —

Fishing

Nestled between the Kootenay River and Brewery Creek in the shadows of the Hughes Mountain Range, this small, highly productive lake is a perfect location to introduce kids or adult beginners to the sport of fishing. With a surface area of 5.7 hectares (14 acres) and a maximum depth of 7.2 metres (23.4 feet), this lake can be fished by canoe, pontoon boat or float tubes and has a small cartop boat launch for easy access to the water. This being said, one of the most productive ways to fish this lake is from shore with a basic spinning rod and reel combo set up with a floater, sinker, and a baited hook. The best spot for bank fishing is on the northern shore, with worms, cooked shrimp, salmon eggs, Powerbait or Trigger X. If fly fishing is more to your liking, anglers will find the fishing excellent right at ice off, carrying on well into late spring. Try using mayflies, damselflies, scuds or leeches as these food sources are well worth imitating.

As this lake is relatively shallow, it experiences fairly regular winterkill. The Freshwater Fisheries Society of BC stocks the lake each spring with 1,500 catchable sized rainbow trout. When released, the trout measure 17–28 centimeters (7–9 inches), growing rapidly as Campbell Lake is rich in aquatic invertebrate life. By mid-summer, these fish can be over 1 kilogram (2 pounds). There are also Eastern brook trout reported here, but with winterkill and no fresh stocking in recent years, the population could be quite thin.

Campbell Lake is one of the first lakes in the East Kootenay to become ice-free due to its low elevation, and thus is a very popular spot for early season fly fishing. The trout that survive the winterkill can be very big and anglers gather in droves to bag a beautiful rainbow.

Directions

Located approximately 20 minutes north of Cranbrook in the beautiful East Kootenay, Campbell Lake can be found between Fort Steele and the Bummer Flats Wildlife Reserve. At the junction of Highway 93/95 and the Wardner/Fort Steele Road, travel approximately 3.2 kilometres (2 miles) north to the CampbellLake rest area on the right hand side. From here you can drive through the rest area to the boat launch.

Facilities

While there are no facilities at this lake other than a rudimentary day-use rest area, the closest wilderness camping would be Lakit Lake Recreation Site, located north of Campbell Lake along the Lakit Creek Forest Service Road. This site has space for four campsites in an open meadow setting on this shallow, man-made lake. The **Horseshoe Lake Recreation Site** is another option further south from the lake off the Wardner-Fort Steele Forest Service Road, providing 17 camping units amongst a stand of pine and aspen. Alternately the **Fort Steele Resort and RV Park** lies directly across from the historic town of Fort Steele and provides amenities such as hot showers, pool facilities, internet access, fire pits and toilet facilities.

Other Options

There are several different options for fishing the many lakes in the immediate vicinity of Campbell Lake. **Suagum Lake** to the north and **Bock Lake** to the south are two lakes in the region with adequate trout fishing, while anglers cast along the shores of the Kootenay River literally for kilometres in each direction.

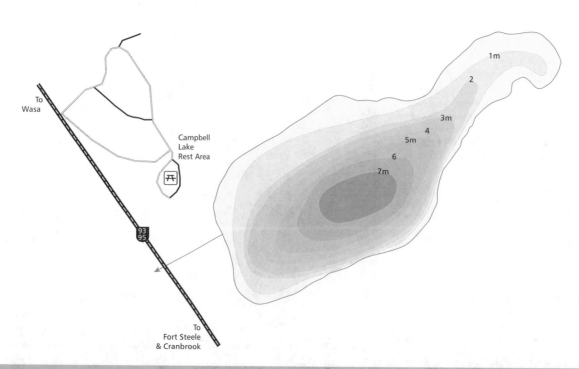

Cartwright Lake

Location: 50 km (31 mi) northwest of Invermere
Elevation: 1,152 m (3,779 ft)
Surface area: 43 ha (106 ac)
Mean depth: 3.4 m (11 ft)
Max depth: 12.2 m (40 ft)
Way Point: 116° 25' 00" Lon - W 50° 48' 00" Lat - N

Fishing

Managed as a quality fishery, anglers can expect to find better than average sized rainbow trout in this popular fishing lake located east of Brisco. Stocked every spring with the Blackwater strain of rainbow, these trout are known to grow over 3 kg (6 lbs) on occasion. However, those are very rare and trout half that size are still something to brag about.

Because the lake is so popular, the larger trout tend to be wary, and it takes a great deal of skill or luck to find the bigger fish. One of the recommended areas in the lake to try your luck is along the shoal areas in the south and north ends of the lake. During the spring trout cruise this shoal area in search of food, while in summer they make furtive excursions into the shallows for food, quickly retreating back into the cooler, safer waters.

Fly anglers will find good chironomid, mayfly, damselfly, dragonfly and caddis hatches here. Freshwater shrimp or scuds and leeches are good alternatives when the hatches are not on and into the fall. Since Cartwright is a clear lake, the trout prefer shallow water in the spring and fall. Earlier in the year use chironomid pupae (black and olive green) patterns followed by Pheasant Tail or Hares Ear mayfly nymphs and then damselfly and dragonfly nymphs into June. Caddis flies worked on top during twilight hours can be a lot of fun during the summer months.

Spincasters should try trolling Panther Martins, Kwikfish and similar type lures. Be sure to work the drop-offs near the shoals and vary your speed and direction to entice strikes.

To help maintain the quality fishery, the limit is only one trout being no less than 50 cm (19.7 inches) in length. In addition there is a single barbless hook, bait ban and no ice fishing allowed on Cartwright. Boaters should note the 10 horsepower motor restriction as well.

Facilities

Cartwright Lake is home to a scenic lakeside forest recreation site that offers two medium sized campsites along with a dock and boat launch suitable for small trailered boats. Between the two sites, there is room for about 17 campers. If these sites are full chances are you probably are best to fish elsewhere. However, there are a number of nearby lakes that also host forest recreation sites and may not be as busy. To avoid the crowds, it is best to visit the area during the week or in spring before the summer weekend warriors come out to play.

Boaters should note the engine power restriction of 10 HP and other special fishing regulations on Cartwright Lake.

Other Options

Just to the north of Cartwright Lake, there are a number of alternative fishing lakes available for exploration. Jade Lake, Topaz Lake and Cleland Lake are a few of the more popular alternatives with good rainbow trout fishing and small forest recreation campsites available for visitors to enjoy. These lakes are described in more detail under Cleland Lake in this book.

Directions

To reach Cartwright Lake, follow Highway 95 to the village of Brisco and turn west onto Brisco Road. This road quickly rises out of the Columbia River Valley to the Bugaboo Forest Service Road. Continue west on this road and turn south onto the Templeton River Forest Service Road. This junction is about 18.5 km west of the highway. Continue south for another 5 km or so where a couple side roads lead to the lakeside camping areas. The southernmost site is the bigger of the two recreation sites.

From the south, the lake is found about 55 km north of Invermere via the Westside and Leadqueen-Frances Forest Service Roads. Turn west at the 39.5 km junction and then follow the Leadqueen-Frances Road north to the lake. Be wary of logging truck traffic when travelling the roads in the areas

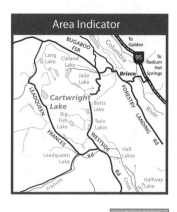

Area Indicator

Species

Rainbow Trout

Cartwright Lake			
Fish Stocking Data			
Year	Species	Number	Life Stage
2013	Rainbow Trout	8,000	Yearling
2012	Rainbow Trout	8,000	Yearling
2011	Rainbow Trout	8,000	Yearling

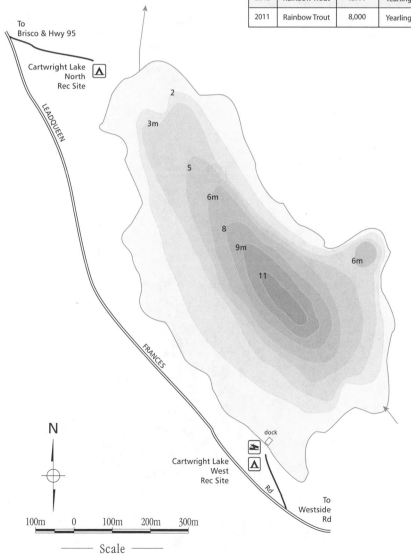

To Brisco & Hwy 95

Cartwright Lake North Rec Site

LEADQUEEN

FRANCES

dock

Cartwright Lake West Rec Site

To Westside Rd

Rd

N

100m 0 100m 200m 300m

Scale

Location: 5 km (3 mi) south of Golden
Elevation: 1,021 m (3,350 ft)
Surface Area: 5 ha (12 ac)
Mean Depth: 11.5 m (38 ft)
Max Depth: 25 m (82 ft)
Way Point: 116° 58′ 00″ Lon - W 51° 15′ 00″ Lat - N

Cedar Lake

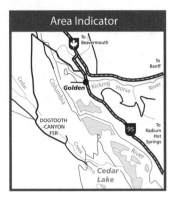

Area Indicator

Species

| Brook Trout |
| Cutthroat Trout |
| Rainbow Trout |

Cedar Lake			
Fish Stocking Data			
Year	Species	Number	Life Stage
2012	Rainbow Trout	2,000	Fry
2011	Rainbow Trout	2,000	Fry
2010	Rainbow Trout	2,000	Fry

Fishing

There are four lakes southwest of Golden that bear the title Cedar. In a fit of pure creativity, they are distinguished by number: Cedar Lake One, Cedar Lake Two, and so on. The most popular and best known of the Cedar Lakes is Cedar Lake One.

Cedar Lake One is stocked annually with rainbow trout, which provide for fair fishing for rainbow up to 1 kg (2 lbs) in size. Anglers can also expect to catch the odd cutthroat trout in the lake, and maybe even a brook trout. However, the cutthroat in the lake are generally small compared to their rainbow cousins, and the brook are a very rare catch indeed.

This lake is quite deep, hence deeper presentations may be required to find those bigger trout. Try trolling a small spoon or leech pattern along the drop off area around the lake. By cruising your lure or fly along this higher percentage area, you should have some success, especially in the spring and fall.

When chironomids are hatching but the trout are not rising, (which usually happens during the day) fly anglers should fish down near the bottom using a long leader on a floating line. For deep hatches, anglers should use a small boat and a sinking line and cast the fly out, letting it sink until it is straight down before very slowly retrieving it to imitate a rising chironomid pupa.

In the early morning, and again in the early evening, the surface of the lake usually calms down, and the bolder fish begin feeding at the surface. While it doesn't happen every night, the intelligent fly angler will watch for the telltale rings that say the fish are rising to feed. When they are rising, a dry fly pattern like a Tom Thumb can work wonders.

The other three Cedar Lakes are also stocked with rainbow trout. However, the lakes are not road accessible, and require a short walk in. This cuts down on the amount of anglers these lakes see. It also makes getting a small craft to the lakes difficult, though not impossible. The fishing in the other three lakes is basically the same as in the Cedar Lake One, with the exception that these lakes don't hold anything other than rainbow trout.

There is a powerboat restriction on the lakes.

Directions

From the city of Golden, follow the signs west towards Kicking Horse Resort. At the 9 km mark on the Kicking Horse Road, the Dogtooth-Canyon Forest Service Road branches southeast. Recent improvements to the recreation site allow for easy 2wd access most of the year. There is also a separate day use area for parking and boat launching.

Facilities

The **Cedar Lake Recreation Site** has recently been upgraded to include 10 campsites, a large day use area with a sandy beach and swimming float. Found close to Golden, it is a popular site for water sports, sunbathing and fishing. In addition to the short 1 km walk to a small, secluded lake near Cedar Lake, the recreation site acts as a staging area for mountain bikers exploring the extensive Moonraker Trail system. A fee is charged on weekends to camp.

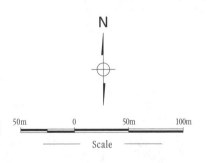

Chain Lake

Location: 33 km (20.5 mi) northeast of Princeton
Elevation: 1,006 m (3,300 ft)
Surface Area: 42 ha (104 ac)
Mean Depth: 5 m (15 ft)
Max Depth: 6 m (20 ft)
Way Point: 120° 16′ 00″ Lon - W 49° 41′ 00″ Lat - N

Fishing

Chain Lake is the first of a series of easily accessed roadside lakes found alongside the Princeton Summerland Road. Despite the easy access and constant stream of anglers, the lake continues to provide plenty of nice sized trout.

Because the lake is relatively large, the preferred method of angling is trolling. There is a boat launch at the forest recreation site, and getting a small boat out onto the water will assist you greatly. Trolling around the edge of the lake with a lake troll (Willow Leaf, wedding ring and bait) can work wonders. Anglers also troll small spoons or even an attractor fly pattern like a Carey Special.

Fly-fishing can be productive, but it's a good idea to get out onto the lake. The forest crowds in on the lake, and, while there are a few clearings large enough to cast from, there are not many. If you can find a place to cast, it is not that difficult to cast beyond the drop off since the water drops quickly off from the shore.

There are ample drop offs and shoal areas around the lake to provide for fly-fishing or trolling opportunities. The key to success on this lake is to find what the trout are feeding on. All the normal hatches occur, but knowing what the food of choice is at the time can greatly improve your success on Chain Lake. Use a dip net or, if you catch a fish, a throat pump to help you determine what the fish are feeding on.

The two stream inlets are often good places to concentrate on. Alternatively, the southeastern shore of the lake, where there is a steep drop off at the tip of a prominent point is a good holding area, especially on those hot summer days. However, do note that there is an algae bloom in the summer, and when the bloom is on, the fishing suffers.

To help alleviate the fishing pressure, the lake is heavily stocked annually. The stocking program helps provide a good trout fishery for mostly smaller fish. Trout average about 0.5 kg (1 lb), although can reach up to 3 kg (6.5 lbs) in size.

Ice fishing is not permitted on Chain Lake.

Directions

Northeast of the town of Princeton, you can find Chain Lake off the paved Princeton-Summerland Road. This well travelled road was once called Highway 40, but has been downgraded to backroad status with the addition of the Coquihalla Connector to the north. Chain Lake is the first of a series of easily accessed roadside lakes.

Facilities

The **Chain Lake Recreation Site** is a scenic shore side camping area. The area is easily spotted off the side of the access road and offers a small boat launch, outhouses and picnic table facilities set within a semi-treed area. There are a total of 31 enhanced campsites along the north shore of the lake. Accessible by RVs, fees are charged from the end of April until early October. In addition to the ever popular Kettle Valley Railway/Trans Canada Trail to explore, visitors will also find a number of private cottages and homes around Chain Lake.

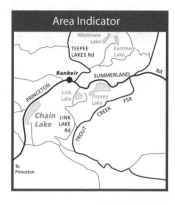
Area Indicator

Species
Rainbow Trout

Chain Lake Fish Stocking Data			
Year	Species	Number	Life Stage
2013	Rainbow Trout	7,500	Yearling
2012	Rainbow Trout	7,500	Yearling
2011	Rainbow Trout	7,500	Yearling

N

100m   0   100m   200m   300m
— Scale —

Other Options

Further down along the Princeton-Summerland Road you will encounter a few more quality fishing lakes including **Link, Osprey** and **Thirsk Lakes**. All three lakes offer angling opportunities for rainbow trout and host of small Forest Recreation campsites for visitors to enjoy.

Champion Lakes

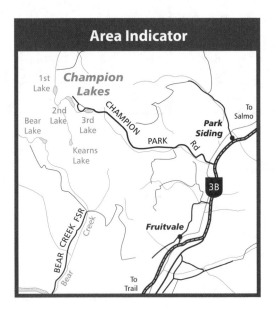

Directions

Champion Lakes Provincial Park lies in the hills above Castlegar and Trail. The park access road is found off Highway 3B to the east of Trail and Fruitvale. The Champion Park Road is a paved, but steep road that climbs 10 km (6 miles) to the park. The first lake you come across will be the Third Champion Lake, which sits alongside the road. There is a day use area on one side of the lake, and a campground and boat launch on the other.

The campground sits between the Third and Second Champion Lakes. Continuing on the main road will bring you to the north end of the Second Lake. If the gate is open, it is possible to drive to the lake to hand launch small craft.

The First Lake is accessed on a 1 km (0.6 mile) trail from the Second Lake. If you are bringing a canoe, you can cut a few hundred meters off the trip by paddling to the west end of the second lake and pulling out there.

Facilities

Champion Lakes Provincial Park offers a popular 89 unit campsite next to the Third Lake. There is also a paved boat launch and a nice sandy beach on the lake. For reservations, visit www.discovercamping.ca. There is also a rustic boat launch onto the second lake, while a maintained trail system links the three.

Fishing

There are three lakes that make up the Champion Lakes that are protected within the confines of the Champion Lakes Provincial Park. The most popular is the third lake, due to its close proximity to the popular camping and beach areas of the park. Due to the high elevation of the area, fishing does not get going until May after the ice begins to break up and remains fairly consistent into October. All three lakes are stocked by the Freshwater Fisheries Society of BC to help maintain the fishery.

The Third Champion Lake is the hardest fished lake in the chain and it shows, as the fishing can be marginal. Although the mainstay of the action is from small pan sized rainbow trout, there are a few reports of decent sized trout that can be caught in the lake.

Fly-fishing is the recommended method of fishing the lake due to the fact that the trout can be quite spooky towards lures and spinners. Most visitors love to cast a line or two into the lake and by the time summer roles around, the trout have smartened up. However, they seem to remain quite aggressive at times towards a well presented bead head nymph or dry fly. The trout consistently seem to hone in on this more natural food choice. Try trolling a leech pattern or larger type nymph to find those bigger trout. Earlier in the year (late May or June), fishing a chironomid pattern from a tube or small boat, using a long leader at the drop offs can also be effective. Try using a copper or green pattern, size 10–14.

Within a few minutes drive of the Third Champion Lake, the Second Champion Lake offers better fishing for bigger fish. The lake is stocked annually with rainbow trout that grow over 1.5 kg (3 lbs) in size. These bigger fish are usually fished out quickly and by the time summer comes trout in the 25 cm (10 in) range are the norm.

Although there are definitely some good sized rainbow trout, fishing in the second lake can be frustrating at times. The inconsistency is most likely due to the number of anglers that fish the lake throughout the summer months. Therefore, the best time to try the lake is late spring or in the fall. Fly anglers can often sight fish the smaller trout with top water flies, although to find the big ones, a dedicated and observant angler needs to work the lake. There is plenty of weed growth in this lake and rainbow tend to cruise the weed lines in search of food. The lake is virtually divided into two separate portions, with both providing results. However, many say that the big trout tend to be found in the southeast portion of the lake.

Watch for the hatches. While the lake has a good chironomid hatch, when the mayflies hatch, using a mayfly nymph will often produce well. Towards evening, try switching to a dry mayfly pattern. Another option that works well is to fish an emerger pattern just below the surface, using a dry dun imitation on a sink tip line, which will drop the fly a couple feet below the surface. Using a slow retrieve will give the fly a lifelike appearance.

Spincasters can also fish here with decent success after the fly-fishing only season is over. At this time, a lake troll with Wedding Band and bait is a deadly combination. Locals say that this is really the only thing that works if you are not into fly-fishing.

Out of the three Champion Lakes, the First Lake offers the best fishing lake of the three to fish, mostly because accessing the lake is so difficult. The lake is only accessible by trail or if you prefer, portage. The trail is an enjoyable walk that travels through a second growth forest. Along the trail you will pass lush moss covered forest floors with many of the trees sporting heavy lichen growth.

The first lake is stocked annually and provides good fishing throughout the season. Focus your efforts is in the southern end of the lake. Two flies that seem to produce consistently are the Carey Special and leech patterns. Work these patterns in the deeper zones of the lake along the drop off areas. Although it is possible to fish from shore at the southeast end of the lake, a canoe or float tube is a real advantage. Carrying either in, however, is not an easy task.

Dry fly-fishing on a still day (usually in the morning or evening) can be fast and furious on this lake. Try working the hatches, or, when there's no obvious hatch, break out a Tom Thumb, which is a great general pattern for fishing dry and even works well for top water trolling.

In the fall, a small chironomid pattern can work quite well, but most people stick to a leech or an olive or black Woolly Bugger on a sinking line with a 1 m (3 foot) leader.

There is a powerboat restriction on all three lakes. Be sure to check the regulations for other restrictions.

Champion Lakes

Location: 16 km (10 mi) south of Castlegar

1st Lake

2m

2m

2m

2m

4

6m
8
10m
12

Landis Cr

Kearns Cr

Landis Cr

2m

Champion
Lakes
Provincial
Park

2nd Lake

8
6m
4

Dry
Island

Dry
Isl

4
6m
8

10m

N

Lookout

Landis Cr

Play Area

dam

Castor Cr

3rd Lake

20 18 16
22
24m

14 12 10 8
floating 6m
wharf 4
2m

Picnic
Area

CHAMPION

PARK

P

Rd

To
Hwy 3B

Upper Champion Lake

Upper Champion Lake			
Fish Stocking Data			
Year	Species	Number	Life Stage
2012	Rainbow Trout	6,000	Fry
2011	Rainbow Trout	6,000	Fry
2010	Rainbow Trout	6,000	Fry

Species
Rainbow Trout

Middle Champion Lake

Middle Champion Lake			
Fish Stocking Data			
Year	Species	Number	Life Stage
2013	Rainbow Trout	3,000	Yearling
2012	Rainbow Trout	3,000	Yearling
2011	Rainbow Trout	3,000	Yearling

Species
Rainbow Trout

Lower Champion Lake

Species
Rainbow Trout

Lower Champion Lake			
Fish Stocking Data			
Year	Species	Number	Life Stage
2013	Rainbow Trout	2,000	Spring Catchable
2012	Rainbow Trout	2,000	Spring Catchable
2011	Rainbow Trout	2,000	Spring Catchable

Upper Champion Lake (#1)
Elevation: 1,051 m (3,448 ft)
Surface Area: 14 ha (35 ac)
Mean Depth: 10.1 m (33 ft)
Max Depth: 24.3m (80 ft)
Way Point: 117° 36'00" Lon - W 49° 11'00" Lat - N

Middle Champion Lake (#2)
Elevation: 1,049 m (3,442 ft)
Surface Area: 15 ha (37 ac)
Mean Depth: 2.3 m (8 ft)
Max Depth: 11 m (36 ft)
Way Point: 117° 37'00" Lon - W 49° 11'00" Lat - N

Lower Champion Lake (#3)
Elevation: 1,044 m (3,425 ft)
Surface Area: 11 ha (27 ac)
Mean Depth: 2.4 m (8 ft)
Max Depth: 13 m (43 ft)
Way Point: 117° 38'00" Lon - W 49° 11'00" Lat - N

100m 0 100m 200m 300m 400m 500m
— Scale —

Region 4

Location: 32 km (20 mi) southeast of Cranbrook
Elevation: 1,201 m (3,940 ft)
Surface Area: 38 ha (94 ac)
Mean Depth: 6.5 m (21 ft)
Max Depth: 13 m (43 ft)
Way Point: 115° 32' 00" Lon - W 49° 10' 00" Lat - N

Cherry Lake

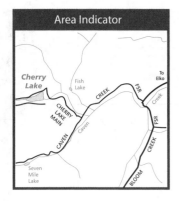

Area Indicator

Species
Rainbow Trout
Cutthroat Trout

Fishing

Cherry Lake is a higher elevation lake found tucked up in the McGillivray Mountains. While the lake is not as high elevation as some, the terrain surrounding the lake keeps both the air temperature and the water temperatures cooler, which means fishing is usually consistent throughout the open water season.

Both rainbow trout and cutthroat trout inhabit the lake in good numbers. There sheer number of fish allows for some pretty good fishing no matter what tactic you use. Fly-fishing, bait fishing or spincasting all produce fish that average 20-30 cm (8-12 in) in size, with the odd 1 kg (2 lbs) trout being taken.

Cherry Lake has a unique bottom structure, with significant drop off that surrounds much of the lake. Trolling along this shoreline drop off area should produce good results, although the shoal along the eastern shore right off the boat launch is an obvious area for trout to hold since there is a deep hole right next to the shoal area. Another great spot will be towards the western end, where there is a large shoal. Move your boat or float tube back from the shoal and hole area and try casting towards the two areas to find consistent action.

In the late spring, after the sun has begun to warm the lake and the hatches have begun, the fish will take to a dry fly. Some popular patterns include size 12–16 pale morning duns, Tom Thumbs and blue wing olives. While getting out on the water will improve your chances, it is quite easy to cast from shore on a summer's evening from right around the boat launch.

For spincasters, try a Panther Martin, Mepps or Blue Fox.

Facilities

The **Cherry Lake Recreation Site** lies along the heavily treed eastern shore of the lake. The rustic site offers space for 10 groups along with picnic tables and outhouses. There is a cartop boat launch suitable for small boats or canoes.

Directions

Sandwiched between Highway 3/95 to the west and Lake Koocanusa to the east, Cherry Lake is tucked away in the McGillivray Mountain Range. Access is gained by following the Kikomun or Jaffray Baynes Lake Roads from Highway 3 near Elko. These paved roads lead across the Bailey Bridge over Lake Koocanusa. A second left leads to the Caven-Gold Creek Forest Service Road. Follow this road southwest for about 32.5 km where the road forks. Continue right (northwest) on the Lower Caven Creek Forest Service Road to the 39 km mark. A right (northwest) here should lead you to the Cherry Lake Main Road. Another 3 km later, continue right and look for the recreation site and lake on your left or south.

Due to the difficult nature of finding this lake, it is recommended to pick up a copy of the *Backroad Mapbook for the Kootenay Rockies BC*. In addition to aiding in backcountry travel, the book contains information on many other fishing opportunities, campsites, trails and much more. A high clearance vehicle and a copy of the *Backroad GPS Maps for BC* are also recommended for your travels.

Other Options

To the south of Cherry Lake lies **Seven Mile Lake**, which is found off the Caven Creek Forest Service Road. The lake is inhabited with cutthroat trout that provide good action at times. The lake is also home to a small recreation campsite.

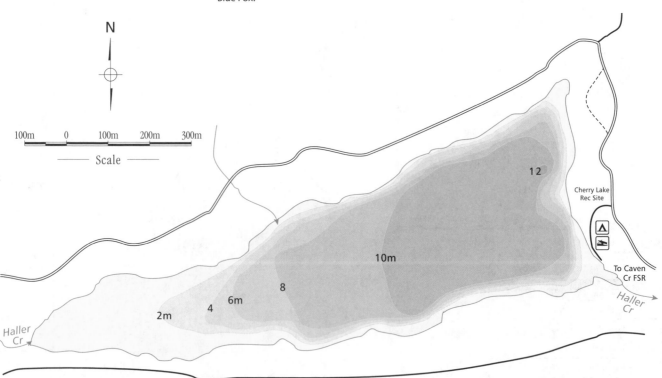

N

100m   0   100m   200m   300m
Scale

Cherry Lake
Rec Site

To Caven
Cr FSR

Haller
Cr

Haller
Cr

12

10m

8

6m

4

2m

Christina Lake

Location: 19 km (12 mi) east of Grand Forks
Elevation: 446 m (1,463 ft)
Surface Area: 2,509 ha (6,197 ac)
Mean Depth: 36 m (118 ft)
Max Depth: 54 m (177 ft)
Way Point: 118° 15′ 00″ Lon - W 49° 07′ 00″ Lat - N

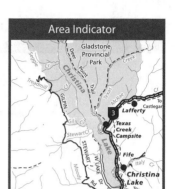

Area Indicator

Species
Bass
Bull Trout
Burbot
Kokanee
Rainbow Trout
Whitefish

Directions

This big lake is easily accessed off Highway 3 east of Grand Forks. There is no shortage of access points on the lake, just look for the familiar blue boat launch or park signs that will direct you to the public access points at either end of the lake.

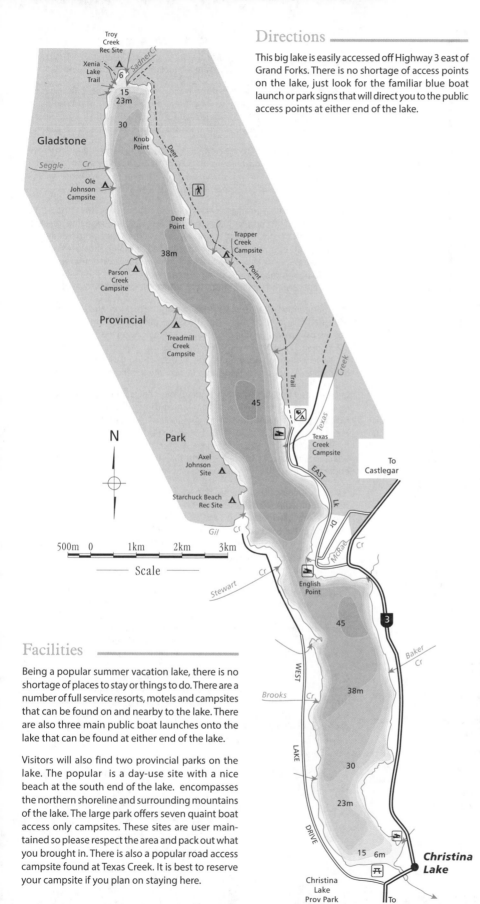

Facilities

Being a popular summer vacation lake, there is no shortage of places to stay or things to do. There are a number of full service resorts, motels and campsites that can be found on and nearby to the lake. There are also three main public boat launches onto the lake that can be found at either end of the lake.

Visitors will also find two provincial parks on the lake. The popular is a day-use site with a nice beach at the south end of the lake. encompasses the northern shoreline and surrounding mountains of the lake. The large park offers seven quaint boat access only campsites. These sites are user maintained so please respect the area and pack out what you brought in. There is also a popular road access campsite found at Texas Creek. It is best to reserve your campsite if you plan on staying here.

Fishing

Christina Lake is a popular recreational lake that has long been a favourite destination for people in the area. Most of the development is taking place in the south, while the north end is protected by a large provincial park. Despite the number of water skiers, jet skis and power boats buzzing around, finding a quite stretch of lake to fish is not that difficult since the lake is over 20 km (12 mi) long and up to 2 km (1.2 mi) wide. Anglers will find a diverse sportfish population with rainbow trout, kokanee, burbot, bull trout, smallmouth bass, largemouth bass, sunfish and whitefish all lurking in the depths.

In recent years, the bass fishery has really taken off. There are many smaller bays that hold bass. Look for largemouth to hold around the heavy cover and in shallow water, while smallmouth prefer rocks and logs to hide in. To be more specific, the marshy shoreline across from the marina is a good area to find largemouth. Working your way north, the gravel bays are more adept to hold smallmouth. At the north and south end of the lake the creek mouths are also good areas to try. The nice thing about bass is they can be very aggressive and will attack most well presented offerings. Using surface lures, like a bass popper for fly anglers or a Hula-Popper for spincasters, is one of the most fun ways of fishing bass. Using a special bass lure designed to not snag the weeds will help, but plastic worms rigged Texas or Carolina style are the most popular way to go.

Trout and kokanee anglers also have a lot of area to work. As a result, trolling is the preferred method of fishing for these sportfish. The best areas to work are around the drop offs of points and around the many feeder streams that bring in nutrients for the fish to feed off of. A lake troll with a wedding ring or other small spinner tipped with bait should attract the smaller fish, while bigger lures and spoons might entice a larger strike. If fly-fishing is your thing, try casting or trolling searching patterns near the creek mouths.

Region 4

Cleland, Jade, Cub, Topaz Lakes

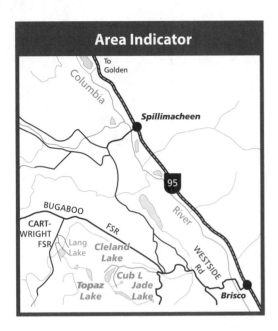

Area Indicator

Fishing

To the west of Brisco anglers will find a cluster of good fishing lakes. Each offers its own unique charm, while they are all stocked regularly with rainbow trout.

Cleland Lake is the first and biggest in the series. As a result, it also sees the most fishing pressure. Despite this, the lake offers fair to good fishing for stocked rainbow trout that average about 30-40 cm (12-16 in) in size. The lake is quite deep, which helps keep the trout relatively active through the summer.

During the early part of the season, the key to finding the feeding trout in this lake is to work the shoal areas in the 3-6 m (10-20 ft) range. If your success is slow, try trolling around the shoal and drop off areas to cover more water. A float tube or canoe is a big advantage to better work the lake.

Jade Lake lies to the southeast and is also stocked annually with rainbow trout. Managed as a fly-fishing only lake, the small lake can produce some nice sized rainbow with the odd trout reaching 1 kg (2 lbs). The best way to fish the lake is by float tube or boat, as shore fishing is limited. The large shoal areas located at the east and west ends of the lake can provide for good action with a chironomid during the spring. During summer evenings, the shoals can also be a good are to focus, when rainbow cruise into the shallows in search of food.

The chironomid hatch usually takes place during mid day, and the trout rarely rise when it is so bright out. The wise fly anglers should fish down near the bottom using a long leader on a floating line, assuming the hatch is occurring in less than 3 m (10 ft) of water. For deep hatches, anglers should use a small boat and a sinking line and cast the fly out, letting it sink until it is straight down before very slowly retrieving it to imitate a rising chironomid pupa.

Cub Lake is a tiny, but surprisingly deep lake that is found north of Jade and east of Cleland. The shoal area located near the southwestern corner of Cub Lake is a good cruising area for hungry rainbow, especially during the spring. The lake is about 200 m (600 ft) at its widest point, which means that shore fishing is certainly possible for these stocked trout. Some people do bring a float tube and park in the middle of the lake, where they can cover almost the entire lake simply by staying in one place and rotating.

Topaz Lake comes by its name honestly. It is a wonderfully clear blue lake, stocked annually with rainbow trout and fishing can be good at times for rainbow that can reach up to 1 kg (2 lbs) in size. It is found almost due west of Cleland but the road in is very rough. Although you may have to hike the last little way, it is easy enough to carry a canoe or float tube with you. A floatation device is highly recommended since you will need to get out to the deeper areas of the lake to work the drop offs, especially during the summer months.

Trolling can work but the movement of a boat or float tube can be enough to scare the trout. Better yet is to anchor in a deeper area and cast into the shallows, working your lure of fly slowly out towards the drop off. This long, narrow lake has two deep holes, one in the north end and one in the southern portion. These two areas are the main hot spots of the lake, as rainbow will cruise the shallows near the deep areas in search of food.

Fly-fishers should watch for active hatches, and try to match them. When there is no active hatch occurring, or the fish just aren't biting, try working an attractor pattern like a Carey Special or a Woolly Bugger. Typically, you should retrieve slowly, pausing for a few seconds between pulls. However, if that isn't working try altering the retrieve with a fast, jerky pull instead. Spincasters can also have a bit of fun throwing light tackle like a Panther Martin, Mepps Black Fury or Blue Fox.

Jade, Cub and Topaz lakes are electric motors only, while there is a 10 hp limit on Cleland Lake.

Directions

To find the lakes, take Highway 95 to Brisco, then follow Westside Road west for about 6 km. The spur road leading west towards Cleland Lake is found at the 50 km mark of Westside Road. Those hauling trailers may prefer the south access from Invermere or Radium Hot Springs despite the longer distance of logging road travel. The road up from Brisco is rougher and narrower. The last stretch of road into Cleland Lake is also a bit rough.. Continuing past the north end of Cleland will bring you to **Topaz Lake**, although the road becomes all but undrivable before you hit the lake, and you will probably have to walk a little bit. Just before reaching the recreation site on Cleland, another road leads south. To find **Cub Lake**, take the next left on the even rougher looking road. This road leads close to but not quite to the shore of the tiny lake. It might be wiser to simply walk or ATV from Cleland.

Finding **Jade Lake** requires taking the same branch road south before the Cleland Lake Recreation Site but keep straight instead of turning towards Cub Lake. At the south end of Cleland, you will find another side road leading southeast. Follow this road and avoid all branch roads and you should meet Jade Lake. Again, this road is particularly steep and rough.

Facilities

Cleland Lake Recreation Site is actually made up of three separate forested sites on the south, west and east shores of the lake. A boat launch is offered on the northern most site for boat with 7kW or smaller engines. The private nature and mountain views make this a fine camping destination; however, campers with trailers should note the limited turnaround space.

The **Jade Lake Recreation Site** is a quaint single unit camping area on a popular fly fishing lake. There is a dock and a place to hand launch a belly or pontoon boat for those able to drag a boat down the steep and rough road access. The **Topaz Lake Recreation Site** is also a single unit site with rough road access. There is a launch here, but trailers are not advised.

Cleland, Jade, Cub, Topaz Lakes

Location: 47 km (29 mi) northwest of Invermere

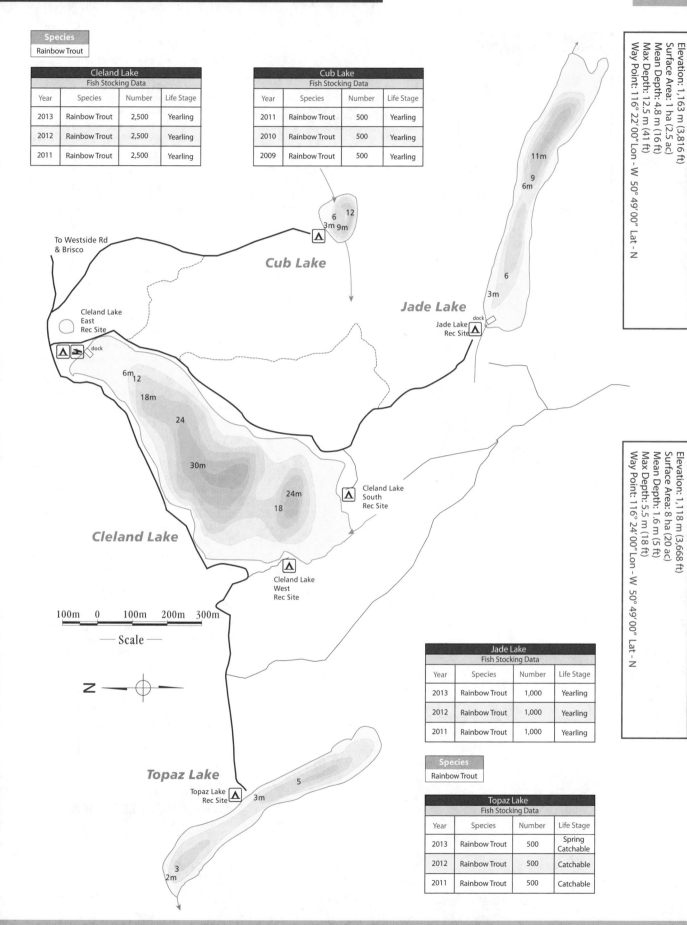

Species

Rainbow Trout

Cleland Lake Fish Stocking Data			
Year	Species	Number	Life Stage
2013	Rainbow Trout	2,500	Yearling
2012	Rainbow Trout	2,500	Yearling
2011	Rainbow Trout	2,500	Yearling

Cub Lake Fish Stocking Data			
Year	Species	Number	Life Stage
2011	Rainbow Trout	500	Yearling
2010	Rainbow Trout	500	Yearling
2009	Rainbow Trout	500	Yearling

Cub Lake

Elevation: 1,163 m (3,816 ft)
Surface Area: 1 ha (2.5 ac)
Mean Depth: 4.8 m (16 ft)
Max Depth: 12.5 m (41 ft)
Way Point: 116° 22' 00" Lon - W 50° 49' 00" Lat - N

Cub Lake

To Westside Rd & Brisco

Jade Lake

Jade Lake Rec Site

Cleland Lake East Rec Site

dock

Cleland Lake

Cleland Lake South Rec Site

Elevation: 1,118 m (3,668 ft)
Surface Area: 8 ha (20 ac)
Mean Depth: 1.6 m (5 ft)
Max Depth: 5.5 m (18 ft)
Way Point: 116° 24' 00" Lon - W 50° 49' 00" Lat - N

Topaz Lake

100m 0 100m 200m 300m

— Scale —

N

Cleland Lake West Rec Site

Jade Lake Fish Stocking Data			
Year	Species	Number	Life Stage
2013	Rainbow Trout	1,000	Yearling
2012	Rainbow Trout	1,000	Yearling
2011	Rainbow Trout	1,000	Yearling

Topaz Lake

Topaz Lake Rec Site

Species

Rainbow Trout

Topaz Lake Fish Stocking Data			
Year	Species	Number	Life Stage
2013	Rainbow Trout	500	Spring Catchable
2012	Rainbow Trout	500	Catchable
2011	Rainbow Trout	500	Catchable

Collier & Upper Collier Lakes

Area Indicator

Collier Lake

Elevation: 1,178 m (3,865 ft)
Surface Area: 12 ha (30 ac)
Mean Depth: 4.1 m (13 ft)
Max Depth: 11 m (36 ft)
Way Point: 118° 55'00" Lon - W 49° 31'00" Lat - N

Species

Rainbow Trout

Collier Lake Fish Stocking Data			
Year	Species	Number	Life Stage
2013	Rainbow Trout	1,000	Fry
2012	Rainbow Trout	1,000	Fry
2011	Rainbow Trout	500	Fry

Upper Collier Lake

Elevation: 1,236 m (4,055 ft)
Surface Area: 7.8 ha (19 ac)
Mean Depth: 3.3 m (11 ft)
Max Depth: 7 m (23 ft)
Way Point: 118° 54'00" Lon - W 49° 30'00" Lon N

Fishing

Collier and Upper Collier are a pair of hike in lakes in the hills to the west of the Christian Valley. Despite their relative remoteness, they do see a fair number of rainbow trout anglers each year. Collier Lake is the easier of the two to access, requiring only a 1 km (0.6 mile) hike and as a result sees the most fishing pressure. Upper Collier is about 1.5 km (0.9 mi) beyond.

Collier Lake can be murky at times and any fly pattern should be dressed with some attractant such as crystal flash or flashabou to help increase success. Leech patterns are often the ideal locator pattern on the lake but the feisty rainbow can be avid top water feeders during hatches. Backswimmer and flying ant hatches are particularly productive on this lake.

Upper Collier Lake is a shallow lake, and a belly boat would go a long way towards improving the fishing experience. In the spring, the resident rainbow can be quite aggressive, striking at any decent presentations. The inlet stream located along the southern shore provides oxygen and water flow, creating a good holding area for trout in the spring. In the late spring, damselfly nymphs will congregate in this region of the lake and hatch near reeds and weeds.

Upper Collier Lake has special quotas and management restrictions, check your regulations before fishing.

Directions

Take Highway 33 to the settlement of Westbridge and then head north along the Christian Valley Road to the Beaverdell State Creek Forest Service Road. Follow this road west over the pass and down to Sago Creek. Across from the Sago Creek Recreation Site, you will find an established trail heading east to Collier Lake. It is 1 km to Collier and about twice that to Upper Collier along a moderately tough trail. A shorter alternative from Kelowna is to take the Beaverdell Road east off Highway 33 near the village of Beaverdell. The road leads about 18 km to Sago Creek site as above.

Upper Collier Lake can also be accessed from the rough, 4wd Dear Creek Road. At the end of the road, an unmarked and unmaintained trail leads about 1 km to the east side of the lake.

Facilities

Both lakes have small campsites that are basically little more than small cleared areas next to the lake.

Species

Rainbow Trout

Upper Collier Lake Fish Stocking Data			
Year	Species	Number	Life Stage
2013	Rainbow Trout	500	Fry
2012	Rainbow Trout	500	Fry
2011	Rainbow Trout	500	Fry

Collier Lake

To Beaverdell-State Creek FSR

Collier Lake Rec Site

1m
2
3m
4
5m
6
7m
8
10 9m

To Upper Collier Lk

N

To Lower Collier Lake

50m   0   50m   100m
Scale

6m

4

Upper Collier Lake Rec Site

2m

To Dear Creek Rd

Upper Collier Lake

Columbia Lake

Location: 2 km (1.2 mi) north of Canal Flats
Elevation: 809 m (2,654 ft)
Surface Area: 2,574 ha (6,358 ac)
Mean Depth: 3 m (10 ft)
Max Depth: 5 m (16 ft)
Way Point: 115° 51' 00" Lon - W 50° 14' 00" Lat - N

Region 4

Fishing

Columbia Lake is the stereotypical Kootenay lake: a long, narrow valley bottom lake that offers pretty good fishing. The lake is at the headwaters of the mighty Columbia River, one of the great rivers of North America, circling north before making its long journey south to the Pacific Ocean in the state of Oregon in the USA.

The lake holds rainbow trout, cutthroat trout and bull trout. Fishing for cutthroat and bull trout is usually slow, but the lake was extensively stocked in the past with rainbow, and, despite the fact that the program was discontinued in 2001, still holds plenty of rainbow. Whitefish and burbot or lingcod also inhabit the lake in fair numbers and are mainly caught in fall and winter by the select few anglers that want to target these fish.

Like the rest of the big Kootenay Lakes, Columbia is a lake built for trolling, which allows you to cover more water as you fish. Sure, there's lots of fish down there, but there's also lots of lake for them to hide.

The lake is surprisingly warm for such a large lake, getting to 18°C (64°F) by July. Such temperatures are uncomfortably warm for cool water species like trout, and so they retreat deeper into the lake. Not too deep, though, preferring to hang out in a layer of water which starts about 4 m (15 ft) down called the thermocline. Here they'll be comfortable and find plenty of oxygen.

What they won't find here is a lot of food, so the trout will usually be found holding where the thermocline and the drop offs intersect. From here, they can mount quick foraging expeditions into the shoals. One area that produces well is the drop off found near the northwest end of the lake. The large shoal drops off quickly to deeper water and is a prime area for foraging trout. Try trolling at various depths around this drop off before moving on to other parts of the lake.

Facilities

Along with a few private campgrounds and resorts, Columbia Lake sports three provincial parks along its shores. **Tilley Memorial Park** is found along the southeast shores of the lake and is a day-use only park with a boat launch, outhouses, picnic table, and a great beach for sunbathing and swimming. **Columbia Lake Provincial Park** is found at the northeastern end of the lake and offers picnic tables for day use. Finally, **Thunder Hill Provincial Park** lies along Highway 93/95 at the southwest end of the lake, but access to this park has been closed off and there are no amenities.

Other Options

Whitetail Lake is one of the best fishing lakes in the Kootenays. The lake can be reached by following the Findlay Creek Forest Service Road west to Whitetail Lake Road, which travels north to the lake. It is described in better detail later in this book.

Directions

Columbia Lake is found just south of Fairmont Hot Springs. Highway 93/95 runs along the western shores of the big lake, and access to the lake is from several places along the highway. The town of Canal Flats and Canal Flats Provincial Park on the southeastern shores of the lake provide one of the main access points to the lake.

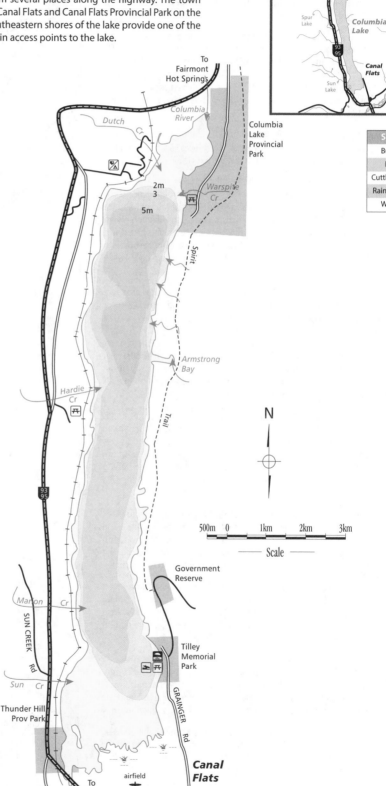

Area Indicator

Species
Bull Trout
Burbot
Cutthroat Trout
Rainbow Trout
Whitefish

Fishing

Where it flows into the Pacific Ocean, marking the boundary between Oregon and Washington State, the Columbia River moves more water than any river on the west side of the Continent. However, a series of major hydroelectric projects has tamed the once wild river, and the salmon that used to spawn all the way up and into BC no longer can make the journey.

But the Columbia is still a giant river, one of the province's largest, and still offers some great fishing. Below the Hugh Keenleyside Dam in Castlegar to the U.S. border at Waneta is a 42 km (26 mile) stretch of free water that has excellent walleye fishing, as well as burbot and some whitefish. But what this section of river is best known for is rainbow trout. It is considered one of the best sections of river fishing in the province and trout regularly top 1 kg (2 lbs) and have been known to reach 4.5 kg (10 lbs) in size.

It wasn't always thus. Stringent regulations, reduced pollution and an active fertilization program in Kootenay and Lower Arrow Lakes have all served to make this section of the Columbia an amazing trout fishing stream.

The upper river doesn't benefit from the fertilization the big lakes, so the trout don't get as big. However, the upper river still flows wild and free through a gorgeous valley. Around Golden, there is good access and good fishing at the confluence of the Kicking Horse River. Another great spot to fish is where the Blaeberry River flows into the Columbia, although access is a little trickier. Most people hike down from the Blaeberry River Bridge on the Trans Canada Highway. The best time to fish is in the fall, when the kokanee spawn. Trout will follow the spawning kokanee and dine on their eggs.

The entire river features huge caddis hatches, and the dry fly fishing is amazing. Pick the right time and the right place on the Lower Columbia and you will witness hundreds (and yes, we mean hundreds) of trout rising at the same time. While the river is best known for it's dry fly fishing, the best time to catch big fish is in April, fishing with sinking tip lines and Woolly Buggers, black General Practitioners or white Muddler Minnows. Spincasters can do well with salmon flies or similar suspended from a bobber. Fish these along the bottom along the edge of gravel bars. By mid to late April, spring run-off forces the water higher, and the river is not fishable until early summer, around mid-June or so.

The Lower Columbia is not a fast moving river, but it moves a lot of water, and is unrelenting in its forward progression. This means that the trout gather in huge back eddies. As an added bonus for the trout, Mayflies, midges, and caddis flies by the millions get trapped in this slowly rotating pool of water, and the trout can gorge themselves. These eddies form on the inside of sharp corners and behind erosion control structures. There are trout in the main river channel, but they are spread thinly throughout. Look for the eddies and you'll find the trout.

If the trout aren't rising, try a Clouser Minnow or Muddler Minnow. Cast towards the bank, and retrieve with short, fast strips. There are plenty of small whitefish in the river, and the trout love feeding on the whitefish fry. Another option is to fish a fly, and or grasshopper pattern; these work best in late summer and into the fall. Get your boat into this current, and allow it to carry you around in lazy circles.

In July, there is a huge caddis hatch. Fishing during this time can be amazing. It can also become frustrating, as there are just so many caddis on the water, finding a fish can sometimes be near impossible. In order to catch a fish during this hatch you have to land the fly right on their snout. Watch for places where the current washes the caddis together into a sort of living, edible raft.

Nymphs like bead head Pheasant Tails, Copper Johns, Deep Sparkle Pupae, or Kaufmann's Metallic Caddis (green) can work, too, but figuring out the current in these eddies can be tricky. Having a couple mayfly or terrestrial patterns as alternative offerings is a good thing. By early fall, the hatches taper off, and the trout move out into the main channel where they will winter near the bottom.

Don't forget those walleye. This fishery is becoming very popular with 30 to 40 fish days possible for walleye over 3 kg (6 lbs) possible. Casting from shore around places like the mouth of the Pend d'Oreille River can be dynamite using small jigs.

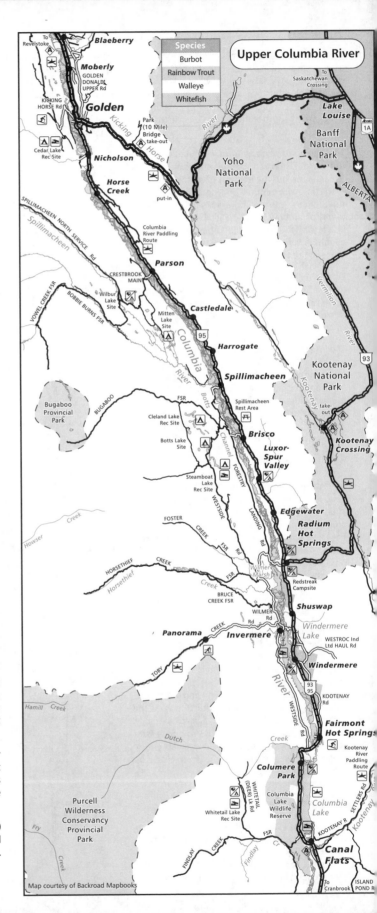

Map courtesy of Backroad Mapbooks

Columbia River

Directions

The Columbia is rarely without a major highway for companionship as it makes its way across the province. From Columbia Lake, the river flows north, followed by Highway 93/95 to Radium Hot Springs, then by Highway 95 to Golden. Although private property or the large sections of swamplands can limit shore access, the river is gentle enough to be drift fished in a small boat or canoe. Look for one of the road crossings to gain access to this section of the river.

North of Golden, the river leaves the highway and flows into Kinbasket Lake, one of the largest lakes in the province. Kinbasket Lake drains directly into Lake Revelstoke. There is a short section of river between Lake Revelstoke and Upper Arrow Lake, near Revelstoke that receives a fair bit of attention. Inquire locally for the better locations and what to use.

The Columbia then flows out of Lower Arrow Lake at Castlegar. This section of the river is a high volume river that provides numerous back eddies from which to sample. There are numerous holes and places to access the river around Castlegar and then off of Highway 22 south to Trail. When driving the highway, you will notice vehicles pulled off the side of the road at popular holes. Alternatively, you can get out in a boat (be wary of the strong currents and back eddies) to cruise from hole to hole.

South of Trail, the river is followed by Highway 22A to the US Border. Places like Beaver Creek and the mouth of the Pend d'Oreille River are known hot spots, but locals also have there own private holes to fish. Similar to above, private property can limit shore access so many prefer to get out in a boat.

Facilities

Covering such a large area, there is no shortage of services to be found. The southern section runs between Castlegar and Trail where all amenities can be found. Be sure to stop in on the local tackle shops to find out what is hot and where they are biting. Riverside facilities are actually quite limited with a few city parks such as Zuckerberg Island in Castlegar and Gyro Park in Trail providing good access. There are boat launching facilities in both cities, while **Beaver Creek Provincial Park** south of Trail provides a small campsite and a paved boat launch.

From Golden to Columbia Lake there are many places to access the river and several private campsites. Hotels and motels as well retailers are also found around the larger centres that include Golden, Radium Hot Spring and Invermere. Parks are limited to day use facilities designed more for wildlife viewing than accessing the river, however, the **Bluewater Creek** and **Waitabit Creek Recreation Sites** north of Golden do offer camping near the river.

Columbia River			
Fish Stocking Data			
Year	Species	Number	Life Stage
2007	White Sturgeon	4,030	Fingerling

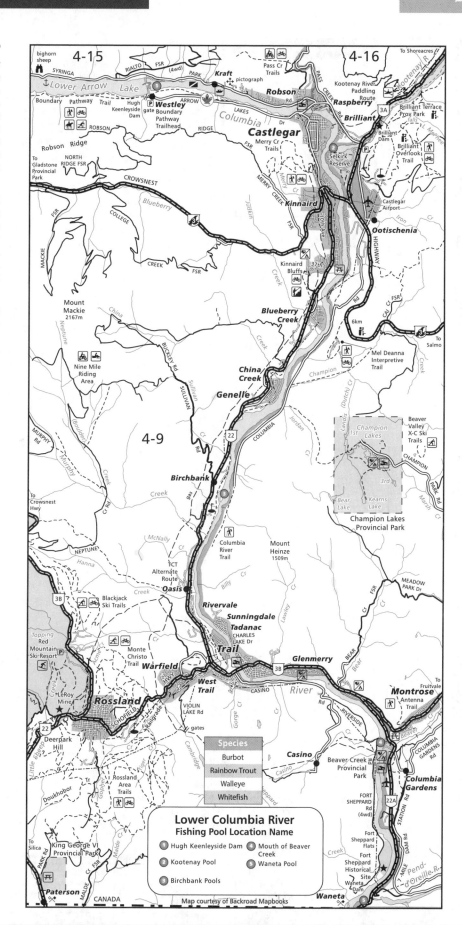

Lower Columbia River
Fishing Pool Location Name

1 Hugh Keenleyside Dam   4 Mouth of Beaver Creek

2 Kootenay Pool   5 Waneta Pool

3 Birchbank Pools

Species
Burbot
Rainbow Trout
Walleye
Whitefish

Map courtesy of Backroad Mapbooks

Region 4

Comfort & Help Lakes

Help Lake

Elevation: 983 m (3,225 ft)
Surface Area: 10 ha (25 ac)
Mean Depth: 1.2 m (4 ft)
Max Depth: 2.4 m (8 ft)
Way Point: 117° 26'00" Lon - W 51° 39'00" Lat - N

Area Indicator

Fishing

There is a string of lakes along the Bush River Road north of Golden and east of Kinbasket Lake. Comfort and Help Lakes are the middle two lakes in the chain.

Comfort Lake was stocked until 2003 with rainbow trout, and, although the stocking program has ended, you will still find some rainbow here. More likely than not, though, you'll find brook trout, which call the lake home, and have managed to survive here better than the rainbow have.

Help Lake was also stocked with rainbow trout until 2003, and, like Comfort, you will still find them here in ever diminishing numbers. The brook trout seem to prosper here, but there are also rumours of the occasional cutthroat, but we can neither confirm nor deny such speculation. If you happen to catch a cutthroat, do let us know at updates@backroadmapbooks.com.

Since the lakes are no longer being stocked, the fishing here is evolving from what it was to something new. The rainbow are slowly being fished out, leaving the lakes to the native brook trout. This is not a bad thing, but some anglers can find fishing for brookies a bit more challenging. Fly-fishing in spring can be very productive for brookies, as the bulk of their diet in the spring is insects such as chironomids and other insect larvae. For spincasters, try small spinners or trolling small spoons. Some proven spoons include the Little Cleo or Gibbs Gypsy. As for spinners, almost anything with a smaller profile can work well in silver or gold, such as a Blue Fox or Panther Martin.

Since the lakes are not very deep, there are only a couple good holding and/or cruising areas for the remaining rainbow that make ideal places to fish throughout the open water season. In the late spring and early summer, there is a decent weed growth in the lakes. Look for both species of trout cruising near the weeds. As the lake warms, the fish often hold in the deeper water next to the drop offs and move in to the shallows, as the heat of the day diminishes. In summer it is best to try off the drop off sections in each lake where there is a significant quick drop in the depth level.

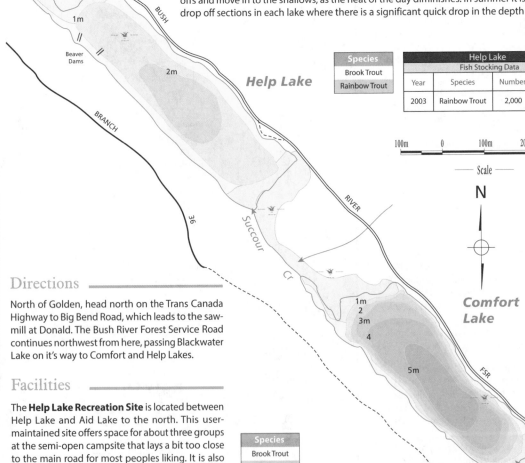

Species
Brook Trout
Rainbow Trout

Help Lake			
Fish Stocking Data			
Year	Species	Number	Life Stage
2003	Rainbow Trout	2,000	Yearling

Comfort Lake

Elevation: 982 m (3,222 ft)
Surface Area: 7.5 ha (19 ac)
Mean Depth: 3.3 m (11 ft)
Max Depth: 5.5 m (18 ft)
Way Point: 117° 25'00" Lon - W 51° 38'00" Lat - N

Directions

North of Golden, head north on the Trans Canada Highway to Big Bend Road, which leads to the sawmill at Donald. The Bush River Forest Service Road continues northwest from here, passing Blackwater Lake on it's way to Comfort and Help Lakes.

Facilities

The **Help Lake Recreation Site** is located between Help Lake and Aid Lake to the north. This user-maintained site offers space for about three groups at the semi-open campsite that lays a bit too close to the main road for most peoples liking. It is also possible to hand launch small boats at Help Lake.

Other Options

To the north of Comfort and Help Lakes lies **Aid Lake**. Like Comfort and Help, Aid Lake is no longer stocked. Anglers can still find the rainbow as well as cutthroat trout here.

Species
Brook Trout
Cutthroat Trout
Rainbow Trout

Comfort Lake			
Fish Stocking Data			
Year	Species	Number	Life Stage
2003	Rainbow Trout	2,000	Yearling

Conkle Lake

Location: 33 km (20.5 mi) northeast of Osoyoos
Elevation: 1,067 m (3,500 ft)
Surface Area: 120 ha (297 ac)
Mean Depth: 22.3 m (73 ft)
Max Depth: 49 m (161 ft)
Way Point: 119° 06′00″ Lon - W 49° 10′00″ Lat - N

Region 8

Fishing

Visitors have come to this secluded lake in the Okanagan Highlands, northwest of Osoyoos for many years to camp, fish, sunbathe, swim or hike the various trails. This 3 kilometre long lake is framed by steep hillsides and is fed by East Creek. Because of the rustic nature of the park, the beautiful setting and decent fishing, the lake sees fairly heavy fishing pressure.

Fly-fishing, trolling, and ice fishing are all successful techniques used to catch rainbow trout that average 30–38 cm (12–15 in), with the odd fish reaching an impressive 60 cm (24 in) in size. Stocked annually by the Freshwater Fisheries Society of BC, anglers are assured a good fight on their line.

There is a lack of shoals on Conkle Lake. Shoals are often called the lake's kitchen, and Conkle's kitchen is very small indeed. As a result, most fly fisherman will target the mouth of East Creek and in front of the campsites. Patterns like the blood leech and Knouff Lake Special fished deep, closer to shore, will entice the rainbow. Casting dry flies to rising fish in June and July in the south shallow bay can also be quite exciting.

Deep trolling is popular with lake trolls, Flatfish, small Panther Martins and Apex lures. Target the shorelines of the east and west sides of the lake. The north end of the lake is best fished early and late in the day to avoid the crowds. For those who like to ice fish, the only winter access is by snowmobile. The north end is a popular ice fishing area with ¼ oz jigs tipped with powerbait or meal worms.

If you are heading out ice fishing on the lake, make sure the lake is frozen solid. Rainbow trout can get sluggish in the winter time, but will still take to a variety of lures. As using bait is illegal in the winter, you need to get the attention of the trout some other way; the most common is to jig a flashy silver lure.

Remember to check the regulations before heading out. There is a boat motor restriction of 7.5 kW (10 hp) on Conkle Lake.

Facilities

Conkle Lake Provincial Park encompasses the entire lake and provides 34 vehicle accessible campsites, including two group campsites; one being a walk-in site. There is also a day-use area at the north end of the lake, with a natural sandy beach created by wave action. Due to high winds that frequent Conkle Lake, summertime brings windsurfing opportunities. The park facilities are quite basic, with a boat launch suited for smaller trailer boats, outhouses and picnic tables for visitors to enjoy. A hiking trail circles the lake as well as leads to the west from the campground to the scenic falls.

Other Options

Little Fish Lake lies to the south of Conkle Lake and is accessible via trail from the Conkle Lake camping area. The shallow lake is not known for its great fishing, but the early spring and late fall might produce a few small trout.

Directions

There are two ways to access the backcountry lake. Both require negotiating narrow winding Forest Service Roads that are not suited for RV's or larger trailers. It is 16 km to the entrance from Highway 33, just north of Westbridge and 26 km from Highway 3, six km east of Bridesville. Follow signs along the forest service roads. The two accesses join a kilometre before reaching the park.

Conkle Lake			
Fish Stocking Data			
Year	Species	Number	Life Stage
2013	Rainbow Trout	8,000	Fry
2012	Rainbow Trout	8,000	Fry
2011	Rainbow Trout	8,000	Fry

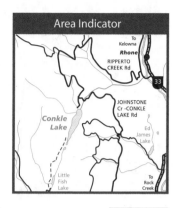

Area Indicator

Species
Rainbow Trout

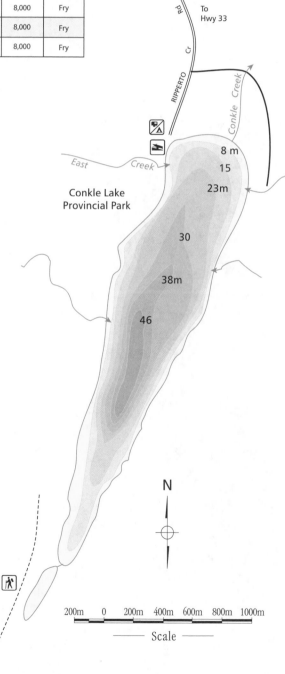

Conkle Lake
Provincial Park

8 m
15
23m
30
38m
46

N

| 200m | 0 | 200m | 400m | 600m | 800m | 1000m |

Scale

To
Little
Fish Lake

Location: 76 km (47 mi) north of Rock Creek
Elevation: 1,083 m (3,553 ft)
Surface Area: 19.5 ha (48 ac)
Mean Depth: 4 m (13 ft)
Max Depth: 9 m (29.5 ft)
Way Point: 118° 48′00″ Lon - W 49° 41′00″ Lat - N

Copper Kettle Lake

Area Indicator

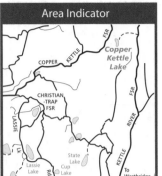

Species
Rainbow Trout

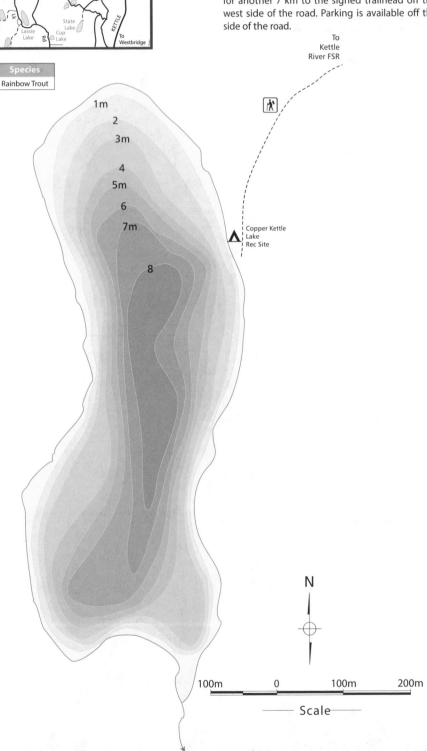

Directions

Copper Kettle Lake is a picturesque lake lying next to the Kettle River Valley. It can only be accessed by foot along a 3 km trail. To reach the trailhead, you must first access the Christian Valley Road from Highway 33 near Westbridge. About 59 km (36 mi) along the Christian Valley Road, the road branches and the pavement ends. Follow the west branch, which is now the Kettle River Forest Service Road, for another 7 km to the signed trailhead off the west side of the road. Parking is available off the side of the road.

Fishing

Copper Kettle Lake is a pretty hike-in lake in the Kettle River area to the north of the Christian Valley. Managed as a fly-fishing only lake, Copper Kettle also benefits from seeing low angling pressure over the year. These factors have allowed the lake to establish a reproducing population of rainbow trout and created a good fishery for all to enjoy.

The lake was stocked throughout the mid-eighties and has developed a thriving and self sustaining population of rainbow. However, trout numbers are impacted by how well they can spawn up the creek at the south end of the lake and there are often beaver dams restricting the waterway.

Fishing in the lake can be good at times for decent sized rainbow that have the reputation to put up a fantastic fight when hooked. As usual, your best bet for success on the lake is to try during the spring or fall periods, as the fishing does slow down in summer. Although the lake's bottom drops quickly off from the shoreline, it is worth the effort to haul a belly boat to the lake.

A good place to start fishing is near the outlet stream at the south end of the lake or along the large shoal area near the southwest side of the lake. Chironomids can be quite effective on the lake, especially in spring, while the lake begins to experience all the normal hatches characteristic of the region. Later in the season caddis fly hatches can be a ton of fun, especially in the evenings. Hatches can occur any time from June to early September can produce some exciting top water action. Adult caddis sits on the water surface drying their wings, and trout will often jump right out of the lake in their attempt to grab the caddis before it makes its escape. This hatch is best fished with a Tom Thumb, Elk Hair Caddis or a green or gray-bodied sedge imitation, such as a Carey Special, drawn across the surface of the water in the same manner as the insect is acting.

Ice fishing is not allowed.

Facilities

If you enjoy hike-in wilderness camping, Copper Kettle Lake provides the perfect backdrop for a fantastic camping experience. The lake hosts a small, rustic camping area that is essentially a cleared area next to the lake for tenters to set up camp.

Other Options

Well before you reach the fork in the Christian Valley Road, you will pass the Christian-Trap Forest Service Road. Follow this road west up a steep rough climb past the State Lake trailhead to the **Sandrift Lakes.** The road dissects the two lakes and provides car top access to the lakes. Along with a few enjoyable Forest Recreation campsites, the lakes offer angling opportunities for rainbow trout.

Cottonwood Lake

Location: 8 km (5 mi) south of Nelson
Elevation: 890 m (2,920 ft)
Surface Area: 6 ha (15 ac)
Mean Depth: 7.3 m (24 ft)
Max Depth: 14.9 m (49 ft)
Way Point: 117° 15′ 00″ Lon - W 49° 25′ 00″ Lat - N

4 Region

Fishing

Cottonwood Lake is a small, roadside lake next to Highway 6 south of Nelson. Because of its proximity to both the highway and to the city, the lake sees heavy fishing pressure throughout the year.

The lake is stocked annually by the Freshwater Fisheries Society of BC with catchable size rainbow trout on a put and take basis. The trout are plentiful but small and are known to be quite aggressive. They are readily caught with a small dry fly, wet fly, small spinners or spoons, or even just a worm and bobber. Because the trout are so feisty, and take so well to most anything you throw at them, Cottonwood Lake is a good spot to take the kids.

In addition to the stocked rainbow, the lake also holds brook trout and kokanee. Trolling a lake troll with a Wedding Band and bait can also attract kokanee. Kokanee are primarily plankton feeders, and so don't go after the same sort of lures as trout. Some other good lures are the Tomac Wee Tad Plug or the Luhr Jensen Needlefish. In the early morning, kokanee seem to prefer green and chartreuse lures, but as the day gets on, they favour bright red, pink and even a hot orange, perhaps with a flash of silver.

Kokanee fight like crazy when they get to the top of the water, and often tear the lure right out of their mouths. If you are trying to net a kokanee and it begins to thrash, lower the tip of your rod to let the fish start swimming again. Play the fish a little longer before attempting to net it again.

Shore fishing is possible and there are trail systems around the lake to help gain access to most of the shoreline. While there is no official launch, it isn't too difficult to hand launch a small boat or canoe. If you do have a canoe or float tube, a good area to try is off the small point along the west side of the lake. There is a good drop off area near this point and it seems be a good holding area for trout.

To help maintain the peaceful park setting, boats are restricted to electric motors only.

Directions

Cottonwood Lake lies off Highway 6 south of Nelson. The lake is home to a quaint little regional park, which provides a nice picnic/parking area at the north end of the lake.

Facilities

Cottonwood Lake is the focal point for **Cottonwood Lake Park**, which is a small, local day-use park. There is a parking area at the park as well as scenic trails around the small lake. During the winter, a number of locals use the park for access to a variety of cross-country ski trails. Overnight facilities and other amenities are readily available in the nearby town of Nelson.

Other Options

Highway 6 provides good access to the **Salmo River** and a number of its tributaries, including **Porcupine Creek**. Despite the easy access, pressure is not that heavy and as a result, the fishing for the rainbow, cutthroat and eastern brook trout can be very good after the high water recedes in June. The fish in the river are often much larger than the cold, fast flowing feeder streams produce.

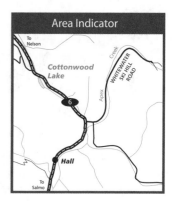
Area Indicator

Species
Brook Trout
Kokanee
Rainbow Trout

Cottonwood Lake			
Fish Stocking Data			
Year	Species	Number	Life Stage
2013	Rainbow Trout	2,055	Catchable
2012	Rainbow Trout	2,550	Catchable
2011	Rainbow Trout	1,150	Catchable

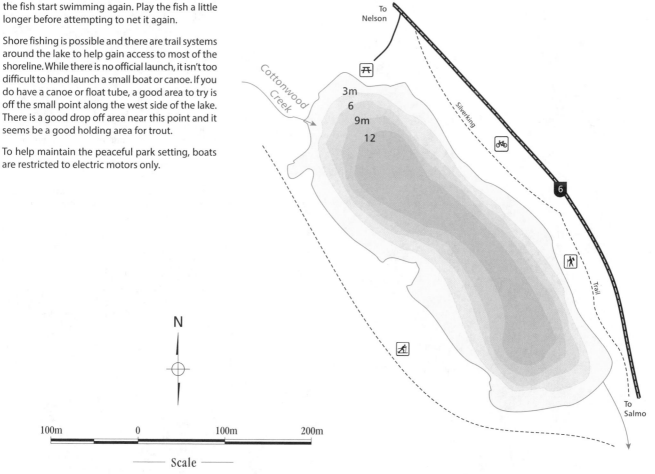

Location: 19 km (12 mi) northwest of Summerland
Elevation: 1,556 m (5,105 ft)
Surface Area: 20 ha (49.5 ac)
Mean Depth: 4 m (13 ft)
Max Depth: 8 m (26 ft)
Way Point: 119° 55′ 00″ Lon - W   49° 42′ 00″ Lat - N

Darke Lake

Directions

Darke Lake lies in the heart of the Okanagan between Summerland and Peachland. The lake and park are easily reached on the Fish Lake Road, which is off the well-signed Princeton-Summerland Road. The park is not designed to accommodate RVs, although smaller units are usually okay. The lake is about 16 km (10 mi) from the highway.

Facilities

Darke Lake is found at the heart of **Darke Lake Provincial Park**, which offers a rustic campground at the south end of the lake. There are no designated sites or even picnic tables, but there is room for about five trucks or camper units. The campsite is open year round and is user-maintained. It is also asked to keep campfires in the designated fire rings.

Fishing

Sometimes called Fish Lake by the locals because of the great rainbow and brook trout fishing, Darke Lake is just far enough off the beaten path to make it feel remote. It is also close enough to Summerland to make a nice day trip.

The lake is surrounded by rolling pine and fir forests, and is protected by a provincial park. Although the park remains undeveloped, there is an informal campsite and a few trails from which to access the lake. To help maintain the fishery, the lake is stocked with rainbow trout from the nearby Summerland Trout Hatchery. These rainbow can reach up to 1 kg (2 lbs) in size, although average much smaller.

Fly-fishing is the most popular angling method on the lake since there are some inviting shoals to explore. Generally, most of the fishing action occurs around the middle or deeper portion of the lake. However, during spring the trout can sometimes be caught while cruising the shallows at the north and south ends in search of easy meals.

Trolling can also produce decent results, especially along the drop off alongside the 8 m (26 ft) hole. The trick when trolling around the lake is to use lighter gear and adjust your speed to allow the lure or fly to roam through different depths.

Unfortunately, the low elevation lake has a tendency to suffer from the summer doldrums. On the other hand, the lake is extremely popular for ice fishing. The lake usually begins to freeze over by early December and anglers soon head out. Be sure to check to make sure there is at least 15 cm/6 inches of ice to bear weight before heading onto the ice.

Brook trout remain more active in the winter than rainbow, and you'll probably wind up hooking them almost exclusively. Some think there isn't really much in the way of technique other than drilling a hole in the ice and dangling a hook through it. This is sort of true, but it is all about the location of the hole. Most of the fish will be found feeding where the water is less than 3 metres (10 ft) deep. So stick close to shore, preferably over known shoal areas. Bait works well, but fish are also attracted to flashy lures that are jigged.

Other Options

Munro Lake is found to the west of Darke Lake via a rough 4wd road off the Princeton-Summerland Road. The small lake is stocked annually with rainbow trout, which provide for decent fishing in the spring and fall.

Darke (Fish) Lake Fish Stocking Data			
Year	Species	Number	Life Stage
2013	Brook Trout	2,000	Fry
2013	Rainbow Trout	2,000	Fry
2012	Brook Trout	2,000	Fry
2012	Rainbow Trout	2,000	Fry
2011	Brook Trout	2,000	Fry
2011	Rainbow Trout	2,000	Fry

Species

Rainbow Trout
Brook Trout

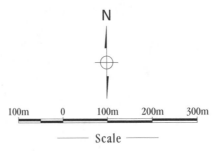

N

100m   0   100m   200m   300m

Scale

Darke Lake Provincial Park

Darke Lake Provincial Park

Silas Creek

2m

3

5m

6

8m

3m

2

Darke Cr

To Summerland

Davis Lake

Location: 32 km (20 mi) southeast of Merritt
Elevation: 1,019 m (3,343 ft)
Surface Area: 23 ha (75 ac)
Mean Depth: 12 m (39 ft)
Max Depth: 18 m (59 ft)
Way Point: 120° 43'00" Lon - W 49° 51'00" Lat - N

Region 8

Fishing

Davis Lake is one of the busiest lakes in the scenic Voght Valley southeast of Merritt. To help maintain the popular fishery and offset the red sided shiners, the lake is stocked regularly with rainbow trout by the Freshwater Fisheries Society of B.C. Fishing is fairly consistent for rainbow that can reach a feisty 2 kg (4.5 lb) in size. Fish in the 0.5 kg (1 lb) range are the norm.

This oddly shaped lake has many shoals and sunken islands allowing for a variety of areas to focus your attention. It is also a shallow lake, and contains an abundance of insect life that makes it a fly anglers' dream lake. The best times to fish the lakes are June, July and autumn.

The shoals and sunken islands are ideal for a variety of damsel or dragonfly nymph patterns, while fishing with chironomids or blood worms is better in the deeper sections of the lake. This can prove to be helpful in hot weather conditions. Visitors will also find that sedges emerging throughout the summer months around those sunken islands. For added excitement, dry fly-fishing off the shoals with Mikulak Sedges, Tom Thumbs and Elk Hair Caddis can often coax the trout to the surface, especially in the evening.

There are a few places that shore fishing is possible. The most accessible is to simply fish off the shore from the recreation site. Spincasters can use smaller spinners, or a worm and bobber. Another popular way to fish the lake is trolling. Using a Panther Martin or Flatfish along the east shoals and south end can bring good action.

During winter, the lake remains a popular fishing destination. While trout can be found most anywhere in the lake, most people don't wander too far on the ice, preferring instead to fish the area around the recreation site.

Area Indicator

Species

Rainbow Trout

Davis Lake Fish Stocking Data			
Year	Species	Number	Life Stage
2013	Rainbow Trout	6,000	Yearling
2012	Rainbow Trout	6,000	Yearling
2011	Rainbow Trout	6,000	Yearling

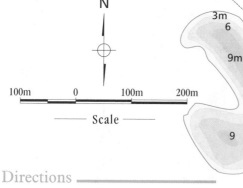

Directions

There are several ways to get into Davis Lake. The quickest is to follow Highway 5A south for about 8 km from Highway 97C to Coalmont Road. Follow the paved Coalmont Road for 11 km and turn north (right) on to the Voght Valley Road. This good gravel road leads to Davis Lake and beyond.

From the Coquihalla Highway (Hwy 97C), take the Coldwater Exit (Exit 256) south of Merritt. Continue north for 4 km to the Kane Valley Road, which branches east. This road soon turns to gravel as it winds around some ranch land. At the 9 km mark, the Voght Valley Road branches south passing by Tahla and Boss Lakes on its way to Davis Lake.

Facilities

Probably the most popular lake in the Voght Valley, **Davis Lake Recreation Site** is also the largest and busiest. Despite offering over 50 RV accessible sites and charging a fee, finding an empty site can be a challenge during the weekend. There are also a couple boat launch areas on the east side of the lake.

Other Options

If you continue east along the Kane Valley Road, you will come across a fine collection of interior fishing lakes, **Englishmen, Harman** and the **Kane Lakes**. This is another popular chain of lakes that are highlighted in our *Southwestern BC Fishing Mapbook*. The plump trout, the scenic camping areas and easy access lures anglers from around the province to this area.

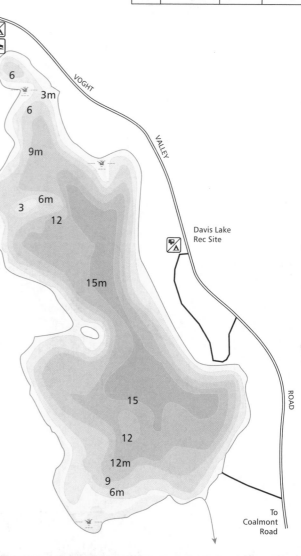

Dee Lake Chain

Area Indicator

To Vernon

ABERDEEN LAKE Rd

Hidden Lake
Doreen Lake
Aberdeen Lake
Dee Lake
Island Lake
Flyfish Lakes
Haddo Lake
Deer Lake Crooked Lake
Grizzly Lake

Species

Rainbow Trout

Dee Lake
Fish Stocking Data

Year	Species	Number	Life Stage
2013	Rainbow Trout	30,000	Yearling
2012	Rainbow Trout	30,000	Yearling
2011	Rainbow Trout	30,000	Yearling

Dee Lake

Elevation: 1,351 m (4,432 ft)
Surface Area: 39 ha (46 ac)
Mean Depth: 3.5 m (11 ft)
Max Depth: 9 m (30 ft)
Way Point: 119° 09' 00" Lon - W 50° 06' 00" Lat - N

Island Lake

Elevation: 1,349 m (4,424 ft)
Surface Area: 48 ha (118 ac)
Mean Depth: 5.5 m (18 ft)
Max Depth: 12 m (39 ft)
Way Point: 119° 10' 00" Lon - W 50° 05' 00" Lat - N

Directions

Best accessed from the south and the Beaver Lake Road, the route into Dee Lake is well signed and fairly easy to follow. Even though it is about 26 km from the highway to Dee Lake Resort, most vehicles should be able to navigate the logging roads.

The Beaver Lake Road can be picked up from the south end of Lake Country, just as you enter town. Follow this road east, up and out of the valley. The pavement ends soon after you leave the valley floor and you will need to be careful on the steep, windy road. At about the 13.5 km mark keep left and follow the signs towards Dee Lake Resort. Shortly before the resort, the Island Lake Recreation Site provides access to Island, Deer and Crooked Lake. The resort provides the best access onto Dee.

If you are really keen to drive into Crooked, you can follow a rough road from about the 30 km marking on the Dee Lake Road. This 4wd road bumps its way to the debris cluttered shoreline of the lake. There is, however, a dam at the south end of the lake from which to shore fish. We recommend launching at Island Lake and paddling into the lake.

Dee Lake

Island Lake

Facilities

Dee Lake is home to a nice wilderness resort, while **Island Lake** offers a well cared for recreation site to camp at. Both sites offer decent boat launches. The recreation site has room for about 15 parties. If these sites are full, it is possible to camp off one of the side roads leading to Deer or Crooked Lake. If you don't have a canoe or small boat, you can rent from the Dee Lake Resort. Contact the resort for more information: (250) 212-2129, or visit their website at www.deelakeresort.com

Other Options

Fly anglers will also be delighted to know there are several fly-fishing only lakes on the plateau. In fact, there are 17 other fishing lakes within a 7 km radius. Continue along the Dee Lake Road and you should soon find **Doreen Lake**. A little further along and a bit trickier to find are the **Flyfish Lakes**. All three lakes offer good fishing for stocked rainbow. Also located nearby is **Beaver Lake**. In fact, the lake is so close, that you can easily pick up your canoe (assuming you are using a canoe) and portage it into the lake.

Dee Lake Chain

Fishing

In the hills to the southeast of Vernon and northeast of Kelowna anglers have a wealth of options to choose from. There are dozens of lakes to choose from, but the Dee Lake Chain is one of the easier places to access and a great place to spend a weekend.

The Dee Lake Chain is made up of four small lakes: Dee Lake, Island Lake, Deer Lake and Crooked Lake. These interconnected, man-made lakes can all be easily accessed with the help of a canoe or a belly boat. While all the lakes have been stocked with rainbow in the past, these days only Dee Lake is being stocked. The lakes all have natural spawning stream, and nature has taken over for the Freshwater Fisheries Society of BC. However, the 30,000 stocked trout added to Dee Lake annually certainly doesn't hurt the fishing. Some of the fish have been known to reach 45 cm (18 in) in size, and trout in the 30-35 (12-14 in) range are the average, not the exception.

Despite being a resort lake, Dee Lake is known to produce many of the bigger fish. The small shallow bays and shoals at the north end of the lake are good areas to anchor a boat and fish chironomids or dragonfly nymphs near the bottom. A slow troll just off of these shallow areas with a '52 Buick, Doc Spratley or blood or black leech also works well in all the lakes. The people at the resort recommend using a hint of red in fly patterns. However, all the bays in the chain are shallow; therefore, trolling in the deeper areas will help avoid hang ups on the bottom.

Finding the original channel of the lake in Island and Deer will yield more fish during the warmer months of the year, as the fish tend to hold here. Further south, Crooked Lake is the most difficult lake to troll because of the shallow areas and floating log debris throughout the lake. Working the area adjacent to the floating grass islands in the middle of Crooked Lake will provide some of the best fly-fishing. There is limited access for shore fishing throughout the chain. However, if you don't have a canoe or belly boat, or just really need to get out and stretch your legs, the dam at the south end of Crooked Lake offers the best opportunity.

Early mornings and late evenings in June and July can provide the fly-fisherman with incredible dry fly-fishing in the entire chain. Casting to rising trout with a Tom Thumb or Mikulak Sedge can be thrilling especially when there are numerous obstacles like floating logs and lily pads. If the fish are rising, but not taking to a dry fly, you can try using a sinking tip line and fly to get your presentation a few inches under the surface.

If you are not a fly angler, try using small spinners, Panther Martins, red Wedding Rings and Flatfish in black and silver or chrome.

All four lakes are closed to fishing from December 1st to April 30th. Always be sure to check the regulations before fishing a new lake.

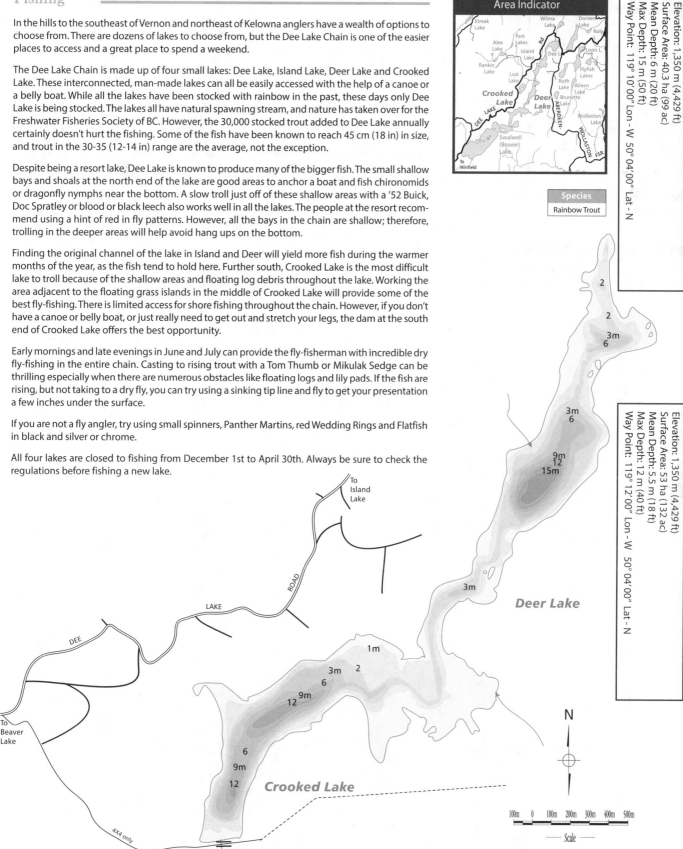

Area Indicator

Species
Rainbow Trout

Deer Lake
Elevation: 1,350 m (4,429 ft)
Surface Area: 40.3 ha (99 ac)
Mean Depth: 6 m (20 ft)
Max Depth: 15 m (50 ft)
Way Point: 119° 10'00" Lon - W   50° 04'00" Lat - N

Crooked Lake
Elevation: 1,350 m (4,429 ft)
Surface Area: 53 ha (132 ac)
Mean Depth: 5.5 m (18 ft)
Max Depth: 12 m (40 ft)
Way Point: 119° 12'00" Lon - W   50° 04'00" Lat - N

Deer Lake

Crooked Lake

N

Scale
100m 0 100m 200m 300m 400m 500m

Location: 12 km (7.5 mi) west of Radium Hot Springs
Elevation: 1,076 m (3,530 ft)
Surface Area: 8 ha (20 ac)
Mean Depth: 2.5 m (8 ft)
Max Depth: 9.1 m (30 ft)
Way Point: 116° 13' 00" Lon - W 50° 38' 00" Lat - N

Dogsleg Lake

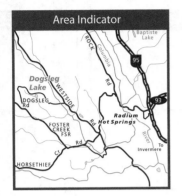

Area Indicator

Species
Rainbow Trout
Brook Trout

| Dogsleg Lake ||||
| Fish Stocking Data ||||
Year	Species	Number	Life Stage
2013	Rainbow Trout	1,000	Spring Catchable
2012	Rainbow Trout	1,000	Catchable
2011	Rainbow Trout	1,000	Catchable

Fishing

Dogsleg Lake isn't really a dogs leg; more of a backwards 'F'. The lake is generally shallow, with only one hole deeper than 3 m (9 feet). The lack of depth, and relatively high elevation means that the lake is prone to winterkill.

As a result, the Freshwater Fisheries Society of BC has started stocking the lake with a small numbers of catchables each year (usually 500), in an attempt to promote a catch and keep fishery for rainbow trout. Surprisingly, there are still reports of the odd brook trout being pulled from these waters even though it has been nearly forty years since the shallow lake was last stocked with brook trout.

Because the lake is so shallow, trolling is not the best option here; the fish are easily spooked by moving objects on the surface of the water. In the earliest part of the season, it is possible to fish from shore at the recreation site. But as the water warms up, the fish retreat to the deeper section of the lake, and a small boat or float tube will help you get to where the fish are. In fact, other than for a short time at the start of the year and again near the end, the majority of the lake is too shallow and too warm to hold trout in any great numbers.

When fishing the lake, first try working either a streamer or leech pattern for fly anglers or a small spinner for spincasters. Try the deeper northern portion, especially off either one of the large points on the lake. The drop off area around the 9 m (34 ft) hole found in the northern section is a good holding when the lake warms.

In the early evenings when the water is calm and the bugs plentiful, watch for the trout rising near the shore. This is a magic time for fly anglers, as it is possible to present a dry fly on the surface of the water (if you can't figure out exactly what the trout are rising for, try a Tom Thumb).

Directions

This small lake lies to the west of Radium Hot Springs. To reach the lake from Radium, follow Westside Road past the junction with the Horsethief Creek Forest Service Road. Continue north on Westside Road to the 21 km mark where the Dogsleg Road branches west. It is another 3.5 km to the lake along the unmarked road that is often difficult to drive during wet weather. Parking is available at the forest recreation site on the northeast shore of the lake.

Facilities

The **Dogleg Lake Recreation Site** is a small forested, lakeside campsite. There is space for a couple groups along with a place to hand launch small water craft. Alternatively, there are motels and bed and breakfast accommodations in nearby Radium Hot Springs.

Other Options

On your way to Dogsleg Lake, you will pass over **Forster Creek.** The creek offers fishing for cutthroat trout and is best experienced after high water during the summer months. Similar to most small streams in the area, Forster Creek also holds good numbers of small cutthroat trout for anglers to chase.

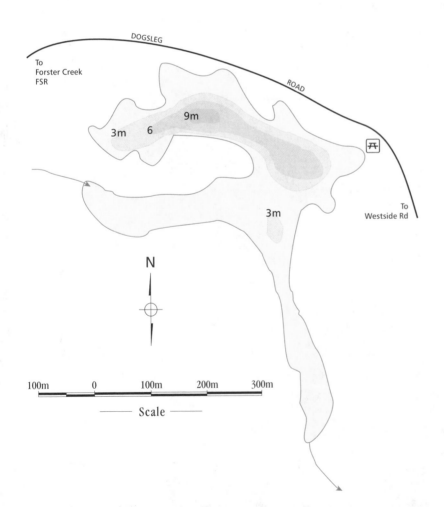

To Forster Creek FSR

DOGSLEG

ROAD

9m

3m   6

3m

To Westside Rd

N

100m   0   100m   200m   300m

Scale

Duck Lake

Location: 15 km (9 mi) north of Creston
Elevation: 536 m (1,759 ft)
Surface Area: 1,693 ha (4,183 ac)
Max Depth: 2.4 m (8 ft)
Way Point: 116° 37′ 00″ Lon - W 49° 13′ 00″ Lat - N

4 Region

Fishing

Anglers in BC have been raised on rainbow, cut their teeth on cutthroat, and sing the praises of steelhead and salmon fishing. Many consider bass an unworthy, unwelcome species. But to a growing population of fans, bass fishing is becoming not just something to do in the summer when the trout aren't biting, it is becoming a hobby, a passion, a lifestyle. As an added bonus there is also a decent perch fishery here.

Located in the Creston Valley Wildlife Management Area, Duck Lake is one of, if not the best, lakes in the province for largemouth bass. In fact, it is one of the best lakes in the country for bass, which have been known to grow over 4.5 kg (10 lbs) in size.

Of course, the average size of the largemouth is closer to 1.5 kg (3 lbs), but that's still a good size catch. The lake has hot summers, mild winters, lots of forage and far less pressure than lakes further east, where bass are much more popular. Still Duck Lake sees upwards of 5,000 angler days a year, many of whom come from Alberta, where bass is a much more popular sportfish. In fact, anglers come from across North America just to fish here.

The lake is part of a large wetland delta formed where the Kootenay River enters Kootenay Lake. Milfoil, an invasive aquatic weed, has taken over the shallow lake and provides great coverage for the bass. In fact, there is very little shore structure. Instead, you will find bass where ever you find weeds, and it isn't unusual to see people fishing the middle of the lake for bass. Watch for bigger, broadleaf weeds that provide the bass cover without restricting their movement.

Larger bass are naturally suspicious, especially after they've been snagged once or twice. They tend to hide deeper in the weeds and only come out later at night. The big bass are also quite suspicious when they hear the sound of an aluminum boat being rowed. As a result, many are starting to use float tubes to fish here.

Traditionally, Mepps spinners and Rapala lures have been extremely popular, but as the sport catches on, anglers are trying other methods. Dark coloured rubber worms and slugs, like black and purple, work early in the season, while later on, crankbaits work well. Because there are lots of perch in the lake, a short, broad bait usually works best. Yellow and orange work well, as does white.

In the heat of the day, the bass head for cover, and you'll need to fish down for them. When the sun isn't on the water, though, it is possible to lure them to the surface with a bass popper or other top water presentation.

The lake is part of the Creston Valley Wildlife Management Area, a federally protected waterfowl viewing area. Motors, even electric ones, are not allowed on the lake.

Facilities

There is no camping allowed in the Creston Valley Wildlife Management Area. Hotels and other amenities are available in Creston.

Directions

Duck Lake is located north of Creston at the south end of Kootenay Lake. To get there, take Highway 3A north to Wynndel. Turn left onto Lower Wynndel Road, then right onto Duck Lake Road about 0.5 km (0.3 miles) later. (Lower Wynndel Road can also be accessed heading east from Creston along Highway 3. It will be your first right turn. Take the Highway 21 exit back towards Creston, then turn onto Lower Wynndel Road, which passes under Highway 3.

Species
Largemouth Bass
Yellow Perch

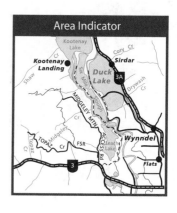

Area Indicator

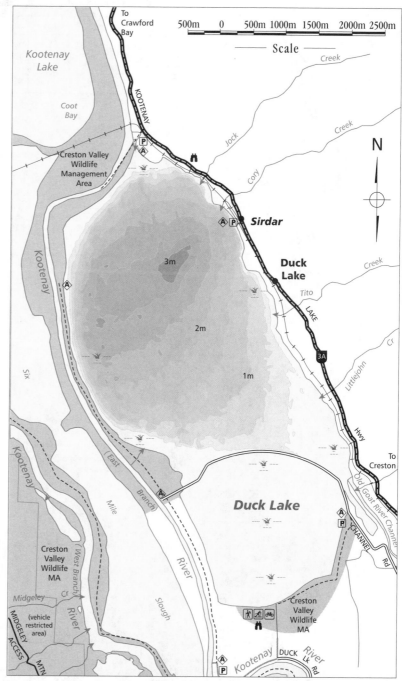

Location: 45 km (28 mi) north of Kaslo
Elevation: 547 m (1,799 ft)
Surface Area: 7,140 ha (17,636 ac)
Mean Depth: 52 m (170 ft)
Max Depth: 118 m (387 ft)
Way Point: 116° 55′ 00″ Lon - W   50° 18′ 00″ Lat - N

Duncan (Reservoir) Lake

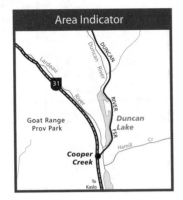

Area Indicator

Directions

Duncan Lake is found just north of Kootenay Lake, off Highway 31. Drive 35 km (22 miles) north of Kaslo to Meadow Creek. Turning right onto Duncan Lake Road will bring you along the east side of the lake. However, the best access is along the southwest side of the lake at Howser Park Recreation Site. To find this site, continue north of Meadow Creek on Highway 31 for just over 8 km. After crossing over the Lardeau River, turn right (east) on Howser Station Road. Follow this road through Howser for 2 km. A left leads to the Howser Park Recreation Site, while a right leads to the Glayco Beach Day Use Area.

Fishing

One of the many, long, narrow valley bottom lakes in the Kootenays, Duncan Reservoir was originally a much smaller lake. In 2007, after a nearly twenty year stocking hiatus, 50,000 Gerrard strain rainbow were dumped into the lake. Such a gap between stockings is par for the course on the lake, which is stocked once or twice every couple of decades.

The Duncan Reservoir was created in 1967 with the creation of the Duncan Dam, one of three major dams built as a result of the Columbia River Treaty. Its has no powerhouse; instead, it's only purpose is to control the flow of water from the Duncan River into Kootenay Lake to assure that there is enough water for the Kootenay Canal and Corra Linn projects downstream.

The lake was originally 25 km (15.5 miles) long, but is now 45 km (28 miles) long, with an annual drawdown of up to 30 m (98 ft). While the reservoir was logged before flooding, in winter when the water levels get low the bleached white stumps are revealed. There are also some signs of the town of Howser, which was flooded by the creation of the lake.

The lake is best known for its phenomenal bull trout fishing, which can get to 5 kg (12 lbs) or more. Right after ice-off, for about six weeks in March and April, the bull trout can be found closer to the surface. By June, they begin to head for the deeper waters, making them harder to find. Bull trout can be quite aggressive, and like to feed on eggs and small fish. One of the most productive methods of catching bull trout is to troll a green or orange Flat Fish or Krocodile. Also, try fishing around creek mouths with bait balls or jigging a bucktail and flasher. Fly anglers can try working large leech patterns.

Of course, the lake also holds good numbers of rainbow trout, which are best caught by trolling small spoons or spinners around the edge of the lake. The best fishing is in spring and fall. Shore fishing isn't the most popular method of fishing for rainbow here, but it can be done, especially around the mouths of streams.

Duncan Lake is also home to one of the few populations of White Sturgeon in BC, but currently the entire region is closed to sturgeon fishing. It should also be noted that bull trout are a slow maturing species and have been over fished in the past. There are tight regulations on the species; make sure you check the regulations before heading out.

Duncan Lake Fish Stocking Data

Year	Species	Number	Life Stage
2013	Rainbow Trout	122,157	Yearling
2012	Rainbow Trout	56,872	Yearling
2011	Rainbow Trout	30,498	Yearling

Facilities

Found north of Meadow Creek off Howser Station Road, **Howser Park Recreation Site** offers space for 5 campers, while the nearby beach and boat launch provide good access to the lake. On the opposite side of the lake, **Glacier Creek Regional Park** is found on the south side of Glacier Creek. This water access park offers a beach area and a place to camp or picnic next to the lake. Fishing, swimming and windsurfing are popular pastimes on the big lake.

Species

Bull Trout
Rainbow Trout

N

500m   0   1km   2km   3km

— Scale —

Echo Lake

Location: 50 km (31 mi) east of Vernon
Elevation: 840 m (2,756 ft)
Surface Area: 57 ha (187 ac)
Mean Depth: 16 m (52.5 ft)
Max Depth: 50 m (164 ft)
Way Point: 118° 42′ 00″ Lon - W   50° 12′ 00″ Lat - N

Fishing

Located just outside of Lumby, Echo Lake is one of the Okanagan's most picturesque lakes. It is set in a steep valley which create an echo, giving the lake its name. Helping protect the natural beauty of the area is Echo Lake Provincial Park, which surrounds the lake. Although the park remains undeveloped, there is a nice resort and a few trails from which to access the lake.

The clear turquoise coloured water and excellent fishing for large rainbow, lake trout and kokanee make Echo Lake a popular recreational destination. Due to the fairly heavy angling pressure throughout the year, the Freshwater Fisheries Society of BC stocks thousands of rainbow trout annually. Despite the large number of fish stocked, the lake is being managed to become a quality rainbow trout fishery. On top of the introduction of freshwater shrimp into the lake ecosystem, fisheries stock the lake with larger strains, such as the Gerrard strain, as well as sterile fish to help increase the number of larger, brighter fish available. Fishing can be quite good at times for trout that have been known to reach the 2 kg (5 lbs) size on occasion.

Lake trout and larger rainbow are primarily caught by deep trolling with large spoons and plugs. Apex Lures in green, pink and black using a downrigger or lead line produces well. Lake trolls with a wedding band will entice both the rainbows and kokanee. Trollers should focus on the two narrows or off one of the many shoal areas found along this lake. Be wary of sudden winds in the narrow valley.

Fly anglers should not be put back by the size of the lake, as fly-fishing can be quite effective. The shoals on the north side and west end of the lake are great places to cast a line. In June and July, use full sink lines and strip or troll a dragonfly nymph, shrimp or blood leech slowly near the drop offs and weedbeds. Chironomid fishing on the shoals with a strike indicator and a bit of patience is productive in early summer and autumn.

Ice fishing on Echo Lake is a popular family activity since the road access throughout the winter is maintained. Popular tactics include suspending a hook baited with cooked shrimp or a jig tipped with maggots.

Directions

Located 50 km east of Vernon, follow Highway 6 to Lumby. Turn right onto Creighton Valley Road and follow this road for about 22 km to the lake. Although the road turns to gravel, cars and larger tailored units should have no difficulties accessing the resort, which is at the far end of the lake.

Facilities

Echo Lake Provincial Park is an undeveloped park that is utilized for day-use only. In addition to anglers, canoeists enjoy exploring this elongated shape lake, while sunbathers frequent the trail access picnic area. There is also an old dock at the picnic area near the southwest corner of the lake that can be used to cast a few lines.

For lake access and overnight accommodations, the **Echo Lake Resort** is found on a lovely bay on the northeast end of the lake. In addition to cabins, there is a large campsite, boat and canoe rentals as well as a boat launch. Visit www.echolakefishingresort.com for more information.

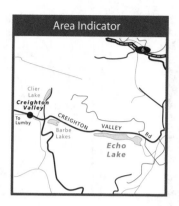

Area Indicator

Species
Kokanee
Lake Trout
Rainbow Trout

Echo Lake			
Fish Stocking Data			
Year	Species	Number	Life Stage
2013	Rainbow Trout	2,000	Yearling
2012	Rainbow Trout	2,000	Yearling
2011	Rainbow Trout	2,000	Yearling

N

100m 0 100m 200m 300m 400m 500m
— Scale —

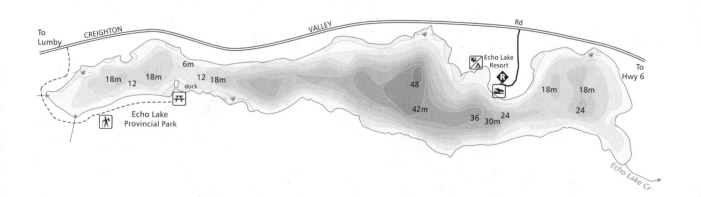

Echo Lakes - North & South

Echo Lake North

Species
Rainbow Trout

Elevation: 887 m (2,910 ft)
Surface Area: 7 ha (17 ac)
Mean Depth: 1.5 m (5 ft)
Max Depth: 6.5 m (21 ft)
Way Point: 115° 48' 00" Lon - W 49° 52' 00" Lat - N

Echo Lake South

Elevation: 885 m (2,904 ft)
Surface Area: 12 ha (30 ac)
Mean Depth: 3.6 m (12 ft)
Max Depth: 12.3 m (40 ft)
Way Point: 115° 48' 00" Lon - W 49° 52' 00" Lat - N

Directions

These small lakes are located west of Skookumchuck not far from Highway 93/95. Just south of the prominent curve on the highway, look for Farstad Road. This road leads west to where the Skookumchuck River Road leads along the south side of the creek. After passing the hydro lines, look for a rough access road leading south to the northern Echo Lake. The southern lake (Echo Lake Two) can be reached by portage or on foot from the first lake. There is also an old road system cum trail accessing the southern lake from the south. Regardless of what route you take, a 4wd vehicle, a GPS and a good map are highly recommended to access these hidden lakes.

Fishing

There are two lakes that share the name Echo here, named, originally enough, Echo Lake One and Echo Lake Two or Echo North and Echo South depending on who you talk to. While both of the lakes are road accessible, getting from one lake to the other involves a fairly long, roundabout drive, and the road to the second lake is very rough. Most people drive to the northernmost lake and make the short portage between the two lakes.

Because of this, the second lake is not fished as frequently, and offers slightly better fishing for small rainbow. Most trout average about 25-30 cm (10-12 in) and are best caught on the fly. Some can get bigger, and there is a 50 cm size restriction for any trout you're planning on keeping.

In both lakes, try working alongside the deep holes found around the lakes. The adjacent shallows can produce well, especially just after ice off and into early summer. Working a leech pattern in deeper water can find trout during the heat of summer. In spring, there are a number of hatches that can produce well.

For spincasters, metal finishes with a lot of chrome tend to attract the rainbow. Some good colours include chrome and blue or chrome and green.

There are three factors that dictate where you will find trout: safety, food and comfort. Rainbow like to hang out where the water is around 13–15°C (55–60°F). In the spring, this is usually just a few feet below the surface, but in the summer, this layer of cool water usually forms at around 4–6 m (15–20 ft). Here there is a large concentration of oxygen, meaning the fish are quite happy to hang out in the deeper areas of the lake, making the occasional trip to the shallower waters to find food. When the sun isn't beating down on the lake, and the surface is calm, the fish will often rise to feed on bugs that are on the surface. This is usually in the early morning or late evening.

Be sure to check your regulations before heading out. There are a number of restrictions such as a bait ban, single hook, special quotas and seasons for trout in the Echo Lakes.

Facilities

Although there are no established facilities, it is possible to pitch a tent or launch a canoe along the shoreline of the lakes. Please practice no trace camping and be bear aware.

Other Options

Just to the north of the Echo Lakes, you can find **Skookumchuck Creek**. Most of the creek is accessible by the main access road used to find the Echo Lakes. The creek offers fishing opportunities for cutthroat trout and bull trout. Be sure to check the regulations before fishing the creek.

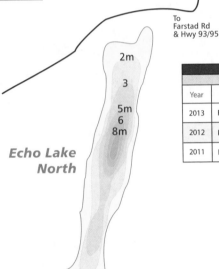

To Farstad Rd & Hwy 93/95

Echo Lake North

2m
3
5m
6
8m
2m

Echo Lake South

5m
3
2m
3m
6
9m
12m
12m

Echo Lake North — Fish Stocking Data

Year	Species	Number	Life Stage
2013	Rainbow Trout	1,000	Spring Catchable
2012	Rainbow Trout	1,000	Spring Catchable
2011	Rainbow Trout	1,000	Yearling/ Catchable

Echo Lake South — Fish Stocking Data

Year	Species	Number	Life Stage
2013	Rainbow Trout	1,500	Yearling
2012	Rainbow Trout	1,500	Yearling
2011	Rainbow Trout	750	Yearling/ Catchable

N

100m   0   100m   200m   300m
Scale

Edwards Lake

Location: 23 km (14 mi) south of Elko
Elevation: 807 m (2,648 ft)
Surface Area: 33 ha (82 ac)
Mean Depth: 3 m (10 ft)
Max Depth: 8 m (26 ft)
Way Point: 115° 06′ 00″ Lon - W   49° 05′ 00″ Lat - N

4 Region

Fishing

Edwards Lake is a fairly popular recreational lake found near the community of Grasmere. There is a small recreation site on the shores of the lake, as well as a number of private cabins. The southern half of the lake is also found in the Tobacco Plains Indian Reserve. Anglers will find that the lake is heavily stocked, although in the last few years, fewer rainbow trout have been dumped in the lake than in the past.

Edwards Lake is most popular in the spring since it is usually the first lake in the area to be ice free. Anglers have been known to be fishing the lake in late March during milder years. The lake features extensive shoals at the north and south ends. Early in the year, the fish are more likely to be found cruising the shores, while in summer, they will usually be found holding in the deeper water just off these shoal areas. Anglers should try off the point found along the eastern shore, which features a sharp transition zone between the deeper water and the shoals. The rainbow in this lake can reach good sizes and provide consistent action throughout the year, even during the heat of summer.

If you are fly-fishing, chironomid patterns work well during the spring, while leech patterns can work well all season long. During the summer or fall, terrestrials like black ants and grasshoppers can create a frenzy on this lake. Watch for these opportunities, as rainbow will be seen splashing on the surface while leaping after these flying insects. It doesn't happen every day, but when the trout are chasing terrestrials, it can be some of the finest dry fly-fishing you ever did see.

Spincasters can try the usual assortment of spoons and spinners. Rainbow like to chase spoons with lots of silver that are retrieved quite fast, as these imitate minnows. Trolling is usually not recommended on lakes as small and shallow as Edwards since the fish are easily spooked by the boat passing overhead. Instead, pick a spot on the lake in deeper water but near a drop off, and cast the lure into the shallow, letting it sink down to near the bottom before retrieving.

There is an electric motor only restriction on the lake.

Directions

To find Edwards Lake, take Highway 93 south from the town of Elko to Grasmere. At Grasmere, take the Grasmere-Dorr Road west off the highway. Continue a short distance and just past the school house, look for the access road to Edwards Lake on the left (west). The recreation site and parking area found about 2 km down this road.

Facilities

The **Edwards Lake Recreation Site** is a small, partially treed site on the north side of the lake. There is space for up to 6 groups here. It is also possible to launch small, electric motor only boats at the lake. Visitors will also find a series of old roads that can be explored on foot or bike.

Other Options

Loon Lake is easily accessible to the north of Edwards Lake and can be accessed by most vehicles. The lake has been stocked regularly and provides for fishing opportunities for nice sized rainbow trout. Check your regulations before fishing Loon Lake, currently there is an electric motor only restriction and an ice fishing ban.

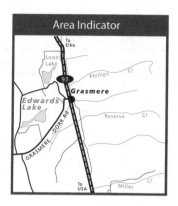
Area Indicator

Species
Rainbow Trout

Edwards Lake Fish Stocking Data			
Year	Species	Number	Life Stage
2013	Rainbow Trout	10,000	Yearling
2012	Rainbow Trout	10,000	Yearling
2011	Rainbow Trout	10,000	Yearling

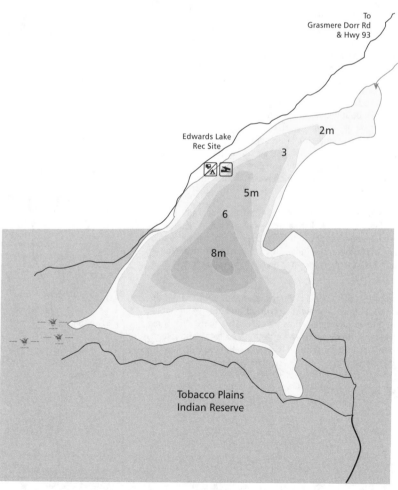

To Grasmere Dorr Rd & Hwy 93

Edwards Lake Rec Site

2m

3

5m

6

8m

Tobacco Plains Indian Reserve

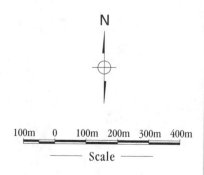

N

100m   0   100m   200m   300m   400m

— Scale —

Region 4

Upper Elk River
Location: North of Sparwood
Stream Length: 213 km (132 mi)
Geographic: 114°54'00" Lon - W   50°1'00" Lat - N

Elk River - Upper

Fishing

Welcome to the single greatest river fishing experience in the world. Or so fans of the Elk would have you believe, and who are we to argue? The boisterous mountain river is a Class II protected stream which means you need a special license (stamp) to fish here, and that the river is highly regulated. But with nearly 150 km (90 miles) of fishable water, the Elk is considered one of the best dry fly-fishing rivers in the country.

The Elk is a big freestone river where spring run-off can end as late as mid-July, though fishing usually get underway about a month before that. It has its headwaters in Elk Lakes Provincial Park, draining Lower Elk Lake. It passes through Elkford, Sparwood, Fernie and Elko before emptying into Lake Koocanusa.

The river is famous for its Westslope Cutthroat, which can get to 1.5 kg (3 lbs), but it also holds bull trout in the 2.5 kg (5 lb) range and lots of Rocky Mountain whitefish. Some of the bull trout in the lower reaches (below the dam Elko) are known to top 6.3 kg (14 lbs).

The great thing about fishing the Elk is the way you approach each species is totally different. The cutthroat is the perfect fish to dry fly, working the surface of the water with the realistic presentations. Experienced anglers will fish the river with a variety of deer hair caddis patterns with size 14 to size 8 hooks in a variety of colours: green, yellow, brown and orange. If those patterns aren't working, a size 16 or size 14 mayfly pattern in olive, tan or grey might work. Having a few nymph patterns will help, too, like a size 8 weighted golden stonefly nymph pattern.

Because the river has irregular, often mixed hatches, there is no need to exactly match the hatch, and fishing a floating stonefly or grasshopper can also induce a strike. In fact, the cutthroat of the Elk are known for chasing almost anything people will throw at them. The larger fish tend to hang out around log jams and close to the shore. This is a good way to lose your flies, and the bigger trout have seen a lot of presentations, and have probably been hooked more than a few times, so it is always a satisfying experience when you convince one of these wily veterans to strike. Doing it without losing your favourite fly in the process is even better.

The Elk is a mid-sized river, and, while it is possible to fish the river from the shore, having a boat will be much more productive. The river is a classic mix of whitewater runs followed by deep pools, riffles and numerous side channels. Most people don't fish exclusively from the boat, but will often get out and wade the shallower sections. Note that the river above Elko is fairly easily navigated by boat. Below Elko, however, there are some rather large rapids. This section is best done with the help of an experienced guide.

The bull trout are best taken with a large (size 2) streamer or bucktail that imitates a small whitefish or kokanee. In the fall, the kokanee begin to turn red, so match your flies appropriately. The bull trout will also take well to a variety of spoons and spinners. The biggest bull trout are found below the dam at Elko, which presents a barrier to fish coming upstream from Lake Koocanusa.

The best time to fish this river is in August and September, when the water levels are a bit lower, the weather is good, and the fish are active. However, keen anglers have been known to get out there when the snow is flying. Sections of the upper river are designated catch and release only, and you'll find the biggest fish in these areas. Be sure to review the regulations before fishing.

Species
Bull Trout
Cutthroat Trout
Whitefish

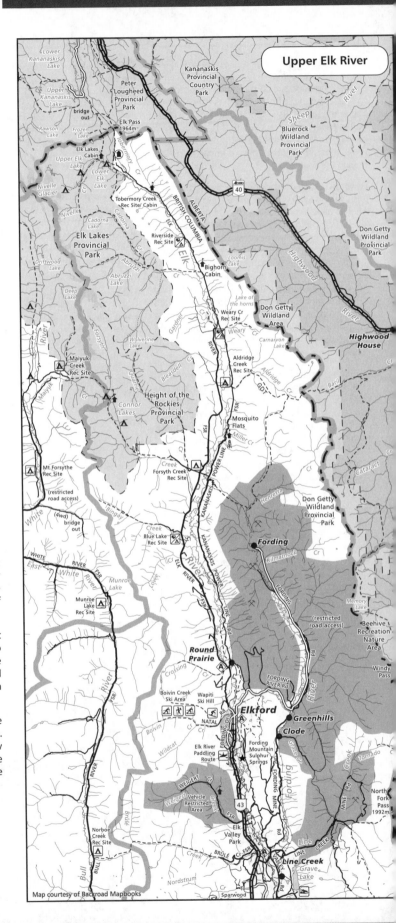

Upper Elk River

Map courtesy of Backroad Mapbooks

Elk River - Lower

Lower Elk River
Location: Flows through Fernie
Stream Length: 213 km (132 mi)
Geographic: 115° 3'00" Lon - W 49° 31'00" Lat - N

4 Region

Directions

The Crowsnest Highway (Highway 3) follows the Elk River for most of its mid section, picking up the river near Elko until the highway branches east at Sparwood. There are numerous holes and access points that literally call out to any would be angler as they drive this beautiful section of highway. Below Elko, the best place to access the river is at the Highway 93 bridge, 14 km (8.5 miles) south of Elko. Access in between Elko and the highway bridge is limited, but there are a few small side roads and some great holes to look for. Be wary of private property along these sections.

Above Sparwood, the river is accessed by a variety of roads including Highway 43 and the Elk Valley Roads, which parallel the river for a short stretch north of town. The Highway 43 bridge in Elkford is a popular spot to access the river, but there are also a few other road crossings to take advantage of in this stretch.

Even further upstream, the Elk River Forest Service Road takes over. This good gravel road is drivable in most vehicles and provides fairly good access to most of the upper reaches. The fish tend to be a bit smaller upstream, but the trade-off is a lot more seclusion and a gorgeous mountain setting. The best access points are from the numerous recreation sites along the river.

Facilities

A number of towns have sprung up alongside the Elk River, offering everything from accommodations (hotels, B&Bs, private campgrounds), to fuel to tackle shops to grocery stores. Be sure to check in at Fernie Fly and Tackle Shop for the latest reports and what is working best at the moment.

For those looking for their accommodation a little more outdoorsy there are several parks and recreation sites in the area. A popular campsite is the **Mount Fernie Provincial Park**, which is home to 38 campsites, several trails and a great bull trout fishing hole. Further upstream the recreation sites include: **Krivinsky Farm** (10 groups in an open area); **Blue Lake** (4 forested sites next to a small fishing lake); **Forsyth Creek** (6 sites but not next to the river); **Aldridge Creek** (a small out of the way site); **Weary Creek** (a small 2 unit site); and **Riverside** (a partially treed 3 unit site). All of these sites are easily accessed of the Elk River Forest Service Road and provide good access to the river itself. If that is not enough, there are also a couple cabins along the river including the **Tobermory Creek Cabin and Recreation Site**, which is available on a first come, first serve basis. For more details on these and other recreational activities in the area, be sure to pick up a copy of the Backroad Mapbook for Kootenay Rockies BC.

Species
Bull Trout
Cutthroat Trout
Whitefish

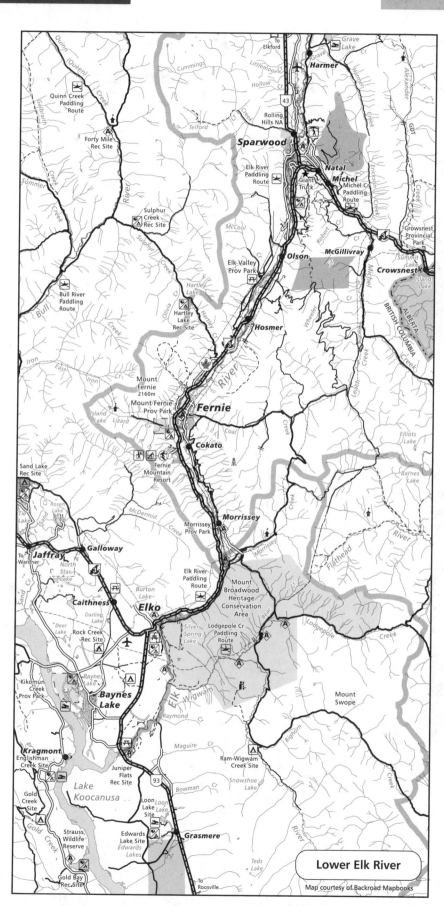

Lower Elk River

Map courtesy of Backroad Mapbooks

Elinor & Naramata Lakes

Elinor Lake

Elevation: 1,280 m (4,199 ft)
Surface Area: 8.2 ha (20 ac)
Mean Depth: 3 m (10 ft)
Max Depth: 5.5 m (17.5 ft)
Way Point: 119° 32' 00" Lat- W 49° 40' 00" Lon- N

Naramata Lake

Elevation: 1,280 m (4,199 ft)
Surface Area: 13.5 ha (33 ac)
Mean Depth: 3.5 m (12 ft)
Max Depth: 6 m (20 ft)
Way Point: 119° 32' 00" Lon - W 49° 39' 00" Lat - N

Area Indicator

Species
Rainbow Trout

Elinor Lake
Fish Stocking Data

Year	Species	Number	Life Stage
2007	Rainbow Trout	1,000	Fry
2006	Rainbow Trout	1,000	Fry
2005	Rainbow Trout	1,000	Fry

Elinor Lake

Naramata Lake

Species
Rainbow Trout

Naramata Lake
Fish Stocking Data

Year	Species	Number	Life Stage
2013	Rainbow Trout	0	Fry
2012	Rainbow Trout	1,000	Fry
2011	Rainbow Trout	0	Fry

N

100m 0 100m 200m 300m
— Scale —

Robinson Creek

Fishing

These two small, narrow lakes are found northeast of the town of Naramata in the hills above Okanagan Lake. The lakes are part of a dam system along Robinson Creek and offer good fishing at times for small rainbow trout.

Fly-fishing is the preferred angling method on the lakes, although spincasting small spoons and spinners can be productive. Since the lakes are part of a dam system, draw down can hinder productivity later in the summer. As a result, fishing is best in the spring.

Of the two, Naramata Lake is slightly bigger, slightly deeper and slightly more popular. As a result, the Freshwater Fisheries Society of BC stocks the lake with 1,000 rainbow fry every year to help maintain the fishery. There is an island towards the north end of the lake, as well as a point on the eastern shore that attract fish in the spring and fall. However, you are better off working the deeper southern end of the lake when the water warms up, as the north half is quite shallow.

On Elinor Lake, the small narrows is a good area to try. A good idea is to cast towards the drop off from the deeper part of the narrows.

In the spring and fall, searching patterns such as black broadhead leeches or Woolly Buggers can be effective. During summer, troll leeches or nymph patterns such as dragonflies deep during the day and watch the surface for signs of an emerging hatch as evening approaches. During hot summer evenings winged black ants can create a flurry of top water activity. While jumping fish will make any angler excited, it is best to look for subtler rises or rings in the water. Smaller fish tend to jump, while the larger, smarter ones are often more stealthy.

Directions

North of the city of Penticton, you can find Elinor and Naramata Lakes high in the hills above Okanagan Lake. To reach the lakes follow Naramata Road north from Penticton to the Chute Lake Forest Service Road. When the main road veers north towards Chute Lake, keep straight. Elinor Lake is about 10 minutes down this road, while Naramata Lake is about 15 minutes. Most 2wd vehicles should have no trouble travelling these roads.

Facilities

There are no boat launches at either lake, but hand launching a small craft is fairly easy. It is also possible to set up a wilderness campsite at previously used sites. Please practice no trace camping and try to leave the area cleaner than when you arrived. Alternatively, Penticton offers all amenities and is found a short distance to the south, while **Chute Lake Resort** is found just north of the lakes. The resort offers both cabins and a campsite along with a nice restaurant.

Erie Lake

Location: 5 km (3 mi) west of Salmo
Elevation: 711 m (2,333 ft)
Surface Area: 33 ha (82 ac)
Mean Depth: 5 m (16 ft)
Max Depth: 13.7 m (45 ft)
Way Point: 117° 20' 00" Lon - W   49° 11' 00" Lat - N

Fishing

Erie Lake is a popular ice fishing lake found west of Salmo. In the past, the lake was stocked with brook trout. Although it is no longer stocked, the brookies have survived and thrived in this shallow, weedy lake. Because of the extensive shoal areas and weeds, the lake is difficult to fish from shore, except during the first few weeks of spring when the ice starts coming off the lake. At these times, the fish do cruise the shallows close to shore looking for food and may take to a line cast from the shore.

More often than not, though, the lake is fished from a small boat or floatation device. The deepest hole is found just out from the rest area off Highway 3, near the west end of the lake. Get into the deeper water, and cast towards the shallows, letting your lure or fly sink down nearly to the bottom before retrieving. Fish are generally found either near the bottom of the lake or near the top, and unless you are fishing during the early morning or later in the evening, chances are they'll be down low. However, by bottom we don't mean the absolute deepest spot of the lake, but rather at the level where the water is cool enough for the fish to be comfortable, which in the summer is usually down around 5–7 m (15–20 ft) or so.

They also like the cool water that flows in from Divide Creek at the west end of the lake. Not only is the water cooler and oxygenated, but the creek also washes food down into the lake.

Over the last few years, largemouth bass, which were illegally introduced into the lake, have detrimentally affected trout angling. However, bass are a popular sportfish in their own right, and can be found in the lake in fair to good numbers. They readily strike jigs, spinners and top water flies or lures. Largemouth can be found almost anywhere in the lake, although it is best to try near weed structure, especially just before and during dusk hours. Bass average about 0.5-1 kg (1-2 lbs) in size, although some larger bass have been found in Erie Lake.

Ice fishing is also extremely popular on the lake. The brookies will often be found near the top of the lake, swimming close to the ice, while the bass will be found down in the weeds. Yellow perch are also known to take smaller jigs and bait during the winter.

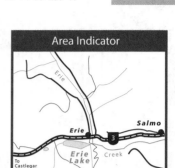

Area Indicator

Species

Brook Trout
Largemouth Bass
Rainbow Trout
Yellow Perch

Erie Lake			
Fish Stocking Data			
Year	Species	Number	Life Stage
2013	Rainbow Trout	6,000	Fry
2012	Rainbow Trout	1,000	Fry
2011	Rainbow Trout	5,000	Fry

Directions

Located west of the historic town of Salmo, Erie Lake lies along the south side of Highway 3. There is a highway rest area where you can park your vehicle. From the rest area, it is a short scramble down a small hill to the lakeshore.

Facilities

The **Erie Lake Rest Area** provides picnic tables and outhouses. Alternatively, the town of Salmo is found nearby and provides a general store, a couple gas stations, as well as various other amenities available for visitors.

Other Options

East of Erie Lake you will both **Erie Creek** and the **Salmo River**. Erie Creek provides good fishing for mostly small brook trout, especially in the remote upper reaches of the creek. The Salmo River flows south towards the Pend D'Oreille River and is accessible off Highway 3 and 6. Rainbow trout are the main species found in the river, while bull trout can be found in a few areas. There are some wonderful pools to cast a fly or lure into.

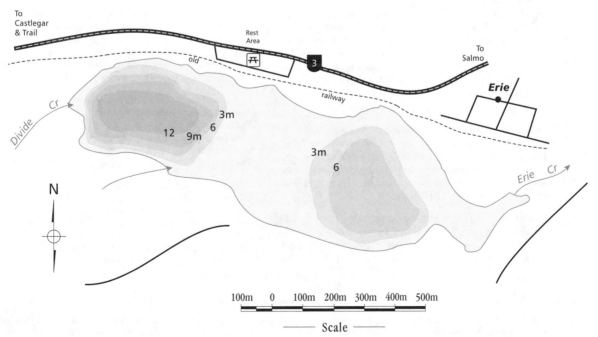

Region 8

Eneas Lakes

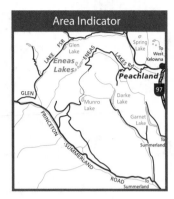

Area Indicator

Island Lake

Elevation: 1,500 m (4,921 ft)
Surface Area: 6.5 ha (16 ac)
Mean Depth: 4.1 m (13.5 ft)
Max Depth: 7.6 m (25 ft)
Way Point: 119° 56'15" Lat-W 49° 45'00" Lon- N

Tsuh Lake

Elevation: 1,500 m (4,921 ft)
Surface Area: 10.5 ha (26 ac)
Mean Depth: 7.6 m (25 ft)
Max Depth: 15.2 m (50 ft)
Way Point: 119° 56'38" Lat-W 49° 45'04" Lon- N

Directions

Found west of Peachland, Eneas Lakes Provincial Park is difficult to access. In addition to no signage, the road was deactivated in 2002 and is no longer maintained. You will have to negotiate almost 20 km of rough, gravel road that is often littered with obstacles. As a result, only 4wd vehicles equipped with a chainsaw or a saw to clear away trees and other debris are recommend.

To find the lakes, you will need to navigate to Munro Lake Forest Service Road from Peachland. To do this, follow Princeton Avenue west. Once on the outskirts of town, look for McDougald to the south (left). A short jaunt down this road will lead to the Munro Lake Forest Service Road. Continue on this road past the turn off to Darke Lake Provincial Park all the way to the end of the road and the rustic campsite on Big Eneas Lake. Access to Little Eneas and Island lakes is by boat and/or foot, while Tsuh can be accessed by trail or a rough 4wd road off the main road into the park.

A copy of the BC Backroad GPS Maps and a Backroad Mapbook for the Thompson Okanagan area is helpful in finding the lakes.

Facilities

Eneas Lakes Provincial Park protects four beautiful lakes in a pristine fir and pine forest setting. The difficult access and limited facilities makes this park a nice destination for those looking for a wilderness experience with good fishing, canoeing, hiking, horseback riding, wildlife viewing and even snowmobiling opportunities. Open year round, it is possible to camp at Big Eneas Lake where there are 4 undeveloped, user maintained sites. Visitors should be prepared to walk into the campsites as the road into the park is very rough and difficult to navigate. There is also a cartop boat launch on Big Eneas.

The Eneas Lakes Circuit trail connects the four lakes. Similar to the access road, no signs are posted and the trails are not maintained. All hikers exploring the park should be well prepared and experienced. During winter the roads are used by snowmobilers. ATV use in the park is limited to the road to the Big Eneas Lake campground and the road to Tsuh Lake.

In addition, there are two cabins located at the north end of Tsuh Lake. The cabins are maintained by the Peachland Sportsman's Association and open to the public. They can be accessed by trail or a very rough 4wd road and are very popular with hunters in fall.

Other Options

Glen Lake can be found northwest of Eneas Lakes off the Glen Lake Forest Service Road, which is found on the way to Headwater Lakes. Eastern brook trout and rainbow trout up to 1.5 kg (3 lbs) can be caught on the fly or by trolling small lures, Flatfish and spinning gear. The 11 hectare lake is stocked.

Fishing

Protected by the Eneas Lake Provincial Park, the beautiful plateau lake area features a unique lake complex consisting of Big and Little Eneas Lakes, Island Lake and Tsuh Lake. A dam on the outlet of Big Eneas Lake stores water for the Summerland Irrigation District. When the water level is at or near maximum, Big and Little Eneas Lakes form a single 25 hectare lake.

Island Lake is accessible only by boat or foot and has no development along its heavily forested shores. Tsuh Lake is also dammed at the outlet to provide water for irrigation. Two cabins on Tsuh Lake that are open to the public are maintained by the Peachland Sportsman's Association.

The lakes, with their limited access, provide a remote angling opportunity for abundant, but small rainbow trout. Big and Little Eneas Lakes as well as Tsuh Lake offer wild trout, with the odd fish reaching 1 kg (2 lbs). Island Lake was last stocked in the late 1980's, but stocking was stopped to reduce the number of fish in hopes to increase the average catch size. However, the fish remain small due to the low angling pressure.

The moderate elevation of the lakes allows the fishery to last throughout the open water season, even during the warmer summer months. However, fluctuating water levels in the dammed lakes can affect the fishing at certain times of the year. There is an agreement with the District of Summerland to maintain optimum lake levels to benefit angling and other water-based recreation.

Fly anglers should note that the aquatic plants include water lilies and marsh grass. Hyalella shrimp are also present. Both of these are good indicators of what fly patterns to use (leeches and other searching patterns or shrimp patterns), especially early in the open water season. During the summer, the lakes are also known to provide some good dry fly action. The ever popular Tom Thumb or small midge patterns can create some added excitement when fishing on the fly.

Most small lures, such as the locally produced Lyman lures (size 1) or Dick Nites, can also be effective. When trolling it is best to work the drop-offs in a figure-eight pattern to vary the direction, depth and speed of the fly. Generally speaking you will need to go deeper during summer.

Fishing near structure such as logs and weeds, shoals or at the edge of a drop-off produces the best results for spincasters and fly anglers. Food sources also congregate around weeds and inflow or outflow streams and in the thermocline. The thermocline is the area of the lake between the warm surface water and the cold water. Concentrate your efforts in these areas to improve your chances of angling success.

If spincasting or fly casting, a good trick is to use the countdown method to gauge where the trout are holding. With every cast be sure to count the seconds your lure or fly is sinking in the water before you begin your retrieve. Continue counting a little longer each time until you find the strike zone. Then you will know where the fish are holding and be able to repeat your count with each cast.

The forested shoreline of the Eneas Lakes makes shore casting difficult. Although it is possible to cast from shore, the use of a small boat or pontoon boat is recommended. Many prefer to troll their lures or flies, but casting towards the lilies and marsh grass is a very effective way to lure the hiding trout out. Despite being plateau lakes, the forested nature of the shoreline helps keep the wind down and makes it easier to maneuver light watercraft like belly boats.

Eneas Lakes

Location: 13 km (8 mi) west of Peachland

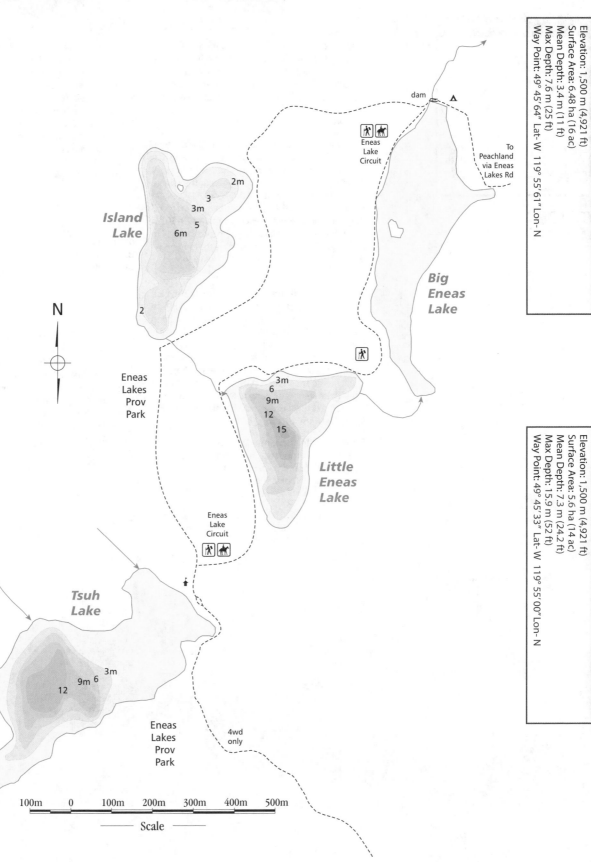

Big Eneas Lake

Elevation: 1,500 m (4,921 ft)
Surface Area: 6.48 ha (16 ac)
Mean Depth: 3.4 m (11 ft)
Max Depth: 7.6 m (25 ft)
Way Point: 49° 45' 64" Lat- W 119° 55' 61" Lon- N

Little Eneas Lake

Elevation: 1,500 m (4,921 ft)
Surface Area: 5.6 ha (14 ac)
Mean Depth: 7.3 m (24.2 ft)
Max Depth: 15.9 m (52 ft)
Way Point: 49° 45' 33" Lat- W 119° 55' 00" Lon- N

dam

Eneas Lake Circuit

To Peachland via Eneas Lakes Rd

Island Lake

2m
3
3m
5
6m
2

N

Big Eneas Lake

Eneas Lakes Prov Park

3m
6
9m
12
15

Little Eneas Lake

Eneas Lake Circuit

Tsuh Lake

3m
9m 6
12

Eneas Lakes Prov Park

4wd only

Tsuh Cr
dam

100m 0 100m 200m 300m 400m 500m
— Scale —

Region 4

Location: 15 km (9.5 mi) northwest of Slocan
Elevation: 1,546 m (5,072 ft)
Surface Area: 267 ha (659 ac)
Mean Depth: 61 m (200 ft)
Max Depth: 155 m (508 ft)
Way Point: 117° 39' 00" Lon - W 49° 51' 00" Lat - N

Evans Lake

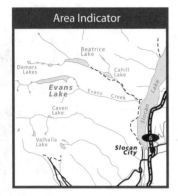

Area Indicator

Species

Rainbow Trout

Fishing

Evans Lake is a beautiful high elevation lake found deep in the interior of Valhalla Provincial Park. Access is by air or by an extremely long, challenging trail. As a result, very few make it to visit this wild, remote, pristine lake. Those that do will find a gorgeous mountain lake surrounded by snow-capped peaks.

They will also find some great fishing. Most high elevation lakes are small, and if they have fish at all, they are usually pretty small due to the short growing season and lack of oxygen in the winter. Evans Lake, on the other hand, is quite large, and the rainbow trout that grow here can get up to 1.5 kg (3.5 lbs). although they average around 25–30 cm (10–12 in) in size. The lake is extremely deep, 144 m (472 ft) at its deepest spot, so despite the long snow-covered season, it does not suffer from winterkill.

Getting a small boat or float tube up to the lake is nearly impossible unless you decide to fly in, which many visitors do. But shore bound anglers will find that the lake depth drops-off quite quickly, making it easy to fish from shore. The north shore is steep, but mostly free of trees. However, it can only be followed about half a kilometre before a rather large cliff blocks your way. The south shore, on the other hand, has no such obstructions, but has a lot more trees. There are some clearings, the biggest of which is actually at the west end of the lake, about 4 km (2.4 miles) from the campsite.

Fly anglers often have good success at this lake. In an attempt to attract the larger trout into striking, try using top water patterns such as a big caddis. Stripping in a Woolly Bugger or large nymph can also help to find bigger trout.

Spincasters will find that spinners work consistently, although not as effectively as flies. Do not be shy to cast a medium sized Flatfish or other minnow imitation lures out there in an attempt to hook into a big one.

Directions

Evans Lake can be found deep within the boundary of Valhalla Provincial Park. The lake can only be accessed by floatplane, helicopter or by bushwhacking along a rustic route from the western shore of Slocan Lake. Most anglers choose to fly into the lake. If you are brave enough to hike-in, the route follows Evans Creek all the way to Evans Lake. To say the least, it is a long and challenging trek. You can reach the creek mouth by boat from Slocan Lake or by trail from Slocan City. Be aware, this is Grizzly bear country.

Facilities

Visitors coming by helicopter will find a landing pad next to the old cabin on the eastern shore. This is also a fine area to camp as there are a few rustic campsites established.

Other Options

The closest fishing alternative to **Evans Lake** is Evans Creek. The creek flows out of the lake all the way down to Slocan Lake. Small rainbow trout can be found in the fast flowing creek in the sections where you find larger pools formed. Adventurous anglers can also make their way west of Evans Lake, to an unnamed lake a few hundred metres beyond and up. It is rumoured to contain rainbow. South of this lake, and a ways up, is the spectacular **Thor Lake,** which holds some brook trout.

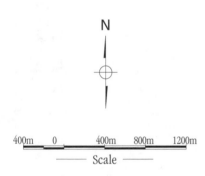

N

400m   0   400m   800m   1200m

Scale

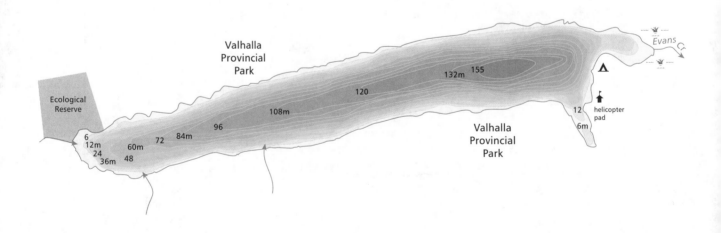

Gardom Lake

Location: 40 km (25 mi) north of Vernon
Elevation: 548 m (1,798 ft)
Surface Area: 73.5 ha (182 ft)
Mean Depth: 8.8 m (29 ft)
Max Depth: 21 m (69 ft)
Way Point: 119° 12′ 00″ Lat W 50° 36′ 00″ Lon N

Fishing

Gardom Lake is a popular fishing and recreational destinationsandwiched between Salmon Arm and Enderby. This family lake is visited throughout the year as it provides fun for both park-goers and anglers alike.

Recently rehabilitated, the lake once again supports some nice sized rainbow trout. The lake is stocked annually with catchable size trout by the Freshwater Fisheries Society of B.C. Reports indicate that these trout are once again topping the scales at 2.5 kg (5 lbs). However, trout half that size are a more regular catch.

Gardom Lake is best fished from a boat, but note the 10 horsepower engine restriction. Anglers who are out on the lake in smaller craft can seek shelter from the winds in around the islands. Try trolling the edges of the drop-offs and around the islands with small spinners, Kwikfish plugs or gang trolls with a wedding band or Flatfish tipped with worms.

The low elevation lake opens up fairly early in the spring. Anglers will find better luck at this time and again through early autumn. The best months for fly-fishing takes place in May and June and again in September.Fly anglers will find good chironomid, mayfly, damselfly and dragonfly hatches here. Be sure to bring along a selection of larvae, pupa and nymph patterns and match the hatch. At other times, trolling the deep portions of the lake using a full sink line with leeches, Woolly Buggers, minnow patterns and Doc Spratleys can be effective. Casting with dry flies on the shoals during the summer months can also be quite exciting with rainbow rising to the challenge.

Although there is limited access to suitable shore fishing areas, there is a well-developed trail system around the park. Most casting from shore prefer to cross the floating bridge that accesses the main island to fish from there.

Due to the good road access, ice fishing is also very popular on Gardom Lake. Meal worms, maggots and powerbait on glo hooks yielding decent results. Berkley Gulp and fresh cooked shrimp are other possible winter baits.

Due to the recent eradication, the lake no longer holds smallmouth bass and perch. These fish were illegally introducedseveral years ago and had severely affected the trout fishery.

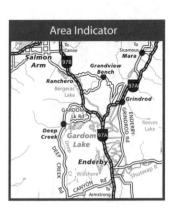

Area Indicator

Species
Rainbow Trout

Gardom Lake			
Fish Stocking Data			
Year	Species	Number	Life Stage
2013	Rainbow Trout	13,000	Spring Catchable
2012	Rainbow Trout	10,000	Catchable
2011	Rainbow Trout	8,000	Catchable

Directions

This lake is easily accessed by car since road signs direct you from the highway to the park. From Vernon, travel north on Highway 97A through the town of Enderby and turn left at Highway 97B leading towards Salmon Arm. The next major left is Gardom Lake Road, which leads to the park and lake.

Facilities

Gardom Lake Park is day-use only park with picnic tables, pit toilets and a playground for kids. Also located within the park is a boat launch suitable for cartop and small trailered boats.

Other Options

Next to Highway 97A, the **Shuswap River** is a meandering stream that is known to produce a variety of sportfish. Although it produces resident trout throughout the year, the stream is better known as a salmon bearing stream. From large Chinook to feisty chum salmon the river comes alive in late summer and fall with several impressive runs.

Location: 12 km (7.5 mi) northwest of Summerland
Elevation: 630 m (2,067 ft)
Surface Area: 40 ha (98 ac)
Mean Depth: 6 m (20 ft)
Max Depth: 20.5 m (67 ft)
Way Point: 119° 47' 00" Lon - W   49° 41' 00" Lat - N

Garnet Lake

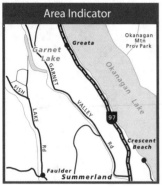

Area Indicator

Species

Rainbow Trout	5
Brook Trout	20

Kokanee 5

Fishing

Garnet Lake is an odd shaped lake that was formed by the damming of the Eneas Creek. The lake is stocked annually with both brook trout and rainbow trout making for an interesting mix when fishing. Both species are much more active in the spring and fall, although the lake can produce well throughout the summer months.

Since the lake is a reservoir, the northern section of the lake is quite shallow, while the southern half of the lake is comprised of two deep areas that reach up to 15 m (49 ft) in depth. Fishing should be concentrated along the drop off areas next to these deep sections. The area next to the inflow of the small creek is also a higher success area. Try working these areas with a beadhead nymph or a Woolly Bugger.

Once the water starts to warm up the trout will be found at about 8–10 m (25–32 ft) in depth where ever there is structure It is important that you get your lure down to where the fish are. Sure, you might have the perfect lure, but if it is passing ten feet, or even five feet over the trout's head, it's not going to do much good.

It is possible to hand launch a boat from the south end of the lake, although a float tube will work just as well. Try trolling from the boat launch to the midsection of the lake, then back along the other side of the arm. A small spoon or spinner will work, as will a searching fly pattern like a Doc Spratley or a leech.

In the winter, ice fishing is quite popular. Although the occasional rainbow trout may be taken, the brook trout remain much more active in winter. Brook trout are usually found less than 3 m (10 ft) under the ice, and usually in the shallows of the lake. Your eyes should flick over to the map now to see the large, shallow area towards the north of the lake, possibly accompanied by a "hmm". While brookies do still tend to favour being near places where there is deep water and some structure, when they head into this area, it's because they are looking for food. However, if this area isn't being productive, you can always try towards the south end of the lake.

There is an electric motor restriction on Garnet Lake.

Directions

Garnet Lake is located north of the town of Summerland approximately 10 km (6 mi) down the Garnet Valley Road. Garnet Valley Road is a good condition 2wd dirt road that can be picked up from Jones Flat Road in Summerland. The lake is about 100 m from the side of Garnet Valley Road. Parking is available off the side of the road.

Facilities

Other than a rustic car top boat launch, there are no facilities immediately available at Garnet Lake. Hotel and other overnight accommodation are available in Summerland and vicinity. If you prefer to spend a few nights in a campground, **Okanagan Lake Provincial Park** and **Darke Lake Provincial Park** are both within a twenty-minute drive from Garnet Lake.

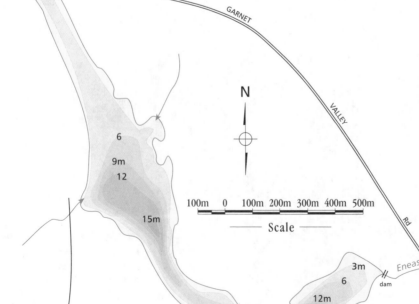

Garnet Lake			
Fish Stocking Data			
Year	Species	Number	Life Stage
2013	Brook Trout	1,000	Fingerling
2013	Rainbow Trout	1,000	Yearling
2012	Brook Trout	1,000	Fingerling
2012	Rainbow Trout	1,000	Fingerling
2011	Brook Trout	1,000	Fingerling
2011	Rainbow Trout	1,000	Fingerling

Gladstone Lake

Location: 36 km (22 mi) north of Princeton
Elevation: 1,001 m (3,284 ft)
Surface Area: 6 ha (15 ac)
Mean Depth: 5.8 m (19 ft)
Max Depth: 14.3 m (47 ft)
Way Point: 120° 38′00″ Lon - W 49° 45′00″Lat - N

8 Region

Fishing

Gladstone Lake is the first in the series of productive fishing lakes found in the popular Pike Mountain Recreation Area. It is a fairly popular lake due to the nice setting and the easy access off of Highway 5A. The lake is stocked annually with rainbow trout by the Freshwater Fisheries Society of BC, which helps keep the trout fishery quite active.

There are two sections to the lake, which are divided by a shallow stretch in the middle of the lake. The eastern half is the deeper portion, with depths of up to 14 m (46 ft) in some sections. The steep drop off on this side of the lake tends to be good holding areas for cruising rainbow. However, there are ample shoals that rear insects and the trout can be found searching these areas for an easy meal on occasion.

A chironomid pattern fished in the 6-10 m (20-30 ft) range around the drop offs can be very productive during spring. There are two ways to fish a chironomid pattern. One is to use a floating line, a long leader and a strike indicator to get the fly to dangle down about a foot off the bottom. This only works with leaders up to about 8 m (25 ft) or so. To fish deeper, use a sinking line. Anchor your boat above where you want to fish, then cast out, allowing the fly to slowly sink down until it is directly beneath the tip of the rod before beginning a very slow retrieve.

Later in the spring and into early summer hatches of damselflies and dragonflies become more prevalent. Fly anglers can have a lot of success with larger nymph patterns.

Other Options

Guilford Lake is located north of Gladstone Lake and can be accessed via the forest service road that branches north from the Pike Mountain Forest Service Road just past Gladstone Lake. Guilford Lake offers angling opportunities for small rainbow trout. Alternatively, Kump, Lodwick and Thalia Lakes are all found in the vicinity and offer decent fishing for stocked rainbow trout.

Directions

You will find Gladstone Lake right next to Highway 5A, about 25 km (15.5 mi) south of the Aspen Grove turn-off on the Coquihalla Connector or 36 km (22 mi) north of Princeton. There is a short access road off the west side of Highway 5A that leads to an informal launching site on private land. Alternatively, there is a short access road off of the north side of the Pike Mountain Forest Service Road that can also be used to get down to the lake.

Facilities

Gladstone Lake is a nice roadside lake offering a couple small picnic areas and rustic cartop boat launches. The site on the east side of the lake rests on private land, while a similar site is found on the south shore off the Pike Mountain Forest Service Road. Visitors are asked to respect the rights of the private land owner that currently allows access to the east side of the lake and owns most of the northern shoreline.

If you are interested in camping in the area, there are several recreation sites in and around the **Pike Mountain Recreation Area**. Signs further along the Forest Service Road direct you towards Kump, Lodwick and Thalia Lakes.

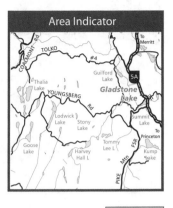

Area Indicator

Species
Rainbow Trout

Gladstone Lake			
Fish Stocking Data			
Year	Species	Number	Life Stage
2013	Rainbow Trout	2,335	Yearling
2012	Rainbow Trout	2,670	Yearling
2011	Rainbow Trout	2,670	Yearling

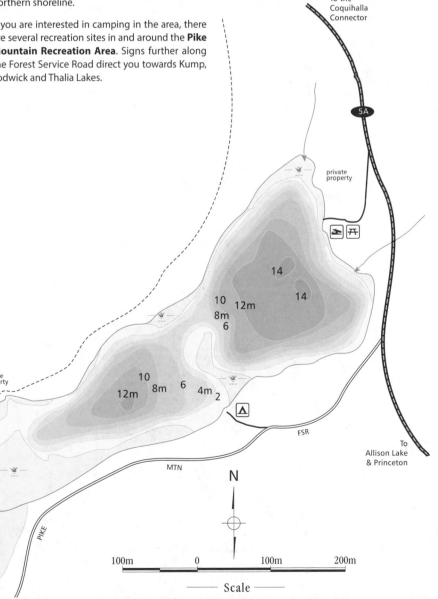

Region 8

Location: 17 km (10.5 mi) west of Peachland
Elevation: 1,144 m (3,753 ft)
Surface Area: 11 ha (27 ac)
Mean Depth: 4.5 m (15 ft)
Max Depth: 13.7 m (45 ft)
Way Point: 119° 58' 00" Lon - W   49° 47' 00" Lat - N

Glen Lake

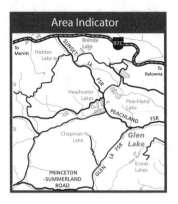

Area Indicator

Species
Rainbow Trout
Brook Trout

Facilities

At the southwest end of the lake, a rough access road leads to a small clearing where it is possible to hand launch small craft. Anglers also set up camp here as there is space for about two groups. Nearby Headwater Lakes provides a more formal forest recreation sites from which to base camp if it is too busy at Glen. We also recommend talking to the local tackle shops, such as Trout Water Fly & Tackle in Kelowna before heading out.

Fishing

Glen Lake is a small lake found in an uninspiring area west of Peachland. It boasts no towering mountain scenery or spectacular vistas. It has no provincial park or even recreation sites on its shores. What it does have are rather large and often feisty rainbow and brook trout. This fact alone keeps anglers coming back year after year.

Fishing in Glen Lake is generally fair for stocked brook trout and rainbow trout. Both species are known to reach up to 1.5 kg (3 lbs) in size and can put up a great fight, especially when hooked with a fly rod. The lake lies at an elevation of 1,160 m (3,806 ft) making for good conditions for much of the open water season. Of course, fishing does slow down at times during the summer.

Much of the lake is quite shallow and fishing should be concentrated in the 3 m (10 ft) to 6 m (20 ft) range during the spring and fall period. Trout tend to revert to the deeper portion of the lake during summer, especially weary brook trout. Trolling small spoons and spinners can provide results, but the large shoal area allows for some decent hatches. Fly-anglers can do quite well here by paying attention to what is hatching. Although there are sometimes multiple hatches here, the usual pattern of chironomids followed by dragonflies, damselflies and then caddisflies should be considered. If no hatches are evident, consider using leeches, shrimp or searching patterns.

The hot spot during spring is the south end near the launch. Working a chironomid or dragonfly nymph is the shoals just off the narrow channel can be very productive.

As always, bringing a small boat or float tube will help when fishing the small lake. It is best to cast from the deeper parts of the lake towards the drop off and slowly retrieve your lure or fly.

Directions

This interior Okanagan Lake is located west of Peachland via the Glen Lake Forest Service Road. To reach the Glen Lake Forest Service Road, follow Highway 97 to Peachland and head west onto Princeton Avenue. Princeton Avenue turns into Brenda Mines Road as it heads west out of town. About 10 km later, the Peachland Forest Service Road branches west. Follow this road another 7 km or so to the Glen Lake Forest Service Road, which branches southwest. Glen Lake is found a short distance later and is visible from the road.

Alternatively, the Glen Lake Forest Service Road is found off the Princeton-Summerland Road. Look for this rougher logging road to the east of Thirsk Lake.

Other Options

Chapman Lake is located to the west of Glen Lake and is accessible via a rough series of logging roads that branch north from the Glen Lake Forest Service Road. Anglers need to be prepared to walk or ATV at least part of the way in. As a result, fishing in the lake is rumoured to be quite good for rainbow trout.

To Peachland FSR

Greata Creek

LAKE FSR

Private Cabins

GLEN

To Princeton-Summerland Rd

3m
6
9m
12

N

100m   0   100m   200m   300m

— Scale —

Glen Lake			
Fish Stocking Data			
Year	Species	Number	Life Stage
2013	Brook Trout	500	Fingerling
2013	Rainbow Trout	2,000	Yearling
2012	Brook Trout	500	Fingerling
2012	Rainbow Trout	2,000	Fingerling
2011	Brook Trout	500	Fingerling
2011	Rainbow Trout	2,000	Fingerling

Grave Lake

Location: 12 km (7.5 mi) north of Sparwood
Elevation: 1,280 m (4,199 ft)
Surface Area: 124 ha (306 ac)
Mean Depth: 17.3 m (57 ft)
Max Depth: 28 m (92 ft)
Way Point: 114° 49'00" Lon - W 49° 52'00" Lat - N

4 Region

Fishing

Over the past five years, over 10,000 rainbow trout have been stocked in Grave Lake annually. This massive stocking program has helped the lake maintain itself as one of the better fishing opportunities in the area. Rainbow trout can reach up to 1 kg (2 lbs) in size and can be caught throughout the open water season. A population of kokanee also exists in the lake.

One area in particular that seems to be a good holding area for both trout and kokanee is the area just off the large point along the northwest side of the lake. The area juts out into the lake and the shoreline has a few decent sized shoals right next to a drop off. Try working your fly or lure along the drop off area, varying your presentation depth in an attempt to find where the fish are holding. Other good areas to try are near the feeder streams coming into the east side of the lake. The cool water of the streams always brings concentrations of oxygen and insect larvae into a lake, attracting sportfish like rainbow.

Rainbow like to chase spoons with lots of silver on a medium to fast troll, as these imitate minnows. Grave Lake is a deep lake that drops off quickly, and most of the fish hang out around these transition zones between deep water and shallow water. Trolling the perimeter of the lake, sticking close to the edge is the best way to fish here.

Trolling a gang troll with a Wedding Band and bait can also attract kokanee. Some other good lures are the Tomac Wee Tad Plug or the Luhr Jensen Needlefish. In the early morning, kokanee seem to prefer green and chartreuse lures, but as the day gets on, they favour bright red, pink and even a hot orange, perhaps with a flash of silver.

Kokanee fight like crazy when they get to the top of the water, and often tear the lure right out of their mouths. If you are trying to net a kokanee and it begins to thrash, lower the tip of your rod to let the fish start swimming again. Play the fish a little longer before attempting to net it again.

Facilities

The **Sparwood Fish & Game Club** helps maintain a rustic camping area and boat launch on the southern side of the lake. Otherwise, Sparwood to the south or Elkford to the north have plenty to offer travellers, including accommodations and other amenities.

Other Options

On the way to Grave Lake, you will cross over the **Elk River**. This cool, clean river offers some World Class fishing for a variety of sportfish species. Anglers can enjoy fishing for cutthroat trout, bull trout and whitefish. The entire river can be productive, from south of Fernie all the way to the river headwaters in Elk Lakes Provincial Park. Fly-fishing can be a lot of fun on the Elk River.

Directions

Grave Lake is located just north of Sparwood. To reach the lake, follow Highway 43 north from Highway 3 and take the Line Creek Mine Road east off the highway. Turn south at the railway crossing and this gravel road leads to the western shore of Grave Lake. Most of the side roads lead to private cabins so it is best to proceed south to the Sparwood Fish & Game Club access area.

Area Indicator

Species
Rainbow Trout
Kokanee

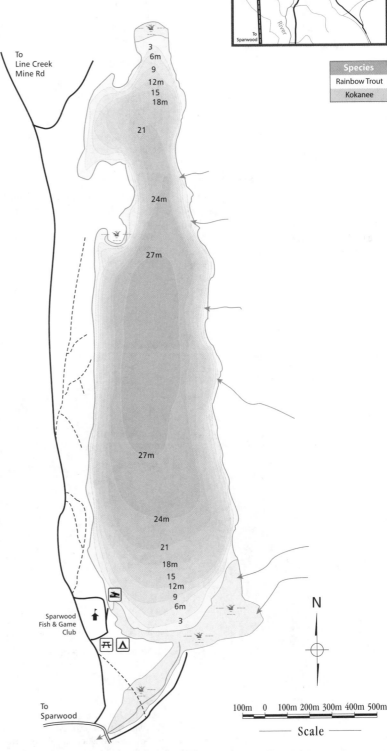

Region 8

Location: 124 km (77 mi) northeast of Vernon
Elevation: 998 m (3,274 ft)
Surface Area: 172 ha (425 ac)
Mean Depth: 31 m (102 ft)
Max Depth: 53 m (174 ft)
Way Point: 118° 20′ 00″ Lon - W 50° 46′ 00″ Lat - N

Greenbush Lake

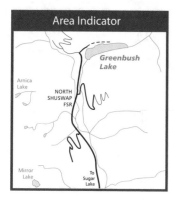

Area Indicator

Greenbush Lake

Arnica Lake

NORTH SHUSWAP FSR

Mirror Lake

To Sugar Lake

Species
Rainbow Trout
Dolly Varden
Whitefish

Fishing

Greenbush Lake is a remote lake at the foot of the Gold Range of the Columbia Mountains. Access to the lake is by a long, rough forest service road. As a result, the lake sees few anglers a year.

That alone should be enough to spark the curiosity of the more adventurous anglers. And, while it would be a stretch to say that this is one of the best fishing lakes in the Okanagan, the fishing can be quite good, especially in the spring and fall.

The lake holds rainbow trout, whitefish and Dolly Varden, Trolling is a preferred method of fishing for visiting anglers, since the lake is quite large. In the spring and late fall, trolling a bucktail at a fast pace can entice some of the larger trout.

The Dolly Varden can get to a comfortably plump 3 kg (6.5 lbs) in size. Dollies often chase down a green or orange Flatfish or a Krocodile lure, but if you want bigger fish, try trolling plugs or larger lures with a flasher. In the spring, try fishing around the mouths of creeks where the feed congregates. Jigging with a bucktail and flasher can be very successful in these areas.

If you plan to bring the fly rod, the many stream flowing into to the lake make for good areas to try. Rainbow have been known to reach up to 2 kg (4.5 lbs) in Greenbush, and will usually take well to attractor patterns like Carey Specials and Doc Spratleys. The lake is not known for its insect hatches, but that doesn't mean they don't occur. Always keep an eye out for what the fish might be eating, especially during the evening when they start to rise to the surface. Spincasters will find the rainbow trout take well to brass or silver coloured lures.

Facilities

In addition to being surrounded by the **Greenbush Lake Protected Area**, the **Greenbush Lake Recreation Site** provides a scenic camping area with space for 3 groups. If you can get your vehicle down the access road, there is a rough cartop boat launch available. A trail also leads along the north side of the lake, but visitors need to be wary of grizzly bears in this high elevation country.

Other Options

Other than Sugar Lake to the south, there are very few lake fishing options in the immediate area of Greenbush Lake. The best fishing alternative is the **Shuswap River**. The northern stretch of the river is home to resident rainbow trout, Dolly Varden and whitefish.

N

Greenbush Lake Protected Area

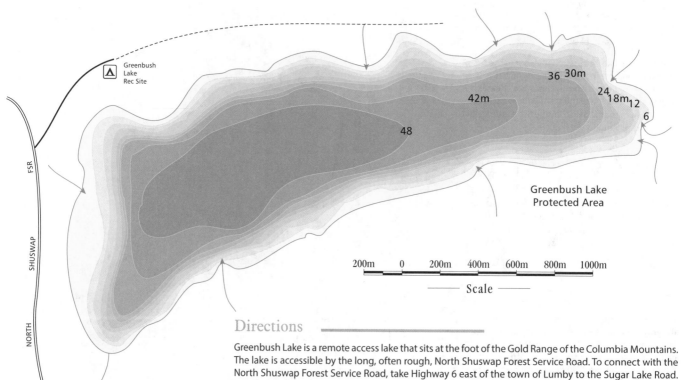

Greenbush Lake Rec Site

36 30m

42m

48

24 18m 12

6

Greenbush Lake Protected Area

FSR

SHUSWAP

NORTH

To Sugar Lake

200m 0 200m 400m 600m 800m 1000m

— Scale —

Directions

Greenbush Lake is a remote access lake that sits at the foot of the Gold Range of the Columbia Mountains. The lake is accessible by the long, often rough, North Shuswap Forest Service Road. To connect with the North Shuswap Forest Service Road, take Highway 6 east of the town of Lumby to the Sugar Lake Road. Follow the Sugar Lake Road north to Sugar Lake where the main road branches, follow the west branch (North Shuswap Forest Service Road). This logging road parallels the Shuswap River for a long distance along the base of the magnificent Sawtooth Range, eventually leading to Greenbush Lake. A 4wd vehicle, a GPS with the *BC Backroad GPS Maps* and associated *Backroad Mapbook for the Kootenay Rockies* is strongly recommended when travelling to the lake.

Haddo Lake

Location: 24 km (14.5 mi) southeast of Vernon
Elevation: 1,268 m (4,161 ft)
Surface Area: 76 ha (188 ac)
Max Depth: 8.5 m (28 ft)
Way Point: 119° 04′ 00″ Lon - W 50° 05′ 00″ Lat - N

Fishing

Haddo Lake is separated from nearby Aberdeen Lake by only a few hundred metres and a dam, which keeps the two lakes separate. Haddo is the smaller of the two lakes, but holds bigger fish, which are rumoured to get to 2 kg (4 lbs). The lake is not stocked, but has a good self-sustaining population of fish.

The fishing here, like most of the lakes in the area, is best in the spring. Just after ice-off, the rainbow can be found in the shallow south end of the lake, but as the weather warms, the fish will move to the deeper north end of the lake.

There are three small islands in the lake, one at the very north end of the lake, and two near the middle. Fishing along the steep drop-off of the middle island is one of the most productive areas, especially as spring wears on. There are also a number of steep drop offs on both the eastern and western shores of the lake which are also good places to focus your energy. Similar to most lakes in this region, Haddo Lake has tea coloured water, even after the spring runoff. Leeches and Woolly Buggers trolled deep work well, even during the warmer months.

Haddo Lake is a great trolling lake. Trollers should concentrate near drop-offs along the larger holes in the lake. A Willow Leaf with a Wedding Band or small lure will work the best, but you can try small, flashy spoons or even a streamer-type fly.

When the trout are feeding in the shallows on insects, it is a prime time for fly fishers who will do well using dragonfly or damselfly nymph patterns. However spincasters need not be left out, as small crankbait like a Flatfish or Hotshot and tiny jigs can often fake it as nymphs or even scuds.

Facilities

Controlled by a dam, many anglers simply cast from shore in this area. Also at the north end of the lake, the **Haddo Lake Recreation Site** provides space for about 4 units as well as a cartop boat launch. The former site on the west side of the lake is now closed, but people still camp here.

Other Options

Spec Lakes are found southeast of Haddo Lake off Philpott Main. They are popular alternatives, especially if you can get out on the water and away from the weeds. The lower Spec Lake is the easiest to access and offers the best fishing if you do not mind smaller fish. The middle and upper lakes are much shallower and the fish are much more finicky resulting in less fishing pressure. The lakes are stocked to help maintain the fishery.

Directions

To find the lake, follow Highway 6 east from Vernon to Learmouth Road. Turn south on Learmouth and follow this windy backroad east to Reid Road, which will take you south to Bluenose Road and eventually the Aberdeen Lake Forest Road. The forest road marks the beginning of the gravel road that is signed with kilometre markings as well a resort signs. Keep left at the 11 km mark and continue straight at the 14 km mark. Just before the 17 km mark on what is known as Haddo (signed Hadow) Main a side road branches to the right; this will bring you past Haddo Lake.

The series of old roads in this network can be confusing, but a good map such as those in the *Thompson Okanagan Backroad Mapbook* or *BC Backroad GPS Maps* will help you find this and the many other lakes in the area. It is also recommended to have a 4wd vehicle, especially during wet weather.

Area Indicator

Species
Rainbow Trout

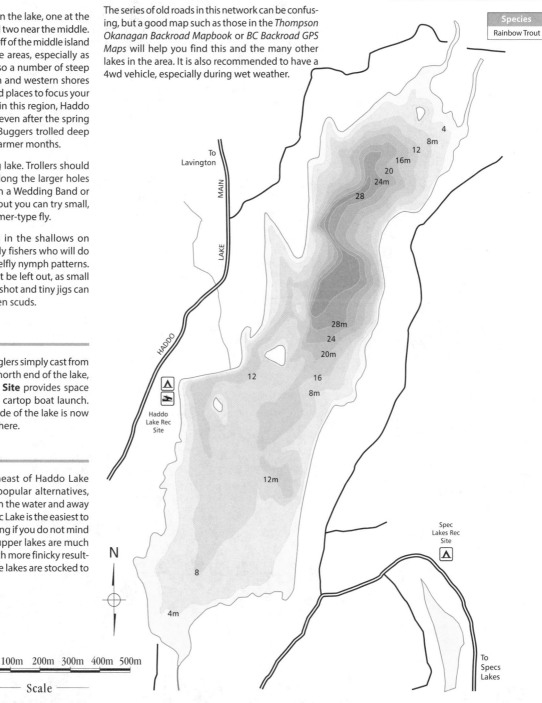

To Lavington

MAIN
LAKE
HADDO

Haddo Lake Rec Site

4
8m
12
16m
20
24m
28
28m
24
20m
12
16
8m
12m
8
4m

Spec Lakes Rec Site

To Specs Lakes

N

100m 0 100m 200m 300m 400m 500m

— Scale —

Region 4

Location: 14 km (8.5 mi) northeast of Kimberley
Elevation: 901 m (2,956 ft)
Surface Area: 54 ha (177 ac)
Mean Depth: 4.5 m (15 ft)
Max Depth: 12.2 m (40 ft)
Way Point: 115° 49' 00" Lon - W 49° 44' 00" Lat - N

Hahas Lake

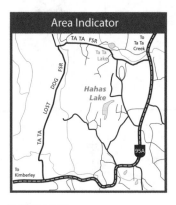

Area Indicator

Species

Rainbow Trout

Brook Trout

Fishing

Not to be confused with nearby Haha Lake, Hahas is a small lake found northeast of Kimberley. The shallow lake is heavily stocked with rainbow trout by the Freshwater Fisheries Society of BC, helping to provide some consistent fishing throughout the season. Brook trout were also stocked in the lake in the past but there have been few, if any, brookies caught in the lake recently.

Upon arrival at Hahas Lake, anglers might be tempted to explore the two long arms that stretch south, as fish like to hold in bays, off points and near islands. However, the eastern arm is extremely shallow, and while it may hold a few fish right after ice off or later in the fall when the water cools down, it is generally devoid of any ichthyological activity for most of the fishing season. Indeed, the tip of the arm is often dry by the end of the summer. The western arm is slightly deeper, and does hold some fish.

A more productive location is just off the tip of the point where the two arms form. This region has an ample shoal area for weed and insect activity ideal for attracting rainbow. Try working a chironomid off the shoal during spring, while a leech pattern can be productive into the summer. During the calm, cool summer evenings, the fish do start to rise to the surface, and will take to various top water presentations; a Tom Thumb or Elk Hair Caddis can be productive into the summer months. Trolling a small spoon in the 3-6 m (10-20 ft) range can also provide decent results. Trolling a silver coloured spoon slightly faster tends to work better for rainbow, as the flashing, quick moving spoon resembles a minnow moving through the water.

While the lake sports fairly extensive shoals at its north end and along its eastern shore, a shoreline angler could work their way around to the western shores of the lake to the point due west of the tip of the point. From here, it is possible to cast into the deeper waters.

Directions

Northeast of the city of Kimberly, Hahas Lake can be found not far from Highway 95A. Look for a well established forestry road off the west side of the highway about 10 km south of Ta Ta Creek. Follow the road north for about 3 km (1.9 mi) and look for a rough road heading west. This is the access road to the north shore of Hahas Lake. Parking is available off the side of the road near the lake. A 4wd vehicle may be necessary when it is wet.

Facilities

There are no facilities available at Hahas Lake, although you could easily pitch a tent just off the road or near the lakeshore. Alternatively, **Wasa Lake Provincial Park** is found to the east or you could always spend a night or two in the quaint little city of Kimberly.

Other Options

To the north of Hahas Lake, you can find **Ta Ta Lake** off the Ta Ta Forest Service Road. The lake has been stocked with brook trout, which are best fished in the early spring just after ice off or in the fall.

To
Hwy 95A

3m

6

9m

N

100m   0   100m 200m 300m 400m 500m

— Scale —

Headwater Lakes

Fishing

There is a series of lakes at the intersection of Trout Creek Main and Peachland Main in the hills west of Kelowna. They were partly formed by the damming of Trout Creek, and they get their name for being the headwaters of this creek.

The First Headwater Lake is stocked annually with brook trout and produces consistently for nice sized brookies. Many anglers have boasted of catching fish in the 3 kg (6.5 lb) trophy class. Both fly-fishing and spincasting can be productive but brook trout rarely resist the temptation of a plump worm on a hook.

Another unique thing about the First Headwater Lake is the floating islands. The islands are literally large chunks of peat moss that broke away from the original shoreline of the lake when the level of the lake was raised by the formation of the dam system. A few of the islands actually have trees growing on them, making for a pretty amazing site. These islands and various areas of the shoreline provide fantastic cover, as the fish can lurk below them in relative safety. Anglers should focus most of their attention around these floating sections of peat. Try casting a Muddler Minnow or trolling a leech pattern. Spincasters can try trolling small spoons or spinners, like a Mepps or Blue Fox. Another hot spot is the western end near the dam. Fly anglers can have success here with Buicks.

Running perpendicular to the first lake, you can find the rest of the Headwater Lake chain. The second lake is the furthest east, followed by the third and fourth lakes (both of which are not charted). The other three lakes are stocked regularly with rainbow trout providing for a decent sport fishery. The shallow nature of the lakes does cause a summer slowdown.

Be sure to check the regulations before fishing the Headwater Lakes. Currently there is a shortened season as well as an engine power restriction.

Facilities

The fishing camp that was located along the shore of the first Headwater Lake is no longer in business (at least at the time of printing). It is unclear if the boat launch is open to the public at this time. **The Headwaters Lakes Recreation Site** is actually found on the third lake and provides seven scenic sites as well as a rustic boat launch. Anglers can also take advantage of the cross-country ski trails to access the lakes.

Directions

The easiest way to access the Headwater Lakes is to travel along the Coquihalla Connector (Hwy 97C) west of Kelowna. Look for the Sunset Exit and follow Sunset Main back east. About 6 km along the gravel road, the Sunset Lake Forest Service Road turns south and eventually passes the mountain lake chain.

From the south, both the Trout Creek Forest Service Road and the Peachland Forest Service Road easily access the lake chain. The good road access allows most vehicles to easily reach the lake chain. A boat launch and campsite are found on the third lake, while a popular resort is found on the first lake.

Area Indicator

Species
Rainbow Trout
Brook Trout

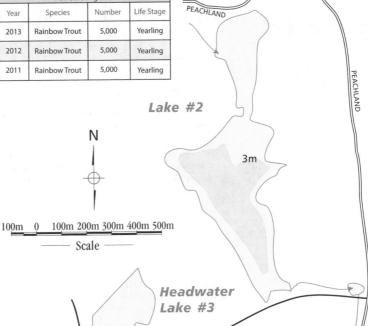

Headwater Lake 1
Elevation: 1,288 m (4,226 ft)
Surface Area: 55 ha (136 ac)
Mean Depth: 4.9 m (16 ft)
Max Depth: 8 m (26 ft)
Way Point: 120° 0' 0.00" Lon - W 49° 48' 00" Lat - N

Headwater Lake 2
Elevation: 1,300 m (4,265 ft)
Surface Area: 17 ha (42 ac)
Mean Depth: 2.1 m (7 ft)
Max Depth: 4 m (13 ft)
Way Point: 120° 0' 0.00" Lon - W 49° 49' 00" Lat - N

Headwater Lake 2 Fish Stocking Data			
Year	Species	Number	Life Stage
2013	Rainbow Trout	5,000	Yearling
2012	Rainbow Trout	5,000	Yearling
2011	Rainbow Trout	5,000	Yearling

Headwater Lake 1 Fish Stocking Data			
Year	Species	Number	Life Stage
2013	Brook Trout	8,000	Yearling
2012	Brook Trout	8,000	Yearling
2011	Brook Trout	8,500	Yearling

Region 4

Location: 15 km (9 mi) south of Cranbrook
Elevation: 929 m (3,048 ft)
Surface Area: 4 ha (10 ac)
Mean Depth: 2.5 m (8 ft)
Max Depth: 5 m (16 ft)
Way Point: 115° 50' 00" Lon - W 49° 23' 00" Lat - N

Hiawatha Lake

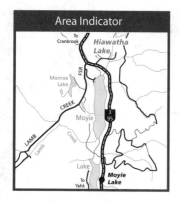

Area Indicator

Species
Rainbow Trout
Brook Trout
Kokanee
Largemouth Bass
Cutthroat Trout

Hiawatha Lake			
Fish Stocking Data			
Year	Species	Number	Life Stage
2007	Rainbow Trout	350	Fall Catchable
2006	Rainbow Trout	350	Catchable
2005	Rainbow Trout	250	Yearling

Fishing

Although rainbow trout are stocked in this lake annually, the lake is becoming better known for its bass fishing. Largemouth bass can be found in the lake in fair numbers, and a small population of kokanee, and the occasional brook trout, cutthroat trout or rainbow/cutthroat cross are also found in the lake.

Because the bass have been taking hold in the lake at the expense of the stocked fingerling rainbow (which usually wound up as bass feed), stocking strategies in the lake have changed. Since 2006, the lake is being stocked with small numbers of catchable-sized rainbow trout, usually only a few hundred or so.

The lake is very weedy, making suitable habitat for bass. These fish can be quite aggressive from late spring through the summer months. Generally as the water gets warmer, the bass become more active.

Largemouth bass are famous for their aggressive behavior, and are known to ambush larger insects like bees or moths that are drowning in the water. They even take mice or small frogs that are on the surface of the water near the weeds or other cover where the bass like to lay in wait. Larger floating lures, known as bass bugs or poppers, are designed to imitate these. Cast these out on a dry line near the weeds or other bass cover, then retrieve very slowly, with short, quick jerks designed to imitate the movement of a creature that is not swimming by choice.

Of course, since you will generally be casting into weeds or lily pads, the chances of getting snagged are much greater. A stronger leader and heavier line will help. Spinners and jigs also work great for the aggressive largemouth.

The best times to find trout is in the early spring and late fall when they are more active. Fly anglers in search of trout should try a leech pattern or Woolly Bugger as the trout in this lake are known to enjoy a meal or two of these creatures. Spincasters will have limited success using a Panther Marten or Deadly Dick tipped with worms.

Facilities

There are no facilities available at Hiawatha Lake. Area visitors can enjoy an overnight stay at the scenic **Moyie Lake Provincial Park**, which is found merely minutes away. The busy site offers 111 campsites, reservations are highly recommended, as well as a nice beach.

Directions

Hiawatha Lake is a very small lake located to the north of Moyie Lake in the East Kootenay. To find the lake, follow Highway 3/95 to the Hidden Valley Road, which is found at the north end of Moyie Lake, not far from the provincial park. Turn east onto the Hidden Valley Road and look for the access to the lake a short distance later.

Other Options

Monroe and **Moyie Lakes** are found in the area and offer some decent fishing opportunities. A good population of rainbow trout and cutthroat trout inhabit Monroe Lake, while Moyie Lake offers angling for rainbow trout, bull trout, cutthroat trout, brook trout, kokanee as well as whitefish. These lakes are described in more detail later in the book.

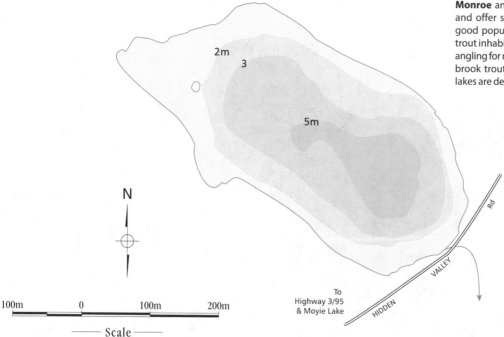

Hidden Lake

Location: 24 km (15 mi) east of Enderby
Elevation: 650 m (2,133 ft)
Surface Area: 131 ha (324 ac)
Mean Depth: 17.8 m (58 ft)
Max Depth: 46.3 m (152 ft)
Way Point: 118° 49' 00" Lon - W 50° 34' 00" Lat - N

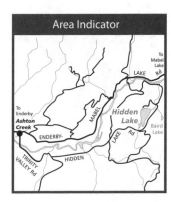
Area Indicator

Fishing

Hidden Lake is a relatively large, scenic lake nestled between two hills east of Enderby. It is a low elevation lake making it a decent early and late season fishery. Good access, lower elevation and its proximity to the town of Enderby, subject this lake to heavy fishing pressure. To augment the fishery, the Freshwater Fisheries Society of BC stocks the lake with thousands of rainbow trout annually. Despite the stocking, Hidden Lake is known to produce larger rainbows up to 4 kg (9 lbs), with the average being 40 cm (16 in) in size. Part of the reason the fish are so big is the no tow regulation is in place on the lake.

Fly fishers using chironomids have success in early spring and late fall at the northwest and south portion of the lake. Fishing near the bottom in 3-9 m (10–30 ft) of water should produce some nice rainbow. If the fish are not on the shoals try the deeper water with blood leeches and Woolly Buggers. In early June, the north and south ends of the lake will have cruising fish feeding in the shallows on damselfly nymphs. Anchoring and cast lures near the reeds, while not trying to spook the trout can be extremely productive. This time of year can also produce well with sedges. If the wind picks up, as it usually does on this larger lake, the south end of the lake has two sheltered bays with nice shoals and drop offs.

The north end of Hidden Lake provides decent success for those trolling a willow leaf or Ford Fender with smaller spinners or an Apex. Reaching the deeper sections of the lake will increase your odds for the larger trout. Lead core line will help get you deeper.

The shallow bays and large shoal on the north side of the lake is also ideal for ice fishing. Fish cruise in the shallows amongst the vegetation during the winter feeding on insects. Using traditional ice fishing tackle like jigs or small spinners with powerbait can be effective. But locals prefer to use cooked shrimp or flies such as beadhead shrimp and leeches.

When heading out on Hidden Lake, be sure to check your regulations for the special restrictions.

Directions

From the town of Enderby on Highway 97A, travel east along the Enderby-Mabel Lake Road. At the community of Ashton Creek, follow the Trinity Valley Road south over the Shuswap River to a junction with Hidden-Shuswap Road. Turn left and follow this road east to the lake.

Hidden Lake Fish Stocking Data			
Year	Species	Number	Life Stage
2013	Rainbow Trout	15,000	Yearling
2012	Rainbow Trout	15,000	Yearling
2011	Rainbow Trout	15,000	Yearling

Species
Rainbow Trout

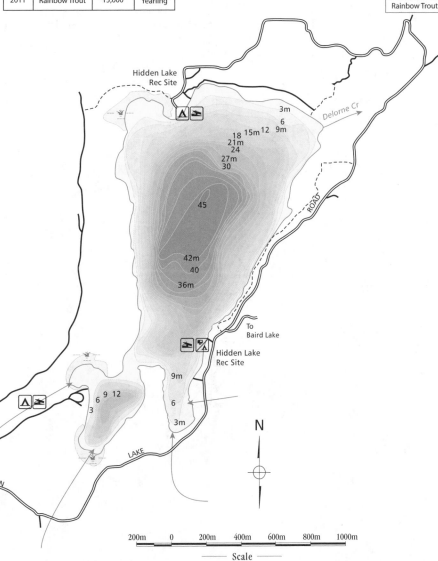

Facilities

Hidden Lake is home to three separate recreation sites with a total of 46 campsites. Each site is home to a boat launch and there are many scenic campsites overlooking the lake. Visitors should be aware that this is an enhanced recreation site and fees are charged from May 1st to September 30th.

Other Options

Baird Lake is a much smaller lake found to the east of Hidden Lake. It is found off a rough branch road on the east side of the bigger lake. The 4wd accessible recreation site is often quieter than many in the area. When coupled with the good rainbow trout fishing, this is a nice place to spend a few days.

Location: 44 km (27 mi) northeast of Vernon
Elevation: 1,512 m (4,961 ft)
Surface Area: 10 ha (25 ac)
Mean Depth: 2.2 m (7 ft)
Max Depth: 8.4 m (28 ft)
Way Point: 118° 40' 00" Lon - W 50° 19' 00" Lat - N

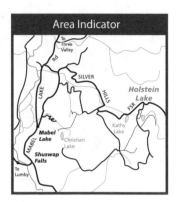

Area Indicator

Species
Rainbow Trout

Fishing

Holstein Lake is a small, marshy lake found northeast of Lumby. It is rather difficult to access and does not get the attention that other lakes in the area receive. As a result, there have been reports of some big fish hooked in Holstein Lake.

The best time to hit the lake is fall, to avoid the spring mud and the summer doldrums. As the fish are starting to fatten up for winter, they are usually a little less fussy, and tend to chase after slightly bigger lures or flies than they might have in the spring. Fly anglers should look at using a leech pattern, or possibly a general attractor pattern like a green or black Doc Spratley or a black Woolly Bugger.

The small roadside lake is quite marshy and shallow around the perimeter and shore casting is virtually impossible. Even float tubers will have difficulty accessing the lake during the spring runoff period when the surrounding lowland area can be muddy or even flooded. Anglers should work the middle portion of the lake where the trout often retreat to. In particular, try fishing off the drop off beside the two recognized holes in the lake.

In the late 1980s, the lake was all but overrun with suckers. Fisheries rehabilitated the lake to get rid of the suckers, and it seems to have worked. They also stock the lake annually and more recent reports indicate the fishery is becoming more consistent. Despite this, the lake is not a heavily used lake and it is not hard to have it all to yourself.

Directions

Holstein Lake is found in the hills northeast of the town of Lumby. To reach the lake, take Highway 6 to Lumby and then follow the Mable Lake Road north off the highway. Follow Mabel Lake Road past Shuswap Falls to the Sigalet-Silver Hills Forest Service Road. Continue along this sometimes rough logging road past Kathy Lake. The next major road should be the Sugar-Holstein Forest Service Road, which leads past the west side of Holstein Lake.

We recommend using a 4wd vehicle and having a copy of the *Backroad Mapbook for Thompson Okanagan* along with a GPS when visiting the lake for the first time.

Facilities

The **Holstein Lake Recreation Site** is a remote access site set amid a mature stand of trees next to the lake. The road access into the recreation site is quite rough and requires a 4wd vehicle to safely negotiate some of the tricky spots. If you can access the lake by vehicle, there is a rough cartop boat launch area available. If access is too difficult, Kathy Lake to the west is a little easier to reach and hosts a small recreation campsite as well.

Other Options

As you proceed along the Sigalet-Silver Hills Forest Service Road towards Holstein Lake, you pass a small lake named **Kathy Lake**. This lake is stocked annually providing angling opportunities for both brook trout and rainbow trout. Visitors will also find a recreation site and car top boat launch.

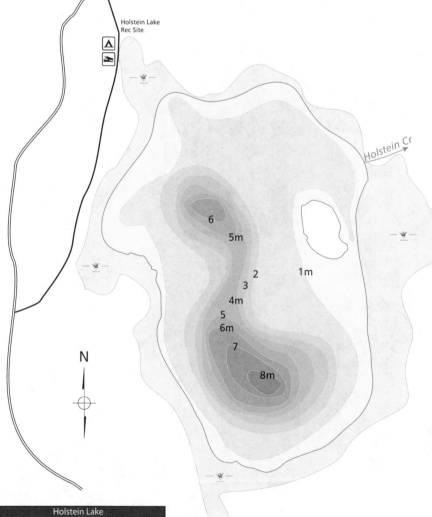

To Silver Hills FSR

Holstein Lake Rec Site

Holstein Cr

N

Holstein Lake Fish Stocking Data			
Year	Species	Number	Life Stage
2013	Rainbow Trout	0	Fry
2012	Rainbow Trout	1,000	Fry
2011	Rainbow Trout	0	Fry

100m   0   100m   200m   300m

— Scale —

Hoodoo Lake

Location: 38 km (23.5 mi) north of Rock Creek
Elevation: 1,226 m (4,022 ft)
Surface Area: 17 ha (42 ac)
Mean Depth: 9.2 m (30 ft)
Max Depth: 27.4 m (90 ft)
Way Point: 118 °57' 00" Lon - W 49° 22' 00" Lat - N

Fishing

In the last few years, the Freshwater Fisheries Society of BC has changed the stock in this lake to Pennask triploid. Some people don't like fishing these fish, because they aren't as aggressive or showy of fighters as other strains of rainbows. Others love their bull doggedness and large size.

The reason for the switch was to counteract the reports that the lake has not been as productive in recent years. Fishery officials think they might have figured out why. At the outflow creek, there is a small concrete dam. The previous fish were heading downstream to spawn, but because of the dam, they weren't able to get back to the lake. Pennask triploids don't spawn, so fisheries are hoping the switch will mean the fishing will improve.

Hoodoo Lake is a high elevation lake, which means that the fishing gets started later in the year. However, the higher elevation combined with the fairly deep nature of the lake does help to extend the lake's productivity well into the summer. Of course the lake does suffer a bit during the heat of summer, but this slow down is short lived before the prime fishing time in early fall. At this time, the chilly high elevation nights help cool the lake to the optimum temperature for trout to stay active.

The north end of the lake features an extensive shoal area. Early in the spring (right after ice off) focus on this area, as this will probably be where the fish are feeding. Once the water starts to warm up, focus on the drop off section next to these shoals. Fly anglers should try chironomid patterns off the shoal areas found along the north and south sides of the lake. One trick is to try to locate early weed growth and work the fly pattern just off these areas. Later in the year trolling a leech pattern or spoon can be productive.

Facilities

At the south end of Hoodoo Lake, you will find a former recreation site suitable for two or three camping parties, more if everyone is in tents. At the campsite, there is also a car top boat launch.

Other Options

En route to Hoodoo Lake, **Peter (or Pete) Lake** is tucked far enough away from the main roads to allow for a fairly decent rainbow trout fishery. There is no longer a recreation site here, but it is still possible to camp at the small lake.

Directions

Hoodoo Lake lies on the eastern edge of the Beaverdell Mountain Range between the Christian Valley and Highway 33. Finding the mountain can be a little tricky with two possible access points. Most prefer to access the lake from the west off the steep, windy Taurus Lake Forest Service Road. This road branches east from Highway 33 north of the settlement of Westbridge. Continue past Taurus Lake and then veer north, eventually picking up the Waddell-Hoodoo Forest Service Road, which should take you by the west side of the lake.

A 4wd vehicle and a Backroad Mapbook are helpful companions when visiting the area.

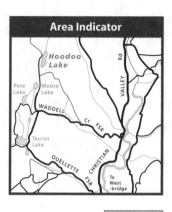

Area Indicator

Species
Rainbow Trout

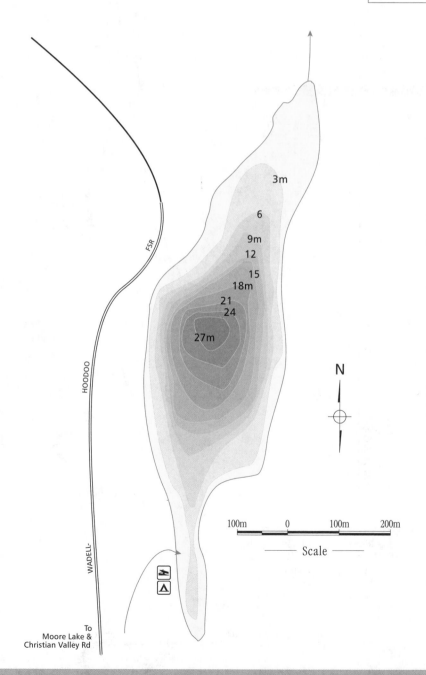

Hoodoo Lake			
Fish Stocking Data			
Year	Species	Number	Life Stage
2013	Rainbow Trout	2,000	Fry
2012	Rainbow Trout	2,000	Fry
2011	Rainbow Trout	2,000	Fry

Hook & Ketchan Lakes

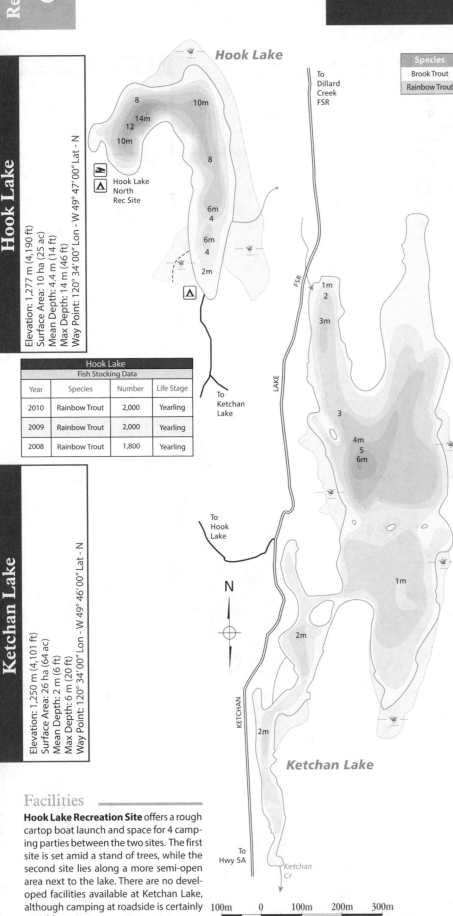

Hook Lake

Hook Lake North Rec Site

8
14m
12
10m
10m
8
8
6m
4
6m
4
2m

Hook Lake

Elevation: 1,277 m (4,190 ft)
Surface Area: 10 ha (25 ac)
Mean Depth: 4.4 m (14 ft)
Max Depth: 14 m (46 ft)
Way Point: 120° 34'00" Lon - W 49° 47'00" Lat - N

Hook Lake			
Fish Stocking Data			
Year	Species	Number	Life Stage
2010	Rainbow Trout	2,000	Yearling
2009	Rainbow Trout	2,000	Yearling
2008	Rainbow Trout	1,800	Yearling

Ketchan Lake

Elevation: 1,250 m (4,101 ft)
Surface Area: 26 ha (64 ac)
Mean Depth: 2 m (6 ft)
Max Depth: 6 m (20 ft)
Way Point: 120° 34'00" Lon - W 49° 46'00" Lat - N

To Dillard Creek FSR

FSR
LAKE

To Ketchan Lake

To Hook Lake

1m
2
3m

3

4m
5
6m

1m

2m

N

KETCHAN

2m

2m

Ketchan Lake

To Hwy 5A

Ketchan Cr

100m   0   100m   200m   300m

Scale

Species	
Brook Trout	
Rainbow Trout	

Area Indicator

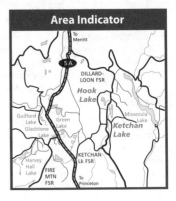

Fishing

Hook and Ketchan Lakes are a pair of lakes north of Princeton. Of the two, Hook Lake has the better fishing.

Hook Lake is stocked annually with rainbow trout and was also recently stocked with brook trout. Fishing in the lake can be good for rainbow up to 2 kg (4.5 lbs) in size, while brookies are often found much smaller than their rainbow cousins.

The eastern shore of the lake is often flooded during the spring runoff period and is a hot spot for hatch activity throughout the season. In the late spring/early summer look for damselflies hatching near the weedy shore area. In the heat of summer, trout tend to congregate more in the deeper western corner of the lake. Since Hook Lake sits at an elevation of 1,265 m (4,150 ft), fishing can be consistent through the summer.

Ketchan Lake is rumoured to hold a small number of large rainbow, but success rates are so spotty, few people bother to fish here. Looking at the depth chart of the lake, it would be best to focus fishing activity near the drop off of the 6 m (19 ft) hole in the northern half of the lake. The added depth in this area is much more hospitably to resident trout. The southern portion of the lake is quite shallow with an average depth of only about 2 m (6.5 ft). Fly anglers can try an attractor pattern or a leech to search out the lake. Spincasters can always use a good old trusty worm and bobber to find those elusive trout.

Directions

The lakes can be reached by travelling along Highway 5A north of Princeton to the Hornet Forest Service Road. The road is found near the summit, but if you hit the highway rest area you have gone too far north. Follow this often rough and bumpy road east and up towards the powerlines. Soon after the powerlines, the road branches with the northern branch leading to Hook and the other branch joining the Ketchan Lake Forest Service Road just south of Ketchan Lake.

From the north, take the Dillard Creek Forest Service Road east from Highway 5A. This road is a little easier to travel en route to its junction with the Ketchan Lake Forest Service Road. Continue south on this rougher road to Ketchan Lake. Either direction requires the use of a 4wd vehicle, especially in wet weather.

Facilities

Hook Lake Recreation Site offers a rough cartop boat launch and space for 4 camping parties between the two sites. The first site is set amid a stand of trees, while the second site lies along a more semi-open area next to the lake. There are no developed facilities available at Ketchan Lake, although camping at roadside is certainly possible.

Horseshoe Lake

Location: 20 km (12.5 mi) east of Cranbrook
Elevation: 846 m (2,776 ft)
Surface Area: 12 ha (30 ac)
Mean Depth: 2.7 m (9 ft)
Max Depth: 11.6 m (38 ft)
Way Point: 115° 31' 00" Lon - W 49° 34' 00" Lat - N

Fishing

Boasting one of the more misleading names of any lake in this book, Horseshoe Lake is a beautiful spring fed lake that is stocked annually with rainbow trout. The lake, which looks nothing like a Horseshoe, offers generally consistent fishing throughout the open water season for usually small trout, although the occasional big one in the 2 kg (4.5 lb) range is hooked.

The lake is very dependent on spring run-off to maintain its water levels. As a general rule, the lake has fairly low water levels in the early spring, but fills with rainwater and runoff by mid-summer. By fall, the water levels have dropped, to begin the cycle once more.

Try working the shoal areas in the 3-4 m (10-13 ft) range during the spring. Chironomids work well in the early part of the season, while leech and shrimp patterns can also be productive at times. There are good caddis hatches on the lake periodically during the summer months. When this hatch is on, there can be some great surface action on the lake.

The lake has fairly large shoals that ring it, making shore fishing difficult except early in the year when the trout are much more prone to cruise the shallows in search of food. Better to bring a small boat or float tube, and cast from the deeper water into the shallower, retrieving across the drop off. Trolling is not a productive method of fishing the lake, as the fish are easily spooked by a moving boat.

Spincasters can try working a small lure like a Blue Fox or Mepps in a silver or other bright colour. Let the lure drift down to near the bottom then retrieve quickly, pausing every so often to imitate the way a minnow swims.

Other Options

To the west of Horseshoe Lake, the **Kootenay River** offers endless angling opportunities. The river is inhabited by good populations of rainbow trout, as well as fair numbers of cutthroat trout and bull trout.

For a nearby lake fishing alternative, **Norbury** and **Peckhams Lakes** can be found to the south of Horseshoe Lake via the Wardner Fort Steele Road. In addition to hosting a beautiful park with variety of facilities (including camping) these lakes are well known for their rainbow trout fishery. Norbury Lake also holds a population of cutthroat trout for anglers to toil after.

Directions

The easiest way to find Horseshoe Lake is to travel to the historical town of Fort Steele via Highway 95/93. The next major road heading east is the Wardner-Fort Steele Road. This paved road leads to the Horseshoe Lake Road about 10.5 km later. Turn left or north and the lake is found within 500 metres. The access road circles the lake and provides access to the many campsites scattered around the lake.

Facilities

The **Horseshoe Lake Recreation Site** is very popular during the summer months and is located in a pine-aspen stand next to the lake. The site is equipped with about a dozen picnic tables as well as outhouses. Along with the fishing at the lake, visitors can also enjoy hiking and biking around this scenic Rocky Mountain area. ATVing and trail biking are also popular in the area.

Please note that motorboats are not allowed on the lake. Hand launching pontoon boats or similar is possible.

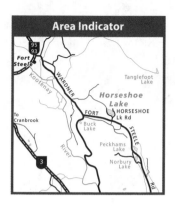

Area Indicator

Species
Rainbow Trout

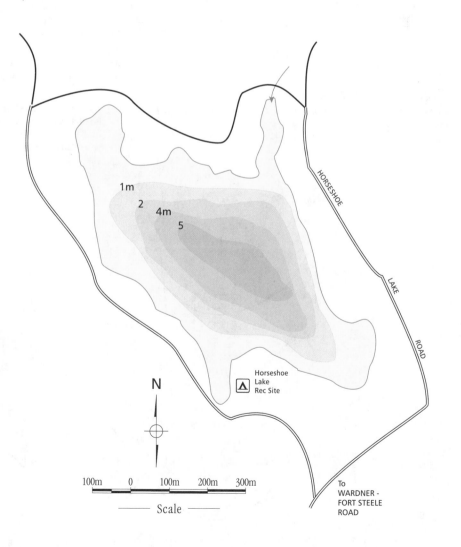

1m
2
4m
5

N

Horseshoe
Lake
Rec Site

HORSESHOE LAKE ROAD

To
WARDNER -
FORT STEELE
ROAD

100m 0 100m 200m 300m

Scale

Location: 26 (16 mi) northwest of Kelowna
Elevation: 1,500 m (4,920 ft)
Surface Area: 25 ha (62 ac)
Mean Depth: 7.5 m (25.5 ft)
Max Depth: 17 m (56 ft)
Way Point: 119° 48′ 00″ Lon - W 49° 59′ 00″ Lat - N

Horseshoe Lakes
(Dobbin & Islaht)

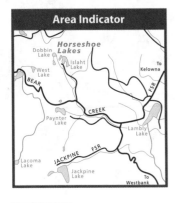

Area Indicator

Species

Brook Trout

Rainbow Trout

Dobbin Lake Fish Stocking Data			
Year	Species	Number	Life Stage
2013	Rainbow Trout	2,000	Fry/Yearling
2012	Rainbow Trout	1,000	Yearling
2011	Rainbow Trout	1,000	Yearling

Fishing

Dobbin, Islaht and West Lakes are a trio of lakes found west of Kelowna that are commonly known as the Horseshoe Lakes. The lakes are within easy access to Kelowna and other urban centres making them a popular choice for a weekend outdoor adventure. Although most of the attention is given to the bigger lakes, West Lake is a good fly fishing lake since the fish get caught here when the water levels are drawn down.

Islaht Lake is an odd shaped lake that was created when the two stream outlets were dammed. Fishing in the lake is fair for small rainbow trout, particularly if you work the main portion of the lake. There are confirmed rumours that brook trout are also found in the south end of the lake. The lake has a variety of nooks and crannies, holes and shallows, making it both an exciting and frustrating lake to fish. Because there are so many places the fish could be hiding, it is sometimes difficult to figure out where they are hiding. A good place to try is near the narrows between the northwest section of the lake and the main body of the lake. During cooler periods, the shoals at the south end can also be very productive.

Dobbin Lake is the deepest of the three lakes, and is stocked annually with rainbow trout. The lake also boasts a thriving population of brook trout, which were being stocked in the lake until 1994. While they are no longer being stocked, they have been able to effectively reproduce since. Both brookies and rainbow tend to revert to the depths of this small lake during the summer; hence, the lake is best fished in the spring or fall period. Both fly angling and trolling can produce results. Try a Deadly Dick for aggressive brookies.

West Lake is connected to Dobbin by a shallow canal that can be navigated in a boat until about mid July. After that you will need to hike in and launch from the west side. The lake can get to about 9 m (30 ft) deep. At the south end there is a nice hole off the point that is a good place to work a gomphus pattern or a Buick. Damsel & dragonfly nymphs work well up the west side, while there is decent caddis and mayfly hatches too. Like all the lakes, scuds or shrimp patterns work well too.

Since each of the lakes is part of a damming system, draw down can hinder angling success at times. Also be sure to check your regulations before visiting these lakes. There is a special season restriction on Dobbin Lake and an electric motor only restriction on Islaht Lake.

Facilities

Although the former recreation sites are no longer maintained, there area places to camp at both lakes. Dobbin Lake also offers a place to launch small boats.

Directions

Locally as the Horseshoe Lakes due to their topographical 'horseshoe' shape, he lakes are located west of Kelowna. Follow the Bear Creek Forest Service Road about 8 km past the resort on Lambly Lake and take the north spur road just before the main road makes a sharp corner to cross the creek. If you hit the right road, you should find Islaht Lake about 3.5 km later. Dobbin Lake is found a short distance later.

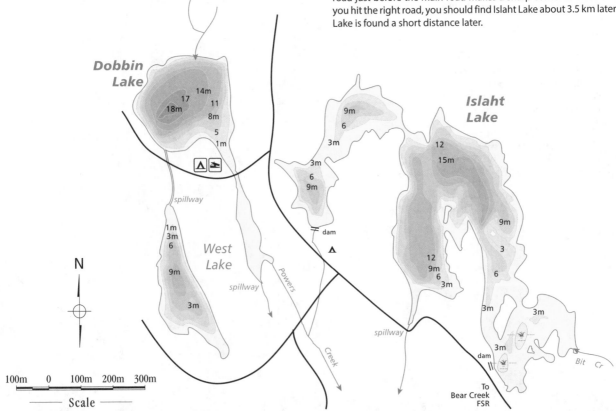

Idabel Lake

Location: 28 km (17 mi) southeast of Kelowna
Elevation: 1,235 m (4,052 ft)
Surface Area: 40 ha (100 ac)
Mean Depth: 5.8 m (19 ft)
Max Depth: 12.8 m (42 ft)
Way Point: 49° 44' 00" Lat - N   119° 14' 00" Lon - W

Fishing

Idabel Lake is a resort lake found southeast of the city of Kelowna. Fly anglers especially will delight in the fishing opportunities Idabel Lake has to offer. The lake is stocked regularly with brook trout and supports a naturally reproducing rainbow trout population. Fishing for both trout species is quite good at times, especially in the spring and fall periods.

Fishing pressure on the lake is fairly heavy, especially on weekends. This is due in part to the fact there is a resort on the lake. The close proximity to Kelowna and the fact the fish are abundant aids in the lakes popularity.

A fine population of freshwater shrimp inhabits Idabel Lake. Fly anglers would due well to try to imitate these crustaceans. The shoal area found just south of the resort along the eastern side of the lake would be a good area to start when visiting this lake. During the spring run off period, near the small inlet stream found just north of the resort can also be a hot spot on the lake.

In the winter, the lake is a popular ice-fishing destination. Although the rainbow trout can be quite lethargic after the lake ices up, the brook trout remain quite active. The best time to visit the lake is early in the winter season as soon as the ice is thick enough to walk on (minimum 15 cm/6 in). At this time, the water is still oxygenated enough and warm enough that the fish are still active.

Most fish are caught in less than 3 m (10 ft) of water, and many in a lot less than that. Drill your holes in the shoal area near the resort. If you don't mind getting cold, try laying on the ice and watching the fish through the hole. As the water is so clear in winter, this can be a fascinating glimpse into the underwater world. Even better, you can watch fish as they take your bait. While a special ice-fishing rod is helpful, many people chose to ice fish using just a lure or jig on some fishing line, pulling the fish out by hand.

Facilities

Along the scenic shores of Idabel Lake, visitors will find the full service **Idabel Lake Resort**. The resort provides a number of different outdoor adventure services to visitors including private cabins along the lakeshore.

Other Options

En route to Idabel Lake, you will pass **Haynes Lake** along the Okanagan Falls Forest Service Road. The higher elevation lake provides fishing opportunities for large stocked rainbow trout. Informal camping areas can be found around the lake.

Directions

Idabel Lake is located southeast of the city of Kelowna. From Kelowna, follow Highway 33 east out of the city. Approximately 8 km (5 mi) past the cut off to the Big White Ski Area you will meet the Okanagan Falls Forest Service Road. Follow this main logging road southwest and across the McCulloch Road. Just past Haynes Lake at the 74 km mark, there is a signed access road heading west off the main road that leads to Idabel Lake Resort. Being a resort lake, all vehicles can easily access the lake.

Area Indicator

Species
Rainbow Trout
Brook Trout

Idabel Lake			
Fish Stocking Data			
Year	Species	Number	Life Stage
2013	Brook Trout	5,000	Yearling
2012	Brook Trout	3,432	Fingerling
2011	Brook Trout	5,000	Yearling

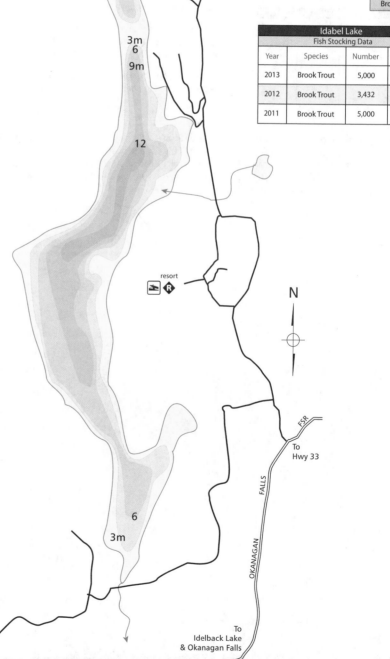

Region

8

Location: 24 km (15 mi) east of Penticton
Elevation: 1,440 m (4,724 ft)
Surface Area: 14 ha (35 ac)
Mean Depth: 3 m (10 ft)
Max Depth: 6 m (20 ft)
Way Point: 49° 30′ 00″ Lat - N   119° 17′ 00″ Lon - W

Idleback Lake

Area Indicator

Species

Rainbow Trout

Idleback Lake			
Fish Stocking Data			
Year	Species	Number	Life Stage
2013	Rainbow Trout	1,000	Fry
2012	Rainbow Trout	1,000	Fry
2011	Rainbow Trout	1,000	Fry

Fishing

Idleback Lake is a small lake east of Penticton that is well known among area anglers as being one of the premier lakes in the area. Fishing in Idleback Lake can be quite good at times for rainbow trout that reach a hefty 2.5 kg (5 lbs) in size. The lake is stocked annually with rainbow trout and is restricted to fly-fishing only. This fishing restriction has helped keep the fishing in Idleback at a high quality with feisty trout that are a thrill to catch on the fly.

The lake is found quite high up in the mountains, and does not ice off until later in the season. Even though it is rather shallow, the lake remains fairly consistent throughout the open water season. However, visiting this lake during the heat of the summer is not recommended.

The depth of the lake drops rapidly along the northern shore, while the southern shore of the lake is generally weedier and gradually recedes to the deeper middle. During the spring and early summer, rainbow can be picked up effectively using chironomid patterns fished off the northern drop off. A blood leech pattern can be particularly productive. Try using a very dark colour, say a deep purple or black for good results. In June, there is a large caddis hatch; dry fly-fishing using an Elk Hair Caddis pattern can provide some great fishing. Caddis are a fairly easy fly to fish. Once they emerge from the water, they sit on surface for a few minutes to let their wings dry; all you have to do is let the fly sit on top of the water, twitching it occasionally, while you wait for the trout to take it.

Fishing around the shallower weedy southern and eastern parts of the lake can also be a good holding area for rainbow cruising the shoals in search of early season insect activity. During the summer months or inactive periods, try working a leech or a dragonfly nymph near the bottom in the 4-5 m (13-16 ft) range.

There are a number of special regulations including a one fish limit and electric motor only restrictions. It is recommended to check the regulations before fishing Idleback Lake.

Directions

East of the city of Penticton you can reach Idleback Lake by first travelling out of the city along Carmi Road. Carmi Road leads into the hills east of the city and passes the Ellis Reservoir before meeting the Okanagan Falls Forest Service Road about 20 km later. At the junction, head north along this main haul logging road. Just before the 44 km mark, you will meet Idleback Lake and the rough lake access road.

Facilities

The **Idleback Lake Recreation Site** is a medium sized campsite with space for about 13 groups and a cartop boat access. Access is good enough to allow RV's. As a result, the site receives heavy use during the summer and can be full at times, especially on weekends.

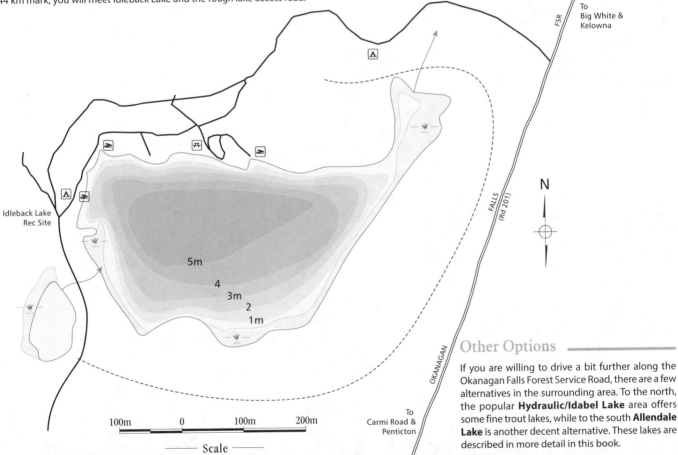

Idleback Lake
Rec Site

To
Big White &
Kelowna

5m
4
3m
2
1m

N

100m   0   100m   200m
— Scale —

To
Carmi Road &
Penticton

Other Options

If you are willing to drive a bit further along the Okanagan Falls Forest Service Road, there are a few alternatives in the surrounding area. To the north, the popular **Hydraulic/Idabel Lake** area offers some fine trout lakes, while to the south **Allendale Lake** is another decent alternative. These lakes are described in more detail in this book.

Jackpine Lake

Location: 24 km (15 mi) west of Kelowna
Elevation: 1,311 m (4,301 ft)
Surface Area: 43 ha (106 ac)
Mean Depth: 4.5 m (15 ft)
Max Depth: 7.5 m (25 ft)
Way Point: 49° 54' 00" Lat - N   119° 48' 00" Lon - W

Fishing

Located in the mountains west of Okanagan Lake, this reasonably high elevation lake is a popular trout destination for anglers out of Kelowna. In fact, it is one of the most popular fishing lakes in the Kelowna area, and can be quite busy on the weekends.

To offset the fishing pressure, Jackpine Lake is heavily stocked with rainbow trout by the Freshwater Fisheries Society of BC. The lake is also managed as a family fishery, meaning that there are plenty of trout in the 30 cm (12 inch) range. Of course the rare lunker is out there and there have been rumours of the odd 2.5 kg (5 lb) trout in the mix.

The tannin-stained lake is a favourite of fly anglers. There is plenty of shoal area in the lake that provides the ideal habitat for finding big rainbow. Depending on the hatch of the day, chironomids and damselfly nymphs used in the spring can both provide good results. However, anglers should note that the lake is a little slower to ice off than lower elevation lakes (mid-May). This results in a lot of overlapping hatches, which can make it a bit more complicated to pick the right fly. Not only do you need to match the hatch, but know you have to figure out which hatch is the one that is attracting the trout. If there is no active hatch using a nymph pattern or a Woolly Bugger on the troll is a popular alternative. Buicks and gomphus patterns are a couple of the local favourites.

In the summer season, the younger rainbow can often be spotted jumping after caddis flies hatching from the lake. This usually occurs early in the morning or later in the evening. At these times, a Tom Thumb or Elk Hair Caddis will provide some exciting top-water fishing.

Also during hot spells, there are occasionally some very large terrestrial hatches, like winged ants. If you show up during these times, you can do very well casting a matching terrestrial pattern. Spincasters can also do well by setting up a bobber and using a flying ant fly pattern too.

There is an electric motor only restriction on Jackpine Lake.

Other Options

The small lake just to the west of Jackpine Lake is called **Gallately Lake**. This small lake has a feeder stream that flows into Jackpine and offers angling opportunities for rainbow trout that are rumoured to reach the 2 kg (4.5 lb) size on occasion.

Directions

From Kelowna, travel west through Westbank to Glenrosa Road. Follow this road north towards the Crystal Mountain Ski Area. Just before the ski hill, you should see the Jackpine Forest Service Road. Follow this road as it descends and then climbs steeply back up. The road should then course west along the northern side of Powers Creek, eventually meeting Jackpine Lake.

Alternatively, the access road can be picked up off the Bear Creek Forest Service Road around the 25 km mark. Just west of Lambly Lake, look for the next major road branching south. Follow this road, which should be the Jackpine-Last Mountain Road, for about 2 km. The Jackpine Lake Forest Service Road branches west and leads another 5 km to the lake.

Facilities

The **Jackpine Lake Wilderness Camp** provides RV sites along with boat rentals. Alternatively, the **Jackpine Lake Recreation Site** is a medium sized site found on the northeast shore. The recreation site can host up to 9 groups and offers a boat launch, picnic tables and outhouses. There is a fee to camp here from mid-May to mid-September.

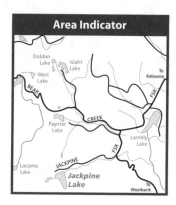

Area Indicator

Species

Rainbow Trout

Jackpine Lake Fish Stocking Data			
Year	Species	Number	Life Stage
2013	Rainbow Trout	3,000	Yearling
2012	Rainbow Trout	8,000	Yearling
2011	Rainbow Trout	8,000	Yearling

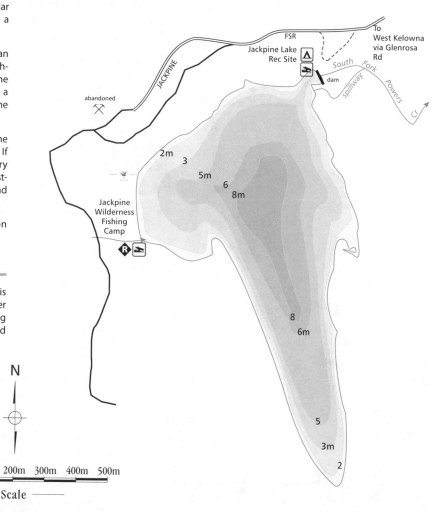

N

100m 0 100m 200m 300m 400m 500m

Scale

Location: 10 km (6 mi) northeast of Greenwood
Elevation: 1,135 m (3,724 ft)
Surface area: 72 ha (178 ac)
Mean depth: 10.9 m (36 ft)
Max depth: 23.8 m (78 ft)
GPS Waypoint: 49° 10' 00" Lat - N 118° 36' 00" Lon - W

Jewel Lake

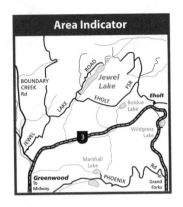

Area Indicator

Species
Rainbow Trout
Brook Trout

Jewel Lake Fish Stocking Data			
Year	Species	Number	Life Stage
2013	Brook Trout	5,000	Yearling
2013	Rainbow Trout	16,448	Yearling
2012	Brook Trout	4,550	Fingerling
2012	Rainbow Trout	15,000	Yearling
2011	Brook Trout	5,000	Fingerling
2011	Rainbow Trout	15,000	Yearling

Fishing

Jewel Lake was known to produce some of the biggest rainbow trout in the province. In fact, rumour has it that a massive 25 kg (56 lb) rainbow was netted decades ago. However, the unfortunate introduction of minnows changed the dynamics of the lake dramatically and reduced the quality of the fishery. Thankfully the Freshwater Fisheries Society of BC releases good numbers of rainbow and brook trout into lakes such as Jewel to counteract the minnow problem. Today, Jewel Lake can once again boast of trout in the 3 kg (6.5 lb) range.

The best time for fishing takes place in June, July and late fall. The most common way to fish Jewel Lake is by trolling the south shoreline with small spinners like the Blue Fox, Mepps and Panther Martin. Using a Willow Leaf or Ford Fender adds to the success. For enticing the brook trout, target the deeper sections with red or chartreuse lures. However, for rainbow, look at fishing the shoals and drop offs with brass or silver colours. Be careful when using bright presentations since the trout can spook easily in the clear waters.

Vast amounts of vegetation throughout the shoals allow fly anglers to use a variety of patterns. Dragonfly and damselfly nymphs are known to work well when casting onto the various shoals. Leeches, Woolly Buggers and patterns like the Doc Spratley can be worked along drop offs or trolled throughout the lake with success. The warm summer months bring sedges to the surface. Fly fishers, using floating lines, can cast to the rising trout in the shallow bays with a Tom Thumb or Mikulak Sedge. This is a fun and rewarding time to catch these great fighting fish.

With good access year round, Jewel Lake is an ideal ice fishing destination. Using traditional ice fishing methods, fish the various shoals found along the lake. Start your day fishing the shallow areas, then, as the day progresses move to deeper water.

There is a 7.5 kw (10 hp) engine power restriction and 8 km/hr speed restriction in place at Jewel Lake.

Jewel Lake Prov Park

6m
12
18m
18
12m
6
6m

Directions

You can find Jewel Lake east of the quaint town of Greenwood by following Highway 3 to the Boundary Creek Road. Take the paved Boundary Creek Road north to Jewel Lake Road and follow signs to the aptly named lake. There are many different access points on the western side of the lake.

Facilities

The first thing you will notice when you reach Jewel Lake is the **Jewel Lake Resort** on the southeastern shore. In addition to cabins, they offer boat rentals and some good advice on where to fish the lake. There is also informal parking areas and several places to launch cartoppers or pontoon boats from the main road.

Further north, the **Jewel Lake Provincial Park** is found at the end of the lake. The park offers 26 vehicle accessible campsites complete with picnic tables, outhouses and a boat launch. The popular park offers natural sand beaches and great views of the Monashee Mountains. It can be busy during the summer, especially on weekends.

To Greenwood

200m 0 200m 400m 600m 800m 1000m
— Scale —

R resort

Jim Smith Lake

Location: 5 km (3 mi) southwest of Cranbrook
Elevation: 1,058 m (3,471 ft)
Surface area: 23 ha (57 ac)
Mean depth: 4.9 m (16 ft)
Max depth: 7.3 m (24 ft)
GPS Waypoint: 115° 51' 00" Lon - W 49° 29' 00" Lat - N

Fishing

Largemouth bass were introduced into Jim Smith Lake a couple years back, most likely brought in illegally as bait for ice fishing. The population is growing very strong, which in turn is having a negative impact on the trout population. But not as much as has happened in other lakes. The lake has extensive shallows, which are favoured by the bass, but it also has an extensive basin where the trout can survive.

Still, in 2002, they stopped stocking the lake with rainbow trout. They stocked the lake for a couple years with cutthroat trout, but in 2004, they stopped stocking the lake altogether. Today, the Freshwater Fisheries Society of BC is keeping a close eye on how the trout populations fares.

There are surviving populations of all three trout species still found in the lake, as well as yellow perch, which have also found their way into the lake illegally. But it is the bass that have become the dominant species here. The fishing for bass can be good at times for largemouth that can reach up to 1 kg (2 lbs) in size.

As the waters of the lake heat up, so does the bass fishing. The bass prefer warm water, and the hotter it is, the more active they become. Some people prefer to jig for bass, as they like to hide in weeds and under sunken logs and anywhere there is some sort of cover. This makes it difficult to get a lure to them without snagging it on something that isn't a fish. Most bass-specific lures have covered hooks, to prevent the lure from snagging. Another option is to use a Carolina or a Texas rig, which uses a worm stretched out over the hook to prevent weeds from hooking.

Fly-fishing for bass has become increasingly popular, and bass take very well to specifically designed bass lures called bass bugs or poppers. These top-water flies resemble bees, moths or some other insect that has fallen into the water. A slow, erratic retrieve that resembles a bug drowning will often produce a rather violent strike. Poppers can be difficult to fish at first since they are hard to cast.

There is a powerboat restriction on this lake.

Directions

You can find Jim Smith Lake southwest of the city of Cranbrook not far off Highway 3. Look for the signed Jim Smith Lake Road off the west side of the highway. The paved road leads to the popular Jim Smith Lake Provincial Park.

Facilities

Jimsmith Lake Provincial Park is open from the beginning of May to the end of October and is home to 29 vehicle accessible campsites. The park also offers a day-use picnic area, canoe launch, outhouses and developed beach. In addition to the fishing prospects, many visitors to the lake also enjoy such activities like sunbathing, swimming and paddling. For reservations call 1-800-689-9025 or visit www.discovercamping.ca.

Other Options

A close by angling option to Jim Smith Lake is **New Lake**. You can reach New Lake by finding the New Lake Road off King Street. Anglers are often pleased with the action at New Lake for its feisty, stocked rainbow trout.

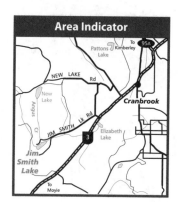

Area Indicator

Species
Cutthroat Trout
Largemouth Bass
Rainbow Trout
Yellow Perch

Jim Smith Lake			
Fish Stocking Data			
Year	Species	Number	Life Stage
2004	Westslope Cutthroat Trout	8,700	Fall Fry
2003	Westslope Cutthroat Trout	5,000	Yearling

Scale

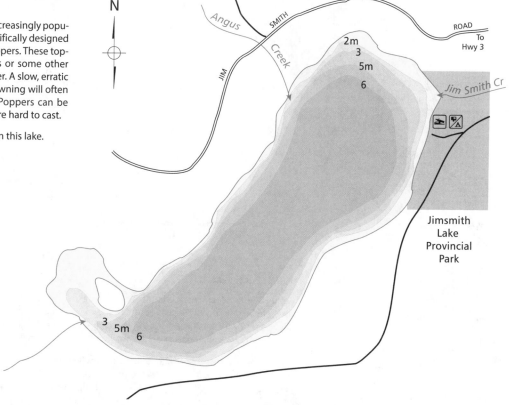

Jimsmith Lake Provincial Park

Region 8

Location: 3 km (2 mi) south of Vernon
Elevation: 392 m (1,286 ft)
Surface area: 2,590 ha (6,397 ac)
Mean depth: 75 m (246 ft)
Max depth: 142 m (466 ft)
GPS Waypoint: 119° 20' 00" Lon - W 50° 09' 00" Lat - N

Kalamalka Lake

Directions

Kalamalka Lake is located south of the city of Vernon. Highway 97 skirts the western shore of the lake providing access to Kekuli Bay Provincial Park and the best boat launch onto the big lake. There is ample parking and a large paved launch at the park. At the north end of the lake, two other paved launches are found on the outskirts of Vernon. Look for the familiar blue boat launch signs off Highway 97 at College Way near the Okanagan Community College or off Kalamalka Road at the south end of town.

People also access Kalamalka Lake through the short channel connecting with Wood Lake to the south. There are a couple boat launches on Wood Lake, including one at the northeast end of the lake off Oyama Lake Road.

Fishing

National Geographic names "the lake of many colours" as one of the 10 most beautiful lakes in the world. It gets its distinctive blue green hues from the calcium carbonate crystals that reflect sunlight.

Anglers will find better luck and the bigger fish from October through to April. With lake trout over 9 kg (20 lbs) and rainbow trout up to 5 kg (10 lbs) there are indeed some trophy class fish in the lake. Kokanee (to 2 kg/4.5 lbs), carp, northern pike minnow and whitefish are also present in this lake.

The lake trout are mainly caught by trolling deep with a downrigger; target the 25–50 m (80–160 ft) depths. Working large lures, such as chrome coloured Apex, William's Wobbler and various coloured Lyman Plugs can produce one of the lunkers.

Preferred regions of the lake for kokanee are near Rattle Snake Point, Cosens Bay or near the rock walls on the east side. Fishing in the 10–15 m (30–50 ft) depths, the lures that work well are Mepps and Blue Fox in red or chartreuse tipped with powerbait or maggots.

Rainbow are not as abundant and are usually caught incidentally with the smaller trout chasing down kokanee gear and the larger rainbow hooking into lake trout gear.

The best shore access is from the park areas. Kekuli Bay Provincial Park provides access to the railway tracks (be cautious since this is an active railway system), while Kalamalka Lake Provincial Park provides access to some nice bluffs at the northeast end of the lake.

Although not as popular, fly-fishing can be productive from spring to early fall in the sheltered bays. Working the drop offs with streamer patterns or a bead head Woolly Bugger can yield the odd rainbow and kokanee. For something different, try fly-fishing the shallow water at each end of the lake with a small beaded hare's ear or pheasant tail nymph that might trick one of those large, finicky carp found there.

Be sure to check the regulations before heading out onto Kalamalka Lake. There are special quotas and boating restrictions. We also ask that you practice catch and release to help preserve those trophy class lakers.

Area Indicator

Species

Species
Carp
Kokanee
Lake Trout
Northern Pike
Rainbow Trout
Whitefish

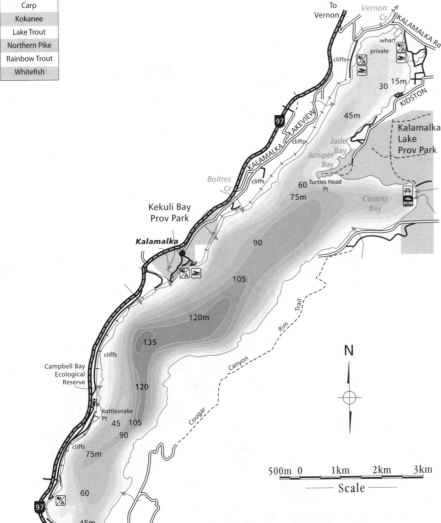

Facilities

Kekuli Bay Provincial Park is found on the western side of the lake off of Highway 97. It features a large concrete boat launch as well as access to the rocky shoreline for casting. There is also camping and a day-use area with small beach area at the park. Other boat launches can be found near Vernon, one by Coldstream Creek and another on the northwest side of Kalamalka Lake.

Day trippers can also enjoy **Kalamalka Lake Provincial Park**. This spectacular park rests on the northeast shore of the big lake and is a great retreat for boaters, cyclists and hikers. On the south shore, **Kaloya Regional Park** is another day-use area with a couple beaches for visitors to enjoy.

Kearns Lake

Location: 18 km (11 mi) south of Castlegar
Elevation: 1,263 m (4,144 ft)
Surface Area: 5.5 ha (13.5 ac)
Mean Depth: 12 m (39 ft)
Max Depth: 26 m (85 ft)
Way Point: 117° 37′ 00″ Lon - W 49° 10′ 00″ Lat - N

Fishing

Fishing in Kearns Lake is not very popular. The fish are extremely finicky, and what might work one day does not work the next. The brook trout are also quite small, averaging under 25 cm (10 in). Having said this, anglers who hit the lake at the right time, and who have the initiative to haul up a float tube or canoe will find that the lake can have its great moments. Spring and fall are the best times to try the lake, as the elusive trout tend to go deep during the summer months.

If you do plan to fish the lake, it is best to work your way along the rustic trail to either the middle or the south end of the lake. If you have a floatation device, try off the small island at the south end of the lake. The trout will cruise the shoal area in search of food during the spring or cool summer evenings.

During summer, it is best to fish deep or early in the day and after sunset. If you are shore casting, it is best to work the steep drop off along the middle of the lake. Your typical Kootenay flies will often work better than casting lures. Spincasters should try either a Panther Marten or Deadly Dick tipped with worm since these lures have proven successful.

Trolling can be effective, working the drop off areas of the lake or around the island at the south end of the lake. Try working a leech, nymph or Woolly Bugger fly pattern. Alternatively, small spinners or even a lake troll with bait can work at times.

Facilities

Kearns Lake is in **Champion Lakes Provincial Park**. Although there are no developed facilities at Kearns Lake, there is a rustic trail system on the east side of the lake that leads to a fine camping area at the south end of the lake. Please practice no trace camping if you plan to stay at the lake. The park, itself, is a full service park offering camping from the months of June through until September. Visitors will find a nice 89 unit campsite near the 3rd lake, which is a popular spot during the summer months. Along with fishing or canoeing in all three Champion Lakes, the 3rd lake offers a sandy beach and a nature trail. For reservations call 1-800-689-9025 or visit www.discovercamping.ca.

Other Options

The three **Champion Lakes** all offer fishing opportunities for rainbow trout. The Third Champion Lake, which is the main recreational lake, is the slowest of the three. The Second Champion Lake is known to inhabit some good sized rainbow trout, although they are notoriously difficult to catch. The First Champion Lake offers the best fishing of the three, although it entails a short hike to access the lake. More details are found earlier in this book.

Directions

Kearns Lake lies within the boundary of the Champion Lakes Provincial Park. The park is located northeast of Trail and can be accessed via the Champion Park Road form Highway 3B. From the picnic parking area at the 3rd Champion Lake, visitors first need to access the nature trail around the south side of the 3rd lake. At the far end of the lake, a moderate but steep trail climbs to Kearns Lake. It is a 4 km (2.5 mi) return hike to the lake.

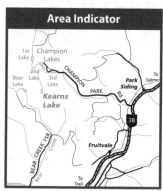

Area Indicator

Species
Brook Trout

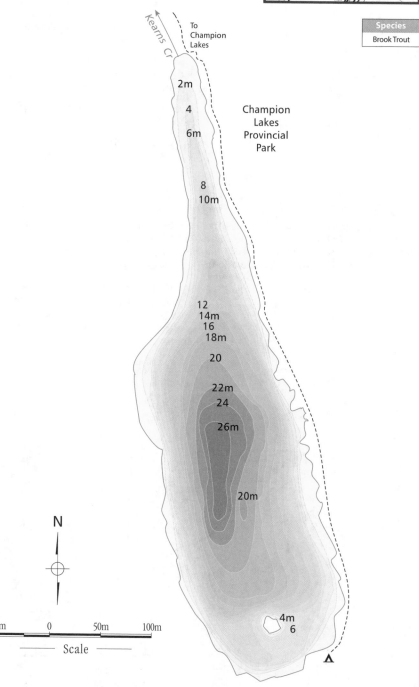

N

50m   0   50m   100m

Scale

Location: 70 km (43.5 mi) east of Vernon
Elevation: 1,356 m (4,449 ft)
Surface Area: 69 ha (170 ac)
Mean Depth: 5 m (20 ft)
Max Depth: 12.5 m (41 ft)
Way Point: 118° 20′00″ Lon - W 50° 07′00″ Lat - N

Keefer Lake

Area Indicator

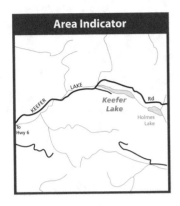

Species

Rainbow Trout
Brook Trout

Fishing

Keefer Lake is the headwaters for the Kettle River watershed, straddling the divide between the Okanagan and the Kootenays. The resort based lake is usually ice free by May long weekend and known to hold plenty of small rainbow and brook trout. It is a great place to fish, and many a Okanagan child has learned the fine art of fishing on these waters.

In recent years rumours have abounded that the fishing is not what it used to be. This is partly true since the lake is heavily fished and there were some inconsiderate souls not abiding by the regulations. Thankfully the resort owners care for the lake and are helping to return this fishery to what it used to be.

The lake is fairly large and deep, with fish averaging in the 20-40 cm (6-15 inch) range. However, some 2 kg (4.5 lb) monsters are caught annually. The best fishing is from the beginning of June until mid-July before the larger fish go deep.

Trolling is the preferred method of angling, although fly-fishing can be quite productive. Fly anglers should focus near the inlet and outlet of the Kettle River. Try stripping various nymph patterns near the river areas. There are some incredible chironomid hatches on the lake in late June and into July. You will need to be patient fishing with chironomids but with a little practice, the reward can be a nice feisty trout.

Trollers should try along the drop offs near the two deeper holes. Bucktails or smaller spoons like the Little Cleo have been known to produce well. Rainbow seem to be attracted to anything orange or green with a bit of silver flash i.e. Wedding Band, or a Red Spratley.

If you do not have a boat or are looking to kill a few hours from shore, you could do worse than to cast a good ol bait and bobber set-up. The smaller trout never seem to tire of worms.

In the winter, ice fishing is very popular as soon as the ice is thick enough to walk on (more than 15 cm/6 inches). Early in the season the fishing is faster, but you'll probably have good luck for brook trout later in the season.

Directions

Keefer Lake is a fabulous wilderness destination. The mountain lake can be reached by following Highway 6 to Keefer Lake Road east of the town of Lumby. The signed logging road is easily spotted off the north side of the highway near the Lost Lake Rest Area. It is about 14 km from the highway to the lake. The road can be rough in sections.

Facilities

Keefer Lake is home to the wonderful **Keefer Lake Wilderness Resort**. The resort offers full service cabins, camping, a boat launch and boat rentals as well as guided trips.

Alternatively, the **Holmes Lake Recreation Site** is found about 5 km to the west. The small, user-maintained site is not the nicest, but does provide a place to camp and possibly launch a boat onto the lake.

Other Options

Just to the east of Keefer Lake you can find **Holmes Lake**. There is a walk-in campsite available at the lake (which is being used by ATVers). It is a small, intimate lake that used to produce large fish. These days, the fishing is still good, but don't expect to find any lunkers, as the lake sees a lot of pressure. Most of the rainbow and brook trout are less than 30 cm (12 inches) in size

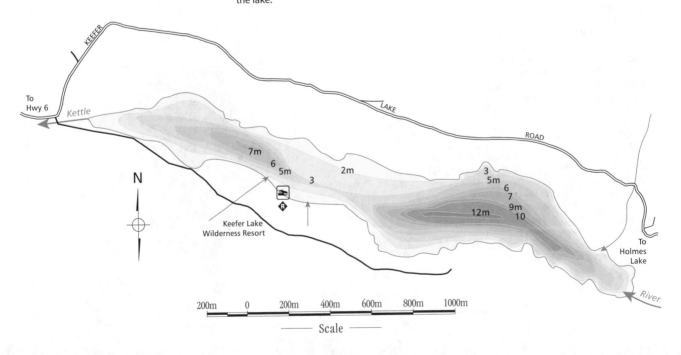

Kilpoola Lake

Location: 9 km (5.6 mi) west of Osoyoos
Elevation: 815 m (2,674 ft)
Surface Area: 17 ha (42 ac)
Mean Depth: 3 m (10 ft)
Max Depth: 8 m (26 ft)
Way Point: 119° 33' 00" Lon - W 49° 01' 00" Lat - N

Region 8

Fishing

Kilpoola Lake is a small, shallow lake stocked annually with rainbow trout by the Freshwater Fisheries Society of BC. The lake is susceptible to winterkill, and fishing is fair for rainbow trout and brook trout that can reach 1 kg (2.5 lbs) in size.

The lake is a low elevation lake near Osoyoos, surrounded by mountains and grasslands. There are very few trees around the lake, and accessing its shores is quite easy. However, the waters get quite warm in the summer, and fishing tends to tail off significantly during the summer months. Because of its low elevation, the summer doldrums strike here earlier than at many other lakes. Of course, the fishing does pick up in the evening once the sun is off the lake. If fishing is marginal through the day, try working a dragonfly nymph or a leech. Once the sun starts to go down look for hatches starting to emerge.

There is a rough boat launch, but a tube or a small hand-launched craft will serve you just as well, if not better, here. If you have a boat, try trolling a leech pattern or a dragonfly nymph near bottom during inactive feeding periods.

Spincasters should try small spinners and spoons, with or without worms. The trick is to make sure that your lure does not run at a constant speed in a straight line. Twitching the rod, speeding up and slowing down, and even stopping will make the lure behave erratically, which makes the lure much more enticing to trout.

Facilities

Kilpoola Lake is located in the **South Okanagan Grasslands Protected Area**, and is found at the heart of one of four separate parcels that make up the park. There are no formal facilities offered at Kilpoola Lake or in the park in general. There is, however, a rustic launching site. The resort town of Osoyoos is nearby and offers a number of first-rate facilities to choose from.

Other Options

For a completely different fishing experience, why not check out **Osoyoos Lake**? This popular resort lake is easily accessed from the town of Osoyoos and provides fishing opportunities for rainbow trout, bass, perch and some kokanee. The lake before Kilpoola is Blue Lake. This lake contains no fish because of high pH levels.

Directions

This 29 hectare size lake is found in the dry mountain belt surrounding Osoyoos. The forestry roads off Highway 3 are poorly marked, making it an adventure to find the lake. A copy of the Thompson Okanagan Backroad Mapbook and a GPS is highly recommended to find this lake.

To find the lake, turn west off Highway 3 onto the Old Richter Pass Road and take the first main road south. This should be the Kruger Mountain Road, which leads past Blue Lake. Keeping south at the next junction should bring you to Kilpoola Lake. You have to pass through a closed gate to access the lake. Make sure you close the gate behind you.

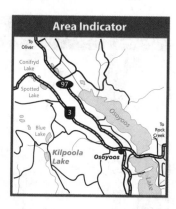

Area Indicator

Species
Rainbow Trout
Brook Trout

Kipoola Lake			
Fish Stocking Data			
Year	Species	Number	Life Stage
2013	Rainbow Trout	1,000	Spring Catchable
2012	Rainbow Trout	1,000	Catchable
2011	Rainbow Trout	1,000	Catchable

To Hwy 3

gate

Lone Pine Creek

2m

3

5m

6

N

Lone Pine Creek

100m   0   100m   200m   300m

— Scale —

To Osoyoos

Kentucky & Alleyne Lakes

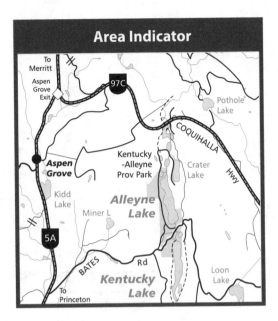

Species

Rainbow Trout

Kokanee

Directions

Found 38 km from Merritt, these lakes are easily accessed. Travel south on Highway 5A from the Aspen Grove Exit on the Coquihalla Connector (Hwy 97C). About 7 km later, Bates Road leads east towards the park. Follow this road for 6 km and continue on the main road to the north end of Kentucky Lake. Alleyne Lake is found on the north side of the road.

Facilities

Kentucky-Alleyne Provincial Park is a scenic park that has long been a favourite of area anglers. In total, there are 58 vehicle/tent campsites, including one group campsite at the north end of Alleyne Lake. Finding a site on the May long weekend through to late October can be a challenge. There are not as many facilities at this park as compared to other parks in the Okanagan (no showers, sani-station or flush toilets) so you should expect a more rustic setting.

Visitors will also find boat launches onto both lakes, although later in the summer launching boats can be a challenge when the water level is down. Trail enthusiasts can take advantage of the many well maintained trails in the park that provide nice viewpoints over the kettle formed lakes. One of the more popular is the 4 km trail that circles Kentucky Lake providing access for shore fishing or a pleasant family walk.

Other Options

Two ponds are located between Kentucky and Alleyne Lakes which feature a "children only – under 16" fishery to foster interest in the sport among the youth. Also known as the **Kentucky Potholes**, the west pond is regularly stocked by the Freshwater Fisheries Society of BC with 500 catchable triploid rainbow. The east pond is stocked, but is hard to fish during low water years.

Fishing

Kentucky Alleyne Provincial Park is well known for its picturesque setting, pristine campground and great fishing in the clear cold waters for larger rainbow. These two kettle lakes form the centrepiece of the park even though the majority of Kentucky Lake lies outside the park's boundaries.

Both lakes are annually stocked with triploid rainbow by the Freshwater Fisheries Society of BC to ensure some good fishing for generally bigger trout. In fact, both lakes produce some nice chrome rainbow that can reach up to 55 cm (22 in) with the average being 35–40 cm. (14–16 in). This is mainly due to the alkalinity levels which create productive conditions. With Kentucky and Alleyne Lakes being clear lakes, trolling deep is the method of choice when fishing. Alleyne Lake, in particular, has sharp drop offs. Even the small, sheltered bay at the lake's south end is 15 m (50 ft) deep.

Those using gear can target the rainbow using small spinners, Flatfish and Dick Nites while trolling just off the shoals in deeper water. Small lures in chrome, black and silver or blue work well. If fishing very deep stay with the chrome lures. Shore fishing is possible in spots along both lakes. Casting from the dock on Kentucky Lake is also possible, but only during high water years. It should also be noted that high winds can hamper fishing but one can head to the south end of either lake for shelter.

Fly fisherman will have success chironomid fishing on the south end of Kentucky Lake during spring and fall. Black Sallies and chromies are popular patterns. Leeches and Woolly Buggers fished with a full sink line at the drop offs can produce well. Casting to cruising fish on the shoals with dry flies can prove to be very productive in June and July. The shoals at the north and north east end of Alleyne Lake are favoured for casting to cruising fish or casting with a damselfly nymph or leech at the drop offs. With the two lakes being so clear, any noise or disturbance on the shoals will spook the fish, so anglers need to approach these areas with caution.

To add to the fishery, Alleyne Lake has also been stocked with kokanee. These landlocked salmon are a popular catch as they are generally easy to catch on the troll. Most anglers use a lake troll with Wedding Band or similar type lure tipped with bait. The addition of a 'snubber' such as those found on the Gibbs Kokanee Katcher can increase the chance of landing one these soft mouthed fish. Troll as slow as possible and in an "S" pattern so your line, will speed up or slow down and change depths as you round the bend. This entices the fish to bite. Trolling with one ounce of weight or less, which takes the lure to 5–15 metres (15 to 45 feet), is the most productive.

While the park is closed in the winter, the lakes are open to ice fishing, assuming that they are well frozen. When fishing for trout, don't go walking out to the middle of the lake to drill your holes. Trout like to hang around the top layer of water, preferably where there is access to food, which means you'll find them close to shore. Usually within 25 m (75 ft) of shore. Watch for points and edges where there may be underwater structure or a drop off in water depth. As a general rule, the farther you can get from the areas that are commonly fished, the better the fishing will be. That said, if you are having no luck, look for holes that have been previously drilled where there are signs of people having caught fish there. That's easier said than done, but if there were fish there last week, there will be fish there today. And make sure you dress appropriately. A trick is to wear neoprene chest waders over polar fleece sweat pants. You can sit on the ice and the neoprene keeps you dry with good insulation from the cold wind.

The road into the lakes may or may not be plowed in winter, and you may or may not need to find alternate methods to get to the park. During the open water season, there is a 7.5 Kw (10hp) motor restriction on both lakes.

Kentucky & Alleyne Lakes

Location: 38 km (23.5 mi) southeast of Merritt

Species

Rainbow Trout

Kentucky Lake
Fish Stocking Data

Year	Species	Number	Life Stage
2013	Rainbow Trout	17,500	Yearling
2012	Rainbow Trout	17,500	Yearling
2011	Rainbow Trout	17,450	Yearling

Kentucky Lake

Elevation: 1,000 m (3,208 ft)
Surface Area: 36 ha (89 ac)
Mean Depth: 16 m (52.5 ft)
Max Depth: 40 m (131 ft)
Way Point: 120° 33' 00" Lon - W 49° 53' 00" Lat - N

Alleyne Lake

Elevation: 994 m (3,261 ft)
Surface Area: 54 ha (133 ac)
Mean Depth: 17 m (56 ft)
Max Depth: 36 m (118 ft)
Way Point: 120° 33' 00" Lon - W 49° 55' 00" Lat - N

Alleyne Lake

100m 0 100m 200m 300m 400m 500m
— Scale —

N

Kentucky-
Alleyne
Provincial
Park

Alleyne Lake
Campground

Species

Kokanee
Rainbow Trout

Alleyne Lake
Fish Stocking Data

Year	Species	Number	Life Stage
2013	Kokanee	5,000	Yearling
2013	Rainbow Trout	22,500	Yearling
2012	Kokanee	0	Yearling
2012	Rainbow Trout	16,425	Yearling
2011	Rainbow Trout	12,500	Yearling

To
Hwy 97C

*Crater
Lake*

To
Hwy 97C

ROAD

Kentucky Lake
Campground

BATES

To
Hwy 5A

Kentucky Lake

100m 0 100m 200m 300m 400m 500m
— Scale —

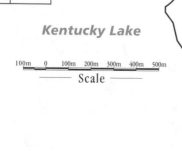

To
Bluey
Lake

Region 8

Kettle River (South)
Location: Between Rock Creek & Grand Forks
Stream Length: 238 km (145 mi)
Geographic: 118° 52' 00" Lon - W   49° 2' 00" Lat - N

Kettle River

Fishing

The Kettle River is a warm, lazy river that makes its way out of the Monashee Mountains through a fairly remote valley before bumping into civilization near Westbridge. From here it follows Highway 33 to Rock Creek and then Highway 3 to Midway, before looping south into the US. The river comes back across the Canadian Border to be joined by the Granby at Grand Forks for a short lived visit back to BC. The river flows through a pretty, sparsely populated area and can be a joy to fish, canoe or even tube on during the summer.

The 282 km (175 mile) long Kettle was once a salmon bearing stream, but the construction of a number of major hydro-electric projects south of the border spelled the end of salmon for the Kettle. However, the river is still a good fishing river. In fact it is a great fishing river with plenty of small rainbow that seem to love to chase after flies. The fish are so easily caught here that fly anglers tell stories of having to be careful on the backcast, lest the fly get too close to the water and snagged by an eager rainbow.

The best fishing in the river happens between Rock Creek and Midway right before and right after spring runoff. The trout seem to really take to single salmon eggs or maggots, although there is a bait ban on the river above Cascade Falls from April 1 to October 31. During these times, spincasters should use try small spoons and spinners. Fly anglers should try a nymph or a dry Royal Coachman. Outside of the falls, there are few hazards to worry anglers if they wish to float the river. Private property in this area does limit shore access somewhat.

However, north of Westbridge and the Christian Valley, the river is much smaller and fishing from shore or wading is the preferred method. Small spinners and spoons as well as the standard trout flies all work in this area. To work the upper Kettle effectively, you need to sneak up on holes to avoid being detected. Work every pocket, pool or seam no matter the size. Some of the biggest fish are hiding in the most unlikely places.

The river also holds lots of mountain whitefish. Similar to trout, they feed mainly on insects, but are much more aggressive and less spooky than trout. Whitefish will readily strike spinners, spoons or shiny lures and can be taken on light fly-fishing gear. In the rivers, bottom fishing with worms or beadhead nymph patterns can be effective. Spincasters can also work maggots or single salmon eggs.

Bass were introduced into Christina Lake in 1901, and can be found in the Kettle River below Cascade Falls. They remain fairly small and not many anglers bother fishing for them. As always, the bass hang around cover such as a sunken log, lily pad or the weeds that line this stretch of the river. They do not move much from their hiding place so you have to get you plug or fly right in close to these types of cover. Larger fish tend to hold in deeper water and rarely come out during the day.

Other uncommon fish found in the river include brook trout and the highly prized brown trout. Fly fishing is the preferred method of finding these very elusive fish (at least on this river). Walleye, which come up the river from Roosevelt Lake in the States, can also be found in the lower reaches. Try casting anything that looks like a minnow or a jig when targeting these predatory fish.

There are catch and release restrictions on certain sections of the river.

Species	
Bass	Rainbow Trout
Brook Trout	Walleye
Brown Trout	Whitefish

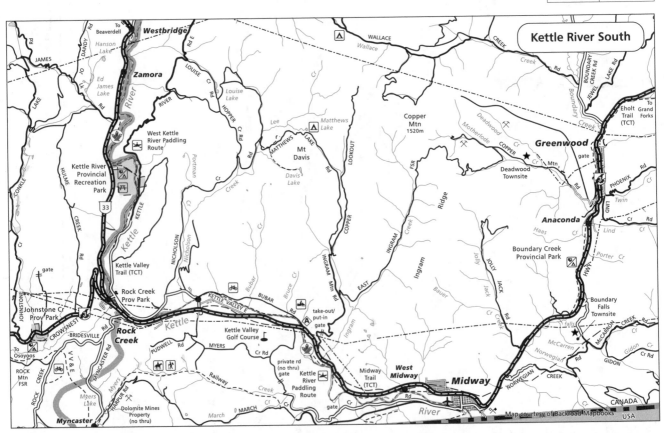

Map courtesy of Backroad Mapbooks

Kettle River

Kettle River (North)
Location: North of Rock Creek
Stream Length: 238 km (145 mi)
Geographic: 118° 55'00"Lon - W 49° 13'00"Lat - N

8 Region

Directions

The upper reaches of the Kettle can be accessed along the Christian Valley Road and Kettle River Forest Service Road north of Westbridge. Outside of a few parcels of private property off the Christian Valley Road, this stretch of river is very easy to access. There are numerous recreation sites and roadside pull offs next to the river.

South of Westbridge, Highway 33 follows the river south to Rock Creek, where the Crowsnest Highway (Highway 3) takes over until Midway. In addition to highway bridges, a popular access point is at the Kettle River Provincial Park. The Kettle Valley Railway/Trans Canada Trail also provides great access to otherwise unapproachable sections of the river.

At Midway, the river flows south across the border. It crosses back into BC near Grand Forks, where it is again accessed by the Crowsnest, as well as dozens of other roads in and around town. The Crowsnest Highway and the Boundary Trail/Trans Canada Trail follow the Kettle River Valley for about 25 km (15 miles) to the junction of Highway 395, where the river heads south again, and this time for good. Drift fishing is common here, but anglers must be wary to portage around the Kettle Canyon.

Facilities

The Kettle Valley Railway section of the **Trans Canada Trail** parallels the river for nearly 100 km. This popular multi-use trail follows an old railgrade through the many small communities along the river. The trail also provides good access to the river in an area that is mostly privately owned.

There are also plenty of places to stay along the river, from roadside motels to campgrounds to quaint little bed and breakfast locations. One of the most popular campgrounds is the **Kettle River Provincial Park**, with 87 vehicle accessible campsites and good access to the river.

Further upstream there are several recreation sites. From south to north they are: **Canyon Flats** (3 RV friendly sites and beach access); **Canyon Creek** (3 forested sites and beach access); **Kettle Bench** (4 sites and beach access); **Kettle Canyon** (a day use site near a waterfall); **State Creek** (10 RV friendly sites); Damfino Creek (2 RV friendly sites); **Sandy Bend** (3 semi open sites and beach access), **Kettle River Crossing** (2 RV friendly, open sites), **Mohr Creek** (3 sites rather close to the road), **Winnifred Falls** (8 forested sites next to a small waterfall) and **Bruer Creek** (4 sites rather close to the road). There sheer number of these sites attests to the popularity of the river. It also makes it easier to find a site all to your own. For more details on these and other activities in the area, be sure to pick up a copy of the Backroad Mapbook for the Kamloops Okanagan region.

Species	
Bass	Rainbow Trout
Brook Trout	Walleye
Brown Trout	Whitefish

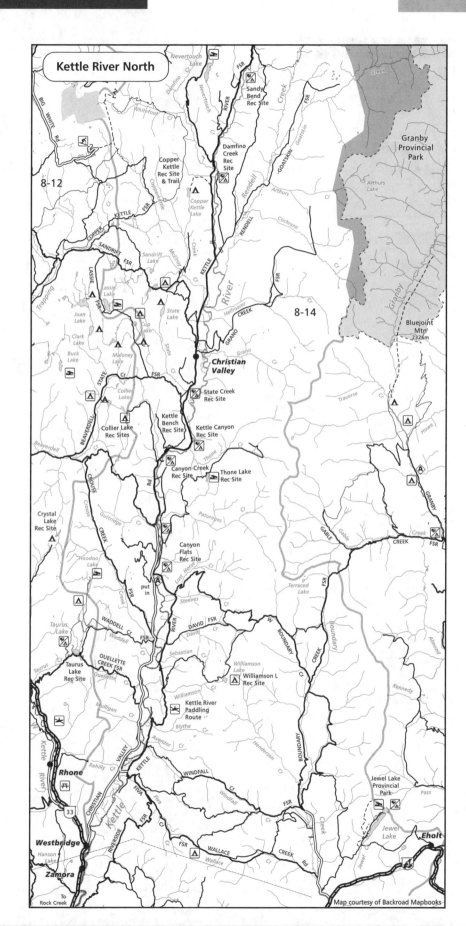

Location: Between Balfour and Argenta
Elevation: 532 m (1,745 ft)
Surface Area: 41,700 ha (103,000 ac)
Mean Depth: 122 m (335 ft)
Way Point: 116° 53' 00" Lon - W 49° 54' 00" Lat - N

Kootenay Lake - North

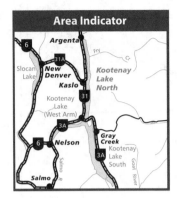

Area Indicator

Species
Bull Trout
Burbot
Kokanee
Rainbow Trout
Whitefish

Directions

With good road access along most of the North Arm, there are several places to access this big stretch of lake. Balfour, Kaslo, Kootenay Bay, Riondel and Argenta all provide good boat launches, while marinas are usually found nearby to the communities around the lake.

Facilities

The North Arm is a semi-developed portion of Kootenay Lake offering a number of facilities and resorts for visitors to enjoy. Kaslo is the biggest centre and can meet almost all the needs of travellers. Visitors can also visit one of the many provincial parks or recreation sites located along the North Arm. The parks include the boat accessible **Campbell Bay & Coffee Creek** sites, as well as the **Davis Creek** and **Lost Ledge** sites that can be accessed by vehicle. The recreation sites include the ever popular **Garland Bay** site as well as the boat accessible **Pebble Beach** site.

The *Kootenay Rockies Backroad Mapbook* describes these sites and countless other recreational opportunities in the area in detail. It is the perfect companion for the *Fishing Mapbook* Series.

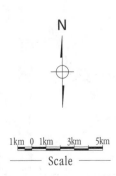

N

Scale
1km 0 1km   3km   5km

Fishing

Kootenay Lake is one of the most famous fishing lakes in the entire province. It is home to the Gerrard strain of rainbow trout, which are the world's largest strain of rainbow. In fact, some of the world's largest rainbow ever caught came from Kootenay Lake, and catches over 18 kg (40 lbs) have been recorded. The lake also holds some extremely large bull trout, good numbers of kokanee, burbot and Rocky Mountain whitefish.

The North Arm is currently regarded as the hot spot for almost all fishing in Kootenay Lake. While you can find good success throughout the entire lake, the northern reaches seem to be providing the most consistent results. Try working near the drop offs at creek mouths or close to the numerous rocky cliff faces.

Rainbow are the most sought after species by anglers, due mainly to the large sizes that commonly top 4.5 kg (10 lbs). The big fish are challenging to catch due to the great depths of the lake; therefore, the best time to fish for these big trout is in the winter when they are found closer to the surface. Try trolling plugs, apex lures or skimming bucktails across the surface. During summer you will have to go deep to find the trout. The best way to do this is by using a downrigger or planer board and trolling in the 10-30 m (30-100 ft) range using a plug or flasher with hootchie. Some popular lures include Lyman, Tomic or J plugs, Apex or Gibbs Hockey Stick lures as well as Coyote, Gypsy, Quick Silver or Road Runner spoons. Trolling a streamer fly pattern that imitates baitfish near the surface will often entice strikes from smaller trout and the odd kokanee throughout the year.

Bull trout are the other big resident fish and can reach 9.5 kg (20 lbs) on occasion. Similar to rainbow, you can catch them by trolling plugs, spoons or Flatfish. They usually hold deeper than the rainbow and the addition of a flasher helps attract the fish. Behind the flasher you can troll Army Truck or Tiger Prawn hoochies, Lyman or Tomic plugs, Whitefish, Wabler or Gader spoons as well as Apex or Hockey Stick lures. They also take bucktails in the winter. An exciting alternative is catching one from shore near larger creek mouths using a worm ball or jig.

Kokanee have benefited from the fertilization program in the 1990's. The fishing is reported to be quite good for generally small fish. The most effective set up is a lake troll with Wedding Band, Dick Nite, Kokanee King or Spin-n-Glo and bait (worm or maggot) trolled slowly in an S pattern. Vary the speed and depth (between 5-25 m/15-80 ft) to entice the kokanee to bite. Lighter tackle and flies provide a bit more challenge and excitement when fishing for kokanee.

Be sure to check the regulations before heading out. There are special restrictions and limits in place that include the north end of the lake being closed from February through June to protect both spawning Gerrard trout.

Kootenay Lake - South

Location: Between Creston and Balfour
Elevation: 532 m (1,745 ft)
Surface Area: 41,700 ha (103,000 ac)
Mean Depth: 122 m (335 ft)
Way Point: 116° 48'00"Lon - W 49° 30'00"Lon - N

Region 4

Fishing

This southern portion of Kootenay Lake stretches from Balfour in the north all the way south to Creston in the south. This stretch of water can provide quality fishing opportunities throughout the year. In addition to the Gerrard strain of rainbow trout, bull trout, kokanee, burbot and Rocky Mountain whitefish, this stretch of water also offers largemouth bass and cutthroat trout.

The largemouth bass are usually found in the shallower shoreline areas. In particular, the shallows around Coot Bay and Kuskanook at the south end are known hot spots. The bass prefer warm water, and become more active as the lake warms in these areas. Jigging or casting weedless lures into the weeds can reveal some nice sized bass. Poppers and other top water lures can be an exciting alternative during overcast or low light periods.

For some reason cutthroat trout are really only found in the southern portion of the lake. Although not in abundant numbers, they can be caught on streamer flies or with spinners resembling baitfish near a few of the inflows of creek mouths.

Anglers targeting the bigger rainbow trout will find Crawford Bay is a good location for finding these large Gerrards. The shelter of the bay and the deep water combine to make a good holding area for the big fish. Large bull trout can also be found in the bay, as well as largemouth bass in the shallower shoreline sections.

Across the lake, Queens Bay is also a known hot spot for big trout as well as well as those feisty kokanee. During the winter, skimming bucktails on the surface can result in some big hits. During the warmer summer, most anglers turn their attention the kokanee. Using a lake troll or streamer fly can attract both kokanee and smaller trout at this time.

The remaining portion of the southern part of the lake often provides consistent action for trout and kokanee. However wind and other weather patterns can hinder results. In addition to paying attention to the weather, be sure to check the regulations before heading out.

Directions

Access to the southern portion of Kootenay Lake is mainly via Highway 3A between Crawford Bay and Creston. You will find boat launches at Kootenay Bay near the ferry landing, Crawford Bay, Lockhart Beach Park, Boswell and Kuskanook. The western side of the lake is very remote and is best accessed by boat.

Facilities

The eastern portion of this part of Kootenay Lake is well developed and easily accessed by Highway 3A. As a result, there are a number of resorts, bed and breakfasts and other accommodations for visitors to enjoy including a number of. Alternatively, visitors can camp at one of the many provincial parks or recreation sites in the region. **Drewry Point** and **Midge Creek Provincial Parks** rest on the quieter west side of the lake while Pilot Bay Provincial Park is found near Crawford Bay. These boat accessible sites offer tenting areas and mooring buoys. The **Next Creek** and **Tyee Creek Recreation Sites** are also accessed by boat. Highway travellers can camp at **Lockhart Creek Provincial Park**, while nearby **Lockhart Beach Provincial Park** offers a nice boat launch.

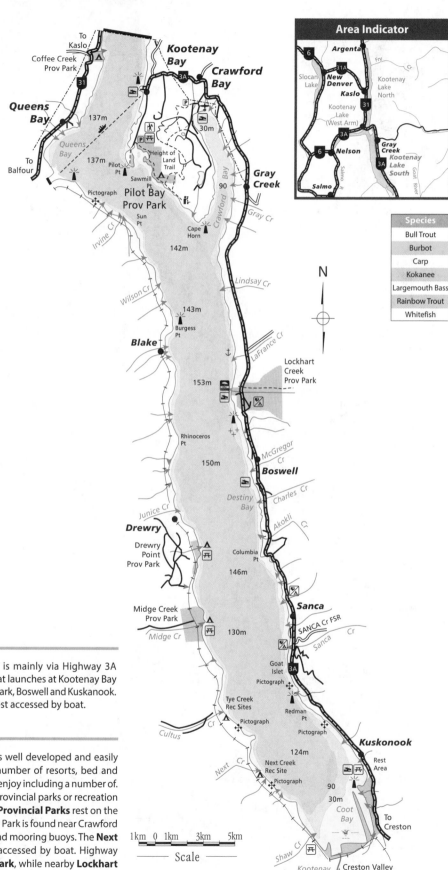

Species: Bull Trout, Burbot, Carp, Kokanee, Largemouth Bass, Rainbow Trout, Whitefish

Region 4

Location: Between Nelson and Balfour
Elevation: 532 m (1,745 ft)
Surface Area: 41,700 ha (103,000 ac)
Mean Depth: 122 m (335 ft)
Way Point: 117° 1'00" Lon - W 49° 36'00" Lat - N

Kootenay Lake - West

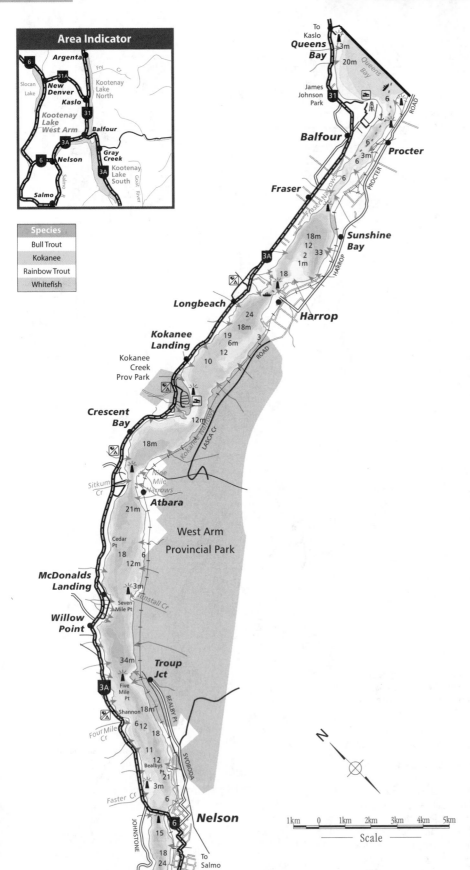

Fishing

The West Arm portion of Kootenay Lake is best known for its kokanee fishing, although anglers can have good success for other sportfish such as rainbow trout, bull trout and in particular whitefish. Fly-fishing has recently become a popular pastime in the West Arm, especially in the narrows around Balfour. Fly anglers can enjoy success in the spring well into summer, with dry fly-fishing the best form June through to the fall. Mosquito patterns, Adams, mayfly emergers and dries can all produce results. A good wet fly selection includes the Woolly Bugger, Carey Special, Muddler Minnow or other minnow type imitation fly.

As with almost all parts of Kootenay Lake, the best way to hook into big fish is to troll. Troll your baits and flies near anomalies in the lake depth, like off the shoal area near Sunshine Bay. Working near these structured areas are your best bet to finding good numbers of trout. For kokanee, a slow troll in the 5- 25 m (16-82 ft) range will produce the best results.

Anglers looking to have a little fun should try fly-fishing or spincasting for whitefish in the shallows of the West Arm. Fishing for these aggressive feeders can be a lot of fun at times, especially if you can get them on the fly.

Directions

The two main access points to the busy West Arm of Kootenay Lake is from the city of Nelson or Balfour. Both centres have marinas available with boat mooring and launching facilities. Another convenient access point is from Kokanee Creek Provincial Park, which is accessible off Highway 3A between Balfour and Nelson.

Facilities

The West Arm of Kootenay Lake is the most developed area of Kootenay Lake. The lake is easy to access and has a well maintained but windy highway travelling along the northern shore. The towns of Nelson and Balfour have plenty to offer visitors, including accommodations and all necessary supplies. The West Arm is also home to numerous resorts, bed and breakfasts and other facilities.

For campers, **Kokanee Creek Provincial Park** has plenty to offer. This full service park has 168 vehicles/tent campsites at two sites (Redfish and Sandspit) as well as a boat launch, beach, outhouses, picnic tables, playground and running water. The main attraction to the park is its spawning channels, where visitors can view the spectacular display of spawning kokanee starting in late August. Reservations are recommended if you plan to camp at the park during the summer months. For reservations call (800) 689-9025 or visit www.discovercamping.ca.

Kump Lake

Location: 34 km (21 mi) northwest of Princeton
Elevation: 1,131 m (3,711 ft)
Surface Area: 17 ha (42ac)
Mean Depth: 8.4 m (28 ft)
Max Depth: 21 m (69 ft)
Way Point: 120° 38' 00" Lon - W 49° 44' 00" Lat - N

Fishing

Managed as a trophy fly-fishing lake, fishing can be good at times for rainbow trout that can reach some decent sizes. It is reported that the trout regularly reach 1 kg (2 lb) in size. The Freshwater Fisheries Society of BC also stocks the lake on occasion to help maintain the fishery, which is best tackled in the spring or fall.

Fly anglers will find some prominent hatches on this lake. The season begins in June (sometimes even late May), with the chironomid hatch. Try fishing a dark coloured chironomid pattern in a deep red or a black. Bloodworm patterns also work well. It is best to try your luck near the small creek inlet on the west side or off the predominant shoal area on the east side of the main part of the lake. The smaller eastern corner is not known to produce many strikes but when the waters are cool in early spring anything can happen.

The next major hatch to occur is the mayfly hatch, which overlaps the chironomids. Mature mayfly nymphs actively swim to the surface, hatch into adults, and fly off to mate. These hatches occur over shoal and drop off areas, and provide the first good dry fly-fishing of the season. Trout actively feed on the emerging adults as they struggle in the surface film and as fully emerged adults floating on the surface. Watch for swallows or gulls actively feeding on a hatch; if you see birds feeding in the air, you know that the fish are doing the same beneath the surface.

The best dry fly-fishing occurs during the Caddis hatch, which starts slightly later in summer. Caddis flies emerge from the water, and then sit on the surface for some time while they wait for their wings to dry. Trout will often try and submerge the flies by splashing, or even leaping out of the water onto the fly. It is quite common for an inexperienced angler to yank on the line to set the hook, only to find there is no fish attached.

Due to the special management status of Kump Lake, there are unique restrictions on such as only fly-fishing is permitted. Be sure to consult the regulations before heading out.

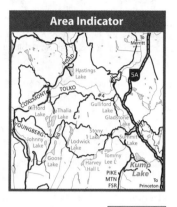

Area Indicator

Species

Rainbow Trout

Kump Lake			
Fish Stocking Data			
Year	Species	Number	Life Stage
2013	Rainbow Trout	2,000	Fry
2012	Rainbow Trout	2,000	Fry
2011	Rainbow Trout	2,000	Fry

Directions

Kump Lake can be reached by following Highway 5A north from Princeton to the Pike Mountain Forest Service Road. Take the forest service road west from the highway and continue straight at the 2 km junction, following the sign to Kump Lake. About the same distance later, a side road leads down to the recreation site and main access point to the lake. The branch road can be a bit rough and may require a 4wd vehicle.

Facilities

The **Kump Lake Recreation Site** is found in the **Pike Mountain Recreation Area.** Popular with everyone from anglers and hunters to campers and ATVers this site can be busy. However, the rough road access does limit larger units. At the lake, visitors will find space for about 7 groups between the two separate sites. There is also a cartop boat launch at the northern site.

Other Options

Gladstone and Guilford Lakes are a couple of the more easily accessed lakes in the Pike Mountain Recreation Area. Both lakes are found just off Highway 5A to the north of Kump. Anglers will find rustic launching sites along with decent fishing opportunities for rainbow trout.

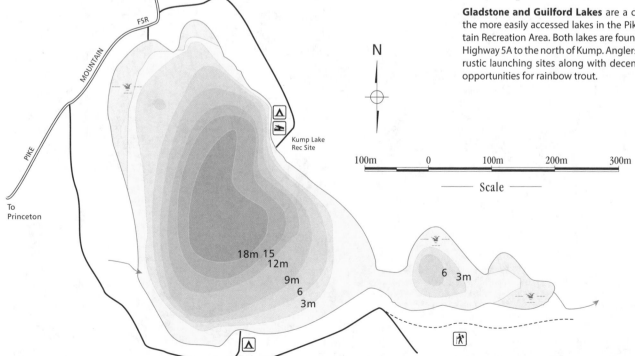

Fishing

It boggles the mind that in the 1970s, it was proposed that the Kootenay be diverted into Columbia River near the headwaters of both rivers. This would have destroyed some great fishing habitat that this river has to offer. Fortunately, it never happened, and the Kootenay lives on as one of the best fishing rivers in the region.

Like the Columbia, though, the Kootenay is no longer the river it once was, with nine dams on the river. The Kootenay flows south out of the province (becoming the Kootenai), but it re-enters BC near Creston, where it forms Kootenay Lake, the largest natural lake in the province. 64 km (38.5 miles) north, the west arm of Kootenay Lake narrows and becomes the Kootenay River again, flowing past Nelson and into the Columbia River near Castlegar.

Needless to say, the Kootenay is one of the largest rivers in BC. It is a freestone river with good populations of bull, cutthroat and rainbow trout. The river also holds burbot, kokanee, whitefish and bass. There are even some big sturgeon in the river, but there is no fishery for them.

Most of the river has long, featureless flat sections with lots of fast moving side channels and braids. It is worth fishing, if only for the scenery and wildlife. Because of the river's size, fishing is best done from drift boats. Flies (dry and streamers) or lures and spinners that represent minnows all work well.

The river is best fished before spring run-off begins. This is usually from April to late May during which the river experiences an amazing caddis hatch. At this time, it is common to see the shallows boiling with rising cutthroat, gorging themselves on the caddis. When the cutts get into a feeding frenzy like this, it rarely matters what you toss at them, as long as it floats and looks sorta edible. Elk or deer hair caddis, or Tom Thumbs are most frequently used at these times.

The skwala stone fly hatches also provide good top water fishing for cutthroat and rainbow. By the end of May, though, the river is running high and dirty for a couple of months due to spring run off. It is possible to get back on in July, but best wait until August. Fishing remains good through to October. The summer and fall see a lot of terrestrials, namely grasshoppers and winged ants that love to land in the river. Once the river clears up again in August, try fishing with a grasshopper or ant pattern. Spincasters can do well suspending these flies off a bobber.

Many people visit the river in spring to fish for bull trout. Try using a small streamer pattern or anything that imitates a small minnow such as small, silver coloured spoons. Nymph patterns also work. Because the water levels are so low, and the water is so clear, it is possible to sight fish for the bull trout.

While the western section of the river is arguably a more remote and more scenic experience, the biggest fish are found in the eastern section of the river. North and east of Canal Flats, the river is fast-flowing and murky, but has some excellent fishing holes. South of Canal Flats, the river is slower moving and warmer, with easy access.

The section between Nelson and Castlegar offers some great fishing. One of the most popular places to fish is the Slocan Pool, where the Slocan River flows into the Kootenay. Back in the early days of the twentieth century, the Slocan Pool was known for its amazing salmon fishing. The last salmon ever caught here was in 1935. These days, this popular hole has both walleye and rainbow trout to 2.5 kg (5 lbs). The fish get bigger the closer you get to the confluence with the Columbia. Another popular fishing area is the section right below the Brilliant Dam near Castlegar.

Continued >>

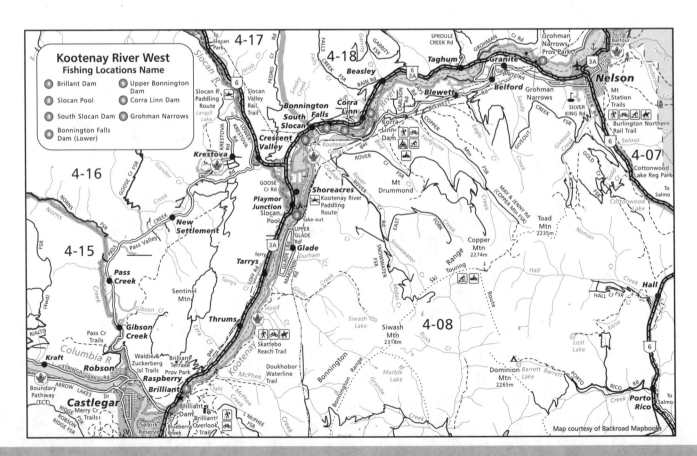

Kootenay River - East

Kootenay River East
Location: Between Kootenay National Park & Cranbrook
Geographic: 115° 38' 00" Lon - W 49° 36' 00" Lat - N

4 Region

Fishing

Continued

Perhaps the quietest stretch of water is that below Kootenay Lake around Creston. This slow meandering stream does not look like much, but bass anglers know better. There are some big largemouth bass that like to hide in the weeds that line the river. Sunfish and other pan fish are also easily found. The trick here is more about accessing the river due to the marshy shoreline and private property in the area. There are, however, several dyke trails as well as the Highway 3 bridge to fish from.

The headwaters of the Kootenay River are found in the national park. Remember that a special license is needed to fish these waters. The season begins June 15 and runs to October 31 during which you will find some great fishing for rainbow and brook trout that can get to 35 cm (14 inches) or so. There is a minimum size restriction of 30 cm (12 inches) for any fish kept from this section of the river.

Always check the regulations before heading out. The Kootenay is a big river, and the regulations for one section can be completely different than the rest of the river.

Directions

The Kootenay River is accessed from many, many locations. It is followed by major highways for much of its route. In the west, Highway 3A links Castlegar with Nelson, while south of Kootenay Lake the river passes through Creston. The eastern section of the river is less populated, but is rarely inaccessible by road. It is paralleled at times by Highways 3, 93 and 95 as well as several logging roads. Few big centres actually rest next to the part of the big river.

Facilities

The Kootenay River has its headwaters in **Kootenay National Park**. Depending where you are planning on accessing the river from, there are cities, parks, or recreation sites on or near the river. In the east there are many areas to camp nearby including **Wasa Lake Provincial Park, Kootenay White, Horseshoe Rapids** and **Cross River Canyon Recreation Sites.** In the west, you are best to look for private campgrounds or motels around Castlegar and Nelson.

Species
Bull Trout
Burbot
Cutthroat Trout
Kokanee
Largemouth Bass
Rainbow Trout
Whitefish

Kootenay River (East) Fish Stocking Data			
Year	Species	Number	Life Stage
2006	Kokanee	412,058	Egg
2005	Rainbow Trout	20,000	Fall Fry

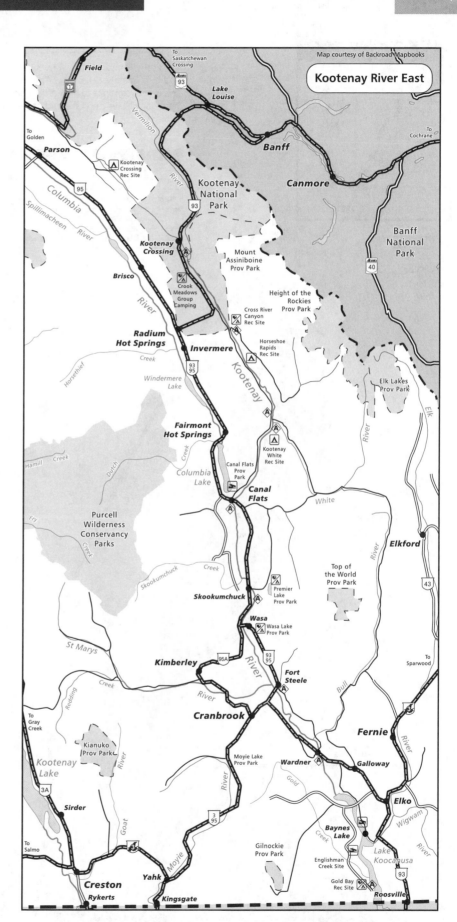

Location: 20 km (12 mi) north of Princeton
Elevation: 811 m (2,661 ft)
Surface Area: 27 ha (67 ac)
Mean Depth: 10 m (33 ft)
Max Depth: 21 m (69 ft)
Way Point: 120° 35' 00" Lon - W 49° 37' 00" Lat - N

Laird Lake

Directions

Laird Lake is easily found off the west side of Highway 5A, approximately 22 km (14 mi) north of Princeton. It is best to continue to the north end of the lake where a small launching site and parking area can be found.

Laird Lake			
Fish Stocking Data			
Year	Species	Number	Life Stage
2013	Rainbow Trout	4,000	Yearling
2012	Rainbow Trout	4,000	Yearling
2011	Rainbow Trout	4,000	Yearling

Fishing

Part of the series of headwater lakes along Allison Lake, fishing can be pretty good in Laird Lake despite the easy access off of Highway 5A. Anglers can attribute the steady fishing to the fact the Freshwater Fisheries Society of BC uses some of the licensing money to help stock the lake annually with rainbow trout. There are also a few small brook trout roaming the lake.

Highway 5A passes close by the lake, and the eastern shores of the lake are mostly accessible from the highway. Although it is a bit steep and traffic whizzes by, there are certainly some good areas to test your luck from shore.

Trolling is a popular angling method on the lake and is reported to be surprisingly productive. Lake trolls, small spinners and searching pattern flies all seem to work on the lake. It is best to work the areas just off the drop offs during cooler periods and work deeper later in the summer. Cast from the deep water towards the shoals, retrieving across the drop off. Trout are opportunists, and would much rather grab something coming towards them than have to chase something heading the other way. Early in the year, try Flatfish type lures in patterns of silver, gold, black and silver and frog patterns. Dick Nite, Panther Martin and Roostertail spoons in smaller sizes are also good bets.

Although some fly anglers may find fishing rather slow, there are an ardent few that will find the lake very rewarding on the fly. If fly-fishing, you should concentrate your efforts around the two predominant shoals located near the middle of the lake. The clear water with a weedy bottom aids the heavy chironomid hatches during spring. If you can find the right depth and colour of chironomids the trout are honing in on, you could be well rewarded. Later in the spring, it is best to switch to nymph fly patterns.

Shoreline fishers can try fishing from the boat launch at the northwest end of the lake. It is weedy close to shore, but fishing from here, especially fly-fishing, is quite productive. However, getting out onto the lake, with a small boat or float tube will usually prove more productive, as you can cover more water.

Facilities

A small, cartop boat launch and parking area is found at the northwest end of the lake, off the side of the highway. Visitors interested in staying overnight in the area can continue north to the campsite at **Allison Lake Provincial Park** or head south and take advantage of the motels and services found in Princeton.

Other Options

There are several decent fishing alternatives in the area, including **McCaffrey Lake, Dry Lake** and **Allison Lake**. One lake in particular, **Borgeson Lake**, is found about 5 km (3 mi) north of Laird Lake along Highway 5A. The small lake hosts a small picnic area and offers fishing opportunities for rainbow trout and brook trout.

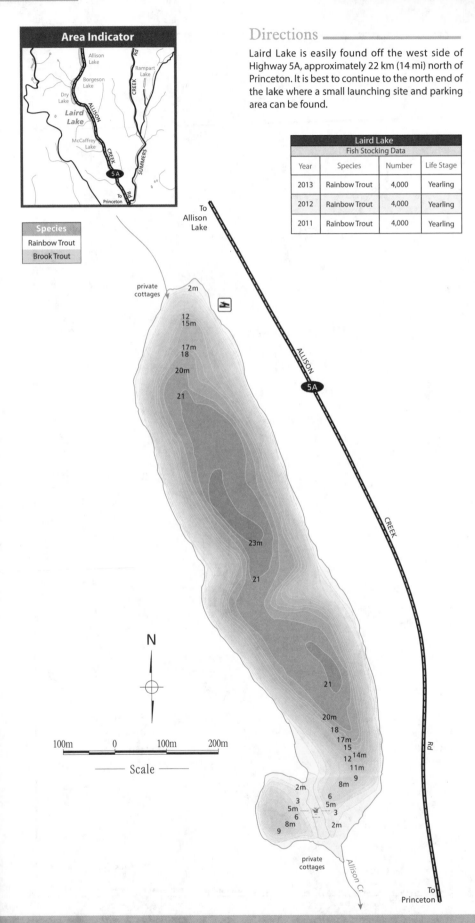

Area Indicator

Allison Lake
Rampart Lake
Borgeson Lake
Dry Lake
Laird Lake
McCaffrey Lake
CREEK
ALLISON Rd
SUMMERS
CREEK
5A
To Princeton

Species
Rainbow Trout
Brook Trout

To Allison Lake

private cottages
2m
12
15m
17m
18
20m
21

ALLISON
5A

23m
21

N

100m   0   100m   200m
— Scale —

21
20m
18
17m
15
12 14m
11m
9
8m
2m
6
3   5m
5m   6   3
8m   2m
9

private cottages
Allison Cr

CREEK
Rd
To Princeton

Ladyslipper Lake

Location: 32 km (20 mi) southwest of Keremeos
Elevation: 2,199 m (7,214 ft)
Surface Area: 27 ha (67 ac)
Mean Depth: 7.6 m (25 ft)
Max Depth: 20 m (66 ft)
Way Point: 120° 11' 40" Lon - W 49° 02' 46" Lat - N

Fishing

Ladyslipper Lake is arguably the best in a series of great fishing lakes in Cathedral Provincial Park. It is a remote hike-in lake that sees very little pressure over the course of a season. Combine that with the fact that it is a high-elevation lake, with a shortened ice off season, means you have a lot of ravenous cutthroat. Add in the spectacular setting, the turquoise coloured lakes and lack of crowds and you have all the ingredients for a truly delightful fishing experience.

The lake has been stocked in the past with rainbow, but they are rarely, if ever, found anymore. Instead, expect plenty of small, feisty cutthroat that will go after most anything you cast. Fly-fishing is the preferred method of fishing up here. Not that you can't spincast, it's just that fly anglers are usually more willing to put the effort in to reach these high alpine lakes. Anglers will want to use light line, so as not to scare the fish.

The lake is found in the sub-alpine, and while there are trees around most of the lake, there are also large open areas, perfect for fly casting. The trouble is that the large open areas means the fish can be quite jumpy. Since the main way to fish here is from the shore (unless you go through the effort to carry a float tube), you want to do whatever you can to keep the fish from being spooked. Approach the shore slowly, keeping an eye out for any movement beneath the water's surface.

Other Options

There are three other lakes in the area, **Quiniscoe, Lake of the Woods** and **Pyramid**, which all offer similar fishing as Ladyslipper. Quiniscoe is the closes to the Cathedral Lake Lodge, and is the heaviest fish, although that isn't saying much.

Directions

Ladyslipper is a remote, hike-in lake in Cathedral Provincial Park. The Ashnola Road leaves Highway 3, 3 km (1.8 miles) west of the Highway 3/3A junction at the west end of Keremeos. Follow this road for 25 km (15 miles) to the Lakeview Trailhead. From here, it is a 16 km (9.8 mile) hike into Cathedral's Core area. However, the Cathedral Lakes Resort offers a shuttle service from the trailhead to the core area for guests of the lodge and campers alike. Transportation is complimentary for lodge guests, but campers will have to pay a (healthy) fee.

Once you've made it to the park's core area, it is still a couple kilometres to hike into Ladyslipper Lake. Take the Centennial Trail east to the junction with the Ladyslipper Trail, which heads south. The trail takes you to the eastern shores of the lake.

Facilities

There is camping in the core area of Cathedral Lakes Provincial Park. **Quiniscoe Lake** has 30 tenting sites, **Lake of the Woods** has 28 sites that are more open and less shaded than Quiniscoe, and **Pyramid Lake** has 12 sites.

For people looking for a slightly more pampered experience, the **Cathedral Lakes Resort** is found at 2,000 m (6800 ft) above sea level, making it the country's highest full-service resort, with cabins and rooms in the lodge. There's even a hot tub.

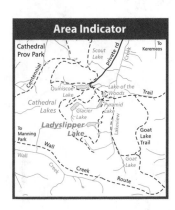

Area Indicator

Species
Cutthroat Trout
Rainbow Trout

N

50m   0   50m   100m   150m   200m

Scale

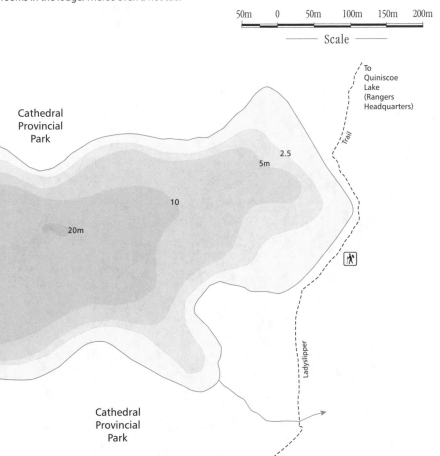

To Quiniscoe Lake (Rangers Headquarters)

Cathedral Provincial Park

Cathedral Provincial Park

Ladyslipper Trail

2.5
5m
10
20m

© Backroad Mapbooks

Region 4

Location: 8 km (5 mi) northwest of Invermere
Elevation: 965 m (3,166 ft)
Surface Area: 18 ha (44 ac)
Mean Depth: 4.1 m (13 ft)
Max Depth: 8.2 m (27 ft)
Way Point: 116° 07′ 00″ Lon - W 50° 32′ 00″ Lat - N

Lake Enid

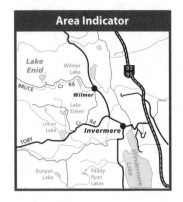

Area Indicator

Species

Rainbow Trout

Brook Trout

Lake End Fish Stocking Data			
Year	Species	Number	Life Stage
2013	Rainbow Trout	5,250	Yearling/ Catchable
2012	Rainbow Trout	5,250	Catchable
2011	Rainbow Trout	5,250	Yearling/ Catchable

Fishing

Lake Enid is a popular year round fishing destination. The lake is stocked annually with rainbow trout and holds a good population of nice sized brook trout. Ice anglers will find the brookies can be quite aggressive during the winter months, while the open water season can be just as rewarding. The trout can get quite large, but finding the bigger fish is often a challenge, as they can be very discriminating about what they eat.

It is wise to examine the bottom structure of this lake, as it is unique and can give big clues to where to find fish in the lake. The first area that sticks out is the prominent underwater point located in the southeastern end of the lake. Using a boat or a float tube, drop anchor just off this point and work the transition zone retrieving from the shallow water towards the deep water. An obvious fallback pattern is a scud, as the lake has plenty of them. A second place that should be tried is a point extending from the eastern shore, found just north of the other underwater point. A third point juts south from the northwestern side of the lake, but does not feature prominent drop offs.

The lake is a popular ice fishing destination. One of the biggest mistakes made by beginner ice anglers is to fish too deep. When snow covers the ice, it blocks the light from reaching the plants, which die. Not only do the plants no longer produce oxygen, the rotting vegetation produces other gases that sink to the bottom of the lake, making it difficult for the fish to inhabit the depths. What oxygen remains in the water tends to be up near the ice. As a result, the brook trout hang out in shallow water, often as shallow as 1–3 m (3–10 ft).

Right after ice-off, the top of the water will be a cruising zone for both brook trout and rainbow trout as they awaken from their winter torpor and begin feeding. Before the insects start to hatch, try using an attractor like a Woolly Bugger, or a terrestrial pattern on the top of the water.

Directions

You can find this small lake just outside of the town of Invermere. To reach the lake, take the Wilmer Road north from town to the Bruce Creek Forest Service Road. Follow the forest road west for about 5 km (3.1 mi) and look for the access rough road off the north side of the road. You can park your vehicle at the forest recreation campsite at the lake.

Facilities

The recreation site at Lake Enid is a day-use only site equipped with picnic tables and a small dock. If you would like a change of pace from the fishing, you can also enjoy the hiking/biking trail around the lake or relax at the small beach area. Of course the trail is used by shore anglers too.

Other Options

There are a couple nearby lakes that offer good fishing alternatives. **Wilmer Lake** to the east is stocked regularly with brook trout and rainbow trout, while **Lillian Lake** to the south also provides fishing opportunities for both species. The only downfall of these lakes is that they are close to Invermere and they receive significant angling pressure throughout the season.

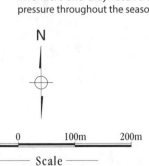

8m   6
      5m   3
              2m

dock
Lake Enid
Rec Site

To Bruce Creek FSR

N

100m   0   100m   200m
Scale

Lake Magog

Location: 48 km (30 mi) northeast of Radium Hot Springs
Elevation: 2,145 m (7,037 ft)
Surface Area: 105 ha (261 ac)
Mean Depth: 20 m (66 ft)
Max Depth: 51 m (167 ft)
Way Point: 115° 37' 00" Lon - W 50° 54' 00" Lat - N

Region 4

Fishing

Set at the base of Mount Assiniboine, Lake Magog is one of the most beautiful lakes in the country. From a purely scenic point of view, there are few lakes in the country that are as picturesque.

But it's not just spectacular scenery that attracts people to the area. Despite the high elevation, Lake Magog produces well for resident cutthroat trout that have been know to grow to 3 kg (6.5 lbs) in size. The average size of cutthroat in the lake is around 35-45 cm (14-16 in) and they are often quite active during the evenings in the summer. The high elevation of this lake limits the fishing season to about three months and as a result, the trout are usually aggressive feeders throughout the open water season.

Shore fishing is possible at Lake Magog, although a floatation device would definitely improve results. Spincasters will find success with small spinners and spoons, while fly anglers should try attractor type patterns. The larger cutthroat are tough to fool, although a well presented fly or lure can produce a trophy sized fish on occasion. Some good flies to take to the lake are Woolly Buggers, streamers and caddis patterns. The lively action of all three flies can make quite a stir at times.

Other Options

Sunburst and **Cerulean Lakes** are two picturesque lakes that provide a good nearby alternative to Lake Magog. Both lakes are accessible by trail north of Lake Magog and lie in a fabulous Rocky Mountain basin. Cerulean Lake is designated a catch and release lake and provides good fishing for nice sized rainbow trout and cutthroat trout. Sunburst Lake is considered as one of the premier fly-fishing lakes in the Rocky Mountains and produces well for good sized cutthroat trout. Within the park, Rock Isle, Larix and Grizzly Lakes are all closed to angling.

Directions

Lake Magog is a remote alpine lake that lies within the gorgeous confines of Mount Assiniboine Provincial Park. The main access to Lake Magog is by trail. There are several possible routes in, but the Bryant Creek Trail starting at the south end of Spray Lakes Reservoir in Alberta is the most popular route in. The challenging trail treks through the Rocky Mountains, passing over the Assiniboine Pass before descending to Lake Magog.

From British Columbia two main trail routes traverse to the lake. One of the more popular routes is via the Simpson River/Surprise Creek Trail that starts off Highway 93 in Kootenay Nation Park. This route treks over the Ferro Pass then continues east towards Lake Magog and other Mount Assiniboine lakes. The other route is the Mitchell River Trail, which passes by Cerulean Lake and Sunburst Lake before reaching Lake Magog.

Facilities

Mount Assiniboine Provincial Park is a scenic Rocky Mountain wilderness park that is a well known hiking and backpacking destination. There are several backcountry campsites throughout the area, including a site on Lake Magog. For those who prefer a roof over their head, there are four cabins and the ever popular **Mount Assiniboine Lodge**. For cabin or lodge reservations call (403) 678-2883. For campsite reservations visit www.discovercamping.ca.

Area Indicator

Goat Lake

Spray

BC   Og Lake

ALBERTA

River

Bryant

Creek

Trail

Lake Magog

Marvel Lake

Spray Lake

Species

Cutthroat Trout

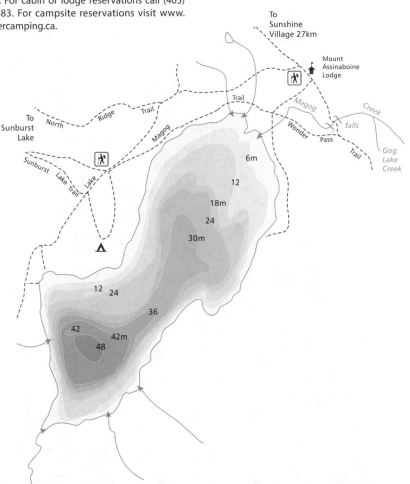

To Sunshine Village 27km

Mount Assiniboine Lodge

Trail

Magog

Creek

To Sunburst Lake

North   Ridge   Trail

Magog

Wonder

falls

Sunburst Lake Trail

Lake Trail

Pass   Trail

Gog Lake Creek

6m

12

18m

24

30m

12   24

36

42   42m

48

N

200m   0   200m   400m   600m   800m

Scale

Location: 17 km (10.5 mi) northwest of Kelowna
Elevation: 1,138 m (3,800 ft)
Surface Area: 82 ha (202 ac)
Mean Depth: 3.7 m (12 ft)
Max Depth: 7.3 m (24 ft)
Way Point: 119° 42' 00" Lon - W 49° 57' 00" Lat - N

Lambly (Bear) Lake

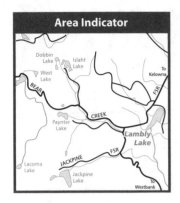

Area Indicator

Species

Rainbow Trout

Yellow Perch

Lambly (Bear) Lake Fish Stocking Data			
Year	Species	Number	Life Stage
2013	Rainbow Trout	5,000	Yearling
2012	Rainbow Trout	5,000	Yearling
2011	Rainbow Trout	5,000	Yearling

Fishing

Also known as Bear Lake, Lambly Lake is a sprawling lake with lots of nooks and crannies to explore. There are coves, islands, points and all manner of habitat for rainbow trout to hide. Even better, the lake is stocked annually with trout by the Freshwater Fisheries Society of BC to ensure a vibrant fishery.

Angling success in Lambly Lake is decent for rainbow trout that can reach up to 1 kg (2.5 lbs) in size. You might expect bigger fish, but perch were illegally released into the lake sometime in the mid-1990s. Despite their size, perch are a ravenous fish, and eat the same sort of food as the rainbow trout. As a result, the rainbow grow slower, and to a smaller size than they might otherwise.

The lake is also used for irrigation in the summer, and the drawdown, coupled with the perch, really doesn't help the trout grow up big and strong. Instead, you'll find good numbers of small trout.

But that's okay. The lake is actually managed as a family fishery, meaning there are plenty of small fish here. You're not going to catch a trophy sized rainbow, but at the same time, you probably won't get skunked. Especially if you go fishing for perch; last year, the local club pulled out close to 500 perch in just a few hours. Perch are a great fish for kids, and can easily be caught right offshore from the campsite. A worm on a #8 hook with split shot and a bobber is about as complicated as it needs to get for perch.

The trout are more likely to hang out across the lake from the campground near the bay with the outlet creek. A boat is necessary to get here. There isn't quite as much shoal, and the drop off is much steeper, making it inhospitable to perch. Try fishing a leech or dragonfly pattern closer to the shoal bottom in this area to entice the bigger trout.

Lambly can get quite windy, which will make it difficult to get out onto the lake with a small boat or a float tube. The wind usually dies down in the evening allowing anglers to get out on the water when the better fishing happens, anyway.

Electric motors only are permitted on this lake.

Directions

West of the city of Kelowna, you can locate Lambly Lake by following Highway 97 to Westside Road. Take Westside Road north along the west shore of Okanagan Lake past Bear Creek Provincial Park to the Bear Creek Forest Service Road. Follow this well-maintained logging road west all the way to Lambly Lake. The lake is found about 24 km up the road.

Facilities

The **Lambly Lake Recreation Site** has recently been upgraded and offers a pair of boat launches for electric motors only. Found in the semi-open area along the northwestern shore of the lake, the 17 unit campsite is RV friendly and managed with fees from mid-April until mid-October. The former fishing camp on the east side of the lake now leases all of its cabins and offers no facilities for area visitors.

Other Options

Cameo Lake can be found by continuing west along the Bear Creek Forest Service Road. The lake offers a small Forest Recreation campsite with a boat launch as well as fishing opportunities for rainbow trout.

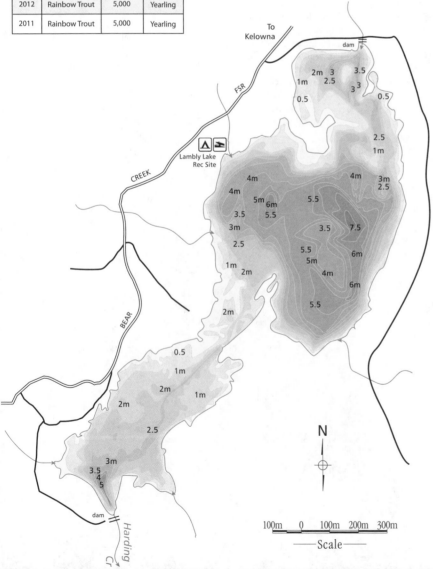

Scale: 100m 0 100m 200m 300m

Larchwood & Tamarack Lakes

Fishing

These two lakes are located near the small town of Skookumchuk, west of the Kootenay River.

Larchwood Lake is known for consistent fishing that can be quite good at times. The lake is stocked annually with rainbow trout and although the trout are not very big, they can be quite aggressive. And if the fishing happens to be slow at Larchwood Lake, one solace is the views are fantastic.

Flies and lures both produce while a worm and bobber can create a lot of action for the kids. Fly anglers can have great results with even a basic bead head nymph worked in the 3 m (10 ft) range. During the evening, a dry fly can also produce quite well. Spincasters should have good luck with a small spinner or spoon as long as they avoid the shallows, especially at the north and south ends of the lake. A good place to focus is the area just out from the boat launch. It is possible to shore fish from here since there are fairly open shores but it is quite weedy near to shore.

Nearby Tamarack Lake is a shallow lake, stocked annually with rainbow trout. There are rumours that brook trout are also resident in the lake in marginal numbers. Fishing can be good during the cooler months (spring and fall) for trout that can be found to 2 kg (4.5 lbs) in size on occasion.

The good size of some of the trout is attributable to their diet, as the larger fish feed on resident minnows. Therefore, fly anglers should try patterns such as a Muddler Minnow or Woolly Bugger. But be wary of making too much noise or movement when out on the lake. The fish, especially the bigger ones, are easily spooked. Fishing from shore is also a challenge (if not impossible) due to the extensive shallows. There is, however, a dock at the access point that can used for casting.

In addition to being a fly fishing only lake, anglers need to note the special season restrictions on Tamarack.

Directions

These lakes can be accessed by a series of logging roads found just east of Skookumchuk. Skookum-chuck is located north of Cranbrook off Highway 93/95. Just before the highway crosses the Kootenay River, Farstad Road branches west. Follow this road west and then north over Skookumchuck Creek. At the next major junction, a left should lead to Tamarack on the aptly named Tamarack Lake Forest Service Road, while keeping straight should lead north along Torrent Forest Service Road. About 4.5 km later, a branch road leads to Larchwood.

Area Indicator

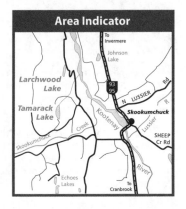

Larchwood Lake Fish Stocking Data			
Year	Species	Number	Life Stage
2013	Rainbow Trout	1,500	Yearling
2012	Rainbow Trout	1,500	Yearling
2011	Rainbow Trout	1,500	Yearling

Tamarack Lake Fish Stocking Data			
Year	Species	Number	Life Stage
2013	Rainbow Trout	4,000	Yearling/ Catchable
2012	Rainbow Trout	4,000	Yearling/ Catchable
2011	Rainbow Trout	4,000	Yearling/ Catchable

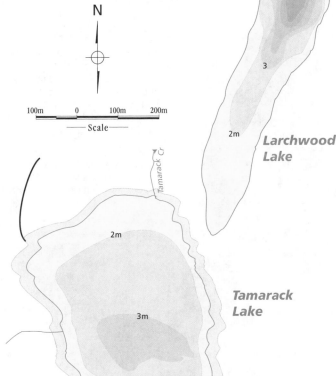

N

100m   0   100m   200m

— Scale —

Larchwood Lake

Elevation: 848 m (2,782 ft)
Surface Area: 16 ha (40 ac)
Mean Depth: 2.9 m (10 ft)
Max Depth: 10.1 m (33 ft)
Way Point: 115° 47' 00" Lon - W 49° 57' 00" Lat - N

Species
Rainbow Trout
Brook Trout

Tamarack Lake

Elevation: 855 m (2,805 ft)
Surface Area: 32 ha (79 ac)
Mean Depth: 2 m (6 ft)
Max Depth: 3.7 m (12 ft)
Way Point: 115° 48' 00" Lon - W 49° 55' 00" Lat - N

Facilities

The **Larchwood Lake Recreation Site** rests in an open area next to the lake. It is a popular place in the summer as the lake warms up to make a nice swimming hole. There is space for about 10 groups with most sites big enough to accommodate trailers. Anglers will appreciate the cartop boat launch.

To the south the **Tamarack Lake Recreation Site** is a little busier during the fishing season. There is space for about 3 campers here, an old dock as well as a place to launch small boats.

Lassie and Cup Lakes

Lassie Lake

Elevation: 1,299 m (4,262 ft)
Surface Area: 36 ha (89 ac)
Mean Depth: 3.8 m (12 ft)
Max Depth: 8.8 m (29 ft)
Way Point: 118° 54' 00" Lon - W 49° 35' 00" Lat - N

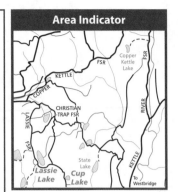

Area Indicator

Species

Rainbow Trout

Cup Lake

Elevation: 1,291 m (4,236 ft)
Surface Area: 9 ha (22 ac)
Mean Depth: 5.3 m (17 ft)
Max Depth: 13.4 m (44 ft)
Way Point: 118° 52' 00" Lon - W 49° 34' 00" Lat - N

Fishing

These quaint Okanagan lakes are both stocked, helping to sustain a good sport fishery for rainbow trout. Of the two, Lassie Lake is the bigger and better stocked.

Lassie Lake is heavily fished throughout the year and can be quite busy during the summer, especially on long weekends. As a result, the rainbow only average about 0.5 kg (1 lb) in size, although a few can be found up to 2 kg (4.5 lb) in size on occasion. Due to the shallow, weedy shoreline, it is best to have a small boat or pontoon boat to fish here.

Anglers should try near the inlet of the small stream into the north end of the lake or near the outlet of Sandrift Creek. The lake experiences a long run off period with dark coloured water; therefore, top water or attractor patterns can be a good choice during this period. Popular patterns that can produce results are a blood leech and modified Buick. Mid June to the end of July produces some good sedge/caddis hatches.

Cup Lake is known for its good fishing and fine backcountry scenery. For these reasons, the lake attracts plenty of visitors throughout summer weekends. A nice time to visit the area is in the cooler fall months when the crowds have subsided. There are two small islands on the lake and the bigger one has a nice campsite for tenters looking to really get away from it all.

The lake is stained a light brown colour by the tannins in the water. A few areas that are often productive in this lake are off the small island and along the north side of the 12 m (39 ft) hole. A leech pattern is a good all around producer, while chironomids in the spring and fall also work well.

The small size of the lake makes it easy for an angler to cover the lake. In fact, a float tube or canoe is the perfect way to explore the lake since casting from shore is difficult due to the weeds that surround most of the lake. No power boats are allowed on the small lake.

Directions

Both lakes lie in the popular Christian Valley of the eastern Okanagan region. The lakes can be reached from several directions. From the southeast, you will need to follow Highway 33 north to Westbridge and the paved Christian Valley Road. Continue north about 45 km to the Beaverdell-State Creek Forest Service Road. Turn east on this good gravel road. After climbing for over 7 km from the valley floor, turn north at the junction and continue another 3.5 km where a left leads past Cup Lake to the Lassie Lake Forest Road. Lassie Lake is found about 5 km further along.

Alternatively, they can be accessed through Beaverdell on Highway 33. Turn east onto the Trapping Creek Forest Service Road and follow it for 11 km. Turn right or east onto the Trapping-Copper Kettle Forest Road for 3.5 km where another right leads to the Lassie Lake Forest Road. Continue south for about 8 km to Lassie Lake. Cup Lake is a short distance further along.

Facilities

Along the southern shore of Lassie Lake you will find the **Lassie Lake Recreation Site** offering seven lake view sites equipped with fire pits and a boat launch. The sites are set amid a decent stand of trees, making for the perfect weekend fishing vacation spot. Alternatively, there are two camping spots at the **Cup Lake Recreation Site**. The lakeshore sites are quite primitive.

Lassie Lake

To Christian-Trap FSR

2m
3
5m
6
8m

Sandrift Cr

6
5m
3
2m

Lassie Lake Rec Site

To Cup Lk

N

100m   0   100m   200m   300m
Scale

To Lassie Lake

Cup Lk Rec Site

3m
6
12
9m
6
3m

To Beaverdell-State Creek FSR

Cup Lake

Lassie Lake Fish Stocking Data			
Year	Species	Number	Life Stage
2013	Rainbow Trout	7,000	Fry
2012	Rainbow Trout	7,000	Fry
2011	Rainbow Trout	7,000	Fry

Cup Lake Fish Stocking Data			
Year	Species	Number	Life Stage
2013	Rainbow Trout	2,000	Fry
2012	Rainbow Trout	2,000	Fry
2011	Rainbow Trout	2,000	Fry

Lazy Lake

Location: 38 km (23.5 mi) northeast of Cranbrook
Elevation: 909 m (2,982 ft)
Surface Area: 35 ha (86 ac)
Mean Depth: 3 m (10 ft)
Max Depth: 10 m (33 ft)
Way Point: 115° 37′ 00″ Lon - W 49° 49′ 00″ Lat - N

Fishing

Also known as Rock Lake or Stevens Lake, Lazy Lake is known for its consistent fishing for small rainbow trout due in part to the aggressive stocking program of the Freshwater Fisheries Society of BC. The lake also holds a fair number of cutthroat trout which were last stocked here in the 1930s but have managed to survive quite nicely.

The shoal areas found at the north and south ends of the lake are good areas to focus your efforts, especially during the spring and fall. Another area that should be worked is just off the small point alongside the western shore of the lake. With the deep hole right next to the point, this area can be productive throughout the year. Spincasters can use small spoons, while fly anglers can try a variety of strategies depending on the time of year. In the spring and early summer, there are a number of insect hatches that occur on the lake that can be matched. When there is no active hatch, try a nymph or attractor pattern like a Carey Special.

If your success is slow, trolling searching pattern flies or lures that resemble baitfish is the best way to try to find where the trout are holding. Vary your speed, depth and location throughout the lake until you experience a few hits. By noting where the fish are responding to your presentation, you can hone your efforts to where the trout are holding out in the lake.

The lake has an open, accessible shore that is a mix of shale, rock and sand, and fishing from shore is easy. Unfortunately, it isn't necessarily all that productive since getting your lure out to where the fish are holding can be a challenge. One of the better casting areas is around the aforementioned point on the western shores of the lake.

There is a speed restriction for motorboats on this lake. Check the regulations for details.

Facilities

The **Lazy Lake Recreation Site** is set in an opening on the west side of the lake. In addition to 12 campsites, there is a cartop boat launch for anglers to use. The site is RV friendly and managed with fees from mid-April until the end of October. If the site is too busy, **Wasa Lake Provincial Park** lies to the west of the lake and offers a more developed, campsite along with a popular beach area.

Other Options

Sowerby Lake is a small hidden lake located to the south of Lazy Lake. The only way to access this secluded lake is via a rough trail off the Wolf Lewis Forest Service Road. The lake provides fishing for stocked rainbow trout that are rumoured to reach good sizes on occasion.

Directions

Lazy Lake is located near Wasa Lake, not far off Highway 93/95. To find the lake, follow Highway 93/95 to the south end of Wasa Lake. Turn east on Wasa Lake Park Drive for a short distance, where the Lazy Lake Road branches right. Continue on this road, which soon turns to gravel as it climbs along the south side of Lewis Creek. Shortly after crossing Lewis Creek, Lazy Lake will appear on the right. It is about 15 km from the highway to the lake. The road is decent enough to allow smaller RV's and trailers to navigate into the recreation site.

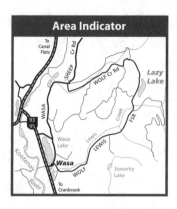

Area Indicator

Species

Rainbow Trout
Cutthroat Trout

Lazy (Rock) Lake			
Fish Stocking Data			
Year	Species	Number	Life Stage
2013	Rainbow Trout	5,250	Yearling
2012	Rainbow Trout	4,000	Yearling
2011	Rainbow Trout	4,000	Yearling

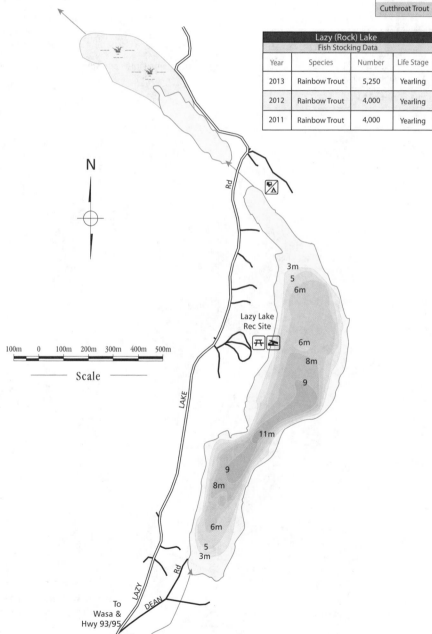

Location: 5 km (3 mi) west of Invermere
Elevation: 945 m (3,100 ft)
Surface Area: 22 ha (54 ac)
Mean Depth: 5.1 m (17 ft)
Max Depth: 11.6 m (38 ft)
Way Point: 116° 05′ 00″ Lon - W 50° 30′ 00″ Lat - N

Lillian Lake

Area Indicator

Species

Rainbow Trout

Brook Trout

Lillian Lake Fish Stocking Data			
Year	Species	Number	Life Stage
2013	Rainbow Trout	6,000	Yearling
2012	Rainbow Trout	6,000	Yearling
2011	Rainbow Trout	6,000	Yearling

Fishing

Lillian lake is a crystal clear lake found just west of the town of Invermere. It has extensive marl shoals that are feature a carpet of green weeds that help make it a very pretty, very colourful lake.

It is also a very busy lake, as its proximity to town means that it's one of the first lakes people think about when looking to head out. And, because it is so pretty, it attracts a variety of other recreators as well. To help alleviate the pressure, the lake is stocked annually by the Freshwater Fisheries Society of BC with rainbow trout. Surprisingly, some good size rainbow (up to 2 kg/4.5 lbs in size) are caught annually. A population of brook trout also exists in the lake.

Fly-fishing seems to be the best angling method and results are better during the spring or fall. In the heat of the summer the lake usually suffers from an algae bloom and fishing slows down nearly to a standstill as the trout retreat to the depths of the lake. Even if you were to successfully snag a fish during a bloom, the algae causes them to taste muddy and they lack any real fight.

In the spring, there are a variety of hatches, the most popular being the chironomid hatch. Fly anglers will want to work a deep line during the day. A common technique involves casting a full sinking line from a boat or tube, and allowing it to sink straight down, and then retrieving using very short, very slow pulls to imitate a rising chironomid. In the evening if the fish are rising, try working the surface with a small dry pattern.

The lake is really divided into three sections, each containing a deep hole with an abundance of shoals. One area that has proven successful is the predominant underwater point found along the southeastern shore of the main body of the lake. This area is a natural attractant for trout as they cruise the shoal for insect larvae.

If you spincasting, small lures and spinners can often entice a strike. Rainbow like flashy lures with silver retrieved quite quickly.

Ice fishing is also popular on the lake. Activity is often best just after the ice is safe enough to walk on (15 cm/6 in). Although the odd rainbow is caught, most of the action is for the brook trout. No matter which species you target, be sure to fish the shallower areas of water since this is where most of the fish cruise in the winter. Jigging small lures and spinners tipped with bait is a common ice fishing method.

During the open water season, anglers should not the electric motor only restriction.

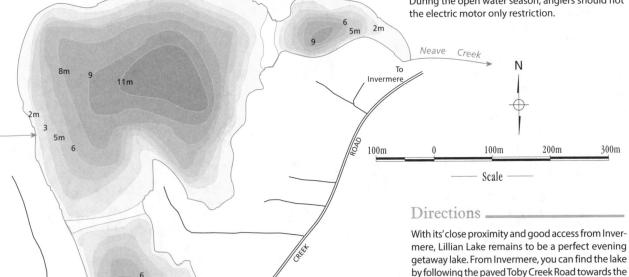

Directions

With its' close proximity and good access from Invermere, Lillian Lake remains to be a perfect evening getaway lake. From Invermere, you can find the lake by following the paved Toby Creek Road towards the Panorama Ski Area. After an initial climb the road levels somewhat and takes you past the southern shore of the pretty lake. There is a recreation site conveniently placed next to the lake to park at.

Facilities

The **Lillian Lake Recreation Site** is a small day-use only site that has picnic tables, cartop boat launch, a beach area and dock for small boats or canoes. The lake was once home to a resort, however, all basic amenities including overnight accommodations, can be found in Invermere.

Link Lake

Location: 35 km (22 mi) northeast of Princeton
Elevation: 1,093 m (3,586 ft)
Surface Area: 18.5 ha (46 ac)
Mean Depth: 4 m (13 ft)
Max Depth: 5 m (16 ft)
Way Point: 120° 13' 00" Lon - W 49° 42' 00" Lat - N

Fishing

Link Lake lies in the heart of the Okanagan, beneath low, rolling mountains. The terrain is made up of a mix of semi-forested slopes and open ranch land giving way to thick forest before reaching Link Lake. The lake is stocked heavily every year to sustain a productive sport fishery. Angling in the lake remains fair for rainbow that have the potential to reach up to 2 kg (4.5 lbs) in size. Both trolling and fly-fishing are productive on this lake.

Success in Link Lake is directly linked to your attention to the immediate conditions on the lake. The lake is full of insect activity throughout the spring and summer. Being able to recognize the proper hatch will produce results, otherwise fishing will often be very poor.

Chironomid patterns are best during May and June. Using a floating line and a chironomid pattern, you can anchor in one place, or allow the wind to push you around slowly. Trout don't usually hit chironomids hard, and you'll need to pay attention. A strike indicator is quite helpful, although some purists don't use them. Chironomids are more often than not fished less than 1 m (3 ft) off the bottom, with a very slow retrieve.

Caddis flies, on the other hand, can offer some extremely exciting fishing, with dramatic takes, with the fish sometimes leaping up and onto the fly. Caddis are generally fished dry, using a Tom Thumb or an Elk Hair Caddis. The best caddis fishing usually happens in the evening after the sun starts to set.

While Link Lake is known for having plenty of insect activity, there are times when there just aren't any hatches. At these times, try a leech or a dragonfly pattern near the bottom of a drop off area. Other options include using an attractor pattern like a Doc Spratley, which you can troll, or cast from an anchored position.

The lake has large shallow area around it, making it imperative to get out onto the water with a tube or small boat. While the wind can kick up here, the lake is fairly well protected. In fact, this is a popular alternative when the wind is too much on nearby Osprey Lake.

There is an electric motor only restriction on Link Lake.

Other Options

Eastmere and **Westmere Lakes** are two walk-in lakes found in the hills above Osprey Lake. Although a challenge to find (the Backroad GPS Maps and Thompson Okanagan Backroad Mapbook are helpful tools to get you there), these lakes are being managed as quality fisheries. This mean the trout are larger and can prove quite the challenge on the fly.

Directions

From Princeton, head north along the paved Princeton-Summerland Road. Just past Chain Lake, Link Lake is easily accessible by taking the Agur/Link Lake Road south off the Princeton-Summerland Road.

Facilities

Along with the various cottages and homes in the area, the **Link Lake Recreation Site** has space for up to 10 groups. Found close to the main road, the sites are RV friendly and managed with fees from the end of April until mid-October. There is also a cartop boat launch available.

For trail enthusiasts, the **Trans Canada Trail** travels right by the northern shore of the lake. The trail follows the historic old Kettle Valley Railway bed through the Okanagan.

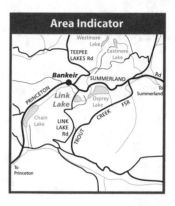

Area Indicator

Species

Rainbow Trout

Link Lake Fish Stocking Data			
Year	Species	Number	Life Stage
2013	Rainbow Trout	8,000	Yearling
2012	Rainbow Trout	8,000	Yearling
2011	Rainbow Trout	8,000	Yearling

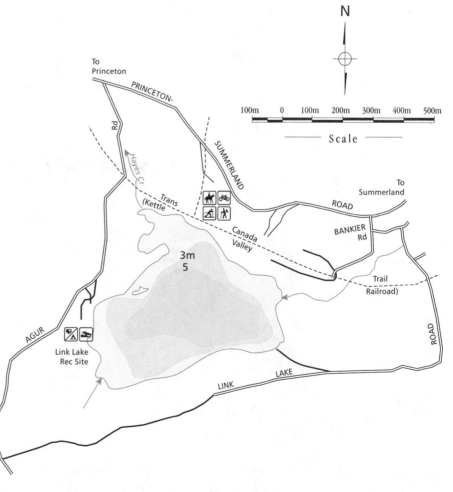

Location: 38 km (23.5 mi) northwest of Princeton
Elevation: 1,129 m (3,704 ft)
Surface Area: 19 ha (47 ac)
Mean Depth: 7.5 m (25 ft)
Max Depth: 18 m (59 ft)
Way Point: 120° 42' 00" Lon - W 49° 45' 00" Lat - N

Lodwick (Ludwick) Lake

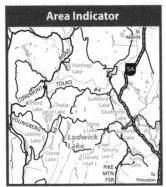

Area Indicator

Fishing

Despite being a difficult lake to find along a maze of backroads north of Princeton, Lodwick Lake receives significant angling pressure throughout the season. To help offset this pressure, the Freshwater Fisheries Society of BC stocks the lake annually with rainbow trout, which provide for good fishing at times for rainbow in the 0.5 kg (1 lb) range. However, it is the trout in the 1.5 kg (3 lb) range that entice the anglers to come here.

Similar to most of the lakes in the Pike Mountain Recreation Area, fly-fishing can be a lot of fun here. The chironomid action can be amazing in the early spring with a host of different coloured and sized hatches occurring sometimes simultaneously. A little later in the spring, damselflies come out in groves and it is not uncommon to see trout picking off flies close to shore where there is weed and reed growth. During slower periods, a leech pattern or dragonfly nymph worked near the bottom along the shoal areas can produce surprising results.

Of course, the trout also respond well to small spinners and lake trolls. No matter what fishing method you enjoy, try working the area around the small islands near the north end of the lake. This area has long been a good holding area for feisty trout.

Directions

Lodwick Lake is found off the Pike Mountain Forest Service Road to the east and Youngberg Road to the west. Although the roads in the area can be a bit rough, most vehicles and moderate size trailers can weave their way into the lake.

From the east, pick up the Pike Mountain Road off Highway 5A between Aspen Grove and Princeton. Follow this road west past Gladstone Lake. At the 2 km mark the Robertson Lake Forest Service Road branches northwest. Follow this road for another 2 km and continue straight, following the signs to Thalia Lake. At around the 5 km mark of this road system, you will need to take the branch road south. This road should take you to the Lodwick Lake Recreation Site.

From the west you will find Youngberg Road at the 22 km mark of the Coldwater Road, which connects Tulameen with Highway 5A. This signed road quickly climbs the hill above the Otter Valley, eventually linking with the Pike Mountain Forest Service Road in the east. Once again, the turnoff to Lodwick is found around the 5 km posting.

A copy of the *Thompson Okanagan Backroad Mapbook* and a *BC Backroad GPS Maps* will help you find the lake.

Facilities

There are two separate recreation campsites available on Lodwick Lake. The site at the northern end of the lake offers a rough boat launch and four campsites, while the southern site also offers four sites without a formal boat launch. The northern site is set amid a good stand of mature trees, whereas the southern site is a little more open. Both camping areas provide splendid views of the lake.

Other Options

As you approach Lodwick Lake from the west, you will pass by the access roads to **Rickey, Clifford** and **Larry Lakes**. These small lakes are a popular alternative to Lodwick Lake and offer angling opportunities for decent sized rainbow trout and beautiful recreation campsites.

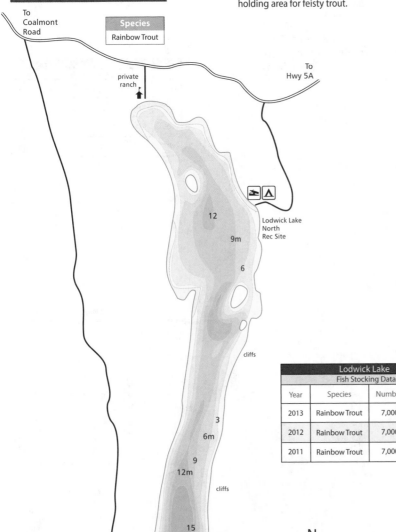

Species

Rainbow Trout

Lodwick Lake Fish Stocking Data			
Year	Species	Number	Life Stage
2013	Rainbow Trout	7,000	Fry
2012	Rainbow Trout	7,000	Fry
2011	Rainbow Trout	7,000	Fry

Scale

100m 0 100m 200m 300m 400m 500m

N

Loon Lake - Balfour

Location: 10 km (6 mi) north of Balfour
Elevation: 892 m (2,926 ft)
Surface Area: 9 ha (22 ac)
Mean Depth: 8 m (26 ft)
Max Depth: 28 m (92 ft)
Way Point: 116° 54'00" Lon - W 49° 42'00" Lat - N

Fishing

The second of three Loon Lakes that offer great fishing in the Kootenays is found just off Highway 31 between Balfour and Ainsworth Hot Springs. This Loon is only stocked every couple of years with rainbow trout, which can get to a decent size, although the average catch is fairly small. The lake is also inhabited by a reproducing strain of brook trout. Brookies were stocked in the lake for many years, but stocking stopped in the 1970s. But they have established a healthy, self-sustaining population.

The shoal areas just off shore are the hot areas for trout in the spring, while the 6 m (20 ft) shoal located in the northern middle portion of the lake is a definite hot spot during warmer weather.

Working a searching pattern like a Woolly Bugger along the shoal areas will often find a few trout in the spring and fall. There are also good hatches on the lake throughout the year to try to match. If you are not a fly-fisher, small lures and spinners can often entice a strike. Rainbow like flashy lures with silver, as these look like minnows. Try trolling or retrieving fairly quickly, as minnows swim quite fast. Fly anglers who troll can stick with the Woolly Bugger, or try a streamer pattern like a Muddler Minnow.

Trolling can work on a choppy, cloudy day. When it is bright out and the lake surface is calm, remain in one place, as a moving boat will cause the fish to scatter, reducing your chance of success.

When the lake freezes over in January ice fishing can be popular for the resident brook trout. The odd rainbow trout can be caught through the ice, although brookies are much more aggressive during the winter months. When ice fishing, start relatively close to shore, and don't fish too deep. A common technique is to drill a series of holes, starting about 3 m (10 ft) out from the shore, and every 3 m thereafter. The fish will flee at the sound of the drill, so drill all your holes at once, rather than drilling a new hole every half hour or so, as this will scare of the fish each time.

The brook trout tend to be found in shallow waters near the shores, as here there is food as well as sufficient oxygen for the trout. Try a small spoon like a Little Cleo or even a miniature white jig for brookies through the ice.

Directions

Loon Lake is found south of the popular Ainsworth Hot Springs, just north of Balfour. From Balfour, follow Highway 31 towards Ainsworth Hot Springs and turn west along the Hansen Forest Service Road. This road eventually veers south and passes by the west side of Loon Lake. You can park your vehicle off the side of the road.

Facilities

There are no facilities available directly at Loon Lake. There are a number of amenities in the area available at **Ainsworth Hot Springs** or at the nearby towns of **Kaslo** and **Balfour**.

Other Options

Krao Lake is located well up the mountainside from Loon Lake. The best access to the small lake is to follow the Cedar Creek Road past the Cody Caves Park to as close as you can make it to the lake. The rough road access, combined with the final bushwhack into the lake means this lake receives few visitors. As a result, you will be rewarded with good fishing for cutthroat trout.

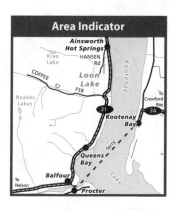

Area Indicator

Species
Rainbow Trout
Brook Trout

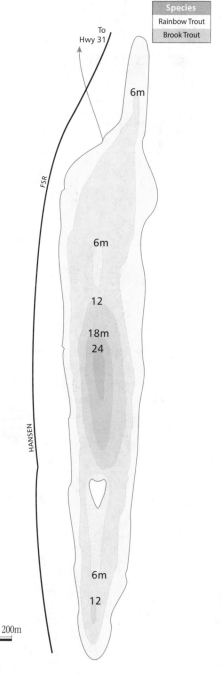

Loon Lake (Balfour Area) Fish Stocking Data			
Year	Species	Number	Life Stage
2013	Rainbow Trout	5,000	Fingerling
2012	Rainbow Trout	5,000	Fingerling
2011	Rainbow Trout	5,000	Fingerling

100m   0   100m   200m

Scale

N

Location: 21 km (13 mi) south of Elko
Elevation: 832 m (2,730 ft)
Surface Area: 33 ha (81 ac)
Mean Depth: 4.1m (13 ft)
Max Depth: 15.6m (51 ft)
Way Point: 115° 06′00″ Lon - W 49° 06′00″ Lat - N

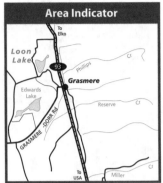

Area Indicator

Species
Rainbow Trout
Brook Trout

Loon Lake (Elko Area) Fish Stocking Data			
Year	Species	Number	Life Stage
2013	Rainbow Trout	5,000	Yearling
2012	Rainbow Trout	5,000	Yearling
2011	Rainbow Trout	5,000	Yearling

Directions

South of the village of Elko, you can find Loon Lake not far from Highway 93. To reach the lake, follow Highway 93 south from Elko to the Grasmere-Dorr Road. Continue a short distance and just past the school house, look for the access road to Loon Lake on the right. The road forks about 500 metres later where a left leads to another fork. A right here should lead to the lake. A good map like the Backroad Mapbook for the Kootenay Rockies or the BC Backroad GPS Maps will help when trying to find lakes like these.

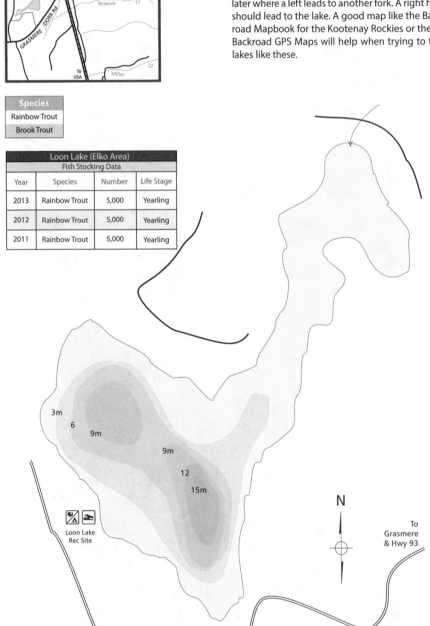

Fishing

There are nearly a dozen lakes in the province with the name Loon Lake, three of which appear in this book. This Loon Lake is found just west of Grasmere off Highway 93 and is stocked annually with rainbow trout, which provide for good fishing throughout much of the season. Brook trout were once stocked in the lake, although it is unknown whether or not the species still exists in the lake in any significant numbers.

The best times to visit the lake is in the spring and fall periods, when the cooler temperatures of the lake help make the trout more active. Since the lake sits at a low elevation in the valley bottom, the lake is one of the first in the region to become ice-free. In some years, fishing is possible as early as late March in Loon Lake. Unfortunately, it is also one of the first to suffer from the summer doldrums

Anglers visiting the lake should focus their efforts in the southern portion of the lake, as the northern arm is quite shallow. The large shoals found around this southern portion can be a buzz of trout activity in the spring. Although trout head into the depths of the lake during the heat of summer days, summer evenings can provide some good fly-fishing action when the trout cruise the shallows in search of food, especially if they're rising to the surface. At this time a dry fly like the Tom Thumb or Elk Hair Caddis can be a lot of fun.

Shore fishing is nearly impossible, as the lake has extensive shoals. Instead, get out onto the lake in a small boat or float tube. While there is a fairly deep hole in the centre of the lake, the fastest drop offs are towards the east end. This doesn't mean that all (or even any) of the fish will be holding in this area, but if they are, they will be easier to find, as they will be holding along the edge of the drop off.

There is an electric motor only restriction on the lake.

Facilities

The **Loon Lake Recreation Site** is a large, partially treed site on the south and west side of the lake. There is space for about 40 groups here and a place to launch small boats. The site can be very busy with RV's and trailers during the summer months due to its close proximity to the highway. Due to the popularity of the site, a caretaker helps maintain the site and there is a fee for camping. Swimming and fishing make up the bulk of the outdoor fun at the site

Other Options

Edwards Lake lies just to the south of Loon Lake and is accessible via the Grasmere-Dorr Road. Edwards Lake is known locally as a productive lake offering fishing for nice sized rainbow trout. The lake is also home to a good sized forest recreation site, so if Loon Lake is too busy, Edwards Lake may be a good camping and fishing alternative.

Loon Lake - Parson

Location: 12 km (7.5 mi) west of Parson
Elevation: 1,241 m (4,071 ft)
Surface Area: 7 ha (17 ac)
Mean Depth: 4.5 (14.5 ft)
Max Depth: 9.1 m (30 ft)
Way Point: 116° 48′ 00″ Lon - W 51° 03′ 00″ Lat - N

Region 4

Fishing

Completing the trilogy of Loon Lakes, is the lake found southwest of Parson. It is a small, shallow lake but extremely popular. The Freshwater Fisheries Society of BC stocks the lake with 6,000 fry stocked here each year to help maintain the fishery. Although the average catch is fairly small, there is the odd decent sized trout caught here annually.

Brook trout were stocked in the lake in the mid-1970s. While they did set up a self-sustaining population, there have been few reports of brookies in the lake over the past few years, and they may be fished out. If you manage to snag a brook trout here, let us know at updates@backroadmapbooks.com.

This Loon Lake is a relatively high elevation lake, which makes for a shorter open ice fishing season for anglers. Rainbow are best found in the lake shortly after ice off in late May. Fly anglers will find using a leech pattern is a good way to begin exploring the lake. As the season progresses, watch for the tell tale signs of feeding activity and try to match the hatch. During the mayfly and caddis hatches, the trout will often rise to a dry fly on calm summer evenings.

In the fall, the rainbow begin preparing for winter, and will usually chase anything that looks like food. Try using a slightly larger pattern than might have worked earlier in the year. Leech patterns will still work, as will attractor patterns like a Doc Spratley or a Carey Special.

If you are a spincaster, small lures and spinners can be productive throughout the season. There is a small dock at the recreation site, and it is possible to reach the drop off areas from here, or from a point just south of the campground. The lake does have an open shoreline, and casting from shore is quite easy. However, your chances of finding the fish will be much improved if you get out on the water in a small boat or float tube.

Directions

West of the community of Parson, you can reach Loon Lake by first following Highway 95 to the Crestbrook Main Road. Take the main road southwest until you reach the Spillmacheen North Forest Service Road. Follow this good forest road west along the Spillmacheen North Forest Service Road at km 17. Follow this good 2wd forest road northwest along the Spillmacheen River. Two roads lead into Loon Lake at km 24 and 24.5. The second allows trailer access.

Facilities

The **Loon Lake Recreation Site** is home to a small dock as well as two separate camping areas. Four forested lakeside sites are located at the main site on the north shore. The south site has a good boat launch and a rough road to a single campsite. During summer, both sites can be quite busy, especially on weekends. If you are seeking solitude, the best time to visit the lake is during the week in the summer or sometime during the spring or fall periods.

Other Options

The closest fishing alternative to Loon Lake is the **Spillmacheen River.** The Spillmacheen North Forest Service Road follows the course of the river making the river relatively easy to access. Fishing in the river can be fair to good in sections for both rainbow trout and whitefish. Fly-fishing is a favourite for anglers visiting this river.

Area Indicator

Species
Rainbow Trout

Loon Lake (Parson Area)			
Fish Stocking Data			
Year	Species	Number	Life Stage
2013	Rainbow Trout	2,000	Yearling
2012	Rainbow Trout	2,000	Yearling
2011	Rainbow Trout	2,000	Fry

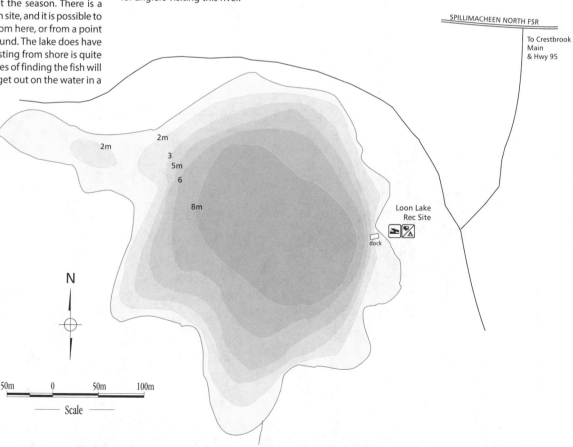

Region 4

Location: 25 km (15.5 mi) east of Cranbrook
Elevation: 794 m (2,605 ft)
Surface Area: 10 ha (25 ac)
Mean Depth: 6.5 m (21 ft)
Max Depth: 18 m (59 ft)
Way Point: 115° 26'00" Lon - W 49° 25'00" Lat - N

Lund Lake

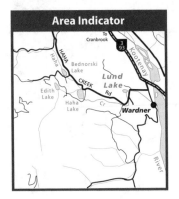

Area Indicator

Species

Brook Trout
Largemouth Bass
Rainbow Trout

Lund Lake Fish Stocking Data			
Year	Species	Number	Life Stage
2006	Rainbow Trout	2,000	Yearling
2004	Rainbow Trout	2,060	Yearling/Adult

Fishing

Lund Lake is a small lake found west of Wardner. The lake was regularly stocked with rainbow until 2004, when the stocking program was discontinued. In 2001 and again in 2003, the lake was stocked with some adult Gerrard rainbow trout, which could bode very well for the size of rainbow found in the future. In addition, the lake was stocked with brook trout in the far distant past, and brookies are rumoured to have established a natural spawning cycle in the lake.

However, the lake has recently been invaded with largemouth bass, which have seriously impacted the fishing in the lake. As a result, the nature of fishing this lake is changing. Historically, fishing was good at times for both trout species, and people can still find trout here. But the lake is becoming better known for its largemouth bass. Largemouth bass are aggressive, predatory fish that like to hide near weeds or other structures, then strike at small fish cruising by. Large insects caught on the surface of the water, and even small frogs and mice that have fallen into the water can also provide a nice meal for these bass.

A common technique for fishing bass is to use large flies called poppers, which look like bees, frogs, mice, or other creatures on the surface of the water. These big, almost ridiculously large flies can be difficult to cast, but do work well. Slow, erratic movements that imitate a drowning insect or mouse can entice the bass to strike. And when they do, look out. Bass are lively fighters and catching them can be addicting.

Spincasters are at a distinct disadvantage when it comes to largemouth bass, as it is difficult to retrieve a lure through the weeds without getting a snag. While bass might be interested in chasing a lure that looks like a minnow, they're not going to bite (literally and figuratively) if the minnow is trailing a bunch of weeds behind it. Jigging can work well, though.

The best way to work the lake for trout is to troll along the drop off areas found next to the shallows. It is important to find the drop off zone as the lake can be deceiving. In some areas, the lake is quite shallow and the drop off is well away from shore.

Directions

You can find this small lake southeast of Cranbrook not far from Highway 3/93. Follow Highway 3/93 to the Wardner Road. The Ha Ha Creek Road branches west from the Wardner Road and passes by the shore of Lund Lake. Parking is available next to the lake.

Facilities

There are no facilities at Lund Lake and the lake is home to a number of private cottages. Please respect private property in the area. The nearby city of offers all amenities including a couple tackle shops, hotels and motels and a variety of places to eat.

Other Options

Nearby **Kootenay River** can be reached within minutes of Lund Lake. The big river provides fishing opportunities for rainbow trout, bull trout, some cutthroat trout, as well as whitefish. As you get closer to Lake Koocanusa, you will also find burbot and kokanee.

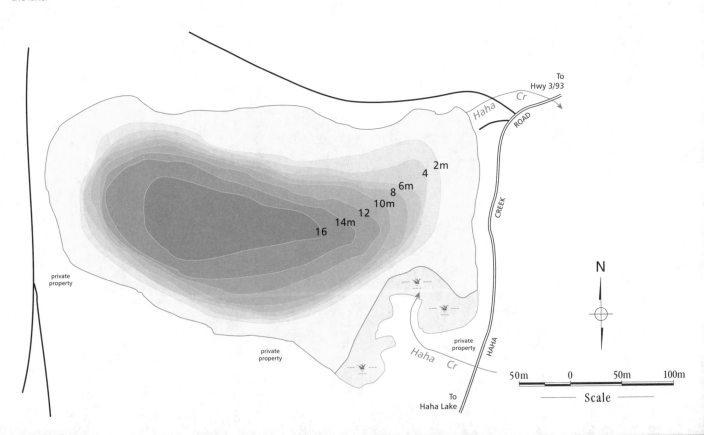

Mabel Lake

Location: 30 km (19 mi) east of Enderby
Elevation: 395 m (1296 ft)
Surface Area: 5,986 ha (14,785 ac)
Mean Depth: 120 m (394 ft)
Max Depth: 200 m (656 ft)
Way Point: 118° 44′ 00″ Lon - W 50° 35′ 00″ Lat - N

Region 8

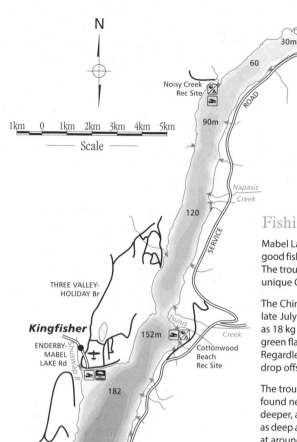

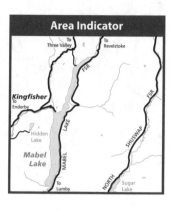

Species
Chinook
Dolly Varden
Kokanee
Lake Trout
Rainbow Trout

Fishing

Mabel Lake is a long, deep wilderness lake in a scenic valley to the east of Enderby. It has good fishing for lake and rainbow trout, Dolly Varden, kokanee, and even Chinook salmon. The trout and dollies are often over 4.5 kg (10 lbs) throughout the year. However, it is the unique Chinook fishery that keeps this lake on some anglers' depth sounder.

The Chinook run up the Shuswap River and are found holding near the river mouths in late July to mid-September. With fish averaging 7–12 kg (15–25 lbs) and some as large as 18 kg (40 lbs) these are big fish. Anglers should try trolling salmon gear such as red or green flashers with pink or green hoochies. Locals also use a silver J plug with a red head. Regardless of the tackle, you will need to work between 12-24 m (40-80 ft) of water near drop offs and ledges.

The trout, char and kokanee are also best caught on the troll. In spring all species can be found near the surface of the lake, but as the heat of summer approaches the fish head deeper, and a downrigger will help reach these portions of the lake. You may need to go as deep as 30 m (100 ft) to find the lake trout, although the other species tend to be found at around 4–6 m (14–20 ft). Be prepared to cover a lot of territory to find fish.

Bucktails and a various assortment of spoons, such as a Gibbs Hockey Stick or Coyote Spoon on a fast troll, can produce trout and dollies. Lakers seem to prefer larger presentations like the size 3 or 4 Lyman Lure. The typical, slow "S" pattern with a lake troll is the proven method to entice those feisty but small kokanee. A general rule of thumb is to use darker colours on dark days and brighter presentations on sunny days.

There are a number of special restrictions on Mabel Lake. Remember, salmon are a federally regulated fish, so check the federal freshwater salmon supplement before heading out.

Directions

There a couple main access points to the lake. From the east, the Enderby-Mabel Lake Road provides access to the resort area known as Kingfisher. There are a couple boat launch sites in the area to use.

From the south, you will need to travel east from Vernon to Lumby and look for the Mabel Lake Road on the north side of the highway. This road starts out paved, but turns to gravel. It is about 33 km (20.5 mi) to the provincial park near the south end of the lake. Further along the road, is the Cottonwood Bay Recreation Site.

Facilities

Mabel Lake Provincial Park is located along the southeast shore of the lake. The first come first serve park offers a total of 81 campsites along with a large day-use area, boat launch and a sandy beach.

There are three recreation sites around the lake. Off the Mabel Lake Forest Service Road, the **Cascade Beach Recreation Site** provides a few scenic lakeside tent sites with a sandy beach area. The 20 site **Cottonwood Bay Recreation Site** is further up the road and has a boat launch and nice sandy beach. The **Noisy Creek Recreation Site** is near the northwest end of the lake, off the Three Valley-Mabel Road. In addition to a paved boat launch, there are over 60 enhanced campsites in a park like setting. Both Cottonwood and Noisy Creek are managed with fees from mid-April until fall.

Location: 10 km (6 mi) west of Oliver
Elevation: 836 m (2,743 ft)
Surface Area: 8 ha (20 ac)
Mean Depth: 9.8 m (32 ft)
Max Depth: 19.8 m (65 ft)
Way Point: 119° 37′ 00″ Lon - W 49° 13′ 00″ Lat - N

Madden Lake

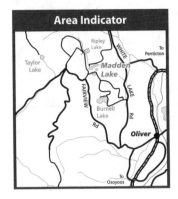

Area Indicator

Species

Brook Trout
Rainbow Trout

Madden (Oliver) Lake			
Fish Stocking Data			
Year	Species	Number	Life Stage
2013	Rainbow Trout	4,600	Yearling
2012	Rainbow Trout	4,000	Yearling
2011	Rainbow Trout	4,000	Yearling

Fishing

Madden Lake is a small lake, hidden in the hills between Oliver and Keremeos. The lake, which is also called Oliver Lake by some locals, is stocked every year by the Freshwater Fisheries Society of BC with rainbow trout. These trout provide for the bulk of the fishing activity although there are still reports of brook trout being caught from time to time.

Since the lake is a low elevation lake in the hot southern Okanagan, fishing success tends to slow significantly throughout the summer season. If you want to find an active fishery, it is best to visit this one during the cooler spring and fall periods.

Rainbow on Madden average about 0.5 kg (1 lb), although some impressive trout in the 2 kg (4.5 lb) range are caught annually. Fly-fishing is usually the most productive fishing method with chironomid hatches being be quite productive in the spring. During slow periods, trolling a leech along the drop offs should result in some success. In the fall, it is best fished by trolling along the south edge of the lake, across from the recreation site, with a leech, shrimp or nymph.

Spincasters can try any of the usual trout lures (small spoons and spinners). Success is hit and miss but if you can find the right depth, a well presented lure might just cause that rainbow to attack. —can sometimes work, but.

The northeast end of the lake is quite shallow and weedy. Fishing here early in the year can be productive, but once the lake starts to warm up, the fish will most likely move to the deeper areas. In fact, fishing around the drop off near the neck of the lake should prove productive.

Directions

The slew of old and active roads can make it quite maddening to find this small lake. From Oliver, follow 350th Avenue west to Fairview Road. This road turns to gravel as it courses north, eventually connecting with the Ripley Lake Forest Service Road (look for the recreation site signs). Continue north and then take the first road right or east, followed by a left or north. If you picked the right roads, Madden Lake should be a short drive away. The roads get progressively worse, so a high clearance vehicle is recommended.

Facilities

The **Madden Lake Recreation Site** offers space for about eight groups in an open area next to the lake. The campsite includes picnic table, outhouses, a boat launch and an established hiking trail around the lake. For more luxurious accommodations the towns of Oliver, Keremos and Osoyoos are all found within easy driving distance. There are plenty of motels and B&B's to choose from.

Other Options

The closest alternative option to Madden Lake is **Ripley Lake,** which is found to the north. To the south, **Burnell Lake** is another good option. There are Forest Recreation sites and with a boat launch available at both lakes. Fishing for rainbow trout can produce some exciting action on these lakes. Ripley is described in better detail later in this book, while the good people at Oliver Home Hardware can give you more pointers on Burnell.

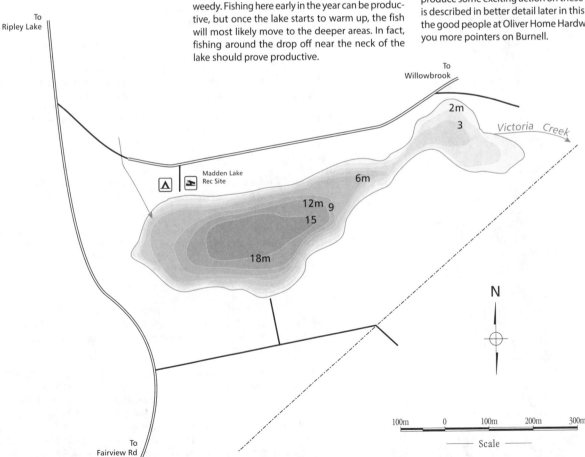

Mara Lake

Location: 16 km (10 mi) west of Salmon Arm
Elevation: 346 m (1,135 ft)
Surface Area: 1,943 ha (4,799 ac)
Mean Depth: 18 m (59 ft)
Max Depth: 46 m (151 ft)
Way Point: 119° 00' 00" Lon - W 50° 47' 00" Lat - N

Facilities

A number of established boat launch facilities are found on Mara Lake. In addition to the boat launches near Sicamous, there are at least two other launching sites on the eastern shore of the big lake. On the western shore there are boat launches at Mara Point Provincial Park and further down the lake off the Old Spallmucheen Road.

For those wishing to stay in the area, there are several full service resorts on the lake as well as accommodation in nearby Sicamous. For day trippers, **Mara Point Provincial Park** (off Old Spallmucheen Road) and **Mara Lake Provincial Park** (off Highway 97A) offer washrooms, picnic facilities and sandy beach areas for visitors to enjoy.

Other Options

Shuswap Lake lies to the north of Mara Lake and boasts over 1,000 km of shoreline. Fishing in the big lake has experienced a tremendous resurgence in the past few years due to regulations imposed on the lake. Rainbow trout and kokanee are the two main species found in the big lake but lake trout and Dolly Varden also inhabit the lake in fair numbers. Some nice sized fish have been caught in Shuswap Lake recently.

Directions

Mara Lake is the scenic backdrop for the town of Sicamous and is easily accessible from Highway 97A south of town. The Old Spallmucheen Road also travels along the western shore of the lake and provides good access to that side of the lake.

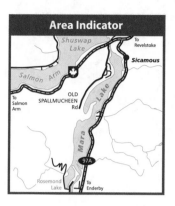

Area Indicator

Species
Dolly Varden
Kokanee
Lake Trout
Rainbow Trout

Fishing

Mara Lake is best known as a summer recreation destination. Sicamous, which sits at the lake's north end, proudly proclaims itself as "the houseboat capital of Canada." Of course, that has to do more with the fact that it abuts Shuswap Lake as well, but Mara Lake sees its fair share of boaters and water skiers and beachgoers. Fishing is often overlooked, despite the fact that it offers pretty good fishing for a variety of sportfish species, including rainbow trout, kokanee, lake trout and Dolly Varden. Rainbow, dollies and lake trout can all be regularly found in the 2 kg (4.5 lb) range but much larger fish do exist.

Mara is a big lake, and trolling is the preferred angling method. Despite its size fishing is best during the cooler spring or fall periods. During summer, trout move to the deeper portions of the lake and a downrigger is required to reach them. When trolling for trout, try a bucktail, Flatfish or a plug to find those elusive big game fish.

For the kokanee, slow down your presentation, and change to smaller gear since most kokanee are caught on small lures or flies. They feed mostly on plankton and small shrimp, not on minnows or small fish. The most popular lure is a Wedding Band, but other gear, like a Tomic Wee Tad Plug or a Luhr Jenson Midge Wobbler can also work. These are usually used in tandem with a dodger or flasher like a Shasta Tackle Sling Blade or a multibladed attractor like a Slim Willies or R&K Spinner Blades. Early in the morning, using green attractors works well, but by mid-day, it's best to switch to something red or pink.

Be sure to check the regulations before heading out. There are special restrictions on this lake.

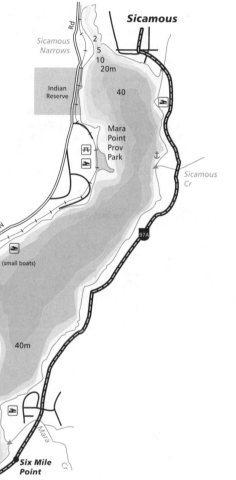

Sicamous

Sicamous Narrows

2
5
10
20m

40

Indian Reserve

Mara Point Prov Park

Sicamous Cr

SPALLMUCHEEN

(small boats)

Black Point

40m

OLD

Pictographs

Mara Cr

Six Mile Point

N

500m 0   1km   2km   3km
— Scale —

20m

10

5
2m

Mara Lake Provincial Park

Rogers Cr

To Shuswap River

To Enderby

Location: 22 km (13.6 mi) north of Princeton
Elevation: 789 m (2,588 ft)
Surface Area: 6 ha (15 ac)
Mean Depth: 6 m (20 ft)
Max Depth: 11 m (36 ft)
Way Point: 120° 34' 00" Lon - W 49° 36' 00" Lat - N

McCaffrey Lake

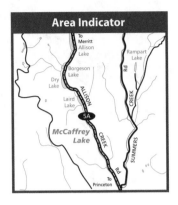

Area Indicator

To Merritt Allison Lake

Rampart Lake

Borgeson Lake

Dry Lake

Laird Lake

5A

McCaffrey Lake

To Princeton

Species
Brook Trout
Kokanee
Rainbow Trout
Whitefish

Fishing

McCaffery Lake is a popular fishing lake. Its popularity is due mostly to its ease of access, as it sits alongside Highway 5A. As a result of its popularity, and perhaps contributing to it as well, the lake is well-stocked annually by the Freshwater Fisheries Society of BC.

Fisheries stock the lake with rainbow, but there are small populations of brook trout, kokanee and mountain whitefish as well. The latter is the least popular of the game species, as it is quite boney to eat. But if you are looking for a good fighting fish that is not as picky as trout, then whitefish will not disappoint.

The fishing is quite productive for rainbow. However, the lake does not produce many big fish despite the fact that there is lots of food for them to eat. This is primarily because they generally get fished out as soon as they reach a reasonable size.

Another factor in raising the popularity of the lake is a fishing pier at the north end of the lake, which is wheelchair accessible, albeit very rough. Anglers will have luck casting from the pier with a variety of lures, including a simple worm and bobber set-up. This works best when there is a bit of a chop to the water to impart some motion to the worm.

Spincasting with a spoon or spinner works well, too. Try Flatfish type lures in patterns of silver, gold, black and silver or frog pattern. Dick Nite, Panther Martin and Roostertail spoons in smaller sizes are also good bets.

Trolling is also popular here, although getting a boat onto the lake is a bit of a challenge. The large shoal area towards the north end of the lake will produce well early in the year or later on. (Don't troll too close to the angling pier if there are people fishing there). Another spot to try is the around the two points that create a wasp waist near the middle of the lake.

Fly-fishing from a float tube is also popular, especially early in the year once the chironomids start hatching.

Directions

McCaffrey Lake is an easily accessible lake that is located just north of the town of Princeton off Highway 5A. The lake is a part of a chain of lakes that dot the Allison Creek Valley.

Facilities

At the north end of the lake, the Princeton Fish and Game Club have established a public fishing pier. There is also a small parking area at this site. Getting a boat onto the lake is challenging, but not impossible. A float tube or canoe can easily be carried down to the lake. The easiest place to launch from is the fishing pier, but there are other places off the highway that will work, too.

For overnight accommodations, **Princeton** is merely minutes to the south, or alternatively **Allison Lake Provincial Park** can be found off Highway 5A to the north.

Other Options

There are several fine options available north of McCaffrey Lake along Highway 5A. One lake worth considering, if drawdown has not drained it too much, is **Dry Lake**. This lake is stocked regularly with rainbow and is known to produce some trophy trout in the 2 kg (4.5 lb) range. There are also some brook trout available in the lake.

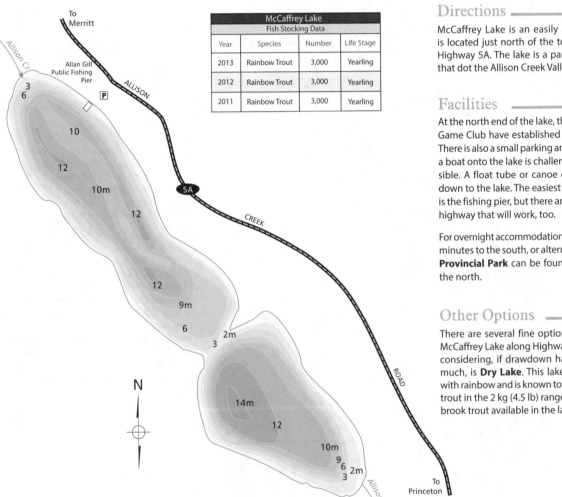

McCaffrey Lake Fish Stocking Data			
Year	Species	Number	Life Stage
2013	Rainbow Trout	3,000	Yearling
2012	Rainbow Trout	3,000	Yearling
2011	Rainbow Trout	3,000	Yearling

To Merritt

Allison Cr

Allan Gill Public Fishing Pier

P

ALLISON

3
6

10

12

10m

12

12

9m

6

2m
3

5A

CREEK

12

14m

12

10m

9
6
3 2m

ROAD

Allison Cr

To Princeton

N

50m   0   50m   100m   150m   200m

— Scale —

McNair Lakes

Fishing

There are three small lakes that make up the chain of lakes known as the McNair Lakes. They are relatively high elevation lakes, and, as a result, the fishing season is a little shorter than some valley lakes. The lakes open up around late May and freeze again by early December. The north or 1st lake has recently seen its stockings switched from Westslope cutthroat trout to rainbow to further enhance the fishery. The south or 3rd lake is stocked with both Westslope cutthroat trout and rainbow, which help to provide generally fair fishing.

The northern lake is set next to the access road and as a result receives the bulk of the angling pressure. Wise anglers looking for better quality fishing will look to the 2nd and 3rd lakes. The cutthroat in all three lakes can be quite aggressive, especially after ice off and in the fall. Try small spinners like a Mepps or small spoons like the Little Cleo to find aggressive cutthroat. Rainbow are also more active during the cooler times of the year and can usually be caught on similar gear as the cutthroat.

Fly anglers can do well throughout the open water season with streamers and on occasion top water flies. The limited season results in crossover hatches, and it isn't uncommon to find three or four insect hatches occurring at the same time. The fish are usually not that selective, but if you are finding that one pattern isn't working, try changing to another. As with anything, the fish usually want the most reward for the least effort. Sometimes that means they will go after the bigger insects. Sometimes that means they will go after the more plentiful hatch.

Mayflies can be very productive on these lakes, while sight fishing with dry flies is a lot of fun. A few dry fly patterns to try are Royal Coachman, Adams, Elk Hair Caddis or Mosquito. Wet flies such as a Doc Spratley, a chironomid or a variety of nymph patterns are also worth a try.

As the waters warm, you will need to fish deeper. During very warm summers, the second lake does tend to warm up, and the fishing slows down. However, the first and third lakes are surprisingly deep, and fishing should remain good. Fishing around the drop offs with fast sink line and long leaders is an option.

Because the lakes are so small, they can easily be fished from the shore. This is particularly true later in the summer when the water levels drop quite a bit.

Facilities

There are no facilities at these small mountain lakes but it is possible to set up camp off the road next to the 1st lake or along the shore of the other two lakes. Please keep the area clean by practicing no trace camping.

McNair Lake (3rd) South			
Fish Stocking Data			
Year	Species	Number	Life Stage
2012	Cutthroat Trout	1,000	Fry
2011	Rainbow Trout	1,000	Fall Catchable
2010	Cutthroat Trout	1,000	Fry

Directions

These three small lakes can be found south of Skookumchuck Creek and north of Cranbrook. To find the lake, look for Farstad Road off the west side of Highway 93/95 near Skookumchuck. Follow the road west to where the Skookumchuck River Road leads along the south side of the creek. The road can be quite rough as it climbs out of the valley, eventually meeting the 1st McNair Lake approximately 11 km (6.8 mi) later. A 4wd vehicle along with a copy of the *Backroad Mapbook for the Kootenay Rockies BC* and a GPS are recommended when travelling to these backcountry lakes.

Area Indicator

Species
Rainbow Trout
Cutthroat Trout

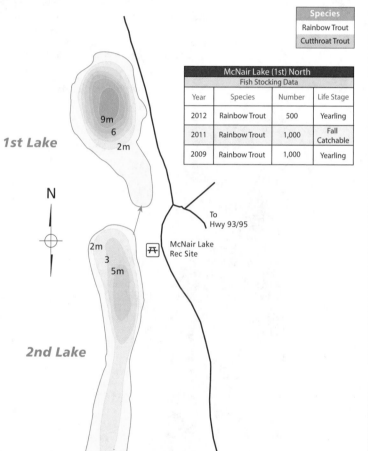

1st Lake
9m 6 2m

2nd Lake
2m 3 5m

3rd Lake
2m 3 5m 6 8m 9

To Hwy 93/95

McNair Lake Rec Site

N

100m 0 100m 200m 300m

— Scale —

McNair Lake (1st) North			
Fish Stocking Data			
Year	Species	Number	Life Stage
2012	Rainbow Trout	500	Yearling
2011	Rainbow Trout	1,000	Fall Catchable
2009	Rainbow Trout	1,000	Yearling

McNair (1st) North Lake
Elevation:1,065 m (3,494 ft)
Surface Area:3 ha (8 ac)
Mean Depth: 4 m (13 ft)
Max Depth:10 m (33 ft)
Way Point: 115° 52' 00" Lon - W 49° 53' 00" Lat - N

McNair (2nd) Middle Lake
Elevation:1,072 m (3,517 ft)
Way Point: 115° 52' 00" Lon - W 49° 52' 00" Lat - N

McNair (3rd) South Lake
Elevation:1,073 m (3,520 ft)
Surface Area: 3.5 ha (9 ac)
Mean Depth: 4.1 m (13 ft)
Max Depth:9.8 m (32 ft)
Way Point: 115° 51' 00" Lon - W 49° 52' 00" Lat - N

Location: 20 km (12.5 mi) south of Cranbrook
Elevation: 1,034 m (3,392 ft)
Surface Area: 7 ha (17 ac)
Mean Depth: 14.4 m (47 ft)
Max Depth: 25 m (82 ft)
Way Point: 115° 51′00″ Lon - W 49° 20′00″ Lat - N

Mineral Lake

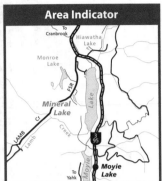

Area Indicator

Species
Rainbow Trout
Cutthroat Trout

Fishing

Clear waters and good fishing await anglers at the easily accessible lake found just west of the much larger Moyie Lake. While the lake is not that hard to find, it offers consistent fishing throughout the open water season. This is due in part to the extensive stocking program by the Freshwater Fisheries Society of BC who stock the lake two or more times a season.

The stocked rainbow trout can be quite aggressive at times and are known to grow up to 2 kg (4.5 lbs) in size. Another advantage of this lake is that it is also inhabited by cutthroat trout, which are usually more aggressive than rainbow. There are also reports of the odd rainbow/cutthroat trout cross located in the lake.

The lake can be fished from the shore, but it is better to work your way east or west around the lake from the recreation site. There are more prominent drop offs along these shores but shore anglers will still have difficulty fishing due to the dense bush and lack of open areas to cast.

The shoal areas along the western side of Mineral Lake can be very active, especially during the spring and fall periods. In the spring, chironomid or bloodworm patterns can be fantastic. Mayfly hatches can also produce some good action during the spring. Watch for the tell tale sign of trout sipping the mayflies off the surface. As the heat of summer sets in the trout revert to the deeper sections of the lake. At this time, it is necessary to use sinking line with searching patterns such as leeches or olive colour damselfly nymphs. Fishing remains quite strong through the summer.

Although fly-fishing is more effective for trout, spincasters and trollers can still see some good results. During the summer, trollers should work the deeper water near the drop off.

Directions

Mineral Lake is located south of Cranbrook near the much larger Moyie Lake. To reach the lake, follow Highway 3/95 to the access road to the Moyie Lake Provincial Park at the north end of the big lake. When the road forks, keep right on the Lamb Creek Forest Service Road rather than accessing the actual park area. After an initial climb, the forest road levels and passes by the pretty little lake. The gravel road is accessible by most vehicles and there is plenty of parking at the recreation site.

Facilities

The recreation site located at Mineral Lake is a day-use only area that is set at the site of a former sawmill at the north end of the lake. Visitors will find a few picnic tables and a good boat launch at the recreation site. This is a popular location during the summer months, especially with local anglers. If you wish to stay overnight in the area, nearby **Moyie Lake Provincial Park** is home to a popular campsite.

Other Options

Just to the north of Mineral Lake, you can easily find Monroe Lake not far off the Lamb Creek Forest Service Road. **Monroe Lake** is a much larger lake mountain lake that offers fishing opportunities for stocked cutthroat trout, rainbow trout and kokanee. This lake is also highlighted in this book.

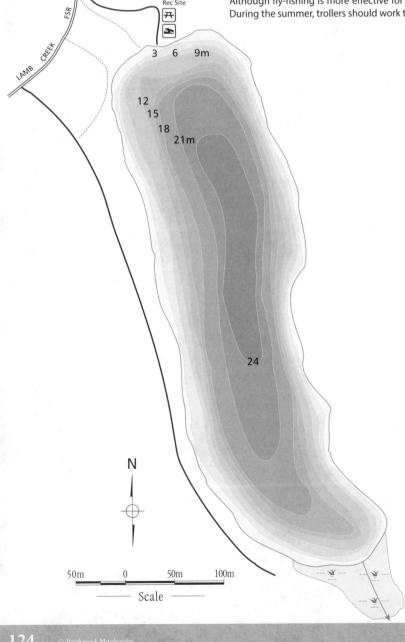

To Hwy 3/95

LAMB CREEK FSR

Mineral Lake Rec Site

N

50m   0   50m   100m
Scale

Mineral Lake Fish Stocking Data			
Year	Species	Number	Life Stage
2009	Rainbow Trout	1,000	Spring/Catchable
2008	Rainbow Trout	1,000	Yearling/Catchable
2007	Rainbow Trout	1,000	Yearling/Catchable

Missezula Lake

Location: 35 km (22 mi) north of Princeton
Elevation: 1,009 m (3,310 ft)
Surface Area: 241 ha (596 ac)
Mean Depth: 30.7 m (101 ft)
Max Depth: 74.1 m (243 ft)
Way Point: 120° 31' 00" Lon - W 49° 47' 00" Lat - N

8 Region

Fishing

Missezula Lake is one of the larger, more popular lakes in the hills north of the town of Princeton. There are cottages at the south end of the lake, and the recreation site at the north end of the lake can be quite busy, especially on a nice weekend.

Fishing in Missezula Lake is generally fair for rainbow trout, brook trout and kokanee. Both rainbow trout and brook trout are stocked in the lake on a regular basis and provide for most of the action in the lake. The kokanee are part of a past stocking program, and have managed to establish a self reproducing population.

Trolling is the main angling method used on the long and narrow lake, although fly anglers can have decent success in the spring and fall. The lake is at a relatively low elevation, and fishing success tends to taper off significantly in the summer. The use of a downrigger in the deeper holes is highly recommended during the warm summer months.

If you do fly-fish or spincast on the lake it is best to try your luck around one of the many inlet streams. The cool streams bring nutrients and insect to the lake as well as helping create oxygen levels preferred by trout. There are two streams within easy walk of the Missezula Lake Recreation site near the north end of the lake. A small craft or float tube can be helpful, although when the wind is blowing, you will get pushed around.

Spincasters can work small lures like Mepps or a Blue Fox, while fly anglers can use a black leech if there is no active hatch happening.

Ice fishing is quite popular on the lake from the time the ice is frozen thick enough to walk on until about the end of February. A popular bait for ice fishing is frozen shrimp from the grocery store, but worms, if you can find some, will work well, too. The best time to catch fish here is at the crack of dawn, which, fortunately is much later in winter than it is in summer. Earlier in the day, you should fish the shallows, sometimes as close as 3 m (10 ft) from shore, since the fish prefer to scour the shoals for food. A common technique is to use a weight to get the hook down until it hits bottom, then crank the lure up a couple twists so it is suspended just off the bottom.

Facilities

This elongated shaped lake offers ten campsites at the **Missezula Lake North Recreation Site**. The recreation site is set amid a nice stand of trees and has a decent boat launch for access. The good 2wd access and water sports make this a popular site during summer. Snowmobiling is also popular in the summer.

At the south end of the lake are several private cottages. Please respect any private property in the area.

Directions

Follow Highway 5A north from Princeton past Allison and Summit Lake, eventually meeting the Dillard Creek Forest Service Road closer to Aspen Grove. Take this good logging road east. Shortly after the long switchback over Bluey Creek, the Missezula Lake Road branches south. This road will take you to northwest end of Missezula Lake.

The south end of the lake is accessed off Highway 5A via the Summers Creek Road and the Missezula Lake Forest Service Road. It is 32 km (19.8 mi) to the south end of the lake.

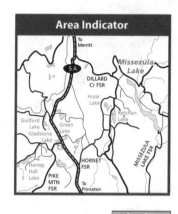

Area Indicator

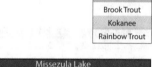

Species
Brook Trout
Kokanee
Rainbow Trout

Missezula Lake			
Fish Stocking Data			
Year	Species	Number	Life Stage
2013	Rainbow Trout	50,000	Yearling/Fry
2013	Brook Trout	25,000	Fingerling
2012	Rainbow Trout	0	Fingerling
2011	Rainbow Trout	136,406	Fry
2011	Brook Trout	0	Fingerling

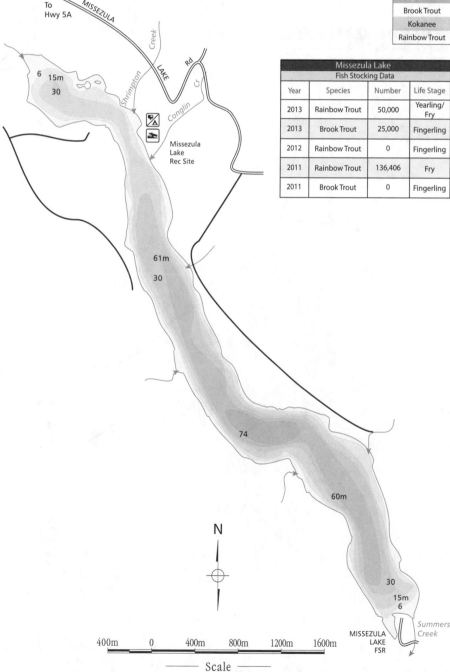

To Hwy 5A — MISSEZULA — Shrimpton Creek — LAKE Rd — Conglin Cr

6 15m 30

Missezula Lake Rec Site

61m 30

74

60m

30 15m 6

MISSEZULA LAKE FSR — Summers Creek

N

400m   0   400m   800m   1200m   1600m

Scale

Region 4

Location: 14 km (8.5 mi) south of Parson
Elevation: 996 m (3,268 ft)
Surface Area: 67 ha (161 ac)
Mean Depth: 5 m (166 ft)
Max Depth: 10 m (33 ft)
Way Point: 116° 34' 00" Lon - W 50° 57' 00" Lat - N

Mitten Lake

Area Indicator

Species

Rainbow Trout

Mitten Lake Fish Stocking Data			
Year	Species	Number	Life Stage
2013	Rainbow Trout	10,000	Yearling
2012	Rainbow Trout	10,000	Yearling
2011	Rainbow Trout	10,000	Yearling

Fishing

Mitten Lake is a popular, medium size lake found south of the town of Parson. With a mix of forested and marshy shoreline, the lake is known to be a good fishing hole and big enough for small trailed boats.

Partially as a result of its popularity, and partially the cause of it, the lake is heavily stocked with Gerrard trout, which are famous for how large they can get. Of course, the size of the lake restricts how large the fish can get, and truth be told, with the amount of fishing pressure the lake sees, the fish are mostly fished out before they can get to any great size. The majority of the fish that are caught in the lake are rarely bigger than 30 cm (12 inches).

There are also rumours that suckers have been illegally dumped in the lake. If this is true, they would be competing for the same food as the trout, which might negatively impact the fishery.

Fishing is best during the spring and fall periods by working the shoal areas around the lake. During the summer the lake warms and as a result the fishing slows down. At this time, early in the morning and again at dusk are the best times to test your luck.

Fly anglers should try working a chironomid or bloodworm along the shoals in early spring. Suspend the fly about 0.5-1 m (1.5-3 ft) from bottom and retrieve very slowly to imitate rising pupae. When the action is slow, the best way to find trout in this lake is to troll a leech pattern near the bottom. For spincasters, small spinners or still fishing with a bobber and worm can produce results. Spinners to try include a small Mepps or Blue Fox. Vary the colour until you find something that works. Another trick is to avoid presenting too much flash with your spinner since this will deter strikes.

Directions

Mitten Lake is a secluded lake located south of the town of Parson. The lake can be found by following Highway 95 to Parson where the Crestbrook Main Road branches south. This road crosses the Columbia River before rising to the benchlands to the west. At about the 6 km mark, turn south on the Mitten Lake Road. Follow this semi-rough spur road for about 14 km to find the recreation site and access to the lake. Despite the road access, people do trailer in boats and camping trailers.

Facilities

The **Mitten Lake Recreation Site** is the most popular of the 11 recreation sites located in the area. Since the water in the lake warms in the summer, the site has become a popular site for water skiing, swimming and boating. The main site features a large dock, small beach, boat launch area for trailered boats, wheelchair accessible toilets and space for over 20 vehicles. Three other sites along the east shore provide camping for another five or so parties. There is a fee to camp here from early May until the end of October.

Other Options

There are a number of good fishing alternatives around Mitten Lake including **Bittern Lake** to the northwest and **Nine Bay Lake** to the southeast. Both are accessed off the Mitten Lake Road, although Nine Bay Lake requires a short hike to reach it. Stocked with rainbow trout, fishing in these lakes can be quite good at times. They are both described in more detail in this book.

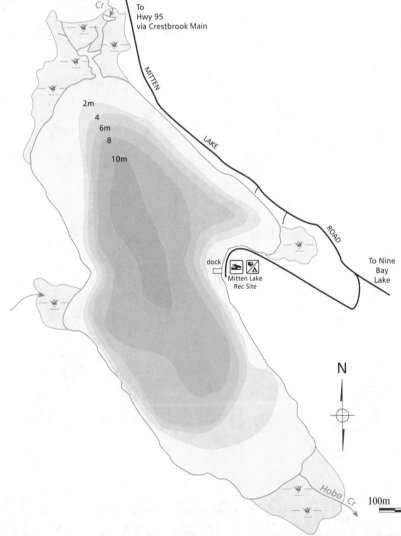

N

100m 0 100m 200m 300m 400m 500m

— Scale —

Monroe Lake

Location: 18 km (11 mi) south of Cranbrook
Elevation: 1,075 m (3,527 ft)
Surface Area: 52 ha (128 ac)
Mean Depth: 12.8 m (42 ft)
Max Depth: 30.8 m (101 ft)
Way Point: 115° 51′ 00″ Lon - W 49° 21′ 00″ Lat - N

Region 4

Fishing

Monroe is a small, Z-shaped lake a couple kilometres off Highway 3/95 south of Cranbrook. It is a popular destination for locals and is currently being stocked multiple times each year with both Gerrard strains of rainbow trout as well as kokanee. The lake also holds a good population of cutthroat and there are reports of a rainbow/cutthroat trout cross inhabiting Monroe Lake. Regardless, fishing for cutthroat and rainbow can be great at times.

The lake is quite deep, and has plenty of food for the trout to grow big on. In the spring, chironomid patterns can literally create a frenzy of consistent action. Work your chironomid along the shoal areas in the 4-6 m (13-20 ft) range very, very slowly. A little later in the spring, the mayfly hatches take over and are known to provide some good dry fly-fishing on occasion. During the summer months, trout revert to the deeper sections of the lake. Finding trout can be a little more challenging at this time, although you can find some success with a sinking line and searching patterns such as leeches or olive colour damselfly nymphs.

Since cutthroat trout are a little more aggressive, spincasters and trollers can have some success with small lures and spinners. You will want a little silver in these lures to help them resemble baitfish that the cutthroat often feed on. It is essential to have a floatation device since the near shore area is quite shallow in this lake.

Kokanee are best caught on a lake troll with a short leader, Wedding Band and maggot. A Flatfish or small pink Spin-N-Glo lures can also be effective. Fly anglers can try trolling slowly with a small red Doc Spratley or Woolly Bugger within a few feet of the surface. In the spring, chironomids and mayflies can also work for kokanee.

Directions

You can find Monroe Lake south of Cranbrook in the mountains above the much larger Moyie Lake. To reach the lake, follow Highway 3/95 to the access road to the Moyie Lake Provincial Park at the north end of the big lake. When the road forks, keep right on the Lamb Creek Forest Service Road rather than accessing the actual park area. As you climb out of the valley, the access road to Monroe branches right, about another kilometre later. This branch road is quite steep and has a few sections that may require a high clearance vehicle. Parking is available off the road next to the lake.

Facilities

Since there are a number of private cabins on the lake, access and camping in the area is somewhat limited. There is, however, a place to hand launch small boats. Nearby offers a large campsite, a nice beach area and a good boat launch onto Moyie Lake.

Other Options

Little Monroe Lake is located to the west of the much larger Monroe Lake. The little lake can be accessed by rough trail from Monroe Lake or by a rough access road from further south on the Lamb Creek Forest Service Road. Little Monroe Lake offers fishing opportunities for stocked cutthroat trout. Most fly anglers that visit the pair of lakes prefer fishing the smaller lake due to its remoteness and size.

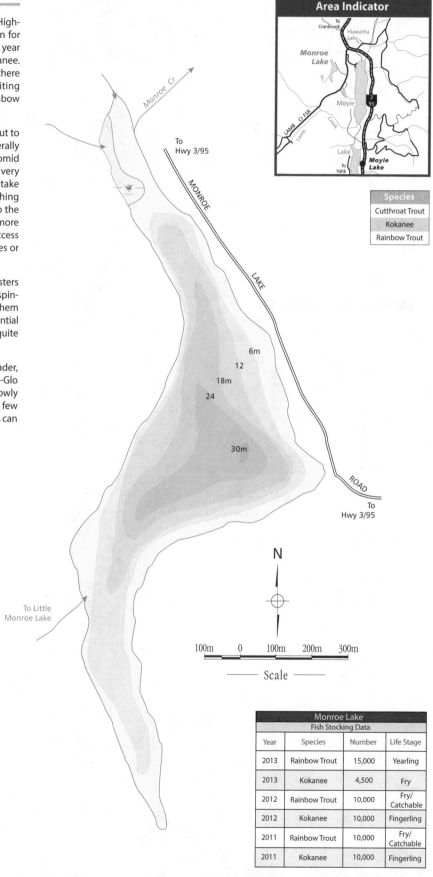

Area Indicator

Species
Cutthroat Trout
Kokanee
Rainbow Trout

Monroe Lake			
Fish Stocking Data			
Year	Species	Number	Life Stage
2013	Rainbow Trout	15,000	Yearling
2013	Kokanee	4,500	Fry
2012	Rainbow Trout	10,000	Fry/Catchable
2012	Kokanee	10,000	Fingerling
2011	Rainbow Trout	10,000	Fry/Catchable
2011	Kokanee	10,000	Fingerling

Location: 18 km (11 mi) south of Cranbrook
Elevation: 927 m (3,041 ft)
Surface Area: 312 ha (770 ac)
Mean Depth: 32.3 m (106 ft)
Max Depth: 57.3 m (188 ft)
Way Point: 115° 50'00" Lon - W 49° 17'00" Lat - N

Moyie Lake

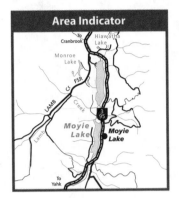

Area Indicator

Species
Brook Trout
Bull Trout
Cutthroat Trout
Kokanee
Rainbow Trout
Whitefish

Moyie Lake			
Fish Stocking Data			
Year	Species	Number	Life Stage
2013	Rainbow Trout	44,960	Yearling
2013	Kokanee	70,000	Fry
2012	Rainbow Trout	30,000	Yearling/Fry
2012	Kokanee	65,000	Fingerling
2011	Rainbow Trout	73,338	Yearling
2011	Kokanee	65,000	Yearling

Directions

South of Cranbrook, you can find Moyie Lake off the west side of Highway 3/95. The lake is actually two water bodies that are nestled in the valley between the Yahk Ridge and the Moyie mountain range. Moyie Lake Provincial Park is the main access area to the upper lake and provides a scenic location to spend the day or weekend. The community of Moyie Lake provides access to the lower lake.

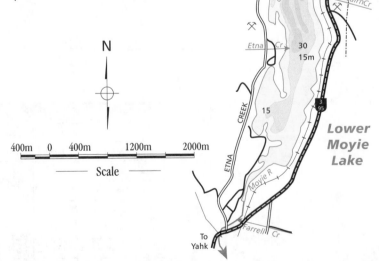

N

400m 0 400m 1200m 2000m
Scale

Fishing

Moyie Lake is a long, narrow lake found alongside Highway 3/95 south of Cranbrook. It is one of the most popular recreation lakes in the area, and during the summer, activity on the lake increases dramatically with an abundance of motorboats, water skiers and folks on the beaches in Moyie Lake Provincial Park. There are two lakes, Upper Moyie Lake and Lower Moyie Lake, which are connected by a short channel.

The two main sportfish sought after are rainbow trout and kokanee. The Gerrard strain of rainbow are regularly stocked in the lake and fishing is often fair for trout that can reach up to 1.5 kg (3.5 lbs). Kokanee are stocked in the lake periodically and fishing success is fair for small kokanee that can be found to 30 cm (12 in).

Other sportfish found in the lake include bull trout, cutthroat trout, brook trout and whitefish. Bull trout can reach the 1.5 kg (3.5 lb) range on occasion, while brookies and cutthroat can grow to 0.5 kg (1 lb).

The main method of angling on Moyie Lake is trolling. Trolling is effective because it allows you to cover more of the lake to find those cruising fish looking for a good meal. In addition to lake trolls, silver spoons seem to be the lure of choice to catch most trout species, as well as kokanee. During the spring you can troll the upper layer of the lake, while a downrigger is recommended to find consistent action during the summer.

Fly anglers and spincasters will find the best results by casting towards one of the many natural points found around both sections of the lake. Another higher percentage area year round is near creek inflows. Spincasting, fly-fishing and even trolling around the drop off can be very effective in this area.

Facilities

This popular lake is home to a number of resorts, cottages, a provincial park and a few privately operated campgrounds. The town of Moyie Lake is found along Highway 3/95 and offers a gas station and general store as well as a popular pub. For more elaborate amenities, including hotels and other services, the city of Cranbrook is a short drive north along Highway 3/95.

Moyie Lake Provincial Park is located along the northern shore of the lake and is a full service park. Facilities include a boat launch, flush toilets and showers as well as a popular picnic and beach area. Visitors can also enjoy the shot interpretive trail that treks through the nearby forest. The park is open to camping from early May to the end of October and is equipped with 111 vehicle/tent sites. This park is busy during the summer and reservations are recommended. For reservations call 1-800-689-9025 or visit www.discovercamping.ca.

Murphy Lakes

Fishing

This small pair of lakes lies within the Coquihalla Mountain Range at the foot of Grasshopper Mountain. They are a long way from any major settlement, and angling pressure is relatively light, although don't expect to have the place to yourself on a weekend.

Both lakes are stocked every year with rainbow trout, which provide for good fishing in the spring and fall. Even though the eastern Murphy Lake is the easiest to access, the lakes are comparable in fishing quality, possibly because the east lake is stocked much heavier than the west.

The small size of the lakes makes it easier to find trout, although they can still be quite elusive at times. For fly anglers, chironomid patterns can be very good in the spring. Try using a darker pattern, even a black. A good technique to determine the depth of the water is to make indicator marks on your anchor rope, which will determine your leader length. Leech and dragonfly patterns are often the perfect recipe for finding trout during those slow periods, while a good old Tom Thumb can provide a lot of action when the fish are rising.

Spincasting from shore using a small spoon like a Mepps can be productive in the spring and fall, while the ol worm and bobber usually always has some takers on these lakes. There are fairly extensive shallows at the west end of the lake, but the rest of the lake features quick transitions into deeper water.

Directions

To reach the lakes from the west, follow Highway 5 to the Coquihalla Summit Recreation Area and take Exit 228 just north of the tollbooth. The Tulameen River Forest Service Road is a good gravel road that climbs up and over the mountain to the Lawless-Britton Forest Service Road, approximately 8 km (5 mi) later. Follow this road to Murphy Lakes.

From the east, the Lawless Creek Forest Service Road heads west from Tulameen. Follow this good gravel road until the Lawless-Britton Forest Service Road junction. This road switchbacks around Lawless and Shwum Creeks before eventually reaching the access road into the lakes.

The main roads are easily passable with a 2wd vehicle, although the final access road requires a 4wd or a hike to the lake. A copy of the Backroad Mapbook for the Thompson Okanagan is quite helpful in locating these lakes.

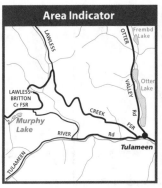

Area Indicator

Species
Rainbow Trout

West Murphy Lake

Elevation: 1,206 m (3,957 ft)
Surface Area: 6 ha (15 ac)
Mean Depth: 1.8 m (6 ft)
Max Depth: 4 m (13 ft)
Way Point: 120° 55' 00" Lon - W 49° 33' 00" Lat - N

East Murphy Lake

Elevation: 1,206 m (3,957 ft)
Surface Area: 7.5 ha (18.5 ac)
Mean Depth: 2 m (6 ft)
Max Depth: 4 m (13 ft)
Way Point: 120° 55' 00" Lon - W 49° 33' 00" Lat - N

To
Tulameen
FSR
-BRITTON

LAWLESS

2
1m 3m 4 5m

1m
2
3m
4

N

To
Coquihalla
Lakes &
Hwy 5

Murphy Lakes
West Rec Site

100m   0   100m   200m   300m

— Scale —

| West Murphy Lake | | | |
| Fish Stocking Data | | | |
Year	Species	Number	Life Stage
2013	Rainbow Trout	3,000	Fry
2012	Rainbow Trout	3,000	Fry
2011	Rainbow Trout	3,000	Fry

| East Murphy Lake | | | |
| Fish Stocking Data | | | |
Year	Species	Number	Life Stage
2013	Rainbow Trout	1,000	Fry
2012	Rainbow Trout	1,000	Fry
2011	Rainbow Trout	1,000	Fry

Other Options

Near the exit on the Coquihalla Highway you will pass the **Coquihalla Lakes** off the west side of the Tulameen Forest Service Road. Surprisingly, the lakes receive low angling pressure for being so close to the highway. Fishing can be good at times for decent sized rainbow trout. Since the lakes are high elevation lakes, the season does not start until usually June and ends in the fall.

Facilities

The **Murphy Lakes West Recreation Site** is a small, 4 unit site on the west end of the lakes. It is a popular spot for anglers and hunters alike and can be quite busy on weekends throughout the year. Visitors will also find a place to hand launch small craft. It is about an 800 metre walk from the campsite to the lake.

Region 4

Location: 23 km (14 mi) southwest of Castlegar
Elevation: 1,266 m (4,153 ft)
Surface Area: 29 ha (72 ac)
Mean Depth: 3.8 m (12 ft)
Max Depth: 7.4 m (24 ft)
Way Point: 117° 56' 00" Lon - W 49° 15' 00" Lat - N

Nancy Greene Lake

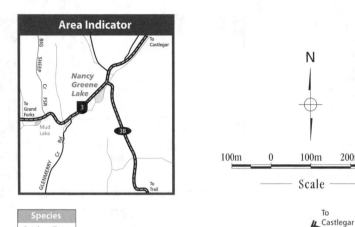

Area Indicator

Species
Rainbow Trout

Nancy Green (Sheep) Lake Fish Stocking Data			
Year	Species	Number	Life Stage
2013	Rainbow Trout	6,000	Spring Catchable
2012	Rainbow Trout	6,000	Catchable
2011	Rainbow Trout	6,000	Catchable

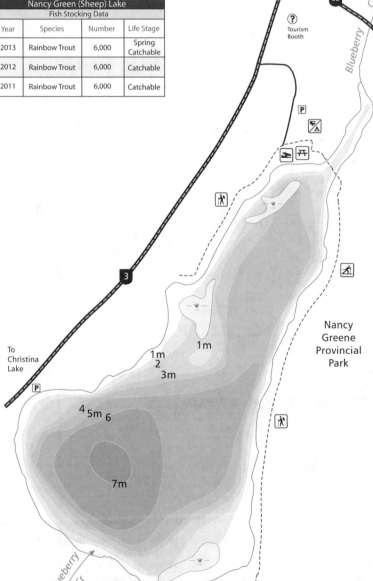

Fishing

Nancy Greene Lake is named after the legendary Canadian Olympic downhill skier Nancy Greene. Also known as Sheep Lake by the old-timers in the area, it is a high elevation lake along the Crowsnest Highway to the west of Castlegar. The lake is being promoted as a catch and keep fishery, and is stocked annually with 1,000 catchable rainbow trout. Fishing success can be hit and miss for rainbow in the 30 cm (12 in) range.

Both fly-fishing and spincasting can produce results when the trout are in the mood. Late spring and summer are the best times to fish here, as the fish seem to take readily to flies like a Carey Special or a Woolly Bugger, although nymph patterns will also work well. The large shoal area found along the western shore is often a good holding area for rainbow. Try stripping in a bead head nymph or casting a small spinner just off the 2 m (6.5 ft) shoal area.

On calm summer evenings, the trout are often seen sipping flies from the surface. A dry fly like a Tom Thumb or a Royal Wulff can work well, depending on what the trout are feeding on.

Fishing from shore is possible in places, but probably won't produce well outside of the first few weeks after ice off. The lake is quite shallow and marshy in places around the edges and is easiest to cast into when the water levels are higher. Still, it is often worthwhile to have a fly rod in the evenings, even if you can't get out onto the lake. Outside of the main beach area, the best place to fish from shore is where Highway 3 passes next to the lake.

Although the trout are lethargic, ice fishing is common in winter. Rainbow are not known for being the best ice fishing fish, but that doesn't stop local anglers from heading out onto the ice. Jigging is the most common technique used for ice fishing, using a small, highly reflective lure. While historically, may people just allowed the lure to dangle, jigging usually works better, as the movement and the sound help attract fish.

No powerboats are allowed on the lake.

Directions

The lake lies near the junction of Highway 3 and Highway 3B, west of Castlegar and northwest of Rossland. The main access point is found in the provincial park. From the parking area, it is a short hike down to the lake. An alternate access can be found west of the highway junction and park access point off the east side of Highway 3. Look for the paved pull out area off the highway. From there it is a short but steep walk down to the lake.

Facilities

Visitors to Nancy Greene Lake will find the small **Nancy Greene Provincial Park** campsite located along the north end of the lake. The park is popular with day-trippers and is equipped with outhouses, picnic tables and a warm up cabin for cross-country skiers. In addition to a good trail system around the lake, there is a place to launch small boats.

Nevertouch Lake

Location: 56 km (35 mi) southeast of Kelowna
Elevation: 1,302 m (4,262 ft)
Surface Area: 52 ha (128 ac)
Mean Depth: 6.7 m (22 ft)
Max Depth: 17.7 m (58 ft)
Way Point: 118° 46′ 00″ Lon - W 49° 46′ 00″ Lat - N

Fishing

In 2007, there was a large forest fire around Nevertouch Lake which burned through the area, charring the forest around the lake. The fire completely surrounded the lake. Although this may have changed the viewscape, fishing remains quite good at times for stocked rainbow trout. The lake can still be accessed; although care must be taken as fire damaged trees are known to just randomly fall over.

Fly-fishing is the preferred angling method used on the lake due mainly to the great success fly anglers often have at the lake. All the normal Okanagan hatches occur, but anglers say the trout are often very aggressive towards terrestrials and other top water flies, such as caddis flies. Try using a flying ant or grasshopper imitation during warmer spells in late spring and through the summer. Other popular dry flies include the Tom Thumb, a general purpose dry fly which is often used to imitate a caddis, as well as the Elk Hair Caddis. Paying attention to the current hatch will always improve success.

There is a large shoal area at the south end of the lake as well as around the corner from the forest recreation site. These are good areas to focus in the spring and fall. As the lake begins to warm, anglers will find success off the small island found in the northern portion of the lake or along the narrow deep band in the southern half. At these times, trolling searching patterns or lake trolls can be effective.

Facilities

The **Nevertouch Lake Recreation Site** was another victim of the wildfires of 2007. Luckily some trees were saved and a new campsite was built in 2008. There are now a total of 15 campsites in two adjacent areas at the north end of the lake. A gravel boat launch, suitable for cartop boats, is available. The quick nature of the repairs can attest to the popularity of the fishery and out of the way lake.

Nevertouch Lake Fish Stocking Data			
Year	Species	Number	Life Stage
2013	Rainbow Trout	5,000	Fry
2012	Rainbow Trout	5,000	Fry
2011	Rainbow Trout	5,000	Fry

Directions

Nevertouch Lake is a remote lake lying in the Kettle River Valley to the east of Big White Ski Area. There are several access options and a copy of the Backroad Mapbook for the Thompson Okanagan along with a GPS and 4wd vehicle is certainly recommended when travelling this far into the backcountry.

To find the lake, you will need to get onto the Kettle River Forest Service Road. This road links the Christian Valley Road and Highway 33 in the south with Highway 6 in the north. From the south, the Nevertouch Lake Forest Service Road is found about 67 km north of Highway 33. From here it is at least another 14 km along this smaller logging road that climbs its way out of the valley and up to the lake.

From the north, the distance from Highway 6 to the start of the Nevertouch Forest Service Road is a bit shorter (just over 46 km), but is quite a bit rougher. Needless to say, the distance travelled requires at least an overnight stay.

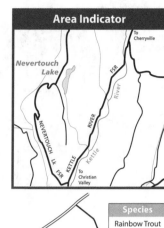

Area Indicator

Species

Rainbow Trout

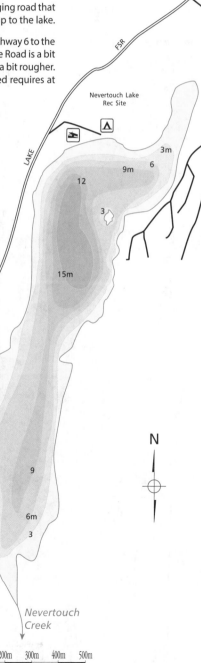

Nevertouch Lake
Rec Site

3m
9m
6
12
3
15m
9
6m
3

N

To
Kettle
River FSR

Nevertouch
Creek

100m 0 100m 200m 300m 400m 500m

Scale

New Lake

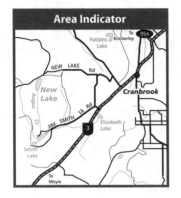

Area Indicator

Species

Rainbow Trout

New Lake Fish Stocking Data			
Year	Species	Number	Life Stage
2013	Rainbow Trout	2,000	Spring Catchable
2012	Rainbow Trout	2,000	Catchable
2011	Rainbow Trout	2,000	Catchable

Directions

You can find New Lake just west of the city of Cranbrook via New Lake Road. New Lake Road is found off King Road, just south of the city centre. There is a small parking area off the road next to the lake.

Facilities

There are no facilities available at New Lake. The city of **Cranbrook** provides all the necessary amenities including tackle shops, hotels and motels and a good selection of restaurants.

Fishing

New lake is a shallow, boggy lake located west of Cranbrook that is often not completely ice free until late April. Because it is so close to Cranbrook, it is a popular lake. As a result, the Freshwater Fisheries Society of BC stocks the lake regularly with catchable sized rainbow trout.

The lake continues to provide good fishing for trout, which grow rapidly due to the presence of freshwater shrimp and other ample food sources. Rainbow in the lake can be found up to 2 kg (4.5 lbs) in size, although they average much smaller. Because of the reeds and the shallowness of the lake, it's best to have a float tube or small boat to get out to deeper water.

The southern and most northern areas of the lake are very shallow, with reeds and lily pads stretching out quite far from shore. At first glance, the lake looks like it is too shallow to hold fish, but there is actually a fairly deep hole towards the north end. The best place to fish are the east and west edges of this hole, as these provide the steepest drop offs. That's not to say that fish won't be found towards the north and south. When the water isn't too warm, the lily pads provide cover for the rainbow trout as they forage for food.

The lake is thick with scuds, which are small shrimp. You'd think that a scud pattern would work well, but they don't really, as there are so many to choose from the fish will rarely find yours. Rather than trying to match what the trout are eating, it is often better to go against the grain, and try an attractor pattern like a Woolly Bugger or Royal Coachman. Alternatively, try trolling leeches and dragonfly nymphs deep during the day when hatch activity is limited.

A lake troll with a Wedding Band and worm or bait is a popular alternative for non-fly anglers. Spincasting with spoons and small spinners cast towards the drop offs also works on occasion. Lures such as a silver Dick Nite, Flatfish, Kamlooper, Mepps or Panther Martin can all entice the fish to bite.

When the water is calm during the evenings, trolling does not work well, as the movement of your boat will scare the fish away. It is best to drop anchor and fish from one location. If the trout are rising, and you have dry fly gear, try working the top of the water.

Other Options

New Lake is the headwater to Angus Creek, which flows south to Jim Smith Lake. **Jim Smith Lake** is a popular recreational area that is easily accessible via the Jim Smith Lake Road from Highway 3. The lake is home to a full service provincial park and offers fishing opportunities for largemouth bass, rainbow trout and brook trout. Look for details on this lake earlier in the book.

To Cranbrook via New Lake Rd

3m
5
6m
8

9m

Angus Creek

N

100m 0 100m 200m 300m

Scale

Nicklen Lake

Location: 24 km (15 mi) southeast of Vernon
Elevation: 1,314 m (4,311 ft)
Surface Area: 89 ha (220 ac)
Mean Depth: 12 m (39 ft)
Max Depth: 41 m (135 ft)
Way Point: 119° 0' 00" Lon - W 50° 08' 00" Lat - N

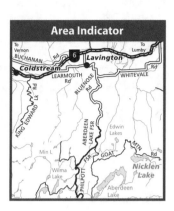

Area Indicator

Species

Rainbow Trout

Fishing

Nicklen Lake is a surprisingly deep lake that offers good fishing for resident rainbow trout that can reach up to 2 kg (4.5 lbs) in size on occasion. Trolling is the preferred angling method used on the lake due to the large size and depth of the lake.

The lake features many nooks and crannies, points and coves as well as islands where the fish will want to hang out. There is an abundance of fish habitat which is both a blessing and a curse; yes, the lake is home to lots of fish, but finding where they are holding can be a bit of a challenge sometime. Using the chart and a depth sounder should help you locate the number of unique shoal areas found around the lake bottom that can provide for good holding areas for trout. During the summer, it is recommended to try trolling with a downrigger along the four deeper holes in the lake. If possible, troll right along the drop off for added success.

Spincasters and fly anglers can also find some success for rainbow near the creek inlets or at the eastern end of the lake during the spring. However, as the water warms up, the fish will move away from the warm water at the eastern end of the lake.

The lake is also open to ice fishing, which usually starts around mid-December. The fish holds rainbow trout, which are not the most active species in the winter. The earlier you get to the lake, the more active they will be. Just make sure the ice is thick enough before heading out. The fish are usually found less than 3 m (10 ft) below the ice in areas where they can feed. This means closer to shore. Frozen shrimp works well, as do worms or maggots.

Directions

Home to a nice resort, finding this lake is relatively easy if you follow their signs. However, it is a fair ways from the highway and visitors with cars or low clearance vehicles should be prepared for a sometimes bumpy drive.

To find the lake, follow Highway 6 east from Vernon to Learmouth Road. Turn south on Learmouth and follow this windy backroad east to Reid Road, which will take you south to Bluenose Road and eventually the Aberdeen Lake Forest Service Road. The Forest Service Road marks the beginning of the gravel road that is signed with kilometre markings. At the 11 km and 14 km mark, keep left. The later junction is the start of the Goat Mountain Road, which winds its way up to the lake. The resort is found about 9 km along the Goat and the recreation site rests shortly after.

Facilities

There are also two recreation sites on the lake. **Nicklen Lake East**, which has space for 5 groups, and **Nicklen Lake West**, which also has space for about 5 groups. Both recreation sites have cartop boat launches, but note that the water levels fluctuate significantly on the lake. There is also a resort on the lake that offers roofed accommodations, RV campsites and boat rentals. Visit www.nicklenlake.com for more information.

Other Options

Goat Mountain Lake is fine fishing alternative located just east of Nicklen Lake. To reach Goat Mountain Lake, continue east along the deteriorating road. If you cannot drive the remainder of the route, you can easily hike to the lake. There is a scenic recreation site campsite and good fishing for resident rainbow trout.

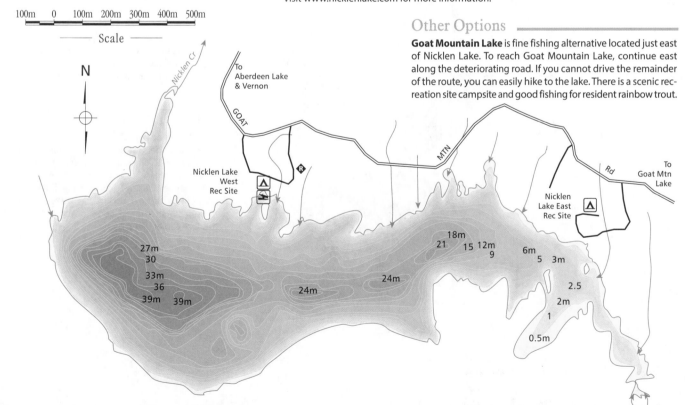

Region 4

Location: 17 km (10.5 mi) south of Parson
Elevation: 963 m (3,159 ft)
Surface Area: 34 ha (84 ac)
Mean Depth: 3.5 m (11 ft)
Max Depth: 11 m (36 ft)
Way Point: 116° 32'00" Lon - W 50°56'00" Lat - N

Nine Bay Lake

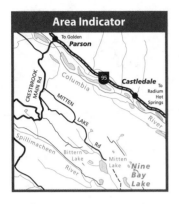

Area Indicator

Species
Rainbow Trout

Nine Bay Lake Fish Stocking Data			
Year	Species	Number	Life Stage
2013	Rainbow Trout	1,500	Yearling
2012	Rainbow Trout	1,500	Yearling
2011	Rainbow Trout	1,500	Yearling/Fingerling

Fishing

Nine Bay Lake is found at the end of a trail (about 200 m/600 ft) from the end of a rough, dead end road. It takes its name from a series of bays that ring the lake, although whether or not there are actually nine bays here depends an awful lot on what you count as a bay.

Even though it is only a short hike in to the lake, it is enough to stop the majority of anglers who prefer their lake access to be roadside. This means that the few anglers willing to make the hike in will find the fishing quite good.

It is possible to haul a small boat or canoe and an electric motor to the lake and use it to troll, but it is easier to bring a belly boat, pick a spot, and fish from there. In fact, the fish are easily spooked by things moving on the surface of these sorts of shallow lakes. Although shore fishing is possible from a few areas, the best fishing is found along the south side of the big island, which is not accessible by foot. This is a great place to fish for stocked rainbow trout, which can get quite big. There have been reports of rainbow up to 3 kg (6.5 lbs) inhabiting the lake.

You might think that the bays on the lake would provide good fishing. Unfortunately. Most of them are simply too shallow to hold no fish. In fact, by the end of summer, some of the bays hold no water. However, there are large shoal areas throughout the lake that are coupled with plenty of weed growth. These are ideal conditions for feeding trout. Work your fly or lure towards these structures in search of cruising rainbow. The best time to fish the lake is in the spring and fall but you will often find success during the summer months, especially as evening approaches.

There are special restrictions at the lake, including a bait ban, single hook requirements and a shortened season from May 1st to October 31st. You can also only keep one trout over 50 cm (15 inches).

Directions

This remote hike-in lake is located south of Parson. The best way to reach this lake is to travel Highway 95 to Parson. At Parson, follow the Crestbrook Main Road west for 6 km and turn east onto the Mitten Lake Road. This spur road travels over 15 km past the northern shore of Mitten Lake. Beyond the recreation site turnoff, the road becomes quite rough. Depending on how far you can drive, it is at least a couple hundred metres into Nine Bay Lake.

Facilities

Visitors to Nine Bay Lake can enjoy the quaint, forested recreation site. The rustic site has room for a few tents and is not heavily used. The 200 metre portage to the scenic lake can deter some visitors from bringing a boat.

Other Options

En route to Nine Bay Lake, you pass by **Mitten Lake.** Mitten Lake offers fishing for stocked rainbow trout and is home to a good size forest recreation site. Due to the easier access, Mitten Lake is more popular than nine Mile Bay Lake, although if the fishing happens to be slow at Nine Bay Lake, it makes a reasonable alternative. Look for more details on this lake earlier in the book.

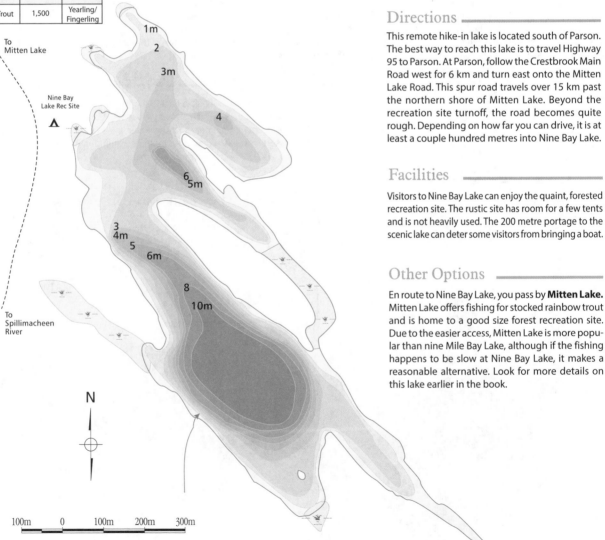

N

100m 0 100m 200m 300m

— Scale —

Nixon Lake

Location: 22 km (13.5 mi) south of Golden
Elevation: 1,331 m (4,367 ft)
Surface Area: 4 ha (10 ac)
Mean Depth: 8.7 m (29 ft)
Max Depth: 16 m (52.5 ft)
Way Point: 116° 57' 00" Lon - W 51° 06' 00" Lat - N

Fishing

Nixon Lake is stocked with a few hundred, maybe a thousand or so rainbow trout, every couple or three years. The amount of fish being stocked in the lake has been steadily declining from the 1970s, when some years there were over 10,000 fish stocked in the lake.

The high stocking numbers simply are not needed, since the lake is so far from the highway and does not receive a lot angling pressure. As a result some good sized rainbow can be found in the lake. The lake is also home to a small population of cutthroat trout.

The high elevation of Nixon Lake also creates a shortened fishing season. The lake is usually open by June but during certain years it can be ice free in late May. The lake ices over sometimes as early as November. As a result, the action is usually pretty steady during the ice free period.

When the lake finally warms up, there is a riot of insect activity on the lake. Fishing the lake right after ice up can be quite productive, as the fish are usually quite hungry. And when the insects start hatching, they all start hatching at once. This can be good and bad. Some days, the fish will take most anything you throw at them, while other days they can be particularly finicky and only take a certain fly at a certain size and in a certain colour. If you happen to be fishing here and see someone having more success why not go over and ask them what they are using. Most anglers are very willing to help out.

The pothole nature of the lake makes shore fishing somewhat difficult. If you have a floatation device, cast towards shore near the drop off area or any structure. On the other hand, the lake is deep enough to troll.

The best way to find rainbow in this small lake is to try an attractor fly such as a Woolly Bugger. Dry fly anglers can also have a lot of fun at this small lake. When the hatch is on, you will find the smaller rainbow hitting the surface after caddis flies and other top water insects. Spincasters should have ample action with small spinners such as a Panther Martin or Blue Fox.

Other Options

The **Spillmacheen River** is a beautiful fast flowing river that parallels the access road to Nixon Lake. The river is inhabited by populations of rainbow trout that can reach up to 0.5 kg (1 lb) in areas. Break out the nymph fly patterns or small spinners and look for those bigger rainbow that hold up in the hundreds of enticing pools found throughout the length of the river.

Directions

Nixon Lake is another remote mountain lake found in the hills above Parson. To find the lake, travel to Parson via Highway 95, and then take the Crestbrook Main Road southwest from the highway. The main road leads to the Spillmacheen Forest Service Road, which travels northwest along the river. It is a fair drive on a generally good forest road (over 21 km from the Spillmacheen/Crestbrook junction) that eventually passes by Nixon Lake. The small lake can be found off the north side of the road.

Facilities

Although there are no facilities available at Nixon Lake, rustic, Crown land camping is certainly possible in the area.

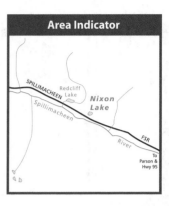

Area Indicator

Species
Rainbow Trout
Cutthroat Trout

Nixon Lake			
Fish Stocking Data			
Year	Species	Number	Life Stage
2013	Rainbow Trout	1,000	Yearling
2011	Rainbow Trout	1,000	Fall Fry

2m
4
6m
8
10m
12
14m
16

To Redcliffe Lake

To Parson & Hwy 95

N

SPILLIMACHEEN

FSR

To Parson & Hwy 95

100m   0   100m   200m

Scale

Norbury & Peckhams Lakes

Peckhams Lake

Elevation: 839 m (2,753 ft)
Surface Area: 14 ha (35 ac)
Mean Depth: 4 m (13 ft)
Max Depth: 9.5 m (31 ft)
Way Point: 115° 29'00" Lon - W 49° 32'00" Lat - N

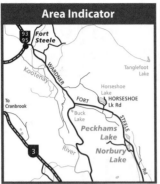

Area Indicator

Species
Rainbow Trout
Cutthroat Trout

Peckhams Lake Fish Stocking Data			
Year	Species	Number	Life Stage
2013	Rainbow Trout	2,000	Yearling/Catchable
2012	Rainbow Trout	3,250	Fingerling/Catchable
2011	Rainbow Trout	3,625	Catchable

Norbury (Garbutts) Lake

Elevation: 836 m (2,743 ft)
Surface Area: 11 ha (27 ac)
Mean Depth: 3.9 m (13 ft)
Max Depth: 8.2 m (27 ft)
Way Point: 115° 29'00" Lon - W 50° 49' 32'00" Lat - N

Species
Rainbow Trout
Brook Trout

Norbury (Garbutts) Lake Fish Stocking Data			
Year	Species	Number	Life Stage
2013	Rainbow Trout	1,500	Yearling/Catchable
2012	Rainbow Trout	1,500	Catchable
2011	Rainbow Trout	2,000	Yearling

Fishing

The provincial park in which these two lakes sit is named after Norbury Lake, which is the southern lake of the two. Actually, only Peckhams Lake sits completely within the park, while just the northern tip of Norburry is in the park.

The lakes receive plenty of attention by anglers throughout the season, as they are easily accessed off the paved Wardner-Fort Steele Road, which cuts through the middle of the park.

In order to maintain the quality fishery, both lakes are stocked with rainbow trout. Norbury Lake is also inhabited by a small population of cutthroat trout and is best fished in the spring and fall periods. Cutthroat tend to hang around the creek mouth whereas the rainbow are found along the drop offs and shoal areas.

Because the lakes are so clear, trolling is not the best strategy, as the shadow of the boat moving above the fish tends to spook them. It is possible to fish the lake from the shore during the spring and fall, and there is a trail around the northern half of Peckham Lake that will help anglers access various spots on the lake. During the summer, it is better to get out onto the lakes with a small boat or tube. Fly anglers can try an attractor fly such as a Woolly Bugger. Spincasters should have ample action with small spinners such as the Mepps or Blue Fox.

Peckhams Lake lies to the north of Norbury Lake and has a fair-sized population of small brook trout along with the stocked rainbow. Fishing in the lake is similar to Norbury Lake, with the best success coming in the spring and fall. During the heat of summer, trout in the lake tend to become lethargic and with the increased fishing and activity on the lake, success drops off significantly. Peckhams Lake is a beautifully clear lake that is surrounded by aspen trees set amid the backdrop of the Steeples. Even if the fishing is poor, the scenery is always magnificent.

No powerboats are allowed on either lake.

Directions

These two small lakes are located east of Cranbrook off the paved Wardner-Fort Steele Road. Follow Highway 95/93 to the historic site of Fort Steele and look for the Wardner-Fort Steele Road off the east side of the highway. The popular lakes are located just south of the junction with the Fenwick Road.

Facilities

The beautiful **Norbury Lake Provincial Park** encompasses Peckhams and part of Norbury Lake. The park is a small park equipped with 46 vehicle/tent campsites on Norbury Lake, as well as a picnic area on Peckhams Lake. Outhouses, a water pump and a boat launch with dock are found at both lakes. The park is set below the scenic Steeples mountain range and is open to camping from mid May to the September long weekend on a first-come, first-serve basis.

North Star Lake

Location: 13 km (8 mi) west of Elko
Elevation: 841 m (2,759 ft)
Surface Area: 25 ha (62 ac)
Mean Depth: 3.3 m (11 ft)
Max Depth: 10 m (33 ft)
Way Point: 115° 15' 00" Lon - W 49° 20' 00" Lat - N

Fishing

Set in an open rangeland between the Crowsnest Highway and Lake Koocanusa, North Star Lake is a small, shallow lake with a very muddy shoreline. Although shore casting is quite limited, those with a small boat or float tube can have a fair bit of success here earlier in the year. The lake is stocked annually with rainbow trout by the Freshwater Fisheries Society of BC to ensure a consistent fishery. As an added bonus, some hefty trout are caught in North Star Lake annually. Some reports say the trout can reach up to 3.5 kg (8 lbs) in size.

With such extensive shallow areas and mud flat, the insect hatches on this lake can be prolific. Fly anglers need simply pay attention to the hatches to have some success. However, the lower elevation of the lake means that the hatches are usually a bit earlier here. Look for chironomid (midge) hatches as early as April. This lake is also a good dry fly lake with some decent evening hatches of mayflies and caddis. During warmer spells in the lake spring, terrestrials, such as ants and grasshoppers, can create a frenzy of action here. If there is no hatch evident, it is best to use a searching pattern like a leech or the ever popular Woolly Bugger.

The best area to work is the area adjacent to the recreation site. This is the deepest section of the lake. Anglers will find good success by trolling either flies or spinners/spoons. Spincasters can try trolling a Flatfish or Little Cleo spoon, or a Willow Leaf gang troll with a Wedding Band and bait. Troll along the drop off around the main body of the lake using a figure 8 pattern, varying the depth, direction and speed of the lure or fly.

Directions

Located south of the village of Jaffray, North Star Lake is a popular recreational lake that can be busy on summer weekends. To find the lake, follow Highway 3/93 to Jaffray and then head south along the Jaffray-Baynes Lake Road. This road is paved but the branch road to North Star Lake can be a little rough in sections as it winds its way to the western shore of the lake. Look for the road off the east side of the Jaffray-Baynes Lake Road, about 4.5 km south of the highway junction. There is a recreation site from where to base your activities.

Facilities

North Star Lake Recreation Site is set in a dry, open ponderosa pine stand along the western shore. The site is equipped with a cartop boat launch and picnic tables for nine groups. RV's and trailers willing to negotiate the road can access the popular site. There are also few private cabins on the west side of the lake.

Other Options

Suzanne Lake is the closest alternative to North Star Lake. You can find Suzanne Lake by looking for the access road off the Jaffray-Baynes Lake Road. Suzanne Lake is about twice the size of North Star Lake and is also home to a popular recreation site. The lake offers fishing for largemouth bass and stocked rainbow trout. Look for more details on this lake later in the book.

Area Indicator

Species
Rainbow Trout

North Star Lake Fish Stocking Data			
Year	Species	Number	Life Stage
2013	Rainbow Trout	4,829	Yearling
2012	Rainbow Trout	4,000	Yearling
2011	Rainbow Trout	4,000	Yearling

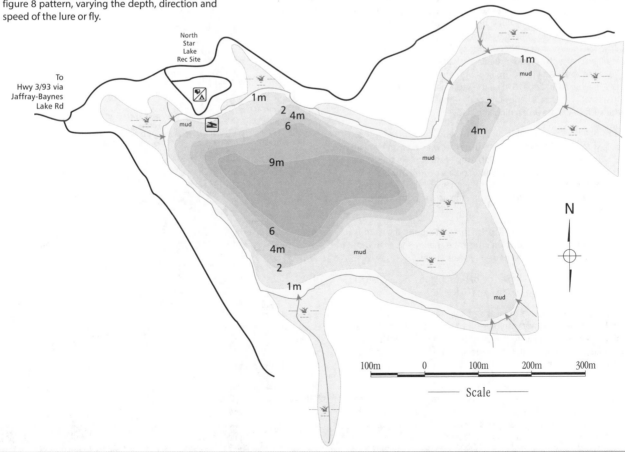

Okanagan Lake - North

Location: North of Kelowna
Elevation: 342 m (1,122 ft)
Surface Area: 35,008 ha (86,470 ac)
Mean Depth: 75 m (247 ft)
Max Depth: 242 m (794 ft)
Way Point: 119° 32′ 00″ Lon - W 49° 48′ 00″ Lat - N

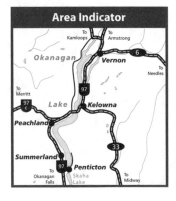

Area Indicator

Directions

Okanagan Lake is the largest lake in the Okanagan stretching from Penticton in the south past Vernon in the north. Although Highway 97 parallels the lake, it really only provides good access to the southern half. There are several provincial parks and communities along this stretch of highway that provide easy access to the big lake. Alternatively, the Naramata Road at the southeast end of the lake also provides access to a nice boat launch and a quieter stretch of the lake.

The northern half of the lake also provides numerous access points including the cities of Kelowna in the south and Vernon in the north. Westside Road, which runs up the west side of the northern half of the lake, provides access to a couple provincial parks and alternate launching areas. Other launches are found off Okanagan Centre and Carrs Landing Roads in Lake Country.

Species
Burbot
Kokanee
Rainbow Trout
Whitefish

Fishing

Stretching 110 km (70 mi) from tip to tail, Okanagan Lake is one of the largest interior lakes in British Columbia. It is also one of the most popular tourist destinations in the province. In the summer, folks flock from far and wide to experience the Okanagan heat and the warm waters of Okanagan Lake. The big lake is better known for its water sports and the legendary Ogopogo than for its fishing. However, anglers in the know will find rainbow, kokanee, burbot and even whitefish scattered around the lake.

If you do head out onto the lake, be prepared for a frustrating experience. Yes, there are lots of fish in the lake. But there's also lots of places they can be hiding. A guide, or at the very least, a fish finder, can help prevent you from searching aimlessly. Concentrating on areas where the fish are more likely to be will also help. This includes around the many points and in the many bays of the lake.

In recent years there has been some good news about the quality of fishing on this large lake. In particular, the kokanee seem to be rebounding and the fishery is once again being opened, albeit only for limited periods. These landlocked salmon are easily recognized by their slender, silver body and are most active in the warmer months. Although not as abundant as in the glory days, trolling a Willow Leaf with a Wedding Band and bait slowly in an S pattern can produce kokanee to 30 cm (12 in). Trolling with one ounce of weight or less, which takes the lure to 5-15 m (15 to 45 ft), is the most productive. Trolling slowly with a small, red Doc Spratley or Woolly Bugger fly pattern within a few feet of the surface can be an exciting alternative.

The best time to fish the lake for rainbow is between October through to June, and people who fish here frequently are usually rewarded with trout in the 1.5–3 kg (3–7 lb) range. The odd 9 kg (20 lb) trophy still lurks in the deep, dark depths. Try trolling a bucktail, spoon or plug on a fast troll. Working a fly or a bobber and bait in the quiet bays, especially ones with feeder streams can also produce nice sized trout. In the summer, the use of a downrigger is a must if you want to try to find trout.

The end of April to mid May is a good time to fish for trout around the various creek mouths. At this time, the trout often cruise the shallows in search of small baitfish. Try using minnow patterns or small Apex lures.

The other main sportfish is burbot. Jigging off of the drop offs around larger creek mouths can produce the odd cod to 4 kg (10 lbs).

Whitefish are an exciting alternative to trout and kokanee. The silvery fish is recognized by their large scales and can be caught to 50 cm (20 in) in size. They feed mainly on insects similar to trout, although they are much more aggressive and less spooky than trout. They will readily strike spinners, spoons or other shinny lures and can be taken on a fly. One known hot spot is the bay just south of Bear Creek Provincial Park.

Be sure to check the regulations before heading out on the lake. We also recommend stopping in at local tackle shops like Trout Waters Fly & Tackle in Kelowna to find out where the current hot spots are and what is working.

Okanagan Lake - South

Location: South of Kelowna
Elevation: 342 m (1,122 ft)
Surface Area: 35,008 ha (86,470 ac)
Mean Depth: 75 m (247 ft)
Max Depth: 242 m (794 ft)
Way Point: 119° 32' 00" Lon - W 49° 48' 00" Lat - N

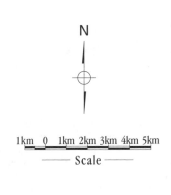

Region 8

Species
- Burbot
- Kokanee
- Rainbow Trout
- Whitefish

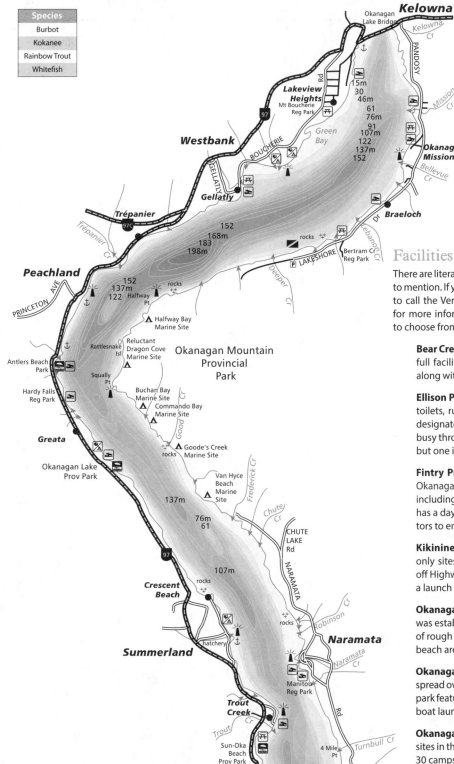

Facilities

There are literally too many resorts and various lodging establishments to mention. If you are looking to stay on the big lake, it is recommended to call the Vernon, Kelowna or Penticton Travel Information Centres for more information. Park enthusiasts also have too many options to choose from. We have listed the majority of the main sites below:

Bear Creek Provincial Park is found north of Kelowna. This busy, full facility park lies off Westside Road offering 122 campsites along with a paved boat launch, day-use area and a sandy beach.

Ellison Provincial Park offers 54 campsites complete with flush toilets, running water and a day-use picnic area. The park was designated as Canada's first freshwater diving park and is quite busy throughout the summer months. There is no launch on site, but one is found further north of Okanagan Landing Road.

Fintry Provincial Park is located along the western shore of Okanagan Lake and offers 50 campsites along with full facilities including showers, flush toilets and running water. The park also has a day-use picnic area along with a fine beach area for all visitors to enjoy.

Kikininee and Sun-Oka Provincial Parks are small, day-use only sites that are located north of Penticton. Easily accessible off Highway 97, both parks are popular with sunbathers. There is a launch at Kikininee.

Okanagan Centre Safe Harbour is found in Lake Country and was established as a safe harbour for boaters to escape to incase of rough weather. It also features two paved launches and a nice beach area for day trippers to enjoy.

Okanagan Lake Provincial Park is a popular destination that is spread over two sites north of Summerland. Open year round, the park features 168 campsites along with hiking trails, a beach area, boat launch and picnic area.

Okanagan Lake Recreation Site is one of the busiest recreation sites in the Okanagan. The site is found north of Fintry and boasts 30 campsites, a nice beach and a boat launch onto the lake.

Okanagan Mountain Provincial Park is a large, remote access park found south of Kelowna. Water enthusiasts will find several beautiful marine access campsites that make a great place to moor at. Hiking trails lead up to some spectacular viewpoints and the interior of the park.

Traders Cover Marine Park is found just north of Bear Creek. This beautiful site offers nice moorage, two swim areas, a covered picnic shelter and a playground for day trippers to enjoy.

Scale: 1km 0 1km 2km 3km 4km 5km

© Backroad Mapbooks **139**

Fishing

The Okanagan River is a small volume, warm river that flows south from Okanagan Lake into Osoyoos Lake before leaving Canada. It is also a unique river in the fact it still supports sockeye salmon run, although there is no fishery for them, an unheralded rainbow trout fishery, whitefish and even bass and yellow perch.

Most of the attention for this river over the last several years has been about trying to reestablish the sockeye runs. The salmon have some challenges. They have to run past four dams on the Canadian section of the river alone. Irrigation ditches have shortened the river and development has also affected the river. These factors have contributed to the Outdoor Recreation Council of Canada labeling this river as "BC's most endangered river" in 2003.

However, things are changing for the better. In February 2006, a fish passage chute was installed at Zosel Dam at the south end of Osoyoos Lake and groups are working hard to conserve and restore both the stocks and the spawning habitat for salmon. Most of this work is happening in the 7 km (4.2 mile) section of river below the McIntyre Dam. This is a good area to watch the sockeye spawn in late October.

That said, the river does offer good fishing for rainbow and whitefish. It might not look like a classic trout stream, but there are some good sections. The occasional rainbow reaches 2.5 kg (5 lb) and there are decent sized whitefish (up to 50 cm/20 long).

The best fishing is early in the season. You can start at McIntyre Dam and work your way down to the creek mouth just below Deer Park, but there is limited public access in this area. Instead, it is best to start from the bridge at the community ball diamond in Oliver. The next three or so kilometres are home to some great man-made riffles and a few nice whitewater tailouts. The riffles were created to help the sockeye spawn and are a haven for the rainbow.

During the warmer days of summer the fishing certainly slows down. However, fishing at day break and after sunset in the evenings can be very rewarding. If visiting the river in the winter, it is best to fish midday (between 11 and 3) when the trout and whitefish are more active.

Due to the abundance of northern pike minnow, fishing a classic bait rig is a frustrating experience. Local anglers prefer to use small spinners and spoons tipped with bait for both rainbow and whitefish. A local favourite is the Silver Bullet.

Check the regulations for closures before heading out. We also highly recommend practicing catch & release to help maintain the trout fishery.

Directions

The river is accessed from a variety of parks and bridges off Highway 97 between Okanagan Falls and Osoyoos. The International Bike Path, which runs along the river banks is also an excellent access point.

Facilities

In addition to the city of Oliver, there are a number of towns along the banks of the Okanagan River that offer a variety services. There are also a few provincial parks along this stretch of river that offer camping and easy access to the river. **Okanagan Falls** has 25 sites, **Vaseux Lake** has 12 sites and **Inkaneep** offers 7 sites.

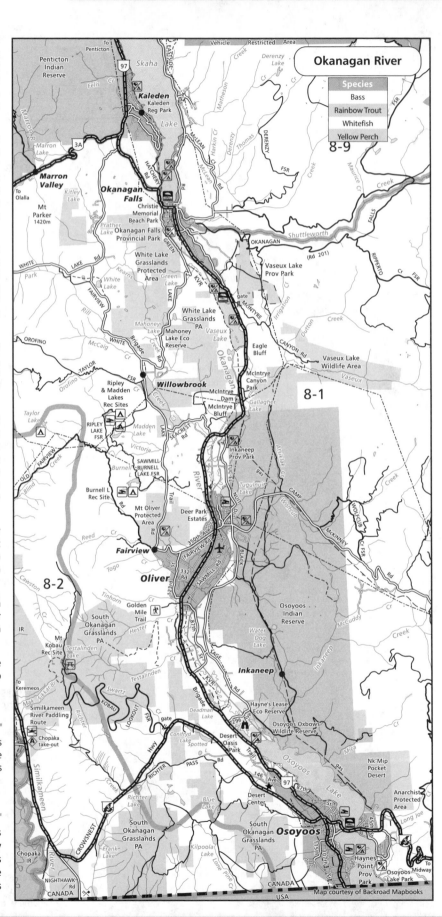

Osoyoos Lake

Location: 0 km (0 mi) from Osoyoos
Elevation: 276 m (906 ft)
Surface Area: 2,300 ha (7,546 ac)
Mean Depth: 14 m (46 ft)
Max Depth: 63 m (207 ft)
Way Point: 119° 27' 00" Lon - W 49° 02' 00" Lat - N

8 Region

Area Indicator

Fishing

Known as the warmest lake in Canada, Osoyoos Lake is a hot bed of outdoor activity during the summer. The lake can be a busy place with boaters, water skiers and jet skiers running up and down the shoreline. Often overlooked, the fishing in Osoyoos Lake can actually be quite productive throughout the year.

Rainbow trout can be found in the lake up to 5 kg (11 lbs) and are mainly caught by trolling spoons or plugs the lake in the early spring or fall/winter periods. Kokanee also inhabit the lake in fair numbers and can be caught by trolling lake trolls throughout the year.

But the largest sport fishery on the lake is the pursuit of bass. Both smallmouth and largemouth bass have established reproducing colonies in the lake and provide for some very good fishing. In fact, Osoyoos Lake has the distinction of producing the BC record largemouth bass at 4.7 kg (10 lbs 6 ounces). Bass are mainly caught in the shallower bays of the lake by spincasting or fly-fishing. When fishing for bass, top water lures and flies can be a lot of fun on this lake. Bass like to hang out where there's lots of cover, so look for areas where the bass can hide out of the sun; this includes weeds, jumbles of rocks, fallen trees and even docks. Because they like to hang out in the junk, top water fishing for largemouth bass is the easiest way to fish for bass, but jigging with a plug or a Texas rig is also popular.

Species
Kokanee
Largemouth Bass
Rainbow Trout
Smallmouth Bass

Directions

Osoyoos Lake is a warm water lake that stretches over the Canada USA border. The scenic town of Osoyoos lies along the shore of Osoyoos Lake as somewhat of a divider between the northern and southern halves of the lake. Most of the western and southern shoreline is developed while the northeastern shore remains part of the Osoyoos Indian Reserve. The lake and the town are easily accessible from Highway 3 or Highway 97.

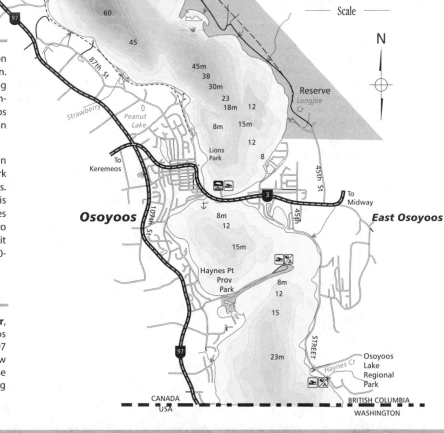

Facilities

Osoyoos Lake is a very popular outdoor recreation lake with water sports being the main attraction. There are several full service resorts located along the shore of the lake as well as various other accommodation facilities. Be sure to contact the Osoyoos Travel Information Centre if you are interested in staying in the area.

Anglers will find a boat launch at the city park in Osoyoos. Found just north of Highway 3, the park also offers a beautiful beach and picnic facilities. Further south **Haynes Point Provincial Park** is located south of Osoyoos and offers 41 campsites along with a beach and picnic area. If you plan to stay at the very popular park during the summer, it is recommended to call Discover Camping at 1-800-689-9025 ahead of time to make reservations.

Other Options

Anglers often overlook the **Okanagan River**, which flows between Skaha Lake and Osoyoos Lake. The river is easily accessible off Highway 97 and provides angling opportunities for rainbow trout, smallmouth bass and largemouth bass. Be sure to check your regulations before heading out on this river.

Location: 36 km (22 mi) northeast of Princeton
Elevation: 1,098 m (3,602 ft)
Surface Area: 39 ha (96 ac)
Mean Depth: 14 m (46 ft)
Max Depth: 11.5 m (38 ft)
Way Point: 120° 12′ 00″ Lon - W 49° 42′ 00″ Lat - N

Osprey Lake

Fishing

Situated in a sort of no man's land between the scrub of ranch land found to the west to the orchards of Summerland in the east, Osprey Lake lies in the middle of the two environments. The lake is surrounded by coniferous forest interrupted by the odd cottage or home along the lakeshore.

The lake is heavily stocked annually with rainbow trout that provide for good fishing during most of the year. Still, some large trout (over 2 kg/4 lbs) are caught regularly. There have even been reports of rainbow over 3 kg (7 lbs) here recently.

Trolling is the main method of fishing the lake; however, fly anglers can be very successful at times, especially during the spring and fall periods. Trollers should focus their attention along the drop off found near the southeastern shore of the lake. Troll with light gear with a Willow Leaf and small, dark coloured spoons or spinning lure. Dick Nites, Blue Foxes, Mepps and Wedding Bands all work well.

Fly anglers will find a blood leech or shrimp pattern fished deep on a sinking line will work well as the lake starts to warm up in the summer. However, the cooler summer evenings are often filled with caddis flies rising off the surface of the lake. A Tom Thumb or Adams can offer some exciting fishing on those days. The west end of the lake has extensive shoal areas, and the trout will come here to feed on the many aquatic insects. Another popular spot is at the narrows at the east end during the spring chironomid hatch.

The Kettle Valley Railway section of the Trans Canada Trail passes alongside the southern shore of the lake, providing excellent access for shore anglers.

Ice fishing in the shallows near the drop offs is a popular winter time activity. The rainbow trout tend to become very slow-witted by the end of the season, so the best time to go is once the ice is thick enough to stand on. A small hook or jig head tipped with a meal worm, powerbait, or pink maggots work best. Anglers have been known to ice fish successfully with flies, using a leech, bloodworm or shrimp pattern.

Osprey Lake has an engine restriction of 7.5 kw (10 hp).

Directions

Northeast of Princeton, you can find Osprey Lake off the Princeton-Summerland Road. This popular lake is easily accessed off the paved road that was once called Highway 40. In addition to the popular recreation site, there are several private cabins on the lake.

Facilities

The **Osprey Lake North Recreation Site** is easily accessed of the Princeton-Summerland Road. Visitors will find nine RV friendly sites along with a good boat launch. There is a fee to camp here from the end of April until mid-October. For those that prefer a comfortable bed, there is a bed and breakfast at the west end of the lake.

In addition to the recreation site, the Kettle Valley Railway/Trans Canada Trail runs along the south side of the lake. Hikers, bikers, horseback riders and even ATVers can enjoy a leisurely outing on this popular trail system.

Other Options

Just to the west of Osprey Lake you can find the Teepee Lakes Road. If you follow this deteriorating road north form the main road you will eventually meet the Teepee Lakes. There are three separate lakes that make up the **Teepee Lakes**, Friday, Saturday and Sunday Lake. The lakes offer very good fishing for small, stocked rainbow trout.

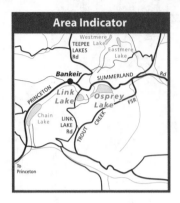

Area Indicator

Species
Rainbow Trout

Osprey Lake Fish Stocking Data			
Year	Species	Number	Life Stage
2013	Rainbow Trout	12,000	Fry
2012	Rainbow Trout	12,000	Fry
2011	Rainbow Trout	12,000	Fry

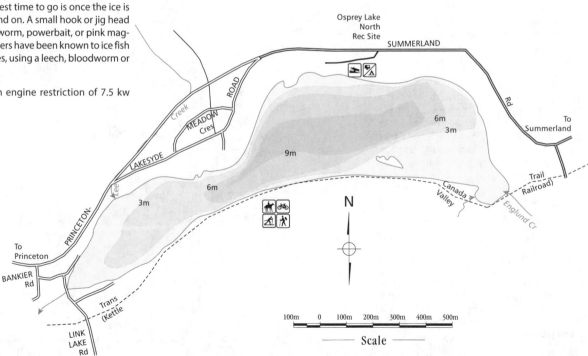

Otter Lake - Tulameen

Location: 22 km (13.5 mi) northwest of Princeton
Elevation: 786 m (2,579 ft)
Surface Area: 205 ha (506 ac)
Mean Depth: 14.3 m (47 ft)
Max Depth: 26.2 m (86 ft)
Way Point: 120° 46′ 00″ Lon - W 49° 35′ 00″ Lat- N

8 Region

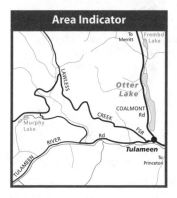

Area Indicator

Species

Rainbow Trout

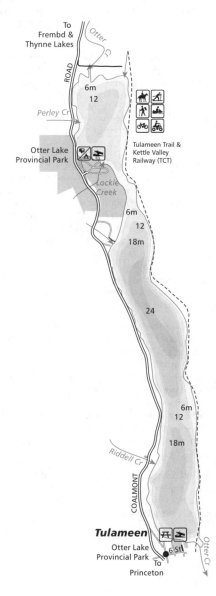

Fishing

With nearly a dozen Otter Lakes across the province, and three Otter Lakes in the Okanagan region, it's sometimes difficult to tell one from another. This Otter Lake is located just north of the town of Tulameen and is one of the most popular fishing lakes in the area.

Once you've been here, though, you will certainly not confuse it for any other lake. On an early morning, with the lake as still as glass, and a light fog hanging in the air, you would swear you were in heaven. Perfect moments like these are rare, but seem to happen here more often than elsewhere.

Thousands of anglers descend upon this lake each season. Because it is so heavily fished, the lake was one of the most heavily stocked lakes in the entire Okanagan, usually with 20,000 rainbow fry. As of 2006, though, the lake is no longer being stocked, with the hopes that the natural reproductive cycle of the fish will keep the fishing as good as it has been in the past.

Unfortunately, the lake's popularity does make the lake somewhat difficult to fish if you are looking for bigger trout. These bigger fish are very wary of anything that doesn't look exactly right (no doubt as a result of being hooked a dozen or more times already), and the smaller fish are often kept as soon as they reach a decent size.

The lake is best fished in the spring or fall by trolling. Since this is a low elevation lake, it heats up significantly during the summer and fishing success slows. In the southern half of the lake, there is a significant shoal area found between the two deeper holes. This is traditionally a good holding area for trout throughout the year, but is particularly good during the summer months.

Directions

Home to a provincial park, Otter Lake can be easily accessed from Princeton. The paved Coalmont Road leads west all the way to the small settlement of Tulameen. Continue through town to access the day-use portion of the park that features a good launching site. The Coalmont Road also links to Highway 5A in the north, about 8 km south of the Aspen Grove Exit. Most of this road is gravel and can be a bit rougher on cars and vehicles with larger trailers.

Facilities

Along with the many private cottages found on this lake, there is the **Otter Lake Provincial Park**. The park has two sites on the western side of the lake with the southern site offering day-use facilities such as picnic tables, outhouses, a beach and a boat launch. The northern site offers 45 campsites available for overnight use as well as a boat launch and outhouses. For hiking and biking enthusiasts, the Kettle Valley Railway portion of the **Trans Canada Trail** travels along the eastern shore of the lake. It is certainly possible to access a few places to cast from shore off this trail.

Other Options

If you continue north past Otter Lake along the Coalmont Road, you will pass by both **Frembd** and **Thynne Lakes**. Neither is considered a great fishing destination, although **Otter Creek** does link these waterbodies together so you should be able to catch a few trout. Much more popular is the creek itself, which is a fine summer destination for small trout. Please be considerate of private property in the area.

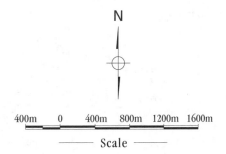

Otter Lake (Tulameen)			
Fish Stocking Data			
Year	Species	Number	Life Stage
2012	Rainbow Trout	12,000	Fry
2011	Rainbow Trout	9,200	Fry

Pinaus Lake Chain

Pinaus Lake

Elevation: 982 m (3,222 ft)
Surface Area: 169 ha (417 ac)
Mean Depth: 13 m (43 ft)
Max Depth: 54 m (177 ft)
Way Point: 119° 35' 00" Lon - W 50° 25' 00" Lat - N

Directions

Northwest of the city of Vernon, you can find the Pinaus Lake Chain south of Falkland and Highway 97. The main access into Pinaus is a little misleading since the actual Pinaus Lake Forest Service Road is a rough 4wd road that is not the main route in. Visitors are best to continue west to the Ingram Creek Forest Service Road, which is found just east of the paved Backroad outside of Westwold. Even the Ingram Creek road can be a bit rough in places as it switchbacks out of the valley and up and over to Pinaus Lake. Resort signs mark the way.

Lady King Lake is found just before Pinaus, while Square Lake is found further east o the north side of the Pinaus Lake Forest Service Road. Little Pinaus Lake is found off a rough side road to the east of the bigger lake. Regardless of which lake you wish to visit, it is recommended to bring a high clearance or 4wd vehicle, especially during wet weather.

Facilities

The **Pinaus Lake Resort** forms the hub of this chain of lakes. It offers a full service campground as well as cabins for rental. Even if not staying at the resort, be sure to check in at the store for local tips and basic supplies.

Campers can also take advantage of a few campsites in the area. The **Pinaus Lake Recreation Site** is a large treed site located along the northern shore of the lake. There is space for at least eight groups along with a boat launch here. Further east, there are user maintained campsites at both **Square Lake** and **Little Pinaus Lake**. These rustic sites offer little in the way of facilities.

Square Lake

Elevation: 1,067 m (3,501 ft)
Surface Area: 10 ha (25 ac)
Mean Depth: 10 m (33 ft)
Max Depth: 21.5 m (71 ft)
Way Point: 119° 33' 00" Lon - W 50° 25' 00" Lat - N

Fishing

Pinaus Lake is the largest of the group of lakes found south of Falkland that include Lady King, Square and Little Pinaus Lakes. All four lakes provide a good fishery for rainbow trout and have been known to produce some nice sized trout on occasion.

Pinaus is a good sized lake at over 3 km (2 mi) in length and is best fished by trolling. Fly anglers can find success throughout the lake, although a keen eye to the hatch is often required to produce any significant results. The lake is heavily stocked and fishing can be good at times for rainbow trout in the 0.5-1 kg (1-2 lb) range. Larger trout in the 3 kg (6.5 lb) range are caught annually. In recent years, the fishing on the lake has been getting better.

Recommended gear for the bigger lake include a plain old worm on a hook, a Wedding Ring with a worm, a pink Panther Martin, Silver Flatfish, powerbait and black Doc Spratley flies. One area that often produces some larger trout is the shoal located just to the north of the prominent southwest bay. The shoal forms somewhat of an underwater point. The area around the stream inlet can also be a hot spot at times, especially in the spring and fall periods.

For something different, you can always try your luck fishing for perch. These feisty fish and are best caught by still fishing worms with a float. Perch are active throughout the year, especially during ice fishing season.

During winter, the big lake is a popular ice fishing destination. Fishing for rainbow is usually best earlier in the season when they are more active. Jigging with a ¼ jig and plastic worms or maggots can usually net decent results.

En route to Pinaus, you will pass by the much smaller Lady King Lake. This small lake is considered one the top lakes in the chain and is stocked annually with triploid rainbow trout. Known to grow faster and to bigger sizes, these trout also benefit from a year round aeration project, ensuring optimum water quality for the fish's growth and insect supply. With the abundance of freshwater shrimp and aquatic insects, the fish grow quickly and are rumoured to be quite acrobatic when caught. Lady King is also managed as a quality fishery in that it is a fly-fishing only lake with single barbless hook and one fish quota. Popular flies include chironomids, shrimp imitations, burgundy leeches, Lady McConnells and sedge/caddis patterns. The lake is small enough to be worked with a float tube and the electric motor restriction ensures a peaceful experience.

To the east of Pinaus, Square Lake offers good fishing for stocked rainbow trout to 1 kg (2 lbs). The lake is quite small, and fly-fishing is the preferred angling method. Fishing success tails off during the heat of the summer, but earlier in the year chironomid hatches are significant during. These flies are best fished just off the 3-6 m (10-19 ft) shoal depths of the lake. There are large shoal areas located along the southern and western shore areas of the lake, which are prime cruising territory for rainbow throughout the spring and fall. When success slows down, try working a leech or dragonfly pattern deeper for those more reluctant rainbow. To help preserve the quality sport fishery, there is a bait ban and single barbless hook regulation on Square Lake.

Little Pinaus Lake is the last lake in the chain and is reported to offer a similar fishery to Pinaus. The smaller lake also boasts of acrobatic rainbow in the 1-2 kg (2-4 lb) range than can be a lot of fun to catch on the fly. Since it is the hardest lake to access, it is also the quietest of the chain.

As always, be sure to check the regulations before fishing these or any other lakes in the region.

Pinaus Lake Chain

Location: 9 km (5.5 mi) south of Falkland

Lady King Lake

Elevation: 984 m (3,228 ft)
Mean Depth: 3.5 m (12 ft)
Max Depth: 7 m (23 ft)
Way Point: 119° 37' 00" Lon - W 50° 25' 00" Lat - N

Little Pinaus Lake

Elevation: 898 m (2,946 ft)
Way Point: 119° 33' 00" Lon - W 50° 25' 00" Lat - N

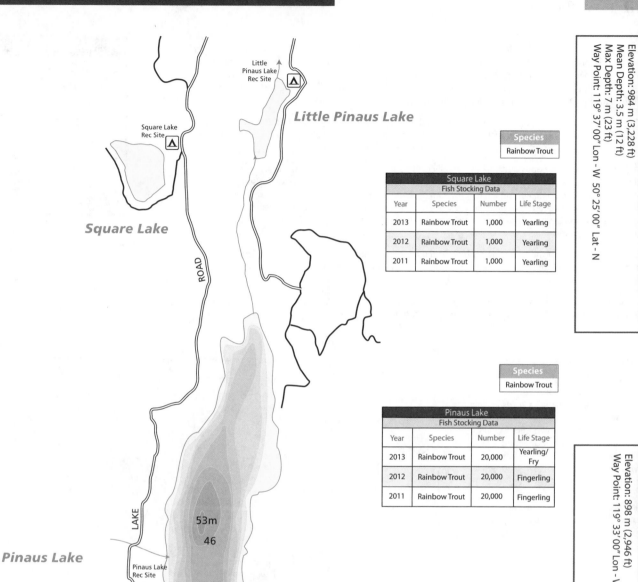

Species
Rainbow Trout

Square Lake Fish Stocking Data			
Year	Species	Number	Life Stage
2013	Rainbow Trout	1,000	Yearling
2012	Rainbow Trout	1,000	Yearling
2011	Rainbow Trout	1,000	Yearling

Species
Rainbow Trout

Pinaus Lake Fish Stocking Data			
Year	Species	Number	Life Stage
2013	Rainbow Trout	20,000	Yearling/ Fry
2012	Rainbow Trout	20,000	Fingerling
2011	Rainbow Trout	20,000	Fingerling

Species
Rainbow Trout

Lady King Lake Fish Stocking Data			
Year	Species	Number	Life Stage
2013	Rainbow Trout	600	Fry
2012	Rainbow Trout	600	Fingerling
2011	Rainbow Trout	500	Fingerling

200m 0 200m 400m 600m 800m 1000m
Scale

Region 8

Location: 17 km (10.5 mi) south of Vernon
Elevation: 1,357 m (4,452 ft)
Surface Area: 227 ha (561ac)
Mean Depth: 6.7 m (22 ft)
Max Depth: 19.5 m (64 ft)
Way Point: 119° 16'00" Lon - W 50° 05'00" Lat - N

Oyama Lake

Fishing

Located in the hills above Kalamalka Lake, Oyama Lake is an extremely popular fishing lake. Historically, it was known for producing big rainbow trout, partially due to the fact that accessing the lake was so difficult. These days, though, the lake is accessible by a 2wd vehicle, and most of the bigger fish have been fished out. Still, the odd big fish is pulled out of the lake, which draws people back.

The lake offers an amazing amount of structure for the stocked rainbow, with 27 islands, many sheltered bays, and plenty of underwater islands. The drop off and shoal areas found off the islands, as well as the underwater islands, are often prime areas for finding cruising trout.

Although trolling is a popular alternative, usually with a spinner or small Flatfish in black, silver or green, fly-fishing can be fabulous on this lake. Be sure to try to visit the lake in June or July for the sedge/caddis hatches. During the hatch, some big rainbow can be taken off the surface with a Tom Thumb or a Mikulak Sedge, making for a ton of fun. The shoal area at the north end of the lake is a great place to work chironomids, damsel fly nymphs, and small dragonfly nymphs. In summer, a '52 Buick or leech pattern are popular options.

The high elevation of the lake allows fishing to remain steady throughout the summer months. At this time, early mornings and evenings are the better times to head out. However, being a reservoir, the lake is subject to draw down from time to time.

Anglers should also be aware of the recently imposed regulations. In addition to catch restrictions, there is also a bait ban. As always, consult the regulations before heading out.

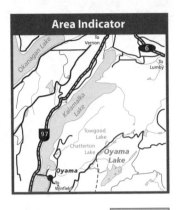

Area Indicator

Species
Rainbow Trout

Directions

This popular fishing lake is found between Kelowna and Vernon to the east Wood and Kalamalka Lakes. Follow Highway 97 to the Oyama turn-off. Continue through town and pay close attention to the signs directing you to Oyama Lake Resort. These should help you find the Oyama Lake Road, which leads up and out of the valley. About 13 km later, a side road leads to the lake. The last section of road (about 2 km long) is quite rough, although usually passable with a 2wd vehicle.

Oyama Lake Fish Stocking Data			
Year	Species	Number	Life Stage
2013	Rainbow Trout	15,000	Fry
2012	Rainbow Trout	15,000	Fry
2011	Rainbow Trout	15,000	Fry

Facilities

Oyama Lake Resort is located along the western shore of Oyama Lake. The resort is a year round resort complete with a small store. They offer cabin, boat and snowmobile rentals.

If you prefer camping, the **Oyama Lake Recreation Site** is also found in this area. The recreation site provides space for about 4 groups as well as boat launch. Boaters should note that the lake water levels do fluctuate significantly throughout the year.

Postill Lake

Location: 12 km (7.4 mi) east of Kelowna
Elevation: 1,392 m (4,568 ft)
Surface Area: 106 ha (263 ac)
Mean Depth: 6.4 m (21 ft)
Max Depth: 13 m (42 ft)
Way Point: 119° 12' 44" Lon - W 49° 59' 26" Lat - N

Fishing

Home to both brook trout and rainbow trout, Postill Lake is the hub of a fantastic fishing area. There are several nearby lakes that also offer good fishing for trout with some impressive sized fish caught each year.

Whether you bring your own boat, rent one from the lodge or simply prefer to fish from shore, there are some enticing bays and shoals to sample on Postill. Due to the higher elevation, fishing really does not heat up until May. The fishing holds relatively steady through the summer and into October. Ice fishing is certainly possible.

With fish in the 20–40 cm (8–16 inch) range, small lures like Flatfish or Mepps and Bluefox spinners seem to work best. Fly anglers should try mosquitoes around mid-June, followed by mayflies. Searching patterns like Doc Spratleys, Grizzly Kings and Golden Pheasants are other productive patterns recommend by the lodge.

Up to 2004, brook trout were being stocked in the lake. More recently, the stocking has switched to the Pennask strain of rainbow trout. These fast growing trout are reported to be doing well.

Due to the size of the lake, it is better suited to small boats rather than belly or pontoon boats. The better holes and shoals are much easier to get to from the water than from shore. Still shore anglers can find some good casting areas, especially around the south end of the lake. Another popular casting area is at the dam.

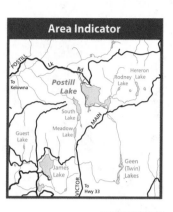

Area Indicator

Species
Rainbow Trout
Brook Trout

Directions

Found north of Kelowna, the lake is easily found by following the Postill Lake Lodge signs off Highway 97. Turn east on Old Vernon Road just north of the Kelowna Airport and follow this road and the signs to Postill Drive. Postill Drive leads to the intersection of Farmers Drive where a gravel road continues straight ahead. This good gravel road continues another 15 km to the lodge. It is about a 30 minute drive from the airport.

Facilities

Postill Lake Recreation Site is located at the north end of the lake, not far from the resort. It is a popular site with 5 official campsites, but room for more. There is a cartop boat launch for anglers, while a series of cross-country ski trails provide excellent hiking and biking in the spring, summer and fall. Shore anglers will find the old road cum trail on the south shore of the lake provides good access to nice fishing holes.

Postill Lake Lodge offers lakefront cottages and cabins as well as campsites. In addition to boat rentals, there is an extensive trail network and a choice of six nearby lakes to test your luck in. The lodge also offers a cabin on Twin Lakes to the south.

Other Options

A visit to Postill Lake would not be complete without visiting at least one of the five smaller lakes in the immediate area. **Heron Lake** (4 km away) and **Roddy Lake** (1.5 km away) are found a short distance to the east and provide trout up to 1 kg (2 lbs). Heron is noted to be a great fly-fishing lake. To the southwest are **South Lake** (500 metres away) and **Meadow Lake** (2.5 km away). Both are fly only lakes with the smaller Meadow Lake rumoured to produce trout in the 2 kg (4 lb) range. Finally **Twin** or **Geen Lakes** are found 5 km to the south. Set at a slightly higher elevation, the lake offers trout up to 1.5 kg (3 lbs) and a cabin.

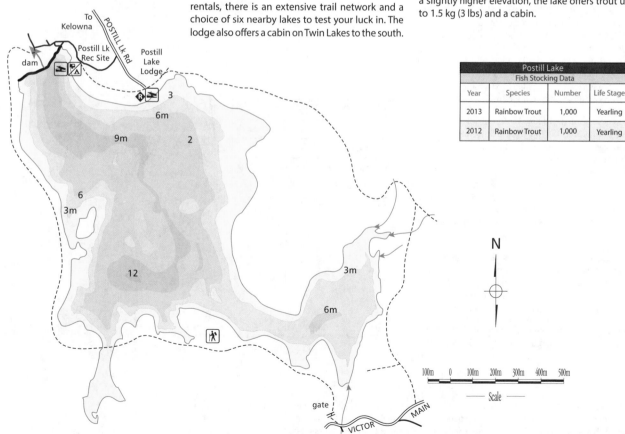

Postill Lake			
Fish Stocking Data			
Year	Species	Number	Life Stage
2013	Rainbow Trout	1,000	Yearling
2012	Rainbow Trout	1,000	Yearling

Location: 52 km (32 mi) north of Cranbrook
Elevation: 877 m (2,877 ft)
Surface Area: 203 ha (502 ac)
Mean Depth: 18.8 m (62 ft)
Max Depth: 32.5 m (107 ft)
Way Point: 115° 39′ 00″ Lon - W 49° 56′ 00″ Lat - N

Premier Lake

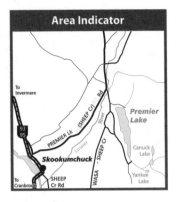

Area Indicator

Species
Rainbow Trout
Brook Trout

Facilities

The popular **Premier Lake Provincial Park** encompasses the southern end of the lake. The park is open for camping year round with full services running from May 15 to October 1. Amenities include 56 vehicle/tent camping sites with picnic tables, an adventure playground, showers and a boat launch. Activities that can be enjoyed include fishing, picnicking, swimming and hiking. The park is also a known wildlife viewing area for larger mammals like elk, deer and bighorn sheep. During the spring, be sure to hike the Staple Creek Trail to the rainbow spawning channel. The channel is quite an impressive sight during the spawning period. Rainbow are trapped in the channel each year to provide the egg source for stocking over 350 lakes and streams throughout British Columbia. For reservations call 1-800-689-9025 or visit www.discovercamping.ca.

Fishing

Premier is one of the better fishing lakes in the East Kootenay if not the province. In fact, the inlet creek is a collecting station for trout eggs that are used to stock hundreds of lakes across the province including this one.

If you are looking for big fish, than this where you should look. There are regular reports of rainbow in the 1.5 kg (3 lb) range along with a few bigger and many smaller trout. There are also unconfirmed reports of chunky brook trout here.

The shoal areas at either end of the lake are good places to start if fishing on the fly. If trolling, you need to cover as much area of the lake as possible. The drop off zone along the cliffs halfway up the lake can be a productive area. Focus your efforts around the edge of the lake in the 4.5–7.5 metre (15–25 foot) range, but not too deep as the lake bottom is weedy. Trout also like to hang out in the dozen small bays that crinkle the shoreline.

Fly anglers will find a good chironomid hatch starting in May and lasting to mid-June followed by mayflies, damselflies, caddisflies and dragonflies. During early summer evenings, there are some good top water hatches on Premier Lake. If you see rises, try to match the hatch. Top water flies that have been known to come in handy include the Adams, Grizzly King and mosquito patterns. At other times try a leech under a strike indicator. The trick is to get the fly down to the level of the fish.

Spincasters can have success with lake trolls and worms, and a good variety of small spoons and spinners. Try trolling a Flatfish with no weight. Remember that the larger trout are wary of things that look unnatural, so presentation is very important.

Be sure to check the regulations for closures and special restrictions as the lake is heavily regulated.

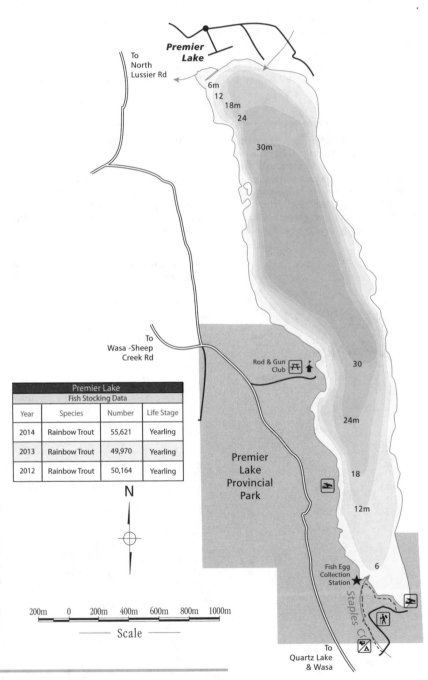

Premier Lake Fish Stocking Data			
Year	Species	Number	Life Stage
2014	Rainbow Trout	55,621	Yearling
2013	Rainbow Trout	49,970	Yearling
2012	Rainbow Trout	50,164	Yearling

N

200m 0 200m 400m 600m 800m 1000m
Scale

Directions

Premier Lake is found east of Skookumchuck not far from Highway 93/95. The easiest way to find the lake is to follow the signs directing the way to the Premier Lake Provincial Park. These signs will direct you from the highway east on the Premier Lake/Sheep Creek Road, which starts coursing north before looping back down to the west side of the lake.

Quartz Lake

Location: 47 km (29 mi) north of Cranbrook
Elevation: 946 m (3,103 ft)
Surface Area: 20 ha (49 ac)
Mean Depth: 9 m (30 ft)
Max Depth: 26 m (85 ft)
Way Point: 115° 38′00″ Lon - W 49° 53′00″ Lat - N

4 Region

Fishing

Found within Premier Lakes Provincial Park, Quartz Lake is often overlooked due to its proximity to one of the best trout lakes in the Kootenays. It is a beautiful lake with rich, azure waters set at the base of a prominent rock bluff, from which it takes its alternate name.

Still, this long, narrow lake is a popular spot during the summer months. Surprisingly, during the spring when the action is best, you will only find a few die hard anglers at the lake. The lake has been stocked with rainbow trout over the years and it holds a good population of cutthroat trout as well as a few brook trout.

Shortly after ice off (in late May to early June), the action can be quite good with both rainbow and cutthroat cruising the shoals in search of anything that looks like food. A particularly good spot in the spring is off the two small mostly underwater islands in the southern portion of the lake. Working a chironomid off this area can be deadly at times. Also, watch for caddis and mayfly hatches as some of the best action can be found off the surface.

As the heat of summer sets in, the trout in Quartz Lake go deep and it is necessary to use sinking line to have any success. Troll attractor type flies for cutthroat, while leech patterns can work for rainbow. Trolling a small, flashy spoon like a Mepps can work well for spincasters.

There are trails around either side of the lake, but these only go a short ways before progress is blocked by sheer cliffs that fall straight into the lake. Still, at the end of the trails are good shore fishing locations. There are good shoals at each end, and a handful of islands to cast around.

Facilities

Quartz Lake lies within the southern boundary of **Premier Lake Provincial Park**. The park is open for camping from mid May through mid September and has 57 vehicle/tent camping sites with picnic tables and many nice amenities to make your stay more enjoyable. For more information on specific parks, visit www.bcparks.ca.

Other Options

Of course, the most obvious location nearby is **Premier Lake,** which is written up previously. To the north of Quartz Lake and Premier Lake Provincial Park, you can find the **Lussier River**. This small river is easily accessible by forest service roads and offers fishing opportunities for rainbow trout, cutthroat trout, bull trout and whitefish. The best time to fish the river is mid season after the spring runoff period. The more northern sections are better since the southern reaches pass through a tight canyon.

Directions

Quartz Lake lies within Premier Lake Provincial Park to the south of the more popular destination. From Highway 93/95 near Skookumchuck, follow the signs directing the way to Premier Lake Park. Continue past Premier Lake and the main park facilities and you will soon reach the western shore of Quartz Lake. A gate may impede travel so come prepared to walk the 2 or so kilometres south.

Area Indicator

Species
Brook Trout
Cutthroat Trout
Rainbow Trout

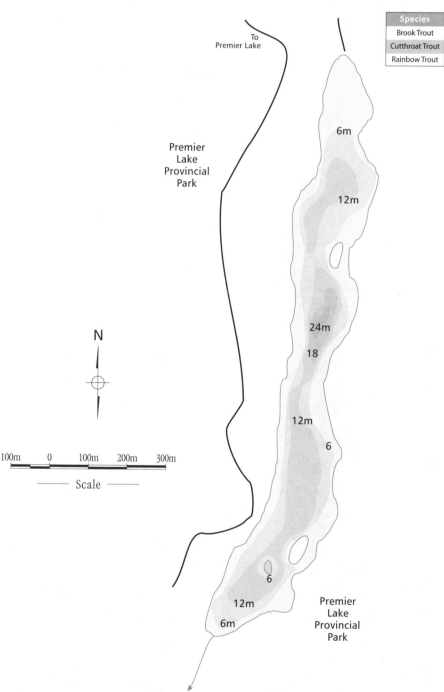

To Premier Lake

Premier Lake Provincial Park

N

100m   0   100m   200m   300m

Scale

6m

12m

24m

18

12m

6

12m

6

12m

6m

Premier Lake Provincial Park

Location: 24 km (15 mi) north of Princeton
Elevation: 1,353 m (4,439 ft)
Surface Area: 15 ha (37 ac)
Mean Depth: 6.8 m (22 ft)
Max Depth: 16 m (52 ft)
Way Point: 120° 29' 00" Lon - W 49° 40' 00" Lat - N

Rampart Lake

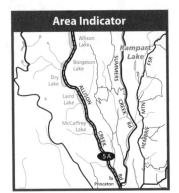

Area Indicator

Species

Rainbow Trout

Directions

Rampart Lake is located north of Princeton via a rough logging road system. Travel north along the Princeton-Summerland Road and look for the Hembrie Mountain Forest Service Road leading north. This road gets progressively rougher as you wind and weave your way up the hillside. There are also many confusing side roads and the branch road leading north to Rampart Lake is found about 15 km from the Summerland Road.

Unfamiliar logging roads can be very confusing to follow. Visitors exploring a new area are always recommended to bring along a good map such as those in the Backroad Mapbook Series along with a GPS.

Rampart (Hans) Lake			
Fish Stocking Data			
Year	Species	Number	Life Stage
2013	Rainbow Trout	4,000	Fry
2012	Rainbow Trout	4,000	Fry
2011	Rainbow Trout	4,000	Fry

Fishing

Also known as Hans Lake, Rampart Lake is a fly-fishing only lake that is stocked annually with rainbow trout. Fishing is quite productive on this lake and if you match the hatch size and colour properly it is not uncommon to catch a dozen trout in an hour. It is also not uncommon to catch a few trout that can reach 2 kg (4.5 lbs) in size.

Chironomid patterns can be very effective in the spring. Work the patterns in the 4-6 m (13-20 ft) range very slowly, varying your depth until you reach a good success rate. During the spring, trout are generally more active after the morning period. This is because the lake heats up as the day progresses, creating greater insect activity in the lake.

A float tube will be a definite asset in the later spring. Around June, the caddis start to hatch, and top water fishing can be fast and furious at times. Trout generally don't rise until the water is calm and the sun is not falling directly on the lake. In other words, dry fly-fishing works best in the evening using a Tom Thumb or Adams.

As spring turns to summer, the lake starts to get a little too warms for the fish, at least on the top layer of water, and so they move into the deeper water, coming into the shoal areas only to feed. The fish remain active into the early part of summer, but by the time August hits the quality of the fishing has dropped substantially.

In the fall, there are still occasional hatches, but most anglers move to leeches, or general attractor patterns like a Woolly Bugger. The fish are getting ready for winter, and will usually chase after larger food sources and fly presentations.

The water level in the lake is maintained by a dam. Unlike other lakes with dams, there is no summer drawdown on Rampart. The lake is also managed as a quality fishery. There are special season, lure and bait restrictions in effect. Consult the regulations for more information.

Facilities

The **Rampart Lake Recreation Site** rests on the southern shore of the lake. In addition to seven campsites, there is a cartop boat launch available. Due to the tricky access, the campsites are not heavily used, making this a good weekend getaway location.

Other Options

The Hembrie Mountain Forest Service Road does link to another series of roads to the east. If you find the right combination, you will find **Spukunne Lake**. The difficult access and regular stocking program help to make this a good destination for generally larger rainbow trout.

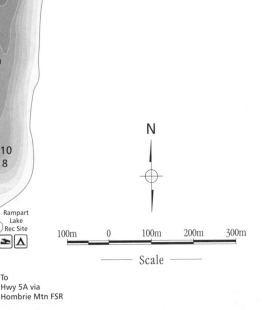

2m

16m

14

12m

10
8
6m
2m 4

Rampart
Lake
Rec Site

N

100m	0	100m	200m	300m

Scale

Rampart Cr

To
Hwy 5A via
Hombrie Mtn FSR

Ripley Lake

Location: 10 km (6 mi) west of Oliver
Elevation: 923 m (3,028 ft)
Surface Area: 6 ha (15 ac)
Mean Depth: 5.3 m (17 ft)
Max Depth: 15 m (49 ft)
Way Point: 119° 37′ 00″ Lon - W 49° 14′ 00″ Lat - N

Fishing

Ripley Lake is another one of those hidden lakes sandwiched in the hills between Oliver and Keremeos. Surrounded by dry grasslands and an open ponderosa pine forest, the lake, which is also known as Bear Lake, is quite popular with anglers, ATVers and campers. However, if you go during the week, or in the spring or fall, there's actually a good chance you will have the place to yourself.

Fishing is fairly good for rainbow that can grow to about 1 kg (2 lbs) in size. Rainbow were originally stocked in the lake in the 1950s and developed a reproducing population; however, increased fishing pressure has resulted in the need to begin stocking once again.

Fly-fishing is extremely popular here since the lake has a shallow, marshy shoreline that has lots of aquatic and emergent growth and good hatches. In fact, the lake has a prodigious number of dragonflies, and in the summer casting or trolling a dragonfly nymph pattern around the shoals at either end of the lake can often be productive. Also, try around the creek mouths. Favourite patterns used by locals include Idaho nymphs, '52 Buicks and Butler's bugs. Leeches and shrimp can be used throughout the year.

Spincasters will find some wide open spaces around the shores of the lake, especially near the recreation site. The campsite also features a small dock that is frequently used to cast out a small spoon or a worm and bobber.

There are two deep holes that are known as holding areas for larger rainbow during the hot summer months. Trolling along the drop offs of these deep holes with a Flatfish or spoon will usually prove productive. Try a small Ford Fender with a red Wedding Band.

Directions

From Oliver, follow 350th Avenue west to Fairview Road. This road turns to gravel as it courses north, eventually connecting with the Ripley Lake Forest Service Road (look for the recreation site signs). Continue north avoiding the fork branching right (that road leads to nearby Madden Lake). Ripley Lake should be about 2 km down this deteriorating logging road.

Facilities

User maintained campsites are found at end of the lake. Both sites have space for about five campsites and a place to launch small boats or pontoon boats. The sites are quite scenic and provide splendid views of the lake and surrounding area. Visitors can also climb to the small knoll south of the campground, which is quite easy to hike up (though it is steep). From here, there are great views of the lake and surrounding countryside.

Other Options

Madden Lake lies to the south of Ripley Lake via the same access road. Madden Lake offers angling opportunities for rainbow trout and is also home to a Forest Recreation campsite and boat launch. This lake is described in more detail earlier in the book.

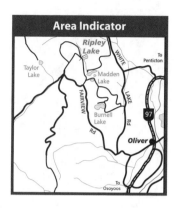

Species

Rainbow Trout

Ripley Lake			
Fish Stocking Data			
Year	Species	Number	Life Stage
2013	Rainbow Trout	3,400	Yearling
2012	Rainbow Trout	3,000	Yearling
2011	Rainbow Trout	3,075	Yearling

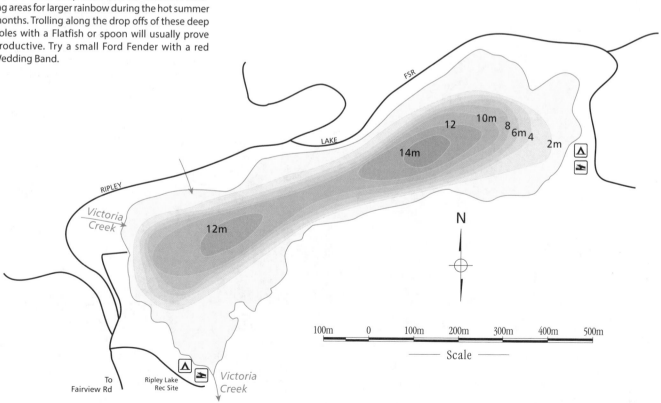

Location: 14 km (8.5 mi) west of Parson
Elevation: 1,442 m (4,731 ft)
Surface Area: 26 ha (64 ac)
Mean Depth: 4.6 m (15 ft)
Max Depth: 14.6 m (48 ft)
Way Point: 116° 46' 00" Lon - W 51° 00' 00" Lat - N

Rocky Point Lake

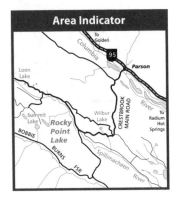

Area Indicator

Species
Rainbow Trout

Fishing

Rocky Point Lake is a narrow lake that is lined with lily pads and other weeds that provide ideal habitat for both insects and trout to hide in. The lake is stocked annually by the Freshwater Fisheries Society of BC with 8,000 trout to ensure a good fishery. Despite the regular stockings, the rainbow are known to reach good sizes with the odd 2.5 kg (5.5 lb) trout caught periodically.

Being a fairly high elevation lake, the fishing season does not get going as early as others closer to the Columbia River valley. On most years, the fishing does not start heating up until late May or early June. Although there may be a bit of a slow down during hot periods, the fishing here remains fairly consistent through October.

For best success, it is best to work the weed areas in the spring and fall. Shore fishing is limited at the lake; therefore, it is recommended to bring a float tube or canoe to better work these areas. At times, the trout in this lake are not very picky and will readily take flies, spinners and spoons. If the trout are a little finicky, try trolling along the perimeter of the lake with a spoon or spinner. In addition to varying your depth until you find the holding areas, you might want to tip the lure with bait.

Fly anglers will definitely find more success if they can match the hatch. However, with limited shoals, many prefer to troll a Woolly Bugger with a little crystal flash or a smaller leech pattern with a touch of maroon just off the weeds.

Directions

This remote lake is located west of the town of Parson set amid the Spillmacheen Mountain Range. and head south to the Spillmacheen North Forest Service Road. Travel northwest along the forest road to the 21 km mark where the Summit A Road branches south. If you pass the access road to Loon Lake, you have gone too far.

The Summit A Road takes you to Summit, Rocky Point and Three Island Lakes along a series of rough 4wd roads. The branch road to Rocky Point is found just over 2 km past the crossing of the Spillmacheen River. A 4wd vehicle along with a copy of the *Backroad Mapbook for the Kootenay Rockies* and the *BC Backroad GPS Maps* are recommended when exploring this area.

Facilities

The **Rocky Point Lake Recreation Site** is a small, semi open site set in a forest next to the lake. This rough road access limits bigger units from coming in and boats must be carried down to the water for launching. There is, however, a small dock from which to cast from.

Other Options

When travelling towards Rocky Point Lake, instead of turning off east after crossing the Spillmacheen River, simply continue and you will eventually pass **Summit Lake**. Summit Lake offers fishing for some good sized brook trout. Summit Lake offers fishing for some good sized brook trout that are stocked regularly. Also in the area is **Three Island Lake**, which is found just beyond Summit Lake. Three Island Lake is stocked with fast growing rainbow trout. Both lakes have limited shore fishing opportunities, but are small enough to fish from a belly boat.

To Summit Lake

Rocky Point Lake Rec Site

dock

3m

6

9m

12

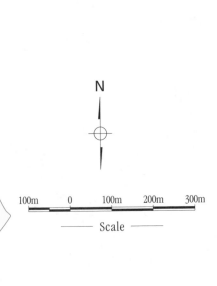

N

100m 0 100m 200m 300m

Scale

Rosebud Lake

Location: 17 km (10.5 mi) south of Salmo
Elevation: 809 m (2,654 ft)
Surface Area: 13 ha (32 ac)
Mean Depth: 7 m (23 ft)
Max Depth: 17 m (56 ft)
Way Point: 116° 46' 00" Lon - W   51° 00' 00" Lat - N

Fishing

Rosebud Lake is a notoriously hit and miss lake for fishing found south of the junction of Highways 3 and 6. It was once a favourite spot with local fly anglers and was considered one of the best lakes in the region. Unfortunately, construction on the lake damaged some of the shoreline areas, creating numerous shoreline washouts. The increased silt in the lake severely hampered fishing success for a number of years, but the quality of fishing is slowly returning.

Part of that is due to the continued efforts of the Freshwater Fisheries Society in stocking the lake, and part of that is just due to the natural regenerative powers of the lake. The lake holds some Gerrard rainbow, which may also help to boost the size of the fish that you will find.

If you do plan to visit Rosebud Lake, a number of different flies can produce results throughout the year. Chironomid hatches can be found year round on the lake, although they are most prevalent during the spring. Try working your fly slowly off the northern shore or along any of the shoal areas found around the lake. As summer approaches, Rosebud sprouts plenty of weed growth, which is where rainbow trout tend to cruise near to feed. Try to match the hatch on the lake. There are quality caddis fly hatches on the lake, especially during mid summer. Many a large rainbow has been caught in this lake on a well presented top water caddis.

Spincasters can do well with bait tipped lures such as a Wedding Band. For best results, try working the area to the east of the deeper hole in the middle of the lake.

The lake is also popular for ice fishing, even though rainbow trout are not the most active fish in the winter. A good strategy for ice fishing is to drill a series of holes, starting at about 3 m (10 ft) from shoreline and working out at regular intervals. The holes should be drilled at the same time, as the drilling disturbs the fish. Better have them run away once and then come back, rather than have them run away each time you decide to drill a hole.

One of the mistakes made by beginning ice anglers is to try and fish too deep. Trout will be found anywhere from a few inches to a few metres below the ice. Try jigging a lure at different depths to see where you get a strike. If a hole proves unproductive, move on to the next one.

Other Options

The closest fishing alternative to Rosebud Lake is the **Salmo River.** Before the damning of the Pend d'Oreille River, the section below Shenango Canyon was a fantastic place to find big rainbow, cutthroat and brook trout. This is still one of the better locations but getting to the holes can be a challenge. Check the regulations before heading out.

Directions

This small lake can be reached via a good gravel road off the east side of Highway 6, south of the town of Salmo. Look for the sign to the lake where the access road meets the highway

Facilities

Rosebud Lake is home to an undeveloped regional park as well as a few private residences that have sprung up around the lake. Visitors will find a small parking area and rustic boat launch at the south end of the lake. There is also an old floating wharf at that end of the lake.

Rosebud Lake Fish Stocking Data			
Year	Species	Number	Life Stage
2013	Rainbow Trout	1,500	Yearling
2012	Rainbow Trout	1,500	Yearling
2011	Rainbow Trout	1,500	Yearling

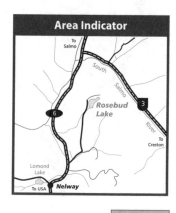

Area Indicator

Species
Rainbow Trout

15m

14

9m

floating wharf

5

2m

Rosebud Regional Park

N

Rosebud Cr

To Hwy 6

100m   0   100m   200m   300m

— Scale —

Location: 3 km (1.8 mi) northwest of West Kelowna
Elevation: 599 m (1,965.2 ft)
Surface Area: 42 ha (104 ac)
Mean Depth: 8.8 m (28.8 ft)
Max Depth: 17 m (55 ft)
Way Point: 119° 33′00″ Lon - W 49° 54′00″ Lat - N

Rose Valley Lake

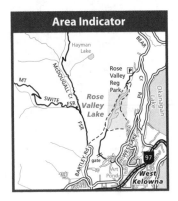

Area Indicator

Species
Rainbow Trout

Fishing

Rose Valley is a scenic man-made reservoir that originated from the time of de-glaciation when melt water formed a channel around a stagnant piece of ice occupying Okanagan Lake. The lake was damned to help provide the Lakeview Irrigation District. As a result, the water levels in Rose Valley Lake can fluctuate.

Rising above the lake are volcanic cliffs, complete with caves on the west side of the lake that are thought to be large air bubbles in the lava. Rose Valley Regional Park helps protect the natural appeal of the surrounding area by being an undeveloped park. Other than a few trails that help anglers access the lake, there are no facilities here.

Considered a good family fishing lake, anglers will find the lake offers plenty of stocked rainbow trout. These trout are best caught in the spring and fall on everything from a worm and bobber to flies. With good trail access around the lake, shore fishing is fairly easy. However, those willing to lug in a belly boat or pontoon boat will be rewarded by trying the small bays and the submerged island near the north end of the lake. The lake has an electric motor only restriction.

The use of a floatation device is highly recommended during the summer to get out to the deeper water where the trout prefer to hold. During the warmer periods, the surface water warms and weed growth develops near the shoreline. Both of these factors limit the effectiveness of casting from shore.

Given the relatively low elevation of the lake, the open water season can start as early as late March. At this time, chironomids suspended just off the bottom or leech patterns trolled slowly seem to be effective. Other searching patterns, such as Wooly Buggers, Doc Spratleys or 52 Buicks are reported to be effective. Smaller trout lures like the Panther Martin or a Mepps Fury also become more effective later in the spring. As always, it is best to check local fly and tackle shops with what is working well before heading out.

Directions

Found in West Kelowna, the easiest access to the lake is found at the north end of the lake via a short 10 minute walk. To find this unmarked trailhead, follow Highway 97 to West Side Road. Follow West Side Road north a short distance to Bear Creek Road. Continue west on Bear Creek Road and look for the Rose Valley Road about 4.5 km later. A short drive down this road brings you to the parking area. The old road/trail is on the left, sandwiched between private property signs. Please avoid crossing private property in the area.

Facilities

Rose Valley Regional Park protects 250 hectares of undeveloped land around the lake. Although there are no facilities in the park, visitors will find a series of hiking and mountain biking trails around the reservoir and in the hills above. These trails link with Westlake Road at the Rose Valley Elementary School in the east and Bartley Road to the south.

Rose Valley Lake			
Fish Stocking Data			
Year	Species	Number	Life Stage
2013	Rainbow Trout	2,500	Yearling
2012	Rainbow Trout	2,500	Yearling
2011	Rainbow Trout	2,500	Yearling

Ruth & Flyfish No 2 Lakes

Area Indicator

Flyfish No 2 Lake Fish Stocking Data			
Year	Species	Number	Life Stage
2013	Rainbow Trout	4,000	Fry
2012	Rainbow Trout	4,000	Fry
2011	Rainbow Trout	4,300	Fry

Species
Rainbow Trout

Elevation: 1,354 m (4,030 ft)
Surface Area: 24 ha (59 ac)
Way Point: 119° 08'00" Lon - W 50° 06'00" Lat - N

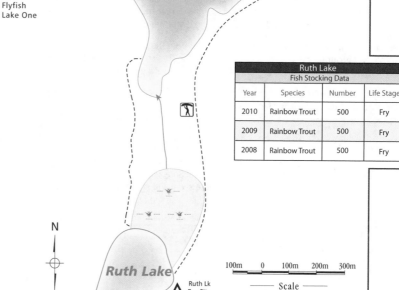

To Loon Lake

Flyfish Lks Rec Site

Flyfish Lake 2

To Flyfish Lake One

Ruth Lake Fish Stocking Data			
Year	Species	Number	Life Stage
2010	Rainbow Trout	500	Fry
2009	Rainbow Trout	500	Fry
2008	Rainbow Trout	500	Fry

Ruth Lake

Ruth Lk Rec Site

To Haddo Lake

N

100m 0 100m 200m 300m
— Scale —

Fishing

There is a usually a law of increasing returns: the harder a lake is to get to, the better the fishing will be. With Ruth being a high elevation lake well away from the nearest road you would think the fishing would be incredible. Think again. Some say it skirts that fine line of whether the risk is worth the reward.

Yes the lake does offer good fishing for rainbow trout, which are stocked annually. The trouble is the lake isn't being maintained as a trophy lake like many in the area. There are no rules in place that would help the fish get nice and big. While there have been fish taken out of here to 2 kg (4.5 lbs), you'll be lucky to find one that gets to half that. But if you are looking for a remote place to catch fish then you could do worse.

Not surprisingly, the same holds true for Flyfish Lake 2 or the eastern Flyfish Lake. The lake is also stocked annually with quick growing trout. But the bigger fish are usually taken long before they have a chance to grow.

Both lakes are quite shallow (thus no chart is available) and the waters are quite rich with tannins, making them a deep brown colour. Even the fish are darker than you would expect from a rainbow. Carrying a float tube or canoe will help you find the fish, which can be taken on a variety of small spinners or spoons, as well as leech patterns, scuds and insect emulations. Because the water is so dark, you'll probably have more success using a brighter coloured pattern.

Due to their shallow nature, these lakes heat up quite quickly and are best fished earlier in the season or later in the year. There are many inviting shoals that the trout often cruise in search of an easy meal. However, the shallow waters make the fish skittish so be sure not to move around too much when out on a boat or canoe.

If you do come in the summer, it is best to fish in the morning or evening. Dry flies, like mosquito patterns or Tom Thumbs can be a lot of fun at that time.

If you do manage to catch a big trout, why not let it go to be caught and released by the next angler?

Directions

From Winfield, head east from Highway 97 along the Beaver Lake Road which becomes the Beaver Dee Lake Road. Follow the road past Beaver and Dee Lake Resorts. Watch for the junction that leads past Doreen Lake to the rough side road marked Flyfish 2. The road is very rough and a 4wd vehicle is recommended, especially during wet weather. It takes you past Loon Lake to the recreation site at Flyfish 2 where you can hand launch small boats.

Once at Flyfish 2, you will need to paddle to the south end of the lake to the short portage or you can lug your gear along a 1.5 km (0.9 mile) trail that leads to the lake. Needless to say, a good map such as those in the Thompson Okanagan Backroad Mapbook will help you find this and the many other lakes in the area.

Facilities

There is a rough campsite at the north end of Ruth Lake which has been developed by the Forestry Service, with space for a couple tents. If you don't want to carry a tent all the way, there are six sites and a good launch site at the 4wd accessible **Flyfish Lake No. 2 Recreation Site**. Portage trails link the two lakes.

Shuswap River West
Location: East of Enderby
Stream Length: 195 km (121 mi)
Geographic: 119° 0' 00" Lon - W 50° 32' 00" Lat - N

Shuswap River - West

Fishing

The Shuswap is a big river, or rather, it is effectively three rivers, its progress broken up by a pair of large lakes. It is at almost exactly the halfway point between Vancouver and Calgary, making it equally accessible. If you were to take and stretch it out, the river would be much longer than in appears on a map, as the river winds and meanders its way across the countryside. The many bends form nooks and crannies where fish can hold.

The upper section of the river begins at its headwaters in Joss Pass, found at the north end of the Sawtooth Range of the Monashee Mountains. This section of the river is cold, clean, and accessible by the Shuswap Forest Service Road. It flows generally southward to drain into Sugar Lake and does not receive the attention the other stretches do. This is partly due to access and partly due to the smaller size of trout.

The middle or east section of the Shuswap flows south from Sugar Lake, then curves north again and empties into Mabel Lake, a much larger lake. The Shuswap Falls are a notable feature on this section. Not only are they a site to behold, they all mark the upward limit of the salmon runs. Beyond here is the domain of trout anglers and there is really good access from Highway 6 and the Sugar Lake Road. Upstream from the falls access is limited, but there are some nice salmon holding areas to look for.

The final or west section of the river runs westward out of Mabel Lake and is easily accessed off the Enderby-Mabel Lake Road. Although trout anglers do come here, this section is busiest when the salmon run during the summer. Access points and bridge crossing are often crowded, so keen anglers often drift the river to find quieter holes (watch for rapids and tricky shallow areas). At Enderby, the river curves north to flow into Mara Lake, which is connected by a short channel to Shuswap Lake, which is ultimately drained by the South Thompson River. This stretch of river runs next to Highway 97A but private property limits access.

The Shuswap is home to several species of fish, including rainbow trout, lake trout (in a few areas), bull trout, kokanee and whitefish, but its real claim to fame is the fact that it is one of the very few rivers in the Okanagan that supports a variety of salmon runs. Currently, the only run that it open to recreational fishing is Chinook, which start around the middle of August, and continues through to mid-September.

In spring, the river is known for its rainbow trout fishing for trout that can get to 2 kg (4 lbs) on a very good day. Most fish you find may be half that size. The best time to hit the river is during the stonefly hatch in late spring. The stonefly is an active insect, and the trout often hit them very hard. Sometimes the trout will try and submerge the fly first, other times they will strike immediately. Be alert, and don't try and set your hook if the trout tries to submerge the fly.

Stoneflies can take up to two years to mature into an adult. This means that there are almost always stonefly nymphs in areas where there are stonefly hatches, and stonefly nymph patterns are good flies to use when there is no active hatch occurring, including into the fall. To fish the nymph effectively, you must fish as close to the bottom as possible, preferably bouncing it along the bottom. A strike indicator will help when fishing nymph patterns.

For bull trout, try using a small, silver coloured spoon. Fly anglers can use streamer patterns like a Muddler Minnow. A leech pattern can work, too.

The river also offers some great whitefish angling. While whitefish are not a favourite eating fish (too boney, many say), they can be quite fun to catch. Between Cherryville and Shuswap Falls, on the middle section of the Shuswap is the best whitefish fishing. This section holds bigger than average whitefish. Spincasters can work maggots or single salmon eggs, while fly anglers will find stonefly nymphs work well.

Continued >>

Shuswap River - East

Shuswap River East
Location: Northeast of Lumby
Stream Length: 195 km (121 mi)
Geographic: 118° 44'00" Lon - W   50° 15'00" Lat - N

8 Region

Fishing

Continued

Shuswap Falls marks another dividing line in the river, as migrating salmon cannot get past the falls. Salmon can be found in the river below the falls in August and September. While there are four species of salmon that spawn here, only Chinook are open to fishing. Casting or drift fishing with cured roe into deep holes seems to be the most effective method. If trout are cleaning the hook of bait, switch to lures, wool (white, red or pink) or flies. Lures of choice include a Kitimat spoon or Spin-N-Glos. The fly angler will need heavy gear and fast sinking lines with short strong tippet to get down to the deep holes. Shooting heads allow increased line control and help maintain a drag-free drift. Patterns mixing bright and dark colours seem to be most effective. Woolly Buggers, Egg Sucking Leeches or Marabou Eggs dead drifted are equally good.

During and shortly after the salmon run is another great time to fish the river, as the rainbow and bull trout gorge themselves on salmon eggs. Both spin-casters and fly anglers will do well to use something that imitates a free floating salmon egg. A egg sucking leech pattern works very well for rainbow and bull trout.

Species	
Bull Trout	Lake Trout
Chinook Salmon	Rainbow Trout
Kokanee	Whitefish

Directions

The Shuswap is a long, meandering river that covers about 200 km (120 miles) as it loops and switchbacks its way from its headwaters to Mara Lake. One of the best places to access the river is between Cherryville and Shuswap Falls on Highway 6, east of Vernon. From Cherryville, the eastern section of river can be followed upstream along the Sugar Lake Road, and then to its headwaters along the Shuswap Forest Service Road. Around Shuswap Falls, the Mabel Lake Road parallels the river for a short distance in this section.

The Mara Lake to Mabel Lake section can be picked from Highway 97A between Enderby and Mara. However, private property limits shore access. The Enderby-Mabel Lake Road is certainly the better route to gain access to this popular stretch of water. The Trinity Valley Road bridge, Cooke Creek Recreation Site and the Kingfisher Hatchery are among the most popular access points.

Facilities

Despite its travels, the biggest centre along the river is the quaint town of Enderby. There is a helpful tackle shop in town along with a variety of accommodations and other supplies. Those looking to camp at or near riverside can also find a variety of places to stay. **Cooke Creek Recreation Site** is a popular spot on the section from Enderby to Mabel Lake. The recently expanded site offers about a dozen riverside campsites and good trail access to fishing holes and the nearby **Kingfisher Interpretive Centre & Hatchery**. The hatchery itself provides interesting displays on the local flora and fauna as well as about the salmon runs.

The next section of river has several convenient campsites. The **Cherryville Recreation Site** is a large open area with a nice beach to access nice swimming or fishing holes. Further upstream, there is a quartet of recreation sites on Sugar Lake. The **Mabel Lake Provincial Park** is also found just north of the river mouth and is a popular 81 unit campsite available on a first come, first serve basis. Closer to Highway 6, the **Shuswap River Hatchery** east of Lumby is another great place to visit and learn more about the local environment and salmon runs on the river. The nearby BC Hydro Canoe Launch is a popular access point for drift fishers.

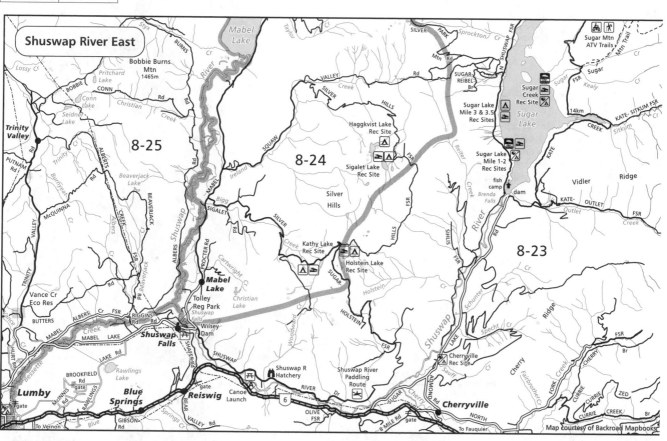

Region 4

Location: 26 km (16 mi) southeast of Nakusp
Elevation: 1,872 m (6,142 ft)
Surface Area: 25 ha (62 ac)
Mean Depth: 29 m (95 ft)
Max Depth: 70 m (230 ft)
Way Point: 117° 34' 00" Lon - W 50° 03' 00" Lat - N

Shannon Lake

Fishing

There are many scenic lakes in the Kootenays. Shannon Lake vies for the title as one of the prettiest. Set in a postcard perfect scene below the towering Mount Vingolf, Shannon Lake is a serene, picturesque mountain lake, and a great place to spend some time exploring the Kootenays.

For the angler at heart, Shannon Lake is home to a healthy population of cutthroat trout. Cutthroat are an aggressive fish that are well known for chasing most anything that looks like food, especially in a high elevation lake like Shannon. The ice comes off in June and returns by November, leaving a short window of opportunity for trout to gorge themselves. The fish can get up to 50 cm (20 inches), but are usually smaller than that.

Try fly-fishing a silver minnow imitation, bait fishing or casting a small silver lure that will resemble small minnows. Fly-fishers can try gold or silver bodied Muddler Minnow or Wool Head Sculpin. Sinking line with short leaders is preferred to work the steep shorelines of lakes. For dry flies, try the old Tom Thumb or other caddis variations. The trick is to present an active target for the trout to hone in on.

Spincasting Kitimat lures, Panther Martin spinners or trolling lake trolls with a small spinner and bait can also be effective. Even still fishing a worm and bobber can often do the trick using light test and a small hook. Cast around the drop off areas or near stream mouths, as the cutthroat tend to cruise these areas in search of food.

The lake has some open places along the shore, from which a line could be cast. However, getting out onto the lake in a tube will improve your chances as you can cover a larger area.

Other Options

The lake that lies to the south of Mount Vingolf is **Wragge Lake**. Wragge Lake can be reached by following the rough Wragge Creek Road from the Shannon Creek Forest Service Road. At the end of the road, another challenging trail leads to the remote mountain lake. The lake offers good fishing for average sized rainbow trout.

Directions

Shannon Lake is a sub-alpine lake set below the majestic Valhalla Mountain Ranges. To reach the lake, follow Highway 6 to the north end of Slocan Lake and look for the Bonanza Road off the west side of the highway. Bonanza Road leads across the meandering creek to the beginning of the Shannon Creek Forest Service Road. Follow this forest road and keep right at the fork in the road at kilometre 3 and 4. The road continues its' ascent along Shannon Creek, eventually reaching the branch road that leads to Shannon Creek Trail at the 12 km mark. It is another 2 km to the trailhead along a rough road that may require a 4wd vehicle.

Facilities

Shannon Lake is a typical backcountry lake that offers a couple rustic areas to camp at lakeside. The **Shannon Creek Trail** is a short but steep trail that climbs 275 m (900 ft) over 1.6 km. Allow an hour to hike into the sub-alpine along a rocky trail that is often slippery. The trail takes hikers along the west side of the lake and up into the Valhalla Ranges. Mount Vingolf is a popular destination for climbers.

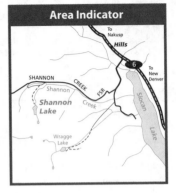

Area Indicator

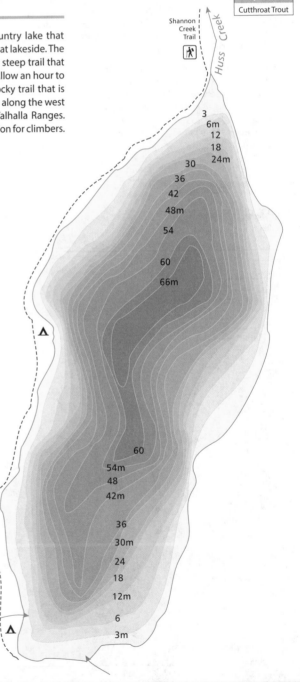

Species

Cutthroat Trout

N

100m   0   100m   200m   300m

Scale

Similkameen River

Location: North of Grand Forks
Stream Length: 197 km (122 mi)
Geographic: 120° 15'00" Lon - W   49° 25'00" Lat - N

Fishing

The Similkameen is a tributary of the Okanogan River (which is what the Okanagan River is called south of the border). The tributary, in fact, is actually bigger than the main river since the Okanogan triples in size when the Similkameen hits.

The river is best known as a place to stop on a hot day's drive down Highway 3. In particular, both Stemwinder or Bromley Rock Provincial Parks offer a good place for a picnic or a dip in the crisp, refreshing water. But the river is also known for its good fishing for rainbow, cutthroat and brook trout as well as Dolly Varden. It is a cold water river, starting high in Manning Park, and flowing east and south towards the Okanagan.

One of the best places to fish the river is at aforementioned Bromley Rock Provincial Park. While the swimming hole should probably be avoided (as hooks and little kids with bare feet don't go together very well), you won't have to walk very far up or downstream to find an enticing patch of water.

Although there are a variety of fish to target, the river is best known for its rainbow trout fishing. Working a small green and yellow stonefly or caddis fly nymph will work well year-round, especially in the middle of the day, when the trout may be hesitant to rise to the surface. Using a sinking line and a strike indicator, bounce your fly right along the bottom. However, when the hatches start to happen along the river, the top water action can be quite fun. Watch for caddis rising to the surface, which will bring the trout after them. Stoneflies actually climb out of the water to hatch, but the females return to the river to lay their eggs. It is when they return to the river that they become targets for the trout, so don't be afraid to land your fly with a bit of a splat. In addition to caddis and stonefly patterns, a Tom Thumb will work well.

Spincasters can work small spoons or spinners, which imitate small minnows and other baitfish. To work this streams effectively, you need to sneak up on holes to avoid being detected by trout. The river runs relatively warm in summer, and wading can be a refreshing break from the heat of the day.

Species
Brook Trout
Cutthroat Trout
Dolly Varden
Rainbow Trout

Directions

The Similkameen starts in the Manning Park, north of the Crowsnest Highway. However, the highway quickly picks up the river valley, and follows it for all but the last few kilometres before the Similkameen flows south out of the province. Access to the river isn't always easy because of cliffs, canyons, thick brush and private property, but it is always close.

Facilities

The headwaters of the Similkameen are in **Manning Provincial Park**, one of the most popular parks in the province. There are 355 campsites, many of which are reservable. Northeast of Manning, the river flows through Princeton, where you'll find full services. East of Princeton, **Bromely Rock Provincial Park** provided 17 first come, first serve campsites along with a separate picnic area with a large natural beach, while **Stemwinder Provincial Park** offers 26 vehicle accessible campsites. Finally, the river flows past Hedley and through the bigger town of Keremeos before heading south and out of the province.

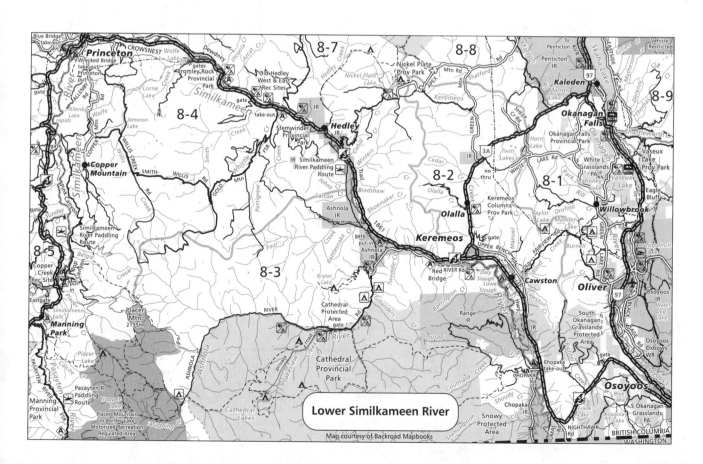

Lower Similkameen River

Map courtesy of Backroad Mapbooks

Location: 1 km (0.6 mi) south of Penticton
Elevation: 339 m (1,112 ft)
Surface Area: 2,010 ha (4,965 ac)
Mean Depth: 26 m (85 ft)
Max Depth: 57 m (187 ft)
Way Point: 119° 34' 00" Lon - W 49° 23' 00" Lat - N

Skaha Lake

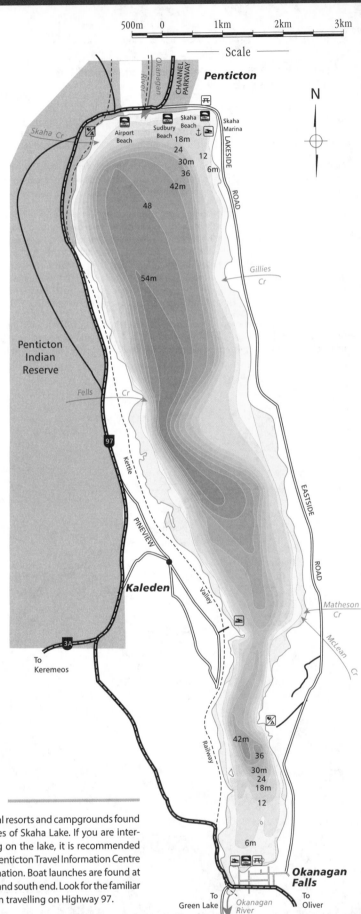

Directions

The lake itself is accessible from several different locations with Penticton being the most notable gateway. Highway 97 travels parallel to the western shore, while Eastside Road parallels the eastern shore.

Species
Bass
Kokanee
Rainbow Trout

Fishing

The cities of Penticton and Okanagan Falls act as book-ends to this popular recreational lake. This big lake is not really known for its quality fishing due mainly to its fame as a fantastic water sports lake. Waterskiing, windsurfing, swimming and just hanging out at the beach are much more popular pursuits. However a growing bass fishery is helping bring this lake back to respectability.

The lake has big bass, both smallmouth and large-mouth, and the number and size of the fish seem to be growing. They aren't as pretty a fish as trout, but they can provide some great action. Largemouth bass, are known for their explosive runs and aerial acrobatics, while smallmouth have more fight in them, pound for pound, than most any fish.

There are as many opinions of what the best way to catch bass is as there are anglers. Spinners, jigs and streamer flies are popular, as are bass bugs and plastic lures designed specifically for bass. The big issue with bass fishing is fishing in the right spot. Bass like to hang out under cover of weeds or fallen trees or overhanging rocks. They love warm water but not the sun. Using top water lures like a bass bug or a Rapala Skitter Pop are great for largemouth. Smallmouth aren't quite so willing to come to the surface and generally hold deeper in the water, although in spring or fall, they are more likely to come to the top. Try a black Rapala on cloudy days, or yellow or chrome on sunny days. Try using a plastic grub in smoke, chartreuse or pumpkin-pepper during the summer.

The most popular area for fishing is at the south end near the outlet of the lake at Okanagan Falls. Here, smallmouth bass as big as 2.5 kg (5 lbs) have been caught from the shore. However, the entire eastern edge of the lake is a mess of weedbeds, providing ideal cover for the bass.

No everyone comes to Skaha to fish for bass and anglers will find a few resident rainbow trout and kokanee. Not that there aren't fish here, there are quite a few, but it's a big lake, and the fish are spread out. As a result, trolling is the most effective way of searching the lake. Try a downrigger with a lake troll, wedding band and bait for the kokanee. The trout are often caught on spoons or flashers with small spinners. Fishing is best in the fall and early winter for trout, while kokanee are best caught in the summer.

Near the end of Main Street in Okanagan Falls is a pier. This is a popular place to fish for trout from, often using just a bobber and worm.

Facilities

There are several resorts and campgrounds found along the shores of Skaha Lake. If you are interested in staying on the lake, it is recommended to contact the Penticton Travel Information Centre for more information. Boat launches are found at both the north and south end. Look for the familiar blue signs when travelling on Highway 97.

Skookumchuck Creek

Location: North of Grand Forks
Stream Length: 65 km (40 mi)
Geographic: 118° 55' 00" Lon - W   49° 58' 00" Lat - N

Fishing

The name "Skookumchuck" means turbulent water, and it is an appropriate name for this creek. Skookumchuk Creek is well known as a great whitewater rafting and kayaking destination. While the river is about 65 km (40 miles) long, only about 20 km (12 miles) of that is considered fishable.

The Skookumchuk (or Skook, as it is known to locals) has a very low flow of water. It boasts steady fishing for cutthroat to 40 cm (16 inches), and some even larger bull trout. The river has many deep holding pools that usually hold a couple of good-sized fish. It is one of the more interesting rivers to fish, with large boulder gardens, endless pocket water and cascades that end in deep blue pools. It is nothing if not beautiful. But it is also quite hard to access.

The river's headwaters are high in the Purcell Wilderness Conservancy, just outside of St. Mary Alpine Provincial Park. Most people who fish the creek do so with a drift boat, raft, canoe, or other means of floating down the river, though it is also a popular wade and walk creek. Really keen anglers will sometimes helicopter in to the headwaters, but if you really want to get as far upstream as you can, there is an old trail to follow. The trail is difficult to follow but will take you to a beautiful area that few people ever bother to get to.

The middle section of the creek is accessed by the Skookumchuck Forest Service Road, while the lower reaches are accessed by logging roads from the settlement of Skookumchuck. In between there is a section of creek that is not really touched by road and sees few anglers.

The river is best known for its cutthroat trout fishing, although it also holds good numbers of bull trout and whitefish as well. The bull trout like to chase after minnow imitations such as the Muddler Minnow, while the cutthroat like to rise to a well-presented Tom Thumb or Elk Hair Caddis. Whitefish also take well to flies.

Do check the regulations before heading out, as sections of the river are closed to angling, and much of the river is designated fly-fishing only. It is catch and release only, and the creek is designated Class II waters meaning you need a special tag to fish here.

Species
Cutthroat Trout
Bull Trout

Directions

The small village of Skookumchuck marks where the creek flows into the Kootenay. From here, the lower section of the river can be accessed by roads, although this section is rarely fished. The upper section of the river is accessed north of Skookumchuck from the Torrent Forest Service Road. This road dead ends at the Skookumchuck Forest Service Road. Turning left onto this road will bring you over Sandown Creek, and then into the Skookumchuck Valley a bit further on. From here, watch for ways to access the creek. A popular access point is from the Buhl Creek Road bridge.

Facilities

Both recreation sites on the creek are worth visiting when in the area. The **Skookumchuck Creek Recreation Site** is a small treed site found near a waterfall, while the **Buhl Creek Recreation Site** sits in an open meadow near the **Buhl Creek Warm Springs**. Both sites are rarely visited and make a fine destination in their own right.

Back at the highway, Skookumchuck is a very small village with less than 100 people, but there is a gas station and a coffee shop. Further north Canal Flats offers only slightly more in the way of services.

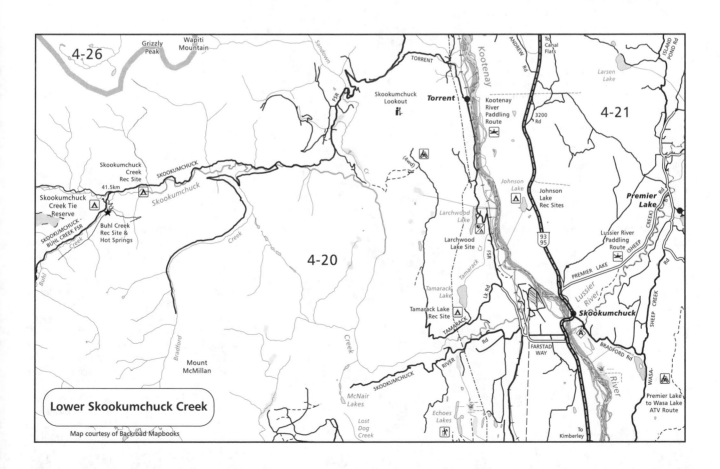

Lower Skookumchuck Creek

Map courtesy of Backroad Mapbooks

Location: North and South of New Denver
Elevation: 541 m (1,775 ft)
Surface Area: 6,929 ha (17,115 ac)
Mean Depth: 171 m (561 ft)
Max Depth: 298 m (978 ft)
Way Point: 117° 21' 00" Lon - W 49° 57' 00" Lat - N

Slocan Lake

Fishing

Beautiful Slocan Lake is one of the bigger lakes of the Kootenays, set below the Valhalla Mountain Range. A large portion of its western shore is protected by the wilds of Valhalla Provincial Park.

Up until 2002, the lake was stocked with 20,000 Gerrard strain rainbow trout, which are famous for their large size, growing up to 5 kg (10 lbs) in size. The lake also holds plenty of large bull trout, and even more small kokanee.

Since Slocan Lake is such a large and deep lake, the best method for finding fish in this lake is by trolling. Work near creek inflows for the big trout, using a deep troll with medium sized spoons or plugs. A few of the more popular lures are the green and yellow Flatfish, the Kamlooper and Rapala plugs. A downrigger is a definite asset during the warmer summer months when Apex lures, Hockey Sticks, coyote spoons and Road Runners are effective in the 10-30 m (30-100 ft) depths. However, like most big lakes the best fishing actually occurs during the late fall and winter. At this time the fish are found closer to the surface and things like a bucktail skimmed on the surface can be an exciting alternative.

For kokanee, the most effective combination is still a Willow Leaf with Wedding Band and maggot or worm trolled near the surface. Troll as slow as possible and in an "S" pattern, with one ounce of weight or less, which takes the lure to 5-15 m (15 to 45 ft). Other kokanee lures include Flatfish or small pink Spin-N-Glo lures, why fly-fishers can try trolling slowly with a small red Doc Spratley or Woolly Bugger within a few feet of the surface.

Fly anglers and other spincasters best bet for success is casting near creek inflows in the spring. During summer, terrestrial flies or a bobber and bait dangled near the drop off of larger creeks can yield the odd big strike.

Directions

This large lake lies in the heart of the West Kootenays, sandwiched in the valley between the Arrow Lakes and Kootenay Lake. The main access points are from Slocan City to the south as well as Silverton and New Denver along the eastern shore. All three towns are home to good boat launches and are accessible from Highway 6.

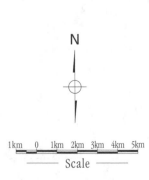

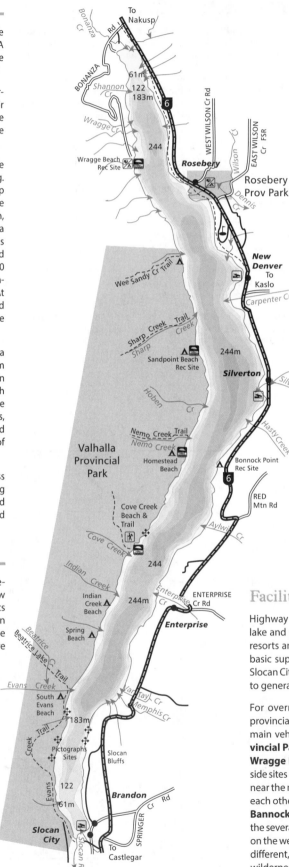

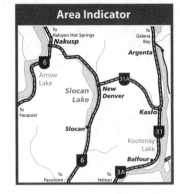

Area Indicator

Species
Bull Trout
Kokanee
Rainbow Trout

Facilities

Highway 6 skirts the eastern shore of the large lake and provides access to a number of lakeside resorts and privately operated campgrounds. For basic supplies and other amenities, the towns of Slocan City, New Denver and Silverton are all home to general stores.

For overnight camping, there are a number of provincial parks and recreation sites to sample. The main vehicle accessible sites are **Roseberry Provincial Park** with 36 sites above the highway and **Wragge Beach Recreation Site** offering 13 lakeside sites and a nice beach area. Both sites are found near the north end of the lake, virtually across from each other. Boaters can also take advantage of the **Bannock Point Recreation Site** on the east side or the several marine sites in **Valhalla Provincial Park** on the western slope of the big lake. For something different, visitors can also explore one of the main wilderness trails in the park.

Snowshoe Lake

Location: 47 km (29 mi) southwest of Nakusp
Elevation: 640 m (2,100 ft)
Surface Area: 19 ha (47 ac)
Mean Depth: 9 m (30 ft)
Max Depth: 20 m (66 ft)
Way Point: 118° 10' 00" Lon - W 49° 55' 00" Lat - N

4 Region

Area Indicator

Species
Rainbow Trout
Brook Trout

Fishing

While it is only 2 km (1.2 miles) from the highway to Snowshoe Lake, the small lake is often overlooked by anglers. The road into the lake is quite rough, and a 4wd is needed, at least when it is wet. And despite it's proximity to a highway, that highway is Highway 6, one of the least travelled highways in the province.

Despite it's relative obscurity, the lake is a great location for anglers, especially fly anglers. The lake was stocked with rainbow trout until 1988, and now a thriving self-sustaining population of rainbow trout exist in the lake. The lake also holds native brook trout, and both species can get quite big here. There are reports of the occasional 2 kg (4.5 lb) trout being caught in the lake.

There is a prominent point southeast of the recreation site at the north end of the lake which may attract some fish, especially in spring and later in fall when the water is cool. However, the area around the point is very shallow, and once the water warms up, most fish will instead hold in the deeper water towards the centre of the lake.

Of course, the fish don't hold in the deepest areas of the lake, but only deep enough that the water temperature is comfortable for them. This area is called the thermocline, and the fish are found where the thermocline meets a drop off. Unfortunately, there are few prominent drop offs or points where the fish will hold, and finding the fish can be challenging. A fish finder would be a real asset here.

Try working the shoal areas in the 3-6 m (10-20 ft) range, especially in the spring. Chironomid patterns will do well earlier in the year and again in the fall, while nymph patterns, such as a dragonfly or damselfly, can also produce results throughout the season. For spincasters, trolling a small spoon or spinner along the drop off areas will certainly have its rewards.

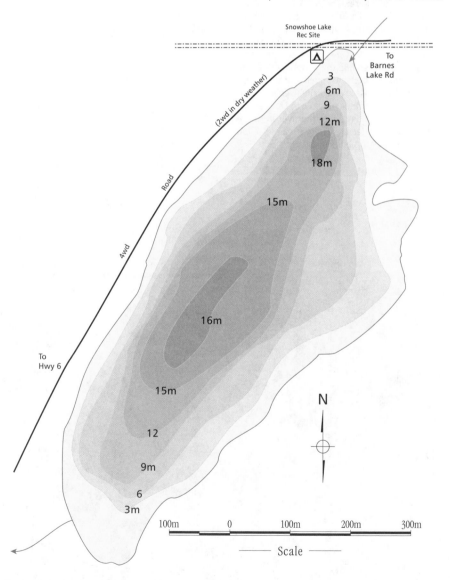

An electric motor only restriction applies to this lake. While there is no boat launch, it is easy enough to hand launch a small craft, which will greatly improve the fishing experience.

Directions

Found west of the Needles ferry terminus, the easiest access into Snowshoe Lake is off Highway 6. Look for the road branching north just before the highway crosses Inonoaklin Creek, about 14.5 km from the ferry. Follow this road through the gravel pit onto a rough dirt road. After crossing a cattle guard at 1.5 km the road forks. Take the right fork, marked with a Snowshoe Lake sign. Continue along this road for another 3 km to the recreation site. Most high clearance 2wd vehicles can access the lake from the south. The access from the Whatshan Lake side is a little trickier and has a steep and narrow section better suited for 4wd vehicles.

Facilities

The **Snowshoe Lake Recreation Site** is tucked into the hills west of the Needles ferry terminal. The site offers space for three groups with a choice of grassy or treed campsites. Hand launching canoes or pontoon boats is easy enough from the access road.

Other Options

Inonoaklin Creek is a large creek that parallels Highway 6 and Edgewood Road west of the Lower Arrow Lake. The creek has good access to the many enticing pools that hold brook trout and rainbow trout to 30 cm (12 in) in size. The best time to try the creek is well after the spring runoff levels subside. Watch for closures.

Location: 17 km (10.5 mi) southwest of Kimberley
Elevation: 976 m (3,202 ft)
Surface Area: 295 ha (729 ac)
Mean Depth: 8 m (26 ft)
Max Depth: 21 m (69 ft)
Way Point: 116° 11′00″ Lon - W   49° 36′00″ Lat - N

St. Mary Lake

Fishing

While the St. Mary River is one of the most popular rivers for fishing in the Kootenays, St. Mary Lake, through which the river flows, is much less well known. Part of that has to do with the general spottiness of the fishing. Although the lake does provide decent results at times, figuring out when those times are not always easy.

The three main sportfish found in the lake are cutthroat, rainbow and bull trout, although whitefish, the odd brook trout and even burbot co-exist in the lake. Trout average about 20-30 cm (8-12 in) in size, although they can reach up to 1.5 kg (3.5 lbs) on occasion.

The bull trout generally eat insects and small fish. Try trolling a green or orange Flatfish or a Krocodile lure. Trolling plugs or larger lures with a flasher can produce big fish. Fishing the creek mouths with bait balls (a large cluster of worms or cured roe) suspended near the bottom can also be very effective. Also, jigging with a bucktail and flasher in the spring near the inflow of the St. Mary can be very successful.

Fishing is often best in the early fall, shortly after the lake begins to cool. The west side of the lake tends to be the most productive, due mainly to the inflow of the St. Mary River. Try trolling a leech pattern or Woolly Bugger along shoal areas, while keeping a keen eye for rises or hatches.

During the heat of the summer, the trout will retreat to the depths of the lake and it is best to work around the deeper hole. For burbot, your best bet is to try during the winter months of February and March. However, this fishery is catch and release only across the region.

The lake's north shore is quite open, and is accessed from the St. Mary Lake Road. Angler's without a way to get out onto the water can try shore fishing from here, or from the end of Lake Front Road on the south side of the lake. While there is no boat launch on the lake, it is possible to hand launch a craft from the end of Lake Front Road.

Directions

You can easily find St. Mary Lake west of the village of Marysville, south of Kimberley. The paved St. Mary Lake Road leads directly to the eastern shore of the lake. A good gravel road continues along the north side of the lake and provides ample places to park and gain access to the shoreline.

Facilities

There are no public facilities offered at St. Mary Lake. All the basic amenities, such as groceries, fuel and accommodations can be found in the town of **Kimberley** to the east. .

Other Options

If you plan to do some serious fishing around St. Mary Lake, you should certainly consider the **St. Mary River**. The river is well known for its hefty cutthroat trout and is also inhabited by bull trout, whitefish and burbot. The resident cutthroat are the river's claim to fame and fishing can be very good throughout the season if you can find the right hole. With the increased restrictions, such as mandatory catch and release in areas, the river is becoming one of the premier rivers in the Kootenays. Many anglers float down the river from the lake. For more details see the streams section at the back of this book.

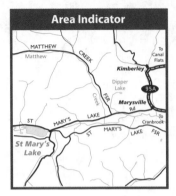

Area Indicator

Species
Brook Trout
Bull Trout
Burbot
Cutthroat Trout
Rainbow Trout
Whitefish

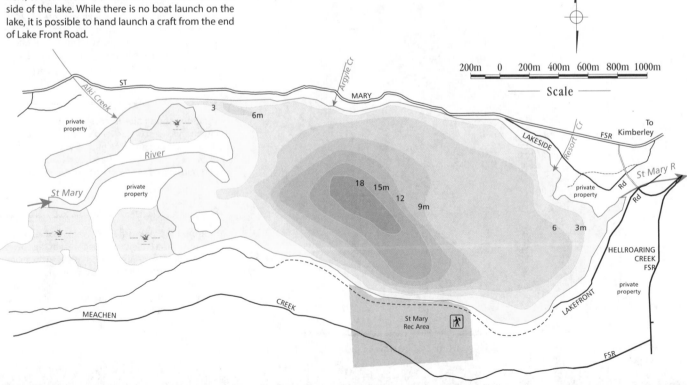

St Mary River

Location: South & West of Kimberley
Stream Length: 116 km (72 mi)
Geographic: 115° 52′ 00″ Lon - W 49° 36′ 00″ Lat - N

Fishing

A Kootenay River tributary with its headwaters deep in the Purcell Mountains, the St Mary River is considered by many to be Southeastern BC's finest cutthroat stream. It is a classic free stone stream, over 100 km (60 miles) from tip to tail. It is a river about which many stories are told, and like most fishing stories, those tales are exaggerated just a bit.

The river is an amazing place to fish with dry flies, and there are plenty of fish; a 30 cm (12 inch) cutthroat is on the big side of average, but there are a few fish up to 50 cm (20 inches). Catch rates have been known to be as high as 50 fish per day, but usually you'll count it a good day if you crack double digits.

The river also has rainbow, Dolly Varden and whitefish, but it's the cutthroat the river is known for. Such quality fishing comes at a price, and that price is access. Getting onto the river can be a bit of a challenge. Most people put in at St. Mary Lake and float down the river in a raft or a canoe. There is lots of private land alongside the river, making bushwhacking into the river difficult.

There are a number of impressive hatches that happen right after spring run-off. The caddis hatch starts around mid-June. A size 10–14 deer or Elk hair caddis or mayfly will work well. Around the same time, there is a fabulous stonefly hatch as well. This is a favourite time to fish the river and many locals who will swear by using a Coachman Dry or a Tom Thumb. However, a weighted stonefly hare's ear stonefly nymph will often work when a dry isn't. A strike indicator will help when fishing a wet fly, but isn't essential.

In the summer, there are plenty of grasshoppers that fall into the river. At these times, the trout tend to hang on the outside of pools or around bends, as the main pools usually hold big, trout-eating burbot. If grasshopper patterns are not working, try an attractor pattern. Terrestrials continue to work into the fall, but a Blue Wing Olive pattern is the fly of choice in October. Try this one around mid-day when it is a bit warmer.

The river is protected as a Class II stream (requiring a special stamp), and is fly-fish, catch and release only on the main stream below St. Mary Lake. There is also a 30 cm (12 in) minimum size restriction to keep on the tributaries.

Directions

Below St. Mary Lake, where the majority of the action happens, the St. Mary River is difficult to access. Since much of the land surrounding it is private, the best way to get onto the river is from St. Mary Lake, with a boat or a raft. You can easily find St. Mary Lake west of the village of Marysville, south of Kimberley. The paved St. Mary Lake Road leads directly to the eastern shore of the lake. A good gravel road continues along the north side of the lake and provides ample places to park and gain access to the shoreline.

Upstream, the St Mary River Forest Service Road takes over allowing for easier access to the less busy upper river.

Facilities

With most of the lower river being private property, there are limited public facilities in the area. The newly established **St Mary Cross-Country Ski Trails** are found on the south side of the river, just east of St. Mary Lake. There is limited river access from this system.

For those looking to overnight in the area, all the basic amenities, such as groceries, fuel and accommodations can be found in the town of Kimberley to the east. There are also a couple private campgrounds around Wycliffe that visitors can use. Upstream, facilities are also limited to a few isolated trails.

Species
Cutthroat Trout
Dolly Varden
Rainbow Trout
Whitefish

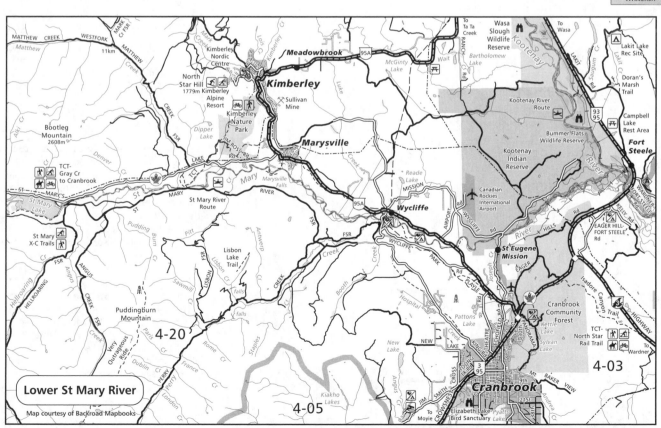

Lower St Mary River

Map courtesy of Backroad Mapbooks

Location: 58 km (36 mi) southeast of Kelowna
Elevation: 1,168 m (3,832 ft)
Surface Area: 17.5 ha (756 ac)
Mean Depth: 4.5 m (15 ft)
Max Depth: 12 m (39 ft)
Way Point: 118° 50′ 00″ Lon - W 49° 35′ 00″ Lat - N

State Lake

Area Indicator

Species

Rainbow Trout

Fishing

As a secluded hike-in fishing lake, State Lake does not see a lot of pressure. Add to that the fact the road into the lake is quite hard on vehicles, and you have the makings of a great fishing lake.

And that's what State Lake is. Not great in the sense of 10 kg (20 lb) rainbow, but great in the sense of good fishing for plenty of good-sized fish. In the past the lake was stocked annually, but that program was discontinued more than 20 years ago, and natural processes have taken over. Fly-fishing only regulations help to protect and maintain the quality of fishing here.

State Lake is best fished in the spring, after the lake turns over. Although the water in the lake does not warm up as much as some other lakes in the Okanagan, it still warms up enough to impact fishing during the summer. There are large shallow areas at both ends, with weeds closes to shore. If you work your way around the east side of the lake, you can manage some shore fishing from there. However, a belly boat is certainly worth the effort to pack in to help reach the trout holding areas.

The lake is one of those dark-coloured, tannin-stained lakes that has limited clarity, especially during the spring runoff. Regardless, the trout seem to be able to easily hone in on surface flies as they readily strike matched hatch patterns. In spring, you can expect mayflies, caddis and some great terrestrial fishing for things like flying ants. State Lake is one of those lakes that can seriously frustrate or excite an angler. Many a time, two side-by-side anglers will have different success, even working the same pattern. Matching the hatch is important, but creating a realistic action is also important. Some insects rise slowly through the water column, some sit patiently on the surface, others kick or skitter around. The (near) fail-safe pattern for this lake is a leech worked deeper along the drop off areas.

State Lake is designated a fly-fishing only lake, and no ice fishing. Check the regulations for more details.

Directions

State Lake is a secluded lake found near the Christian Valley. A variety of logging roads lead into the area and can be picked up off Highway 33 or off the Kettle River Forest Service Road. North of Beaverdell on Highway 33, the Trapping Creek Forest Service Road leads up the creek and over to the Sandrift Forest Service Road. Continuing back down towards the Christian Valley should take you past the trailhead to State Lake on the south side of the road. It is a short 1 km walk into the lake.

A copy of the *Backroad Mapbook for the Thompson Okanagan* shows a few other road options over to and up from the Christian Valley. Regardless of the route, a 4wd vehicle might be necessary during wet weather.

Facilities

The forest service has established a few backcountry tenting sites at State Lake that are rarely used. The first site lies at the end of the trailhead and can be very muddy in the spring. The other two sites lie along the east and west shores at the northern end of the lake. The **State Lake Road Recreation Site** is found at the start of the trail into the lake. The small, treed site only has space for one or so groups.

Other Options

Just to the west of the **State Lake Road Recreation Site**, you can reach the **Sandrift Lakes** via the Sandrift Forest Service Road. There are a couple lakeside recreations sites on the lakes, while all three Sandrift Lakes offer fishing for stocked rainbow trout. The small nature of the lakes makes fly-fishing from a belly boat or similar a nice alternative here.

State Lake
Rec Site

10m

8

6m

4

2m

N

State Creek

100m   0   100m   200m

— Scale —

Streak Lake

Location: 16 km (10 mi) south of Vernon
Elevation: 1,359 m (4,459 ft)
Surface Area: 22 ha (54 ac)
Mean Depth: 9 m (29 ft)
Max Depth: 11 m (36 ft)
Way Point: 119° 14' 00" Lon - W 50° 07' 00" Lat - N

Fishing

Streak Lake is well named. Fishing here seems to run in streaks: a good streak, a bad streak, a completely skunked streak…. The best way to describe the fishing here is unpredictable. The lake is stocked regularly with rainbow trout, although they seem to change their feeding habits from day to day, just to keep anglers on their toes. Both trolling and fly-fishing produce results on this lake when the trout decide to bite.

Rainbow average about 20-30 cm (8-12 in) in size, although can be found larger from time to time. Try trolling over the 5 m (16 ft) hump located in the middle of the lake for greater chances of success throughout the year. Popular trolling lures include Little Cleos, spinners and small Flatfish in black, silver or green. Fly anglers can troll a leech or a '52 Buick.

Fly-fishing can be great, when the bite is on. A popular time is in late spring, during the caddis fly hatch. Dry fly-fishing with a Tom Thumb or a Mikulak Sedge can be productive. The shoal areas at the north and south end of the lake are good places to work chironomids, damsel fly nymphs, and small dragonfly nymphs. In summer, a '52 Buick or leech pattern are popular options.

Ice fishing in the winter is not very popular, as the road to the lake is not plowed. However, it is possible to walk or ski into the lake from Oyama Lake. Oyama has a bait ban, and ice fishing there can be unproductive, but that is not the case on Streak Lake. Try working the area right past where the lake widens near the recreation site. There is a drop off here, plus shoals for the fish to feed in. Rainbow trout don't like to get too deep in winter, so work around the 3 m (10 ft) drop off.

Directions

Streak Lake is located south of the popular King Edward Lake via a rough 4wd logging access road. East from the city of Vernon, follow Highway 6 past Coldstream to King Edward Lake Road. This gravel road is not maintained and can be tricky to follow as it climbs the hills into the popular fishing area to the south. Once you pass King Edward Lake, the access road to Streak Lake can be picked up around the 18 km mark on the south side of the main road (if that is what you call it).

The roads in this area are often rutted and difficult to negotiate even in a 4wd vehicle. It is also a good idea to bring along a good map and a GPS to help track your travels in the backcountry like this.

Facilities

The **Streak Lake Recreation Site** offers about five campsites along the southwest shore of the lake. There is a boat launch at the campsite, although it is definitely more of a cartop access than a trailer access.

Other Options

Streak Lake is connected to **Oyama Lake** by a short channel that can be navigated with a canoe. Oyama Lake offers much more reliable fishing for some nice sized trout. Look for more details on this lake earlier in the book or you can venture north to **High Lake**. This smaller lake can be reached by trail from the Oyama Lake Road and is home to a rustic campsite. Fishing in the lake is known to be decent as the lake is stocked regularly and receives generally light fishing pressure.

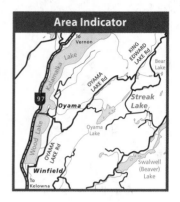

Area Indicator

Species
Rainbow Trout

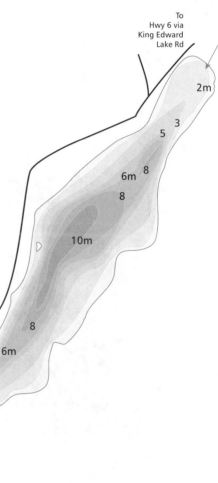

To
Hwy 6 via
King Edward
Lake Rd

2m
3
5
8
6m
8
10m
8
6m
5m
6
11
Streak Lake Rec Site
4m
3
2m

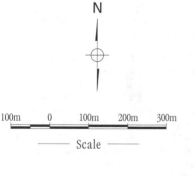

N

100m 0 100m 200m 300m

Scale

Streak Lake			
Fish Stocking Data			
Year	Species	Number	Life Stage
2010	Rainbow Trout	4000	Fry
2009	Rainbow Trout	4,000	Fry
2008	Rainbow Trout	4,000	Fry

Location: 55 km (34 mi) northeast of Vernon
Elevation: 606 m (1,988 ft)
Surface Area: 2,080 ha (5,138 ac)
Mean Depth: 35 m (115 ft)
Max Depth: 83 m (272 ft)
Way Point: 118° 30' 00" Lon - W 50° 23' 00" Lat - N

Sugar Lake

Directions

Sugar Lake is a large lake located northeast of the town of Lumby. To reach the lake, you must first travel east from Lumby along Highway 6 to the Sugar Lake Road, in the small settlement of Cherryville. Watch for Frank's General Store. The Sugar Lake Road lies off the north side of the highway and leads all the way to Sugar Lake. The road has a good gravel surface and should poise no problem for most 2wd vehicles. It is just over 15 km to the south end of the lake from Highway 6.

Fishing

Sugar Lake is a relatively isolated lake, surrounded by the rugged Monashee Mountains. Despite its isolation, it is quite popular, as the wide variety of fish that can reach some impressive sizes keep visitors coming back time and again. Not only does the lake offer the famous Gerrard Rainbow Trout strain, which is stocked, there are Kamloops Rainbow, bull trout, kokanee, mountain whitefish and burbot. The Gerrard Rainbow and bull trout often reach 5 kg (11 lbs), while the feisty Kamloops Trout average about 1 kg (2 lbs). Needless to say, there are some fine fish lurking in the depths of Sugar Lake

Trolling is the preferred angling method used on the lake, although fly-fishing can be productive around the Shuswap River inlet or at one of the many other creek inlets. Trollers should try off the west side of the large island in the north end or off the point that juts out from the Mile 1 & 2 Forest Recreation Sites. All species are generally harder to locate as the heat of summer sets in. At this time, a downrigger is quite useful to find rainbow and bull trout.

Given the size of the lake and fish, trolling lures like the locally produced Lyman lures in sizes 3 or 4 can be effective. Earlier in the day try trolling closers to the surface and then start working deeper to find where the fish are holding. Kokanee are also a common catch using Gang Trolls and Wedding Rings or small spinners. Similar to the trout, success is often better earlier in the day.

There are special restrictions on Sugar Lake, be sure to check your regulations before fishing. Also note that the water levels are regulated by a BC hydro dam. Levels can fluctuate over 7 metres (20 feet).

Facilities

As a large recreation destination lake, Sugar Lake makes a fine spot to spend some vacation time at. The lake is home to a fine resort as well as five separate Forest Recreation camping areas that are often busy during the summer months.

The **Kokanee Lodge and Resort** is found at the south end of the lake and offers boat rentals, a boat launch, campsites, cabins and a restaurant. Next up are the **Mile 1 & 2 Recreation Sites,** which feature a beautiful beach area as well as a boat launch. The Mile 2 site is the largest recreation site on the lake with 40 campsites available, while Mile 1 is a smaller site found just to the south. **Mile 3 & 3.5 Recreation Sites** are found a little further north and are also small sites offering camping, a small beach area and boat launch. On the east side of the lake, the **Sugar Creek Recreation Site** has 12 campsites complete with a scenic beach area and a cartop boat launch.

Area Indicator

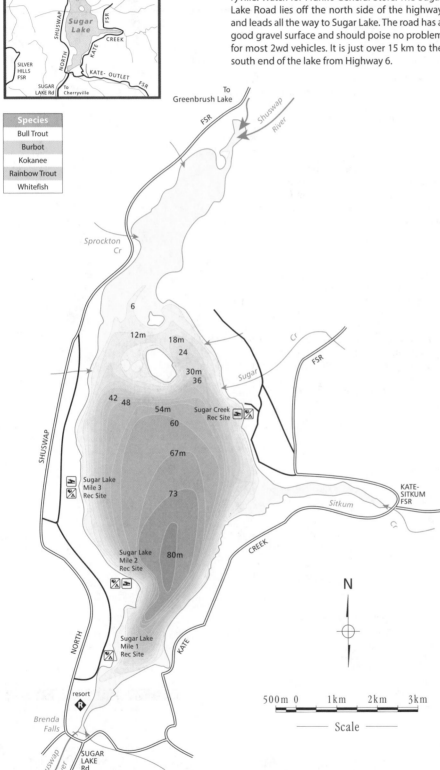

Species

Species
Bull Trout
Burbot
Kokanee
Rainbow Trout
Whitefish

Summit Lake – Merritt

Location: 35 km (22 mi) north of Princeton
Elevation: 1,004 m (3,293 ft)
Surface Area: 4.7 ha
Mean Depth: 9.2 m (30 ft)
Max Depth: 13.5 m (44 ft)
Way Point: 120° 63'88" Lon - W, 49° 75'42" Lat - N

8 Region

Fishing

There are twenty two Summit Lakes in BC, a couple of which are in the Okanagan Region. This Summit Lake is found near the Pike Mountain Recreation Area, next to Highway 5A between Princeton and Aspen Grove. The lake is stocked annually with rainbow trout that provide for fair fishing throughout the season.

Despite the fact that the stocked rainbow are a triploid that are intended to grow bigger faster, the trout in this lake do not get very big. This is probably due to the easy access and heavy fishing pressure. Still it is a great lake for kids and the old worm and bobber usually always meets some success on Summit Lake.

The fishing can be quite good right as soon as the ice melts. At this time, a Flatfish in silver, gold, black and silver or frog pattern can be effective. Dick Nite, Panther Martin and Roostertail spoons in smaller sizes are also good bets. Fly fishers can try dragonfly nymphs, water boatman, shrimp, chironomids and leeches. Fish your lures or flies on the shoal or edge of the drop off where the trout will be concentrated.

The inlet creek located at the southern end of the lake, can be a productive area to cast a line, especially in spring. Fly anglers should look for hatching chironomids at this time. If the hatch is difficult to determine a leech pattern trolled along the drop off area on the southeast side of the lake can produce some decent results.

Other Options

If your luck is slow at Summit Lake, there are plenty of other lakes you could try that are found within minutes. The easiest to access is **Gladstone Lake**, which is a short drive to the north and is also a highway side trout lake. The Pike Mountain Forest Service Road also provides easy access to several decent trout lakes. **Kump** and **Robertson Lakes** are found relatively close to the highway. Detailed descriptions of Gladstone and Kump are found earlier in this book. Like the others, Robertson is stocked with rainbow to help maintain a good fishery.

Directions

You can find Summit Lake off the west side of Highway 5A north of Allison Lake. As the name implies, the lake is found on the summit of the highway. There is a small parking area off the side of the highway that makes a convenient access point.

Facilities

There is a small rest area found at Summit Lake equipped with picnic tables and a cartop boat launch. For overnight stays, there are several Forest Recreation campsites found in the immediate area or **Allison Lake Provincial Park** can be found to the south off Highway 5A.

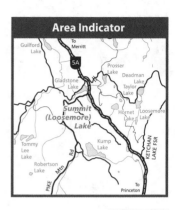

Species
Rainbow Trout

Summit (Loosemore) Lake			
Fish Stocking Data			
Year	Species	Number	Life Stage
2013	Rainbow Trout	2,000	Fry
2012	Rainbow Trout	3,000	Fry
2011	Rainbow Trout	3,000	Fry

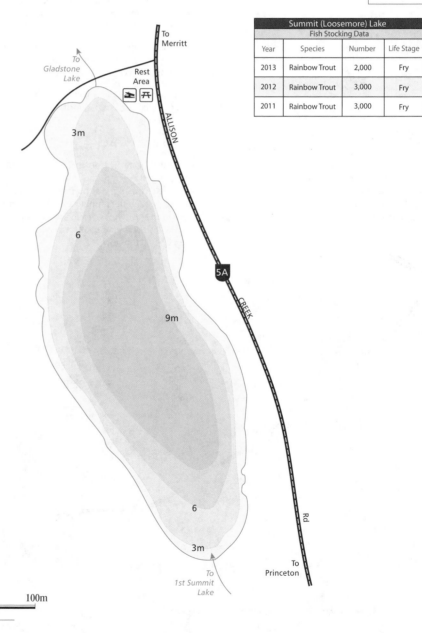

Location: 16 km (10 mi) southeast of Nakusp
Elevation: 764 m (2,506 ft)
Surface Area: 158 ha (390 ac)
Mean Depth: 4.4 m (14.5 ft)
Max Depth: 17 m (56 ft)
Way Point: 117° 38′ 00″ Lon - W 50° 09′ 00″ Lat - N

Summit Lake - Nakusp

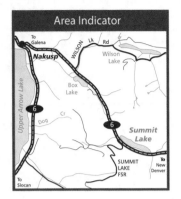

Area Indicator

Species

Rainbow Trout

Summit Lake			
Fish Stocking Data			
Year	Species	Number	Life Stage
2013	Rainbow Trout	5,000	Yearling
2012	Rainbow Trout	5,000	Yearling
2011	Rainbow Trout	5,000	Yearling

Fishing

Despite the name, Summit Lake is not a very high elevation lake, and as a result fishing gets going in early spring. The lake remains a favourite with local fly anglers since fishing for rainbow trout can be quite productive. Up to ten thousand rainbow are stocked in the lake annually and the fish can reach up to 2.5 kg (5.5 lbs) in size, although average about 35 cm (14 in) in size. There are some rumours of trout getting to 4.5 kg (10 lbs), but little evidence. Still, it is rumours and innuendoes like this that bring people to the lake.

The fishing begins in early April. There are artificial fly only and catch and release restrictions in place until May 1. Be sure to check the regulations before heading out.

Summit Lake is known for its quality chironomid and caddis fly-fishing, and chironomids almost always work. Fishing the shoals and weed beds near the islands just off the provincial park camping area and on the west side of the lake are known hot spots. You can also try the shallow bay by the boat launch as rainbow will cruise these shallows in search of emerging chironomids. If you happen to land a rainbow during one of the many ample chironomid hatches, do not be surprised to see your catch with dozens of the small larvae in and around its mouth.

As the water begins to warm and caddis or sedge flies start to hatch, the fishing in Summit can be a lot of fun. At these times try stripping a good sized caddis fly along the top. The rainbow will shoot right out of the lake after these flies at times. On many July evenings, the lake literally boils with rising trout.

If there is no hatch evident, a green Carey Special cast or trolled just below the surface is a good searching pattern year-round. Leeches, dragonfly and damselfly nymph patterns also work well into the summer. The nymphs are best fished in the evening when the fish are feeding on mayflies.

Spincasters can also find success on the lake using small spinners or spoons. The lake is quite shallow for most of its length, but the northeast end is a decent area to troll.

Directions

Summit Lake is located south of the town of Nakusp. Highway 6 travels right past the southern shore of the beautiful lake. Parking is available at the rest area or public access point found along the southern shore.

Other Options

Box Lake is located just down the road form Summit Lake along Highway 6. Look for a small sign off the west side of the highway marking the road to Box Lake. Box Lake offers fishing for plump, but small brook trout and rainbow trout. The lake is also home to a nice recreation site. Look for more details on this lake earlier in the book.

Facilities

There is no shortage of places stay or access the lake from. **Summit Lake Provincial Campground sits** at the north end of the lake and offers 35 campsites with flush toilets, firewood and a sani-station. These scenic, island-like sites are available from the end of April to the end of September on a first-come, first-served basis. There is also a boat launch and dock at the park. Day trippers will find a roadside picnic area near the south end of the lake that has a boat launch, picnic tables and washroom facilities. In addition, **Three Island Resorts and Campground** is at the north end of the lake providing a well-maintained private facility that caters to RV's and fifth wheels.

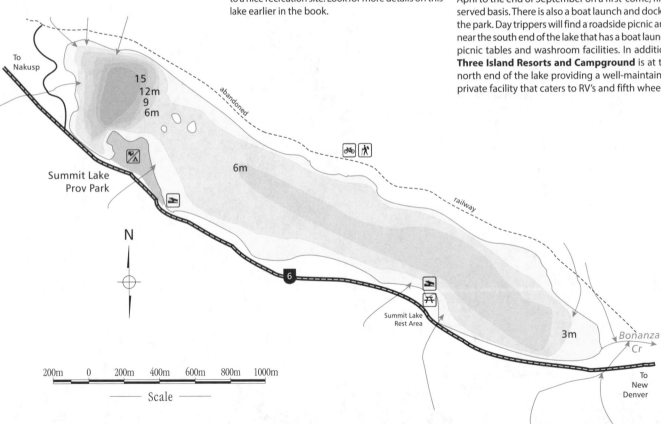

Summit Lake – Sparwood

Location: 16 km (9.9 mi) southeast of Sparwood
Elevation: 1,356 m (4,407 ft)
Surface Area: 18.6 ha (48.5 ac)
Mean Depth: 3.7 m (12 ft)
Max Depth: 5 m (16.4 ft)
Way Point: 114° 41' 43" Lon - W 49° 38' 30" Lat - N

Fishing

Located on the border between British Columbia and Alberta, this highly productive lake is a great fishing destination due to its proximity to Highway 3 and Sparwood. At a maximum depth of 5 metres (16 feet), some anglers call the entire lake one big shoal, with the lake being frost and ice free by early April. Species within this medium sized lake include brook, rainbow and cutthroat trout. The Westslope cutthroat reproduce naturally along the creek systems and shoreline areas, while the eastern brook trout and rainbow trout are stocked every year.

Most fly fishers use chironomids or leech patterns in the shallow depths. The bottom of the lake is a mix of chara, marl and pondweed where invertebrate food sources flourish. Be sure to inspect the shoreline for the appropriate insect and match the colour and size with your patterns.

Chironomids continue to produce between September and November, as will Woolley Buggers and leech patterns trolled on a sinking line. Trolling just below the surface is a good way to search the lake for the sometimes elusive fish. Leeches, dragonfly and damselfly nymph patterns produce throughout the summer months, while large traveling sedges attract many fly anglers in July for some frenzied top water action.

Gang trolls with Wedding Rings, Apex lures and small spoons are popular tackle. Spin fishers do well using Gibbs gypsy spoons, Flatfish and Kwikfish plugs. An added attraction to Summit Lake is that you can literally fish from anywhere along the shore with good results. Check with the local tackle shops for what is working on the lake before heading out.

Fishing regulations include a single barbless hook, a bait ban and a two fish limit. Summit Lake is closed for ice fishing in the winter.

Directions

Access to Summit Lake is quite easy due to its location next to Highway 3 at the Crowsnest Pass and Alberta border. Simply follow Highway 3 east from Sparwood for about 15 minutes. Once at the lake, continue south until you see a side road leaving the highway at the south side of the lake. After the train tracks, you will find a picnic site with a boat launch for cartop and smaller trailered boats.

Facilities

Although there are no formal areas to camp on the lake, people often park overnight at the south end where a rustic boat launch is also found. From here an old road/anglers trail leads along the west side of the lake providing good access for those without a boat. Crowsnest Provincial Park, which is found at the north end of the lake, is a day-use only park with a small picnic area and pit toilets. Accommodations and supplies can be found in Sparwood.

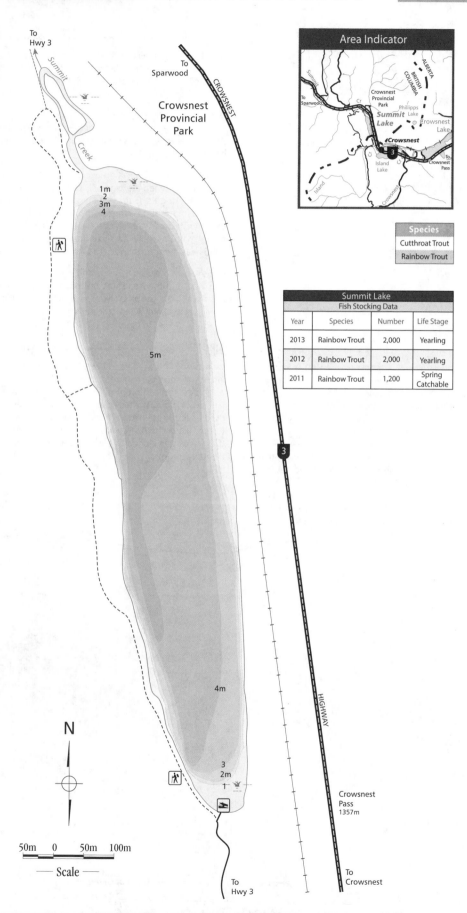

Area Indicator

Species

| Cutthroat Trout |
| Rainbow Trout |

Summit Lake			
Fish Stocking Data			
Year	Species	Number	Life Stage
2013	Rainbow Trout	2,000	Yearling
2012	Rainbow Trout	2,000	Yearling
2011	Rainbow Trout	1,200	Spring Catchable

Location: 45 km (28 mi) northeast of Golden
Elevation: 1,530 m (5,020 ft)
Surface Area: 45 ha (111 ac)
Mean Depth: 11.8 m (39 ft)
Max Depth: 31 m (102 ft)
Way Point: 117° 23' 00" Lon - W 51° 34' 00" Lat - N

Susan Lake

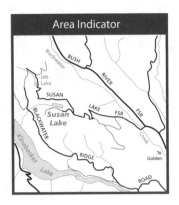

Area Indicator

Species

Brook Trout

Rainbow Trout

Fishing

Susan Lake is a small lake found north of Golden near the south arm of Kinbasket Lake. It holds stocked brook trout, which provide for good fishing mainly in the spring. Brookies average about 30 cm (12 in), although can be found to 2 kg (4.5 lbs) on occasion. There are rumours that rainbow trout also inhabit the lake from past stockings.

Due to the shallow areas near the shoreline, anglers are well advised to bring a float tube or small boat. From the water, it is much easier to cast towards the elaborate shoals, especially at the western end of the lake near the islands. Trolling around the deep hole in the northeast bay during the summer can also be affective.

Susan Lake is a high elevation lake, and doesn't ice off until late in the spring. As a result, the trout are usually quite hungry when the ice finally comes off, and will take hungrily to a fly or lure. Spincasters should try small silver or gold spinners for brookies such as a Panther Martin or a Blue Fox. Another proven angling method for brookies is the Deadly Dick tipped with a worm. Cast these lures along the drop off zones in search of aggressive brookies. Fly anglers can have a lot of fun at this lake as brookies will chase down nymph patterns quite readily during the spring. A few good flies to try are a damselfly nymph or a simple bead head nymph. A mosquito pattern is also quite effective.

In the winter, the Golden Snowmobile Trail Society maintains a snowmobile trail to Susan Lake. It is a short, easy ride, and the ice fishing on the lake is great. As always, caution needs to be taken that the lake is frozen solid, but the brook trout are much more willing to take to a lure or jig in the winter than most other trout species. Shiny lures jigged anywhere from a few inches to a few metres below the ice will work well.

Directions

Susan Lake is a popular lake that is found close enough to Golden to provide a perfect evening getaway. From Golden, follow the Trans Canada Highway north to the Big Bend Road near the village of Donald. Take the Big Bend Road past Donald, to the Bush River Forest Service Road. Continue north along the forest road to the Susan Lake Forest Service Road, which is found around the 15 km mark. The Susan Lake Forest Service Road travels west over the Blackwater Creek then winds its way up to Susan Lake. Most 2wd vehicles will have no trouble accessing the lake. The recreation site provides a good boat launch and plenty of parking.

Facilities

Visitors will find the **Susan Lake Recreation Site** along the southeast shore of the lake. The small, open site comes complete with a cartop boat launch and dock. The terraced campsites are often used by locals as parking spots for day-use access to the lake or the nearby lookout. Be forewarned, the area is often inundated with mosquitoes during the early summer.

Other Options

A good alternative to Susan Lake is **Jeb Lake** to the northwest. The Susan Lake Road continues northeast turning into a rough 4wd road that eventually reaches the eastern shore of Jeb Lake. The tiny lake is home to a small recreation site and offers fishing for stocked brook trout.

Susan Lake			
Fish Stocking Data			
Year	Species	Number	Life Stage
2013	Brook Trout	4,000	Fingerling
2012	Brook Trout	4,000	Fingerling
2011	Brook Trout	4,000	Fingerling

SUSAN   LAKE

To Jeb Lake

3m
6 9m
15m

21 24m 27
18m
12   30
12
9m
6
3m

ROAD

Susan Lake Rec Site

dock

N

SUSAN
LAKE

FSR

To Hwy 1 via Bush River FSR

100m 0 100m 200m 300m 400m 500m

Scale

Suzanne Lake

Location: 8.5 km (5.3 mi) west of Elko
Elevation: 822 m (2,696 ft)
Surface Area: 57 ha (141 ac)
Mean Depth: 5.8 m (19 ft)
Max Depth: 12 m (39.4 ft)
Way Point: 115° 14′ 00″ Lon - W   49° 19′ 00″ Lat - N

Fishing

Suzanne Lake is a popular and productive fishing lake found sandwiched between Lake Koocanusa and Elko. It is heavily stocked with rainbow trout (usually multiple times a year) including some of the renowned Gerrard strain of rainbow. Over the years, largemouth bass have also found their way into the lake and as a result there is good fishing on the lake throughout the open water season. The low elevation of the lake allows fishing as early as late March in some years.

The trout in Suzanne Lake grow to good sizes and can be found in the 2 kg (4.5 lb) range due to the abundant food sources including freshwater shrimp, chironomids, damselflies and dragonflies. These food sources like to congregate around weeds and inflow or outflow streams in the thermocline (the area of the lake between the warm surface water and the deeper cold water).Try your luck in the northern part of the lake where the bottom is littered with weed beds, providing excellent cover and food sources. Trout fishing is best done in the early spring or late fall months while the best time of day is in the early morning or early evening.

Trolling slowly with chironomids or leech patterns suspended just off the bottom seems to be an effective method here, with Wooly Buggers, Doc Spratleys and 52 Buicks also reported as being effective. Smaller trout have been known to be attracted to lures like the Panther Martin or the Mepps Fury. For fly fisherman, try baitfish or deer hair patterns on a fast sinking line.

During the cooler seasons, try various nymph patterns such as a damselfly or dragonfly nymph. The large amount of weeds and reeds in the lake offers an abundance of insect larvae. Anglers will need to trick the trout with a convincing good-sized meal that closely resembles the insect hatches.

When the water warms up in summer, the largemouth bass come out to play. Apparently the bass here aren't that picky and will strike regardless of whether you are baitcasting, spinning or fly-fishing. Since bass like to hang out in weeds or around cover, getting a lure to them can prove to be difficult. Fly-fishers have a bit of an advantage, as largemouth bass love ambushing large insects on the surface of the lake, especially insects that are in trouble. Bass poppers, which can look like a drowning bee or moth or even a mouse can be flipped into the weeds and twitched around to simulate a drowning insect. Streamer patterns can also work, but stand a much greater chance of getting hung up or snagged on weeds.

Spincasters, on the other hand, are at a bit of a disadvantage. Because the bass hang out under cover, the chance of snagging a weed or getting hung up on a fallen log is greatly increased. Jigging for bass works well since you don't need to worry about placing your cast. Another option is a simple Carolina or Texas rigged hook.

Directions

Suzanne Lake is a popular recreational lake found west of Elko. To find the lake, follow Highway 3/93 to the village of Jaffray. From Jaffray, travel south along the Jaffray-Baynes Lake Road and look for the access road to Suzanne Lake about 6.5 km later off the east side of the road. The access road travels to the western shore of Suzanne Lake and a small recreation site. During dry weather, most vehicles can make it into this fine fishing lake.

Facilities

Visitors will find **Suzanne Lake Recreation Site**, a small, heavily treed site along the western shore of the lake. The recreation site offers space for about 10 units and is equipped with a cartop boat launch and wharf. There are also a few private cabins around the lake.

Other Options

To the northwest of Suzanne Lake you can find **North Star Lake**. The access road to this smaller lake is also accessible via the Jaffray-Baynes Lake Road. North Star Lake is home to a recreation campsite and offers fishing for stocked rainbow trout. Look for the write-up earlier in this book.

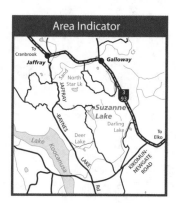

Area Indicator

Species
Rainbow Trout
Largemouth Bass

Suzanne (Manistee) Lake			
Fish Stocking Data			
Year	Species	Number	Life Stage
2013	Rainbow Trout	10,000	Fall Catchable
2012	Rainbow Trout	10,000	Adult/ Catchable
2011	Rainbow Trout	10,000	Yearling

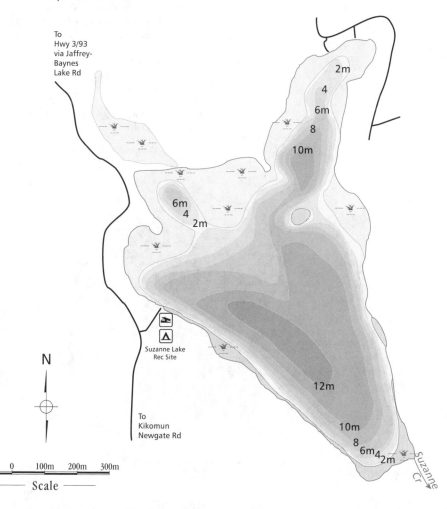

Location: 33 km (20.5 mi) north of Rock Creek
Elevation: 1,164 m (3,819 ft)
Surface Area: 21 ha (52 ac)
Mean Depth: 6 m (20 ft)
Max Depth: 12 m (39 ft)
Way Point: 118° 58' 00" Lon - W 49° 19' 00" Lat - N

Taurus Lake

Area Indicator

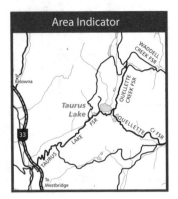

Species
Rainbow Trout

Taurus (Bull) Lake Fish Stocking Data			
Year	Species	Number	Life Stage
2013	Rainbow Trout	2,500	Fry
2012	Rainbow Trout	2,500	Fry
2011	Rainbow Trout	2,500	Fry

Fishing

Taurus is a small, pretty lake located in the mountains between the Kettle and West Kettle Rivers. The lake is stocked annually with 3,000 rainbow trout taken from Pennask Lake that provide good fishing... most of the time. Rainbow average about 0.5 kg (1 lb), although are often found in the 1 kg (2 lb) range.

There are weeds at the north and east ends of the lake, which can provide cover for the trout early in the year. These translate into large shoal areas, which are prime cruising areas for hungry rainbow.

Shore fishing is difficult, but not impossible. Better to bring a tube or a small boat to get out into the deeper areas of the lake. From here, cast into the shallows and retrieve slowly towards the deeper water, as fish tend to be opportunist and will strike more readily at something moving towards them than at something moving away from.

Fly-fishing can be quite productive. Chironomid patterns can work very well in the spring, while leeches and various nymph patterns, imitating damselflies or dragonflies are a regular part of the rainbow's diet in Taurus Lake. Try working these patterns along the bottom of shoal areas, even touching bottom at times in an attempt to stir the deeper holding trout into striking.

Spincasters will find that a small spinner or spoon will work fine, too. The trick is to make sure that your lure does not run at a constant speed in a straight line. Twitching the rod, speeding up and slowing down, and even stopping will make the lure behave erratically, which makes the lure much more enticing to trout.

Trolling the lake is possible, and there is a boat launch on the east side of the lake for small boats. Spoons with a metal finish work well for rainbow trout. Try a Krocodile or a Flutter Spoon in these colours. Spinners also produce well on a troll.

Facilities

The **Taurus Lake Recreation Site** provides space for about nine campsites over three separate sites around the lake. The main site is found on the west side of the lake and offers five treed sites, a gravel boat launch and even a small sandy beach. Small trailers or RVs can use this area. A second site is found on the northwest side of the lake. There are two small campsites in a treed area that are not suitable for RVs due to the steep access. The final site is found on the southeast side of the lake. There are another couple treed sites here that can also be accessed by small RVs.

Directions

Taurus Lake can be reached from two directions. From the west, follow Highway 33 south from Kelowna past Beaverdell to the Taurus Lake Forest Service Road. The steep road can be rough in sections as it climbs northeast into the mountains. Continue right at the junction just before the 6 km mark and the lake is another kilometre down the road.

From the east, the Oullette Creek Forest Service Road can be found about 14.5 km up the Christian Valley Road from Highway 33. Turn left or west on the Oullette and follow this road as it snakes its way up and over to Taurus Lake. It is just over 10 km from the Christian Valley Road. Most prefer to access the lake from the west.

Other Options

There are a few other small fishing lakes in the area that can be a bit tricky to find. The closest is **Peter Lake,** which is found off a side road just after the Waddell Creek Forest Service Road junction to the north. The small, scenic lake offers fishing opportunities for stocked rainbow trout.

To Peter Lake

To Waddel Cr FSR

CREEK FSR

TAURUS Creek

To Hwy 33

Taurus Creek

TAURUS

LAKE

Taurus Lake Rec Site

5m 3 2m
6
6m
9
11m
12

OULELETTE

FSR

OUELLETTE CREEK FSR

To Christian Valley Rd

N

100m   0   100m   200m
Scale

Thalia Lake

Location: 40 km (25 mi) northwest of Princeton
Elevation: 1,083 m (3,553 ft)
Surface Area: 19 ha (47 ac)
Mean Depth: 13 m (43 ft)
Max Depth: 30.5 m (100 ft)
Way Point: 120° 43'00" Lon - W 49° 45'00" Lat - N

Fishing

Not to be confused with nearby Thala Lake, Thalia Lake is part of the popular Pike Mountain Recreation Area. The lake is stocked annually with the Pennask strain of rainbow and offers good fishing for trout that are known to reach up to 1 kg (2 lbs) or larger in size. Fishing can be quite steady on Thalia, especially in the spring and fall periods, when you can literally catch trout anywhere around the lake.

Of course, as the depth falls off so rapidly from the shore, the fish will generally be found in a ring around the lake, sticking close to the shoals where they feed. In the early spring, right after ice off, the fish will stick to the top layer of water, making them easy to find. And, as they are generally ravenous after a long, cold winter, they will take just about anything. However, if they are acting fussy, try a chironomid or water boatman pattern. There is a sandbar at the north end of the lake which is where you should focus your attention early in spring.

Later in the year, try working a leech or dragonfly nymph pattern closer to the bottom of the lake along shoal areas and drop offs.

Trollers should also work these shoal areas and drop offs with lake trolls or small spinners, especially in the spring. In the heat of the summer, it is best to work the deeper parts of the lake. In particular, the point area along the western shore of the lake seems to be a good holding area. Don't work too deep, though, as the fish tend to hang out in a band of water known as the thermocline, which is located about 4 m (15 ft) down.

Directions

Thalia Lake is found off the Pike Mountain Forest Service Road to the east and Youngberg Road to the west. Although the roads in the area can be a bit rough, most vehicles and moderate size trailers can weave their way into the lake.

From the east, you can pick up the Pike Mountain Road off Highway 5A between Aspen Grove and Princeton. Follow this road west past Gladstone Lake. At the 2 km mark the Robertson Lake Forest Service Road branches northwest. Follow this road for another 2 km and continue straight, following the signs to Thalia Lake. Unfortunately, the signs disappear and finding the lake can be tricky. Short side roads branching north, about 4 km later should take you to the lake.

From the west you will find Youngberg Road at the 22 km mark of the Coldwater Road, which connects Tulameen with Highway 5A. This signed road quickly climbs the hill above the Otter Valley, eventually linking with the Pike Mountain Forest Service Road in the east. Once again, the turnoff to Thalia is a bit tricky.

Since the route into the lake is rather challenging, it is a good idea to bring a copy of the *Thompson Okanagan Backroad Mapbook* and a GPS to track the route. The *BC Backroad GPS Maps* are a handy tool that combines the backroad detail with recreational points of interest to easily find hidden lakes and recreation sites. You can even read about your favourite lake or camping area through the Backroad Extras!

Facilities

Along the quaint shores of Thalia Lake there are two recreation camping areas, totaling seven campsites. The southern site lies in more of an open area, while the northern site sits among the trees along the northern shore. There is also a cartop boat launch available at the lake.

Thalia Lake Fish Stocking Data			
Year	Species	Number	Life Stage
2013	Rainbow Trout	9,000	Fry
2012	Rainbow Trout	9,000	Fry
2011	Rainbow Trout	9,000	Fry

Area Indicator

Species
Rainbow Trout

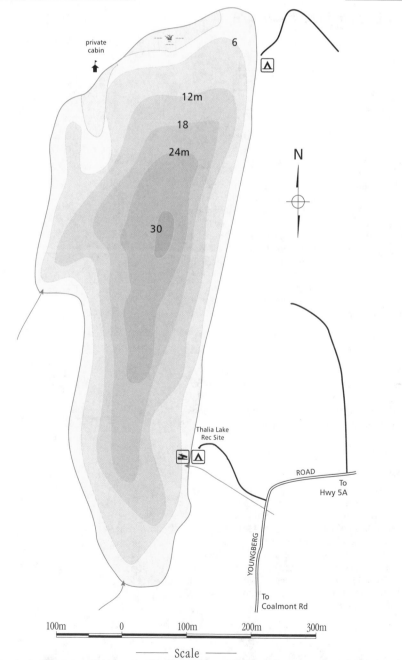

private cabin

6

12m

18

24m

30

N

Thalia Lake Rec Site

ROAD

To Hwy 5A

YOUNGBERG

To Coalmont Rd

100m   0   100m   200m   300m

Scale

Location: 50 km (31 mi) northeast of Rock Creek
Elevation: 1,244 m (4,081 ft)
Surface Area: 10 ha (25 ac)
Mean Depth: 8.4 m (28 ft)
Max Depth: 15.9 m (52 ft)
Way Point: 118° 48' 00" Lon - W 49° 27' 00" Lat - N

Thone Lake

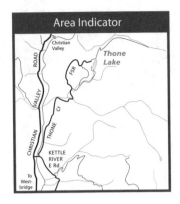

Area Indicator

Species

Rainbow Trout

Thone Lake			
Fish Stocking Data			
Year	Species	Number	Life Stage
2013	Rainbow Trout	2,000	Fry
2012	Rainbow Trout	2,000	Fry
2011	Rainbow Trout	2,000	Fry

Fishing

Found high in the hills above the Christian Valley, Thone Lake is a long driver from the nearest city. Despite its remoteness, the road in is fairly good and the place is often busy with anglers on summer weekends.

Rainbow trout are stocked in Thone Lake each year by the Freshwater Fisheries Society of BC, helping to provide good fishing throughout most of the season. Anglers can find success trolling small spinners and spoons. Popular trolling lures include spoons like Little Cleos or Blue Foxes, spinners and small Flatfish. Fly anglers can troll a leech or a '52 Buick.

Fly anglers will find that the trout here are not very picky, and at times will hit almost any presentation. These aggressive trout are most often the smaller, younger rainbow, but they provide a ton of fun nonetheless.

During the spring chironomid hatch, fish a leader that is long enough to dangle the fly a few feet off the bottom (no more than 1 m/3 ft), and retrieve slowly, with slow strips, followed by pauses of up to 30 seconds. If fishing the hatch isn't producing good results, a leech pattern worked a little slower near the bottom of shoal areas will rarely go unnoticed by Thone Lake trout. During the late spring and early part of summer, caddis hatches can create a frenzy of action on this lake. During this time, trout will often be spotted leaping right out of the lake in their desperate attempt to grab a meal.

There is no boat launch, but it is easy enough to hand launch a canoe or other small craft. The lake has a rocky shore with a sharp drop off and no shoal area. Shore fishing is easy; there are even some rocky bluffs that you can fish off of.

Directions

This remote access lake lies in the eastern Okanagan hills above the Christian Valley. To reach the lake, travel to the settlement of Westbridge via Highway 33. At Westbridge, take the Christian Valley Road north off the highway. At about the 27 km point along the paved road, look for the Losthorse Creek Forest Service Road branching east (right). Shortly after turning onto this road, look for the Losthorse-Thone Lake Forest Service Road leading north. It is about 14 km to the recreation site on this peaceful mountain lake.

Facilities

The **Thone Lake Recreation Site** is a popular treed site offering about nine campsites and a cartop boat launch on the south and northwest side of the lake. The nicely spaced sites can be busy on weekends throughout the year as anglers and hunters frequent the area.

Other Options

Further along the Christian Valley Road, there are over a dozen various lakes found in the mountains to the west of the valley. Some of the more popular fishing lakes in this area include the **Sandrift Lakes**, **Lassie Lake, Cup Lake** and the **Collier Lakes**. Each of these lakes offers fishing opportunities for rainbow trout as well as Forest Recreation campsites for overnight use. For more details on these lakes, be sure to see their descriptions with depth charts earlier in this book.

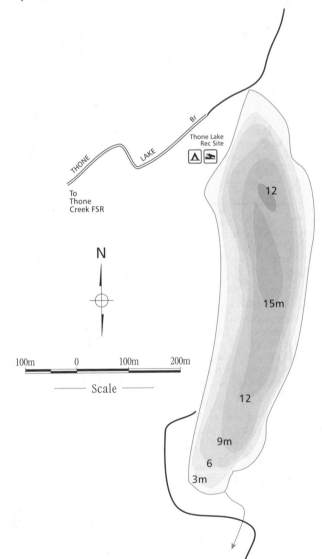

Tie Lake

Location: 35 km (22 mi) east of Cranbrook
Elevation: 850 m (2,789 ft)
Surface Area: 126 ha (311 ac)
Mean Depth: 2 m (6 ft)
Max Depth: 5 m (16 ft)
Way Point: 115° 19'00" Lon - W 49° 24'00" Lat - N

4 Region

Fishing

Tie Lake is a twisting, knotted lake with many bays and points. An angler in a canoe could paddle from one end of the lake to the other in an hour, but spend the better part of a day getting to the same place following the shoreline. It is a perfect lake for a belly boat, as even when it is windy, there is very little chop. There are two boat launches on the lake: one at the recreation site and one at the park, and the lake sees lots of usage from recreational boaters.

Unfortunately for anglers looking for the lake's stocked rainbow or occasional brook trout, most of these bays are very shallow, which means that during the summer, the fish tend not to be found in these areas. In early spring and again in late fall, these bays can be popular places, but as a general rule, the best place to fish for trout to 2 kg (4.5 lbs) is the deeper areas of the lake just out from the Tie Lake Recreation Site, and then only in the spring and fall, before the water warms up.

The lake has a thick silt layer as the bottom with a few spawning areas having gravel bottom. Feed is prolific with freshwater shrimp, snails, leaches and various insects abounding. The only problem for fishing can be winterkill.

Because it is such a shallow lake, it heats up considerably during the summer, bringing the trout fishing to an almost complete standstill. Fortunately, the beginning of summer doesn't mean the end of fishing here, as the lake has a large population of largemouth bass, which love the warm water. These fish can get to 2 kg (4 lbs), though usually are much smaller.

Once the water warms up, the bass move into the shallows, finding cover in the lake's weeds and reeds. Fly-fishers can use bass poppers, which are large top water flies that look like drowning bees or moths or even mice. These should be flipped into or near the weeds and twitched around to simulate a drowning insect. Streamer patterns can also work, but stand a much greater chance of getting hung up or snagged on weeds. Spincasters will find success with spinners, jigs, Texas rigs and top water lures such as a hoola popper or Rapala.

Directions

Tie Lake is a well developed lake with several private cabins surrounding the lake. The lake is easily found via the Tie Lake Road off the north side of Highway 3/93, just east of Jaffray. It is a short drive to Tie Lake where it is possible access the lake from either the recreation site or park.

Facilities

On the south side of Tie Lake you will the **Tie Lake Recreation Site**. The medium sized site is partially treed offering camping, picnicking and a beach area for visitors to enjoy. In total, there are a dozen RV friendly campsites that are available from mid-April to the end of October for a fee. These sites are often full during the summer since the lake is a popular place for water sports.

Further west, there is a small park that is a popular place to picnic with a nice beach and another boat launch. Private cabins also surround the lake.

Other Options

If you continue north beyond the Tie Lake Road, you may be able to reach the Bull River Road. Follow this main road west and you will pass by **Sand Lake**. Sand Lake is a long, shallow lake that is home to a quaint recreation site and a few cutthroat trout.

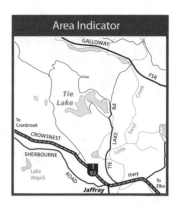

Area Indicator

Species
Rainbow Trout
Brook Trout

Tie Lake Fish Stocking Data			
Year	Species	Number	Life Stage
2013	Rainbow Trout	0	Fall Catchable
2012	Rainbow Trout	0	Catchable
2011	Rainbow Trout	6,400	Yearling

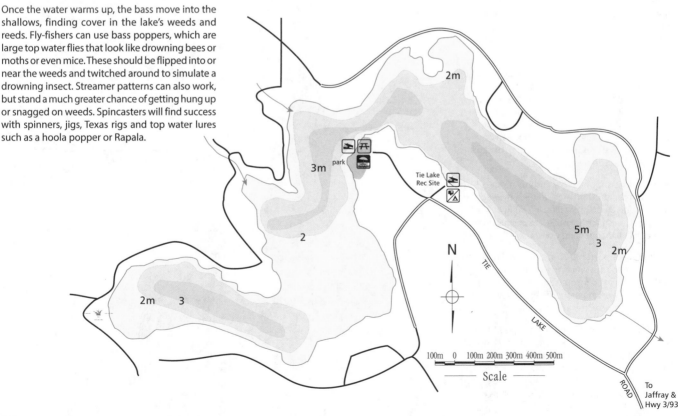

Location: 45 km (30 mi) northeast of Nakusp
Elevation: 721 m (2,365 ft)
Surface Area: 2,784 ha (7,099 ac)
Mean Depth: 128 m (420 ft)
Max Depth: 234 m (768 ft)
Way Point: 117° 24' 00" Lon - W   50° 34' 00" Lat - N

Trout Lake

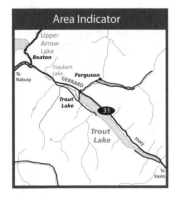

Area Indicator

Species
Bull Trout
Burbot
Cutthroat Trout
Kokanee
Rainbow Trout
Whitefish

Fishing

Set between two fabulous mountain ranges, Trout Lake is a scenic valley bottom lake, connected to Kootenay Lake by the Lardeau River. While Kootenay Lake is home to the largest strain of rainbow trout in the world, the world famous Gerrard Trout is actually named after the small community at the south end of Trout Lake.

In the early 1900s, fishery officials believed the massive trout came down from Trout Lake and named the lake and town after these amazing fish. However, when they set up a net to catch the trout from Trout Lake they discovered the trout were spawning upstream from Kootenay Lake, but not downstream from Trout Lake.

Trout Lake is home to some large rainbow trout in their own right. Rainbow are regularly caught in the 1.5 kg (3 lb) range and are often twice that. The lake also holds fair numbers of bull trout in the 3-4 kg (6.5 to 9 lb) range, as well as kokanee, burbot, some cutthroat trout, a few lake trout and plenty of whitefish. Despite the good fishing, the lake is rarely busy with anglers.

Fishing success for rainbow and bull trout is best by trolling the drop-off areas around the edges of the lake with a Flatfish or plug in spring or fall. For kokanee, try a small Krocodile lure or similar spoon tipped with a maggot and trolled near the surface.

Fly fishing opportunities are mostly limited to the cooler months, when the trout come in close to shore. However, if you want to try your luck in summer, try working around creek inflows, as the cool, oxygenated water attracts trout.

The stream mouths are also good areas for spin-casters to test their luck from shore. Although spinners and spoons can entice a strike or two, you will find better luck still fishing with a bobber and bait. Worms and grasshoppers suspended just off bottom are usually too tempting for rainbow or bull trout to pass up.

Directions

Trout Lake is a large lake located alongside Highway 31, one of the most interesting highways you will ever find. The section between Galena Bay in the west and Meadow Creek in the east is not paved. Adding to the gravel is the series of hairpin corners and steep sections along the north side of Trout Lake that will make all but the most experienced backroad travellers a little uncomfortable at times. The route is quite scenic, however.

The town of Trout Lake provides good access to the northwest end, while the campground is the main access point at the southeast end. Unfortunately, there is no launch at this south end.

Facilities

The town of Trout Lake is quite small, although there is a hotel along with a small store and gas station for your convenience. A maintained boat launch can also be found in town, just off Highway 31.

Goat Range Provincial Park is found at the southeast end of the lake. In addition to a small camping area, a popular attraction is the spawning channel along the Lardeau River. Visitors will be amazed at the sight and size of the large Gerrard rainbow trout during their annual spring spawning.

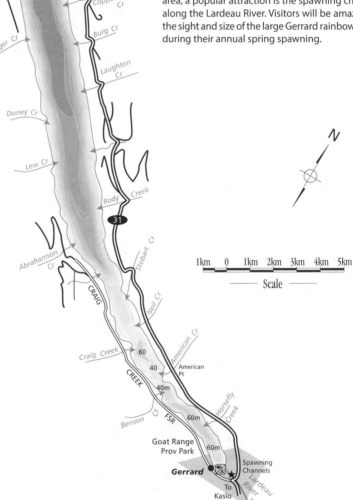

Tugulnuit (Tuc-El-Nuit) Lake

Location: 1 km (0.6 mi) north of Oliver
Elevation: 299 m (980 ft)
Surface Area: 50.5 ha (125 ac)
Mean Depth: 5.7 m (18.8 ft)
Max Depth: 8 m (26 ft)
Way Point: 119° 32′ 00″ Lon - W 49° 12′ 00″ Lat - N

Fishing

Located in the town of Oliver, Tugulnuit Lake is a small, but popular lake. There are public beaches and private campsites around the lake, and getting onto the water is quite easy.

The lake holds good number of trout, bass and perch, but it is best known for its carp fishing. Indeed, the lake plays host to the Great Canadian Carp Off, held every summer.

The carp derby was originally designed as a way to eliminate the carp from the lake, as it was considered a nuisance fish. However, after running the derby for a number of years (it began in 1998), the Southern Okanagan Sportsman's Association discovered that people were actually enjoying fishing for carp. In Europe, the carp is considered a prize sportfish. In BC, carp is not common and considered a pest. Fans of the carp argue that carp can provide good eating (many would argue that they taste better than salmon), when raised in clean waters. Which is true, but they also take on a muddy taste when the waters are not so clean, as is the case with this lake.

Carp are scrappy fighters and many an unwary angler has lost a hook or two to spunky carp that put up a bigger fight than expected on this lake; stories are even told of rods and reels being pulled out of angler's hands by the fish. Carp can quickly grow to 3 kg (6 lbs) or more in the lake, although catches of half that size are more common.

Unlike most of the game fish in BC, carp are bottom feeders. While they will sometimes chase down food, they usually graze the bottom of the lake. A popular strategy is chumming the lake with sweet corn or boiled potatoes, which should draw the carp into the area you're fishing. Then, rig a small, sharp hook (between size 4 and 8, as even big carp have small mouths and they only nibble on the food) with bait. Canned corn flavoured with anything from sugar to schnapps is a popular bait. Toss the hook out … and wait. And wait. As carp are not predatory fish, movement tends to scare them off; a small strike indicator/float is invaluable so you can see the carp start to take the bait. Once they do take the bait, set the hook. Don't have your drag on too tight, or their first run will snap the line.

If carp is not your thing, you can still fish for rainbow in the spring and fall as well as bass and perch throughout the year. Tips and techniques for these sportfish are found the book.

Directions

Tugulnuit Lake is easy to find, east of Highway 97 in Oliver. After crossing the Okanagan River north of Oliver, head south on Tuc El Nuit Lake Road, which leads back down to the lake. You can also take 79th Street off Highway 97 to 71st Street. Turning north will bring you to the lake.

Facilities

There are a number of private resorts and campgrounds on the lake, including **Sunny Beach RV Park** at the north end of the lake and the **Lakeside Resort**, at the south. **Inkaneep Provincial Park** is found to the north and also offers camping. For supplies and fishing tips, the city of **Oliver** is basically on the lakes doorstep.

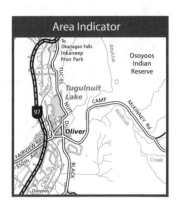

Area Indicator

Species

Species
Bass
Carp
Rainbow Trout
Yellow Perch

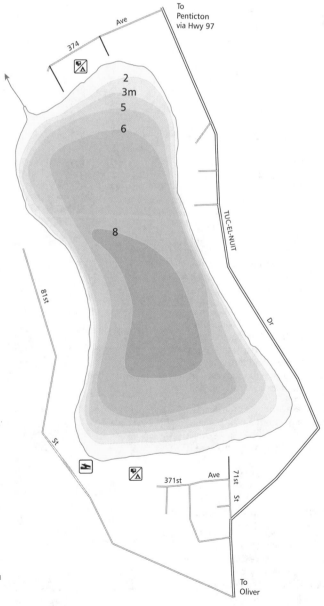

N

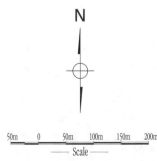

50m 0 50m 100m 150m 200m
— Scale —

Region
8

Location: 10 km (6 mi) north of Oliver
Elevation: 326 m (1,070 ft)
Surface Area: 275 ha (679 ac)
Mean Depth: 6.5 m (21 ft)
Max Depth: 27 m (88 ft)
Way Point: 119° 32' 00" Lon - W   49° 17' 00" Lat - N

Vaseux Lake

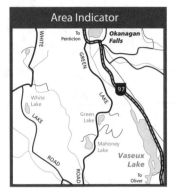

Area Indicator

Directions

Vaseux is a beautiful lake found approximately 25 km south of Penticton and 10 km north of Oliver in the South Okanagan Valley. Highway 97 runs along the majority of the east shore. At the south end of the lake, Sundial Road provides a designated launching site for cartoppers and canoes. Alternatively, there are various hand launching areas along the highway.

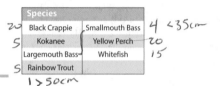

Species	
Black Crappie	Smallmouth Bass
Kokanee	Yellow Perch
Largemouth Bass	Whitefish
Rainbow Trout	

Facilities

Vaseux Lake Lodge is located along the southern shore of this shallow lake and offers all the amenities of home. **Vaseux Lake Provincial Park** is located along the northeast end of the lake and provides twelve campsites and a day-use area with a sandy beach and outhouses. The park is also well known for its wildlife habitat including some fine waterfowl viewing areas. Also stretching along the east side of the lake is the Vaseux Bighorn Wildlife Area. This area is home to Canada's largest herd of California bighorn sheep, which can often be seen in the surrounding cliffs.

Adding to the mix, the old Kettle Valley Railway runs down the east side of the lake. This trail provides shore access for anglers wanting to test their luck from the quieter west side of the lake.

Fishing

Vaseux Lake is arguably the best largemouth bass fishing lake in BC. There are bass over 5 kg (10 lb) bass lurking in the depths while 2.5 kg (5-6 lb) fish are not uncommon. In addition to largemouth, there other main sportfish include smallmouth bass, black crappie, perch, whitefish, rainbow trout and kokanee. Some decent size rainbow (to 2 kg/4 lbs) are also caught here.

The south end of the lake is a popular spot for those targeting bass. The privately owned island provides rocky outcroppings that the smallmouth bass love to hide around. Working your way north, the docks and rafts of the homes along the eastern shore provide convenient ambush spots for the aggressive bass, while the western side sees fewer anglers and is considered the better side to fish. The northern end of the lake is quite shallow and the lily pads provide great cover for the largemouth. Fishing this area can be a challenge due to the shallow water that can be only 15 cm (6 in) deep and the ever shifting channels and oxbows of the Okanagan River that enters here. A flat bottom boat and subtle movements are recommended if you want to target bass at the north end. Shoreline anglers can park at pullouts along the highway. There is a good rocky section along the highway south of the houses that is good for bass fishing.

Soft plastics are the name of the game here. Tubes, Trick Stiks, Texas rigs and traditional jig heads will all work. Some prefer using Rapalas and crankbaits, while poppers can add an exciting top water element. Fly anglers prefer big patterns, such as frogs, oversized leeches or even mice.

The center part of the lake is home to the deepest hole. This is the area to target the trout and kokanee. Lake trolls will attract both trout and kokanee, while fly anglers will delight in the fact that the lake is known to have prolific insect hatches. Matching the hatch is one of the best ways to entice the trout into biting. Fly fisherman should come armed with patterns such as Muddler Minnows, clousers, large leeches, crayfish, hopper and popper patterns.

The lake has a no motor (power or electric) restriction which, in part, reduces the pressure on the lake. Canoes are a good alternative since they allow you to troll effectively or simply park and cast. There are also varied regulations that cover the inflow and outflow of the Okanagan River and the oxbows, so be sure to check the regulations before heading out.

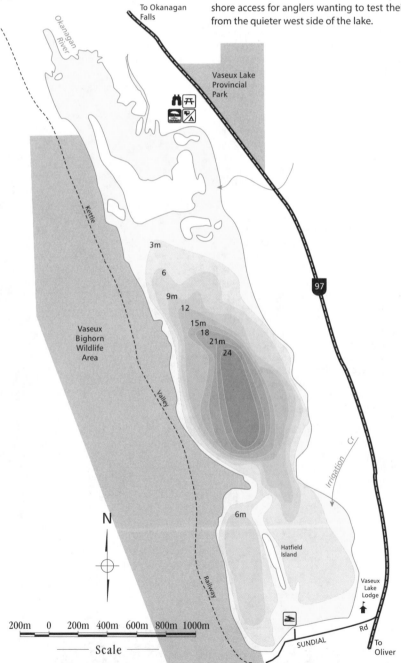

Wall Lake

Location: 143 km (89 mi) southeast of Cranbrook
Elevation: 1,760 m (5,774 ft)
Surface Area: 22 ha (54 ac)
Mean Depth: 14 m (46 ft)
Max Depth: 30 m (98 ft)
Way Point: 114° 5′ 00″ Lon - W 49° 00′ 00″ Lat - N

Fishing

Wall Lake is named for the rather imposing rock wall that rises out of the lake's eastern shore. It is one of the most scenic fishing lakes in the region. It is also inhabited with good numbers of cutthroat trout.

The cutthroat in the lake are known to reach up to 40 cm (16 in) in size and can be caught on a variety of flies and lures. Since the lake is a high elevation lake, there is a limited summer season, making the resident trout quite aggressive feeders during this period. It also means that insect hatches occur concurrently, which means the fish are often feeding on a variety of different sources. It can be tough figuring out what the fish are eating, but as a general rule, they are voracious, and will often take the largest things they can find.

As with most hike-in lakes, it can be quite challenging to haul in a float tube. For this reason, shore fishing is the main method of angling. Shore casting is readily feasible from several points. In particular, the drop off along the rocky point just south of the campsite is particularly enticing. Try using an attractor pattern like a Carey Special or a Woolly Bugger. When the lake is calm, fly anglers should try top water flies such as a caddis fly or something similar that the hungry trout can hone in on. Spincasters will have consistent success with small spinners and spoons.

Caution should be taken when approaching the lake. While the fish are hungry, they are also cautious. All that sparkling clear water makes it easy for predators to spot them, and they know it. Cutthroat can be found anywhere in the cool waters of Wall Lake, even within inches of the shore, and many anglers start working the lake from well back.

Other Options

If travelling from the BC side, you will more than likely pass by the **Flathead River** en route to Wall Lake. The picturesque river lies in a steep valley and is best accessed via the Flathead Forest Service Road. The river offers several recreation sites and has fishing opportunities for cutthroat trout, bull trout, rainbow trout and whitefish. Watch for special restrictions on the river.

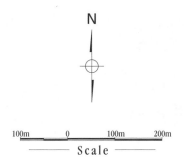

N

100m   0   100m   200m

Scale

Directions

Wall Lake is a scenic lake that lies within the Akamina-Kishinena Provincial Park in the very remote southeast corner of BC. The easiest access is actually from Waterton Lakes National Park in Alberta. From near the end of the Akamina Parkway, it is a 3 km (1.8 mile) hike along an old road and then steep trail into the lake.

From the BC side, the lake is only accessible via a long trail from the end of the Kishena Forest Service Road. To find this road requires travel along several logging roads southeast of Elko. It is recommended to have a good 4wd vehicle and a copy of the *Backroad Mapbook Kootenay Rockies BC* when venturing this far from the highway.

Facilities

Visitors are encouraged not to camp at Wall Lake due to grizzly bear concerns. There is, however, a bivouac to help protect people from the sudden mountain storms that frequent the high elevation lake. Please be prepared for both if visiting the lake.

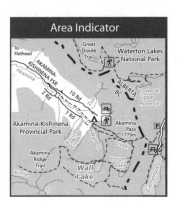

Area Indicator

Species
Cutthroat Trout

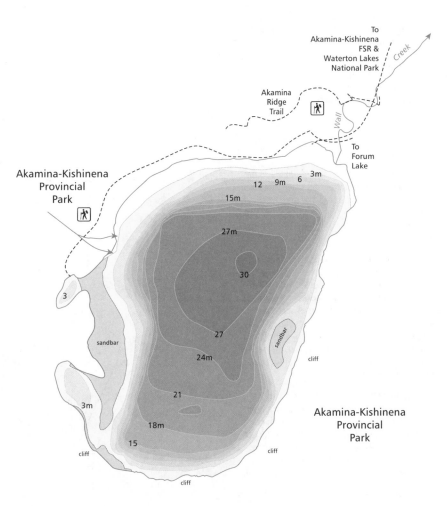

Location: 35 km (22 mi) southeast of Cranbrook
Elevation: 820 m (2,690 ft)
Surface Area: 4 ha (10 ac)
Mean Depth: 5.5 m (18 ft)
Max Depth: 9 m (30 ft)
Way Point: 115° 21'00" Lon - W   49° 23'00" Lat - N

Wapiti Lake

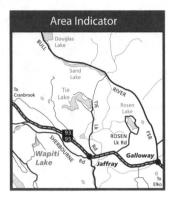

Area Indicator

Species

Rainbow Trout

Brook Trout

Directions

The scenic lake is found off Sherbourne Road, which is found on the south side of Highway 3/93 shortly after crossing the Kootenay River near Wardner. A short access road leads south from Sherbourne Road providing good access to a recreation site on the lake.

Wapiti Lake			
Fish Stocking Data			
Year	Species	Number	Life Stage
2013	Rainbow Trout	1,000	Spring Catchable
2012	Rainbow Trout	1,000	Catchable
2011	Rainbow Trout	1,000	Catchable

Facilities

Located 2 km from Highway 3/93 on a good gravel road, the **Wapiti Lake Recreation Site** offers three campsites in a large, grassy meadow at the north end of the lake. It is ideal for an overnight stop over and can be accessed by trailers and RVs. Being one of the more scenic lakes in the area, it is often busy with anglers and campers alike.

Other Options

Just to the west of Wapiti Lake, you will find the **Kootenay River.** The river is accessible from several nearby roads and offers fishing for rainbow trout, cutthroat trout, bull trout and the odd lingcod. Watch for special restrictions on the river.

Fishing

The word Wapiti is the Cree word for Elk, and yes, there is a chance of seeing an Elk around this small lake, which is little more than a glorified pond. The lake's edges are covered in lily pads, and the Steeples mountain range rises due south of the lake, opposite of the Wapiti Lake Recreation Site. It has been described as a touch of paradise, and while it doesn't have the same dramatic beauty as some high-elevation lakes, it is a pretty lake in its own right, peaceful and still.

Fishing in Wapiti Lake is usually quite good despite the fact the lake lies so close to the Highway 3/93. The lake is regularly stocked with catchable sized rainbow trout, which provide for the bulk of the action. Brook trout are also resident in the lake, although they are most readily caught during the winter through the ice. There are also rumours that kokanee exist in the lake.

Rainbow and brook trout average about 25-35 cm (10-14 in) in size, although they can reach up to 1.5 kg (3.5 lbs) on occasion. Wapiti Lake used to sport plenty of 2.5 kg (5 lb) football sized rainbow but increased angling pressure now keeps the average size down.

Wapiti Lake is best fished by a boat or float tube and is made up of two deep holes. Working the shallows between these two holes, right where the lake doglegs to the west, should prove to be productive. Chironomids are the first insects to start hatching, as soon as the water warms up. By early June, there will be a number of hatches occurring throughout the month, sometimes at the same time. During these times the trout can get particular about what they eat.

The shoal area between the two lakes can be a productive during ice fishing season, especially for brookies, who like to cruise the shallows. Don't drill your holes too far out from shore, as the trout like to stay in the top ten feet of water or so, and will usually stick to the shallows where any food in the lake will remain. Through the ice, try jigging a small white jig or a small spoon like a Little Cleo.

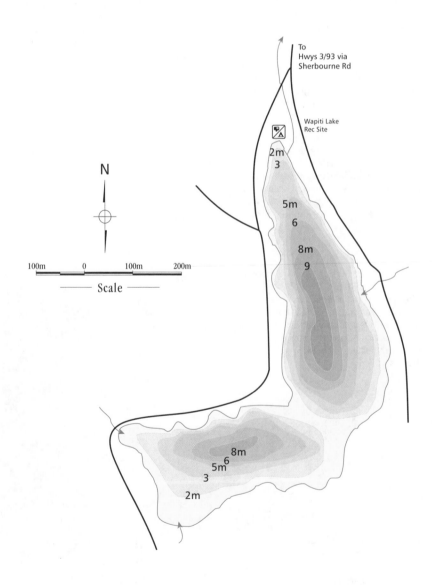

To Hwys 3/93 via Sherbourne Rd

Wapiti Lake Rec Site

2m
3

5m
6

8m
9

N

100m   0   100m   200m

Scale

8m
6
5m
3

2m

Wasa Lake

Location: 30 km (18.5 mi) north of Cranbrook
Elevation: 774 m (2,545 ft)
Surface Area: 102 ha (252 ac)
Mean Depth: 4 m (12.5 ft)
Max Depth: 13 m (43 ft)
Way Point: 115° 44' 00" Lon - W 49° 47' 00" Lat - N

4 Region

Fishing

Wasa Lake is an extremely popular lake alongside Highway 93/95. Locals in the village of Wasa on the shores of the lake advertise the lake as having the warmest water in the Kootenays. Tourists flock to the shores of the lake to lie on its beaches, swim in its warm waters, and water ski on its surface.

While warm water is great for attracting tourists, it is hard on trout. The lake was stocked for a number of years but that program was discontinued way back in the 1960s, as the trout just weren't surviving. While there are occasionally trout pulled from this lake (as there are a couple deep holes where they can retreat in the hottest weather), the lake has become best known for its largemouth bass fishing.

Unlike trout, bass love warm water, and as the temperature rises, so does the activity level of bass. While many local anglers have a low regard for bass, finding them ugly when compared to the lovely rainbow trout, largemouth bass can be a lot of fun to fish for.

Fly anglers can take largemouth off the top with popper flies and other top water variations. Poppers are stripped in a jerky fashion making noise and action on the surface. Largemouth are often stirred silly by this action and will take the fly right off the top in a feeding frenzy. For spincasters, there are a number of good top water lures available such as floating Rapala variations. One particular lure that is a favourite of bass anglers is the 'Pop R', essentially a minnow imitation with a hollowed mouth area and crystal flash tail.

Look for bass in shoreline weed areas or along the freshwater reef found in the lake. When bass are lethargic, try a jig worked slowly along bottom structure.

Other Options

If the fishing is slow on Wasa Lake, a nearby alternative is **Lazy Lake**. Lazy Lake can be reached by following the Wolf Lewis Forest Service Road east from Wasa Lake. The road eventually passes by the western shore of Lazy Lake. In addition to a recreation site, the lake provides fishing opportunities for stocked rainbow trout. Look for more details on this lake earlier in this book.

Directions

Wasa Lake is one of the most popular recreational lakes in the Cranbrook/Kimberley area. In addition to the Wasa Lake Provincial Park, there are several cabins scattered around the lake. The park and lake can be easily reached via Highway 93/95 north of historic Fort Steele.

Facilities

Wasa Lake Provincial Park is a popular park that can be quite busy during the summer. The park is equipped with 104 vehicle/tent campsites, a separate beach and picnic area, a boat launch and much more. Visitors can enjoy a variety of activities including hiking or biking one of the many trails found in and around the park. For reservations call 1-800-689-9025 or visit www.discovercamping.ca.

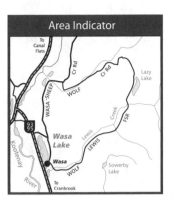

Area Indicator

Species
Largemouth Bass
Rainbow Trout

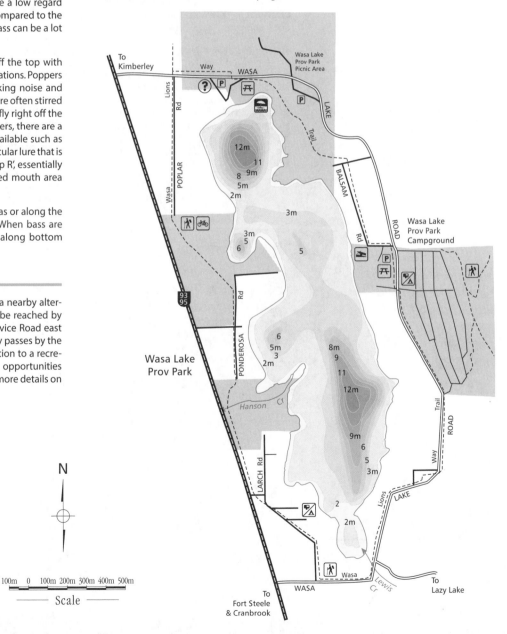

N

100m 0 100m 200m 300m 400m 500m

Scale

Location: 48 km (30 mi) northeast of Radium Hot Springs
Elevation: 1,897 m (6,224 ft)
Surface Area: 17 ha (42 ac)
Mean Depth: 5.5 m (18 ft)
Max Depth: 11 m (39 ft)
Way Point: 115° 41'00" Lon - W 50° 54'00" Lat - N

Wedgewood Lake

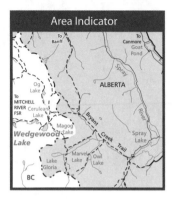

Area Indicator

Species

Cutthroat Trout

Fishing

Stunning alpine scenery, towering mountain peaks and crystal clear waters all come together in Mount Assiniboine Provincial Park to create some of the most spectacular lakes you ever did see. One of the most beautiful is Wedgewood Lake.

However, all that sheer beauty comes at a cost, and the cost is accessibility. Getting to the lake is a long, difficult ordeal, unless you choose to take a helicopter to the Mount Assiniboine Lodge. From there, you still have to hike 5 km (3 miles) along a moderately difficult trail.

The lake holds good numbers of cutthroat trout that average 30-35 cm (12-14 in) in size but can be found to 1.5 kg (3.5 lbs) on occasion. As a high elevation lake, fishing opportunities in Wedgwood Lake are limited to the summer and early fall periods. Since the trout have a short open water season, they can be quite aggressive will readily attack small spinners and fly patterns.

The use of a floatation device would be helpful on Wedgwood Lake for a couple of reasons. The cutthroat tend to travel around the lake in loose schools; therefore, if you can locate a school, your success rate should increase considerably. Also, shore fishing is limited due to shoreline vegetation and the lack of developed trails. If lugging a float tube into the alpine is not feasible, try to access the drop off areas near the middle of the lake from either shore.

Directions

This remote alpine lake lies deep within Mount Assiniboine Provincial Park. From the BC side, it is a grueling trek along the Mitchell River Trail. The trailhead is located at the end of the Cross River Forest Service Road. To reach the forest road, take Highway 93 east of Revelstoke to Settlers Road. Settlers Road travels south eventually crossing the Kootenay River and meeting the Cross River Road. The roads are currently well maintained due to industrial activity in the area.

Alternatively, Wedgwood Lake can be found beyond Lake Magog and the popular Bryant Creek Trail. This trail starts in Alberta, at the south end of the Spray Lakes Reservoir. No matter the route in, it is a long difficult trek into Wedgwood Lake.

For people with more money than time, it is possible to fly into the Mount Assiniboine Lodge. From the lodge, it is only 5 km (3 miles) to the lake along a moderately difficult trail. For information on getting to the lodge, visit www.canadianrockies.net/assiniboine/ or call (403) 678-2883.

Facilities

Mount Assiniboine Provincial Park is a wilderness, trail access only park that offers rustic backcountry camping at mainly designated campsites. Visitors to the park often use Lake Magog to the east of Wedgwood Lake as a staging ground for exploring the park. At Lake Magog, there is a campground as well as four cabins and **Mount Assiniboine Lodge**.

Other Options

Cerulean Lake is another remote Mount Assiniboine Park lake that is found to the east of Wedgwood Lake. The alpine lake is home to a quality rainbow trout fishery during the late summer. There are rumours that the odd 7 kg (15 lb) rainbow exists in the lake.

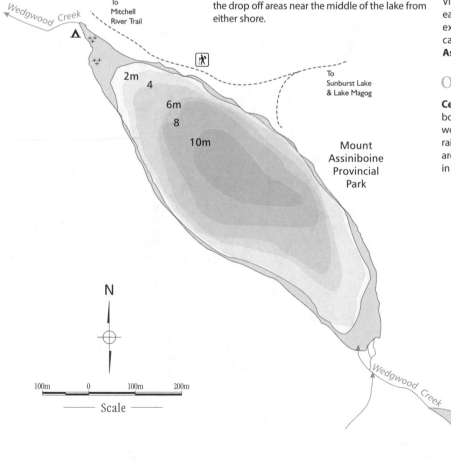

Wee Sandy Lake

Location: 32 km (19.9 mi) southeast of Nakusp
Elevation: 1,942 m (6,371 ft)
Surface Area: 74 ha (183 ac)
Mean Depth: 27 m (89 ft)
Max Depth: 85 m (279 ft)
Way Point: 117° 33′ 00″ Lon - W   49° 59′ 00″ Lat - N

4 Region

Fishing

Set in a magnificent alpine valley, far, far from the madding crowds, Wee Sandy Lake is one of a handful of great fishing lakes in Valhalla Provincial Park. Very few anglers make the trip up here each year, as getting to the lake involves either renting a helicopter or float plane, or a long, difficult hike from a trailhead that is only accessible by boat. Getting to the lake requires a serious commitment of time, energy, or at the very least, cash.

Those who do make the trip will be rewarded with a peaceful alpine lake and quite often nobody else around, although backpackers and climbers do hike into this area occasionally. This deep, secluded lake can be fished any time after ice off, which is usually in mid June. The open water season is short and only lasts about three to four months. During this time the wild rainbow and cutthroat can be quite aggressive at times and will strike any well presented lure or fly.

Because the water is so clear, approach the lake with caution. The waters of the lake are cold enough that the cutthroat can be found anywhere on the lake, and will often be found very close to shore. Simply walking up to the lake will often scare the fish off, ruining you chances of catching a fish for quite a while. The wise angler approaches the shore slowly, often finding a point of land higher up and back from the lake to observe the lake. If things are calm, it will be possible to spot fish moving in the water. If the water is choppy, it becomes harder to see the fish, but it is also harder for them to spot you.

Although shore fishing is limited, there are a few clearings along the shore with room for casting. Fly anglers should try top water flies such as a caddis fly. For larger trout a small streamer fly pattern often works. Spincasters will experience ample action using small silver or gold spinners. Try a silver spoon such as a Little Cleo to try to entice larger trout to strike.

Directions

Wee Sandy Lake lies deep within the rugged Valhalla Provincial Park in the heart of the West Kootenays. Like Beatrice and Evans to the south, Wee Sandy Lake is more easily accessed by floatplane or helicopter. For those who prefer to hike in, the Wee Sandy Creek Trail can be accessed from Slocan Lake, across from New Denver. Do not take this trail lightly; it is a difficult 14.4 km (9 mi) one-way hike that ascends some 1,370 m (4,495 ft) to the lake. Also be aware that this is Grizzly bear country.

Facilities

Wee Sandy Lake offers no formal camping areas, although there are a few clearings that visitors with tents can use. For those hiking in, the **Iron Creek Cabin** is found at around the 11 km (6.8 mi) mark of the trail. Although rustic in nature, it is a nice place to stay on those chilly nights as it has a wood stove.

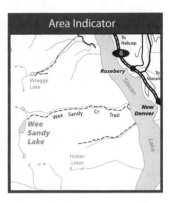

Area Indicator

Species
Rainbow Trout
Cutthroat Trout

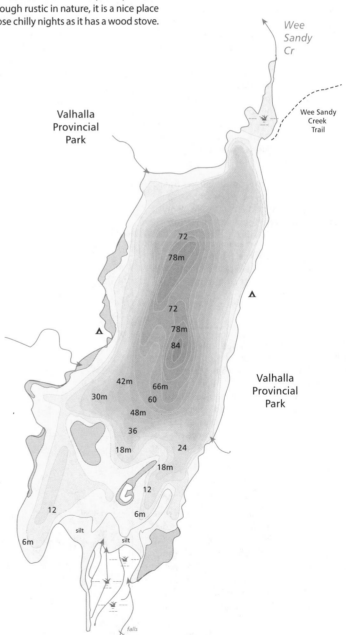

N

100m   0   100m 200m 300m 400m 500m

— Scale —

West Kettle River

Fishing

The West Kettle is the Kettle River's smaller, warmer twin sibling. It has its headwaters in the Graystokes area east of Kelowna, and flows for 90 km (56 miles) to its confluence with the Kettle at Westbridge.

The river has plenty of bug life, which in turn supports the small rainbows that inhabit the river. Fly anglers love the river as it features a huge stonefly hatch, as well as plenty of other surface insects. Using a dry stonefly imitation or a wet, weighted stonefly nymph works extremely well in the spring after spring run-off. The annual spring closure ends June 1, and by that time the water has usually settled down. The river also holds whitefish, brook trout, and a very few of the extremely rare, almost mythological brown trout.

In the summer, the fishing here is not very good. The waters of the river get quite warm, up to 20°C (68°F), which is getting up near the highest temperature rainbows can stand. However, because the fish tend to congregate in the big pools in summer, it makes them easy to find, and fishing pressure has really knocked stocks down. Using a night crawler here is as almost as easy as the proverbial shooting fish in a barrel. Trouble is, the river is catch and release below the Beaverdell Station Road bridge, and the entire river has a bait ban from April 1 to October 31. But the river suffers from non-compliance; some people are still using bait and keeping their big fish below the bridge. Don't add to the problem. The river has some amazing trout habitat, but removing the mature fish from the river seriously impacts the stocks. Above the bridge, anglers can keep one fish a day.

In the fall, the river starts to cool down, and the fishing becomes much more active again. One of the most popular patterns is a grasshopper imitation, as there are plenty of hoppers falling into the river in September and October.

Every once in a while, you will find a rainbow that gets up to 1 kg (2 lbs). Although impressive, this is a far cry from the 2.5 kg (5 lb) fish the river used to produce regularly in the 1960s. Please respect the regulations to help return the river to the glory days of the past.

Directions

Highway 33, between Kelowna and Rock Creek, is a quiet highway that picks up the West Kettle south of the Big White turn-off. As the highway dips down towards the valley, the river is much more noticeable and there are numerous access points along the highway. At Westbridge, the West Kettle joins the main stem of the Kettle. Also providing good access to the river in this area is the Kettle Valley Railway portion of the Trans Canada Trail. The upper reaches of the West Kettle are accessed off the Okanagan Falls Forest Service Road.

Facilities

The West Kettle passes through, or near, a number of small towns, including Beaverdell and Westbridge, where you will various supplies as well as small hotels or Bed and Breakfast accommodations. There are a few private, riverside campgrounds along Highway 33, while the highway also provides a couple convenient rest areas for visitors to access the river from. **Arlington Lakes Recreation Site** to the north and **Kettle River Provincial Park** to the south can also be used as base camps to help explore the river.

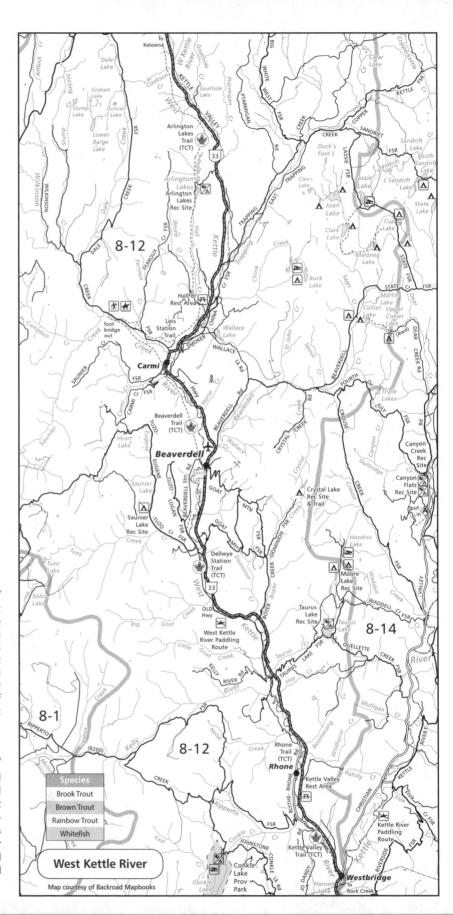

West Kettle River

Map courtesy of Backroad Mapbooks

Species
Brook Trout
Brown Trout
Rainbow Trout
Whitefish

Whatshan Lake

Location: 36 km (22 mi) southwest of Nakusp
Elevation: 643 m (2,110 ft)
Surface Area: 1,692 ha (4,179 ac)
Mean Depth: 48 m (157 ft)
Max Depth: 116 m (381 ft)
Way Point: 118° 05'00" Lon - W 50° 00'00" Lat - N

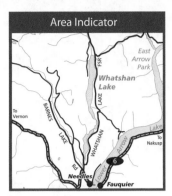

Area Indicator

Species
Bull Trout
Kokanee
Rainbow Trout

Directions

Whatshan is a large lake southwest of Nakusp. To reach the lake from the south, follow Highway 6 to the ferry terminal at Needles. From here, watch for the Whatshan Lake Road, heading north as you climb the highway heading out of the small community. Whatshan Lake Road soon connects with the Whatshan River Forest Service Road, which runs along the east shore of the big lake and provides access to the two recreation sites near the north end of the lake.

If you are coming from the north, take the Lower Mosquito Road from the Arrow Park Ferry. Turn left at the West Mosquito Road at the 9 km mark, then left again onto the Stevens Forest Service Road. After 14 km you will come to the north end of the lake.

The lake can be accessed by most vehicles.

Facilities

Towards the north end of the lake are the **Stevens Creek** and **Richy Recreation Sites.** They are located within a few kilometres of each other. Richy is a user-maintained site that offers space for about five groups, a beach, boat launch and small dock. Stevens Creek is the more established site with space for 13 camping groups in the pine forest along with a day-use area for picnicking or simply enjoying the pea gravel and sand beach. The scenic site offers nice views of Whatshan Peak and the Pinnacles, while swimming is possible during the summer. There is a boat launch onto the fair sized lake, while the road access is good enough for small RV's and trailers to access the site.

Fishing

Located west of Lower Arrow Lake, the man-made Whatshan Lake is a long, narrow valley bottom lake that offers some great fishing for rainbow trout, bull trout and kokanee.

The size of Whatshan can be intimidating for anglers who are used to smaller lakes. Fly anglers especially will find it hard to read the big lake, but the lake is actually quite friendly for flies. Your best chances are found around the mouths of the many streams that flow into the lake, especially from the west side, but if you have a boat, you will be able to access plenty of possibilities. There are numerous points and bays along the shore of the lake.

The lake is divided into two sections by a narrow channel, slightly south of centre. The northern half of the lake is bigger and deeper, and has a couple of recreation sites and a boat launch. The south end of the lake is smaller and shallower, but can still be quite productive, as can be the channel between the two sections.

Springtime seems to be the best time of the year for rainbow trout which are usually caught by trolling. Concentrate on points, inflow creeks or bays, trolling a lake troll with a Wedding Band or small lure and single egg, or a Flatfish, Kitimat or Krocodile spoon. Fly-fishers can use a streamer type fly pattern. Muddler Minnows, Polar Bear or bucktails are popular choices. As the water warms, try an Apex, Lyman plug or flasher with a hoochie in the 10-30 m (30-90 ft) depth. For deep trolling, downriggers with the aid of a heavy weight will enable you to troll your lure deep enough to find holding areas.

However, by summertime, the focus of the fishing has turned to the kokanee. Kokanee are best caught on a lake troll like a Willow Leaf or Ford Fender, with a short leader, Wedding Band and maggot. A Flatfish or small pink Spin-N-Glo lures can also be effective. Troll as slow as possible and in an "S" pattern, with one ounce of weight or less, which takes the lure to 5-15 m (15 to 45 ft). Fly-fishers can try trolling slowly with a small red Doc Spratley or Woolly Bugger within a few feet of the surface.

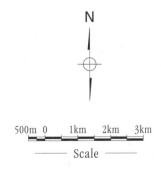

N

500m 0   1km   2km   3km

—— Scale ——

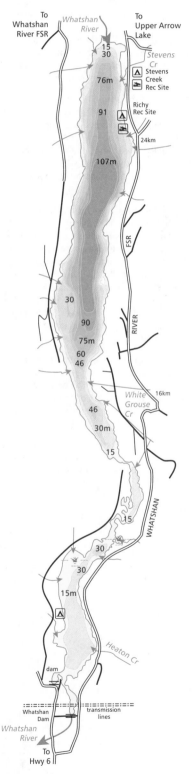

Location: 23 km (14 mi) east of Canal Flats
Elevation: 1,143 m (3,750 ft)
Surface Area: 392 ha (969 ac)
Mean Depth: 13 m (43 ft)
Max Depth: 19.3 m (63 ft)
Way Point: 115° 29' 00" Lon - W 50° 08' 00" Lat - N

Whiteswan Lake

Fishing

Whiteswan Lake is perhaps the most famous fishing lake in the Kootenays, known for its spectacular fishing for Gerrard strain rainbow trout that can reach up to 5 kg (11 lbs).

Because of its fame, it receives constant pressure throughout the ice free season, which is slightly shorter than other lakes in the area, as the lake is at a quite high elevation. The lake is stocked on occasion with rainbow to help supplement the naturally reproducing trout. The lake also holds good number of brook trout that can get up to 45 cm (18 inches).

Fishing is best in the spring and fall. Despite the lake's relatively high elevation, the top layer of water can get quite warm in summer, and swimming is a popular pastime at the beach at the north end of the lake. During these times, the trout retreat to deeper water. Trolling around the drop offs around the edge of the lake can still provide anglers with good success.

Fly anglers should try a leech or shrimp pattern when the hatch is not on. Other fly patterns that are effective are chironomids or bloodworms during the spring and dry flies, such as an Adams or a Humpy during the summer evenings when the trout are rising. The shallows at the northeast end of the lake are a good area to work in spring, but in summer, your best bet is to troll a Carey Special or other attractor type wet fly around the edges of the lake. Use a deep sinking line to get down to where the trout are holding.

The lake is also a popular ice fishing destination, although there is a closure, currently from December 1 to January 2. Although the odd rainbow is taken through the ice, most of the action is for brook trout that prefer to cruise the shallows during the winter.

Before fishing here check the fishing regulations, as there are a number of special regulations in effect, including a shortened season and gear restrictions.

Directions

Whiteswan Lake is the centerpiece of the beautiful Whiteswan Lake Provincial Park. To access the scenic park, take Highway 93/95 south from Canal Flats to the signed Whiteswan Lake Road Turnoff. The good gravel road travels east, past the much smaller Alces Lake, and along the southern shore of Whiteswan Lake. There are boat launches at either end of the lake.

Facilities

Whiteswan Lake Provincial Park has five separate campgrounds with a total of 114 vehicle/tent sites. The Home Basin Campground is the biggest on the lake. The park also spots three picnic sites and two paved boat launches, one at the northeast end of the lake, one at the southwest. Along with fishing, visitors to the park can enjoy a variety of other outdoor activities, such as soaking in the nearby Lussier Hot Springs, hiking along the park's many trails or viewing the park's abundant wildlife. The park is open year round, with winter camping available at the Inlet Creek Campground.

Other Options

To the west of Whiteswan Lake is **Alces Lake**. Alces is part of Whiteswan Provincial Park, and fishing can be quite good at times for stocked rainbow trout. The lake is fly-fishing only; check the regulations for restrictions before heading out. For more information, check out the write up earlier in the book.

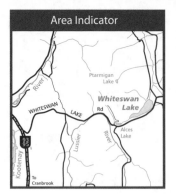

Area Indicator

Species
Rainbow Trout
Brook Trout

Whiteswan Lake			
Fish Stocking Data			
Year	Species	Number	Life Stage
2009	Rainbow Trout	500	Yearling
2004	Rainbow Trout	10,000	Yearling

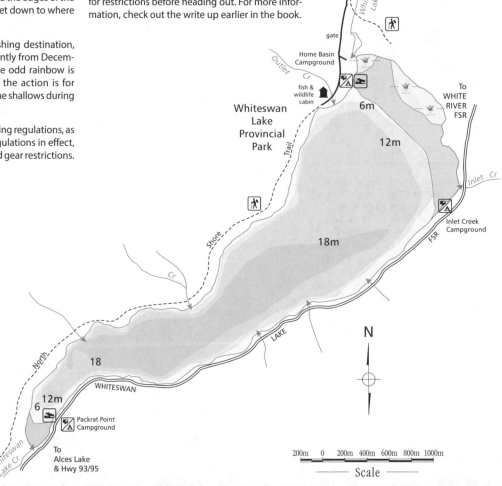

Whitetail Lake

Location: 16 km (10 mi) west of Canal Flats
Elevation: 1,100 m (3,609 ft)
Surface Area: 157 ha (387 ac)
Mean Depth: 9.8 m (32 ft)
Max Depth: 19.2 m (63 ft)
Way Point: 116° 01′ 00″ Lon - W 50° 12′ 00″ Lat - N

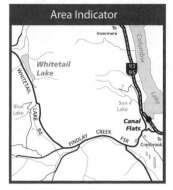

Area Indicator

Species
Rainbow Trout
Brook Trout

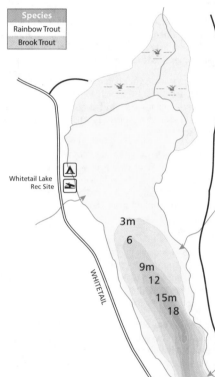

Whitetail Lake
Rec Site

3m
6
9m
12
15m
18

WHITETAIL

LAKE

Rd

To
Findlay
Creek FSR
& Hwy 93/95

Fishing

One of the most beautiful and most popular fishing lakes in the entire province, Whitetail is a deep, clear blue lake surrounded by snow-capped mountains. It is home to Gerrard Rainbow that can get up to 5 kg (11 lbs). It also holds good numbers of brook trout, in the 20–45 cm (8–18 inch) range.

Because the lake is so clear, the weedbeds can be found to a depth of 6 m (20 ft) or so. These provide food and cover for the trout. The lake also has fairly steep shoreline areas, with fast transitions between the shoals and the deeper areas of the lake. The exception is the east end of the lake, where there is a fairly extensive shoal area. The lake is fed by snowmelt, and remains cool all summer. This results in fishing that remains strong, even in the heat of August.

The trout hang out around the rim of the lake, near the transition zone between deep water and shallow. This makes them fairly easy to find. Trolling is the most popular method here using spinners and plugs such as Dick Nites, Flatfish or similar type lures worked along the edge of the drop-off. Trolling wet fly patterns in the transition areas can also produce well.

Fly anglers will find that a chironomid worked in the shoals at the northern end of the lake will produce well in spring. Nymph patterns, such as a grey bead head nymph, can be used as a searching pattern when chironomids aren't hatching. When the mayflies and caddis flies are found on the surface on late summer evenings, the fish will rise to take them. This is a perfect time for some exciting top water fishing with a dry fly that imitates either of these.

Whitetail Lake is a trophy fishing lake, and is managed as such. There are size restrictions, bait bans and seasonal closures, all in an attempt to keep the quality of fishing here up to historical standards.

Directions

Whitetail Lake is found west of Canal Flats off Highway 93/95. From Canal Flats, drive 4.5 km north, to the Findlay Creek Forest Service Road. Follow this road west, watching for the Whitetail (Deer) Lake Road. This good 2wd road leads north shortly after crossing Emily Creek. At km 23.5, do not take the turn to Blue Lake. Instead go straight, keeping right at km 25.5. Watch for the access road to the Whitetail Lake Recreation Site to your right.

Facilities

The **Whitetail Lake Recreation Site** is found along the northeast shores of the lake, just off the Whitetail Lake Road. The popular site is the busiest recreation site in the area. There are 30 campsites here, in two sets, with 22 picnic tables shared amongst them all. Most of the campsites offer shade and easy lake access. The first group of sites reached is accessible by trailers and features a boat launch and a day use area. The second group of sites further south along the lake shore has no trailer turn around area. The sites are generally full each weekend during the fishing season and there is a fee to camp here from mid-April until the end of October.

Other Options

Along the way to Whitetail Lake, you will be travelling along **Findlay Creek**. Fishing in the creek can be good for generally small cutthroat trout and some nice sized bull trout. Fishing success in this creek definitely improves along the more remote stretches of the creek. Watch for bait bans and other special regulations.

Whitetail (Deer) Lake			
Fish Stocking Data			
Year	Species	Number	Life Stage
2013	Rainbow Trout	12,000	Yearling
2012	Rainbow Trout	12,000	Yearling
2011	Rainbow Trout	12,000	Yearling

N

200m 0 200m 400m 600m 800m 1000m

—— Scale ——

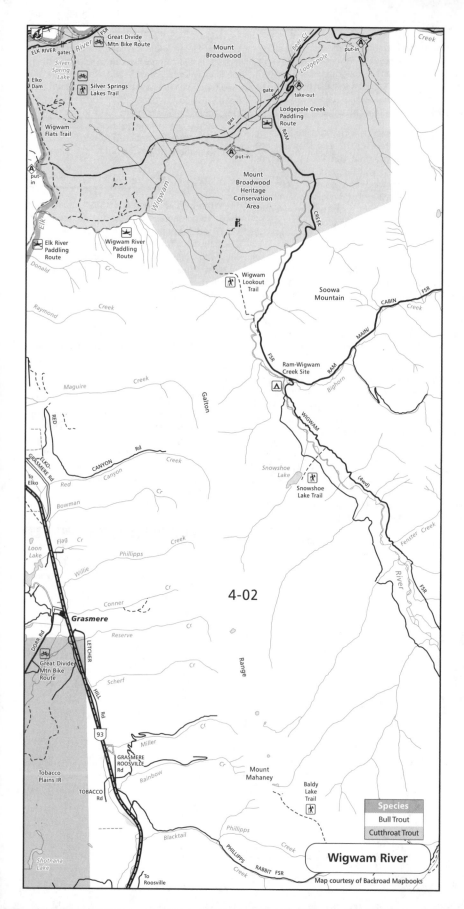

4-02

Snowshoe
Lake Trail

Species
Bull Trout
Cutthroat Trout

Wigwam River

Map courtesy of Backroad Mapbooks

Fishing

The Wigwam is another one in a series of fine cutthroat trout rivers in the East Kootenay. It is an Elk River tributary, but is much harder to access, making it a popular alternative to the often overcrowded Elk. Fans of the river also claim the trout caught here are bigger than the ones you will find in the Elk.

The river also vies for the designation of most beautiful river in the Kootenays. There is stiff competition from a number of other rivers, but the Wigwam is truly gorgeous, with well-polished, coloured stones on the river bottom that shimmer as the crystal clear water is poured over top of them. The river cuts back and forth, creating deep holding pools where the bull trout and cutthroat like to hold. It is a walk and wade fishery as you move from pool to pool.

The river has diverse and prolific hatches. In June, salmon flies begin to emerge, followed by a seemingly endless hatch of green drake mayflies. This is one of the most popular hatches since the cutthroat take the mayflies hard.

In early summer, the caddis begin to hatch. While the cutthroat don't usually hit these as hard (often sipping them off the surface), the fishing is just as good. This is also the time for the P.M.D. Hatch, which is best fished with a sunken spinner or soft hackling.

Experienced anglers will fish the river with a variety of deer hair caddis patterns with size 14 to size 8 hooks in a variety of colours: green, yellow, brown and orange. If those patterns aren't working, a size 16 or size 14 mayfly pattern in olive, tan or grey might work. Having a few nymph patterns will help, too, like a size 8 weighted golden stonefly nymph pattern.

Later in summer and into fall, terrestrial patterns work well, and a #8 foam hopper is a popular choice. There are also lesser hatches of green drakes and caddis in October, and finding the right presentation can be a challenge, as there is still just so much choice.

The Wigwam has one of the largest populations of bull trout in the Kootenay. They are best taken on large streamer (size 2) patterns, but have been known to take to dry flies at time. Finding bull trout over 60 cm (24 inches) is not uncommon.

The Wigwam is a Class II water (special stamp required) and divided into two sections. Upstream of the Ram Wigwam Creek Recreation Site, it is closed to angling from April 1 to October 31. Downstream, it is fly-fishing only and closed from mid-September to the end of October when the vulnerable bull trout spawn. The whole river is catch and release only.

Directions

The Wigwam is found south of Fernie. It is a walk and wade river with fast flowing water through steep terrain. At Elko, it is possible to walk or bike into the upper end of the canyon along the closed road. Alternatively, follow Highway 3 north of Elko to Morrissey Road. Follow this road 17 km to the Lodgepole Forest Service Road, which links to the Ram Creek Road at km 25. This road picks up the Wigwam River and follows it to the Ram-Wigwam Creek Recreation Site. Anglers can also find a few river access points established by paddlers along the lower reaches.

Facilities

The **Ram-Wigwam Creek Recreation Site** is a small, partially treed site accessing the Wigwam River.

Wilbur Lake

Location: 6.4 km (4 mi) southwest of Parson
Elevation: 1,277 m (4,189 ft)
Surface Area: 14.6 ha (36 ac)
Mean Depth: 3.2 m (12.2 ft)
Max Depth: 9.1 m (29.8 ft)
Way Point: 116° 40′08″ Lon - W 51° 1′00″ Lat - N

8 Region

Fishing

Situated between the Spillimacheen River and the mighty Columbia River, Wilbur Lake is a small, relatively productive lake set amongst a number of trout infested waters within the general vicinity. Despite the relatively sparse population in this part of the Columbia Valley, the good forest service road access and fishing makes Wilbur Lake a popular destination.

Relatively shallow, Wilbur Lake is rich in all the important trout food sources such as scuds, mayflies, damselflies and dragonflies. It stands to reason that imitating these food sources when casting can reap big rewards for the intrepid angler. It doesn't seem to matter whether you are trolling, spinning, fly-fishing or baitcasting, the trout in this lake will bite quite frequently.

The Freshwater Fisheries Society of British Columbia stocks this lake each spring with yearling rainbow trout. This Pennask strain of trout are feisty fish that feed heavily on chironomids making this lake a fly fisherman's dream lake. Chironomid fishing can be fun, exciting and highly rewarding when executed correctly. In particular, take the time to learn how to fish the pupae stage. When the pupae rise, it is a feeding frenzy for the trout. These hatches tend to happen during mid-day, and while the majority of hatches happen in shallower water (3–5 m/10–15 ft), you may also find them rising in deeper water as well.

There are also several different lures that may work, with spinners and spoons always a good bet, but plugs also seem to work well. The best time to fish Wilbur Lake is in the evening. The rainbows here seem to prefer the mid-level waters when foraging, so stay between the shoreline and the middle of the lake.

Directions

Located in the beautiful Columbia-Shuswap Regional District, approximately 6.5 km from Parson, Wilbur Lake is easily found by following access road signs. From Parson, follow Sanborn Road across the Columbia River to the Crestbrook Main. About 10 km along the main road look for the turnoff on the right that leads down a narrow 2wd access road.

Other Options

To the southeast of Wilbur Lake lies a great selection of trout lakes. Although road conditions vary, most high clearance 2wd and 4wd vehicles should be able to locate these lakes, especially if they are equipped with a Backroad Mapbook and/or the Backroad GPS Maps. Gavia, Joyce, Mitten and Nine Bay are a few of the more popular lakes in the area. All are stocked with rainbow trout and most offer recreations sites from which to base camp.

Facilities

Wilbur Lake Recreation Site sits on the east shore of Wilbur Lake and offers two medium sized campsites with picnic tables, toilet facilities and a rough boat launch. There is also a small dock at the site. The user maintained campsite is free to use; however, please be considerate and pack out what you pack in as there is no garbage collection here.

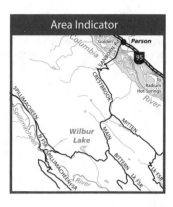

Area Indicator

Species
Rainbow Trout

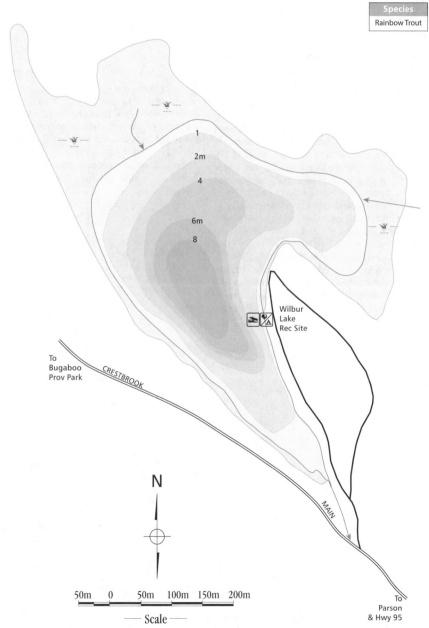

Location: 15 km (9 mi) northwest of Grand Forks
Elevation: 994 m (3,261 ft)
Surface Area: 17 ha (42 ac)
Mean Depth: 8 m (26 ft)
Max Depth: 17 m (56 ft)
Way Point: 118° 32′ 00″ Lon - W   49° 08′ 00″ Lat - N

Fishing

Wilgress is a mid-elevation mountain lake situated between the towns of Greenwood and Grand Forks. It is easily accessed off Highway 3.

The lake is stocked annually with rainbow trout, which provide for good fishing throughout the year. Over the last few years, the Freshwater Fisheries Society of BC has been stocking both yearlings and catchables in the lake. The small lake is also inhabited with a reproducing brook trout population. The brook trout make for an exciting ice fishing season while both species can be caught on the fly or by trolling small spoons and spinners during the ice-free season.

The lake shoreline is muddy and covered in sedge grass, making shore fishing difficult. A boat or float tube is needed to effectively fish the lake. However, the mud and weeds make great insect habitat, and fly-fishing is particularly productive. One area in particular that tends to hold good numbers of trout is the shoal found off the north side of the shallow island located at the south end of the lake.

In the spring, fishing can be quite good on Wilgress Lake using a dragonfly or damselfly nymph. As summer approaches, the trout do revert to the deeper portions of the lake. However, with a little patience, you can be successful even in the summer. Shrimp, damselfly nymphs and leech pattern fished on a full sink line can be effective during the day. As dusk approaches, try sitting about 10 m (30 ft) away from the weed line and cast small nymph patterns or a leech pattern towards the weeds. Using a sink tip with a long leader is often the right combination. Vary your stripping speed until you find a receptive speed that entices regular strikes. This method is a proven winner on this lake in the summer. Of course, if there is a caddis fly hatch on, the fish will start to rise to a dry fly, typically a Tom Thumb or Adams.

Spincasters can try working small lures on light gear along the shoreline. A small Willow Leaf with a Wedding Band can work wonders.

Directions

This pretty roadside lake is located north of Grand Forks off Highway 3. There is a small rest stop off the side of the highway, where you can park and access the lake.

Facilities

Wilgress Lake is the scenic backdrop for a Highway 3 rest area. The rest area has flush toilets along with picnic tables making it a good place to stop for lunch. It is possible to launch small boats in the area. For overnight camping, there is a provincial park at Jewel Lake and a recreation site at nearby Marshall Lake. Roofed accommodation can be easily found in Grand Forks, which is only minutes away along Highway 3.

Other Options

A nearby alternative lake fishing option is **Marshall or Providence Lake**, which can be found off the Phoenix Road. This road climbs past the ski hill and links Highway 3 south of Wilgress Lake with the city of Greenwood to the west. The man-made lake was created by the flooding of an old mine pit and is stocked with rainbow trout. There is a boat launch providing small boat access onto the lake.

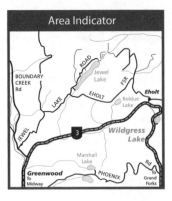

Area Indicator

Species

Rainbow Trout
Brook Trout

Wilgress Lake Fish Stocking Data			
Year	Species	Number	Life Stage
2013	Rainbow Trout	6,500	Yearling/ Catchable
2012	Rainbow Trout	6,000	Yearling/ Catchable
2011	Rainbow Trout	6,660	Yearling/ Catchable

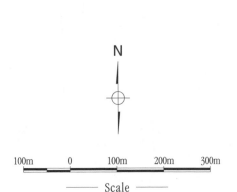

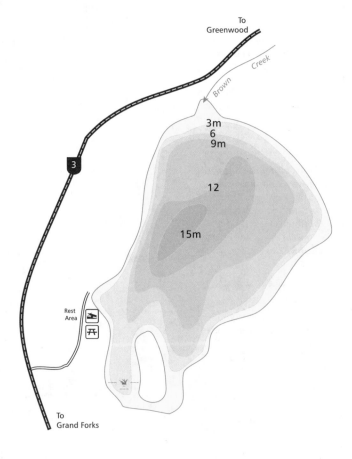

Williamson Lake

Location: 32 km (20 mi) northeast of Rock Creek
Elevation: 1,351 m (4,432 ft)
Surface Area: 13 ha (32 ac)
Mean Depth: 3.5 m (11.5 ft)
Max Depth: 11 m (36 ft)
Way Point: 118° 47' 00" Lon - W 49° 17' 00" Lat - N

8 Region

Area Indicator

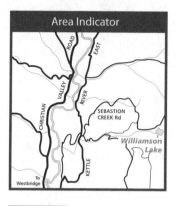

Species
Rainbow Trout

Williamson Lake Fish Stocking Data			
Year	Species	Number	Life Stage
2013	Rainbow Trout	3,000	Fry
2012	Rainbow Trout	3,000	Fry
2011	Rainbow Trout	3,000	Fry

Directions

To find this small lake, first travel to the small settlement of Westbridge via Highway 33. At Westbridge, take the Christian Valley Road north for about 7.5 km. Cross the river to the Kettle River East Forest Service Road, which branches north. After about 11 km, the Sebastian Creek Forest Service Road branches east. This road will take higher into the mountains before eventually meeting the short trail down to Williamson Lake some 10 km later. A 4wd vehicle is recommended to negotiate your way into this remote mountain lake.

Other Options

Williamson Lake is all alone on the east site of the Kettle River Valley, but if you cross over to the west side, you will find over a dozen more fantastic fishing lakes. The lakes lie within the western hills of the valley and are accessible via logging roads and/or hiking trails from either the Christian Valley Road or Highway 33. Almost due west, **Taurus, Moore, Peter** and **Hoodoo Lakes** all offer fishing opportunities for rainbow trout. All but Peter have recreation sites providing access to the lake. Hoodoo and Taurus are also described in more detail earlier in this book.

Fishing

There aren't a lot of lakes east of the Christian Valley Road and the Kettle River and west of Christina Lake. Williamson Lake, located high in the mountains above the river, is one of them.

It is a remote, difficult to access lake that doesn't see anywhere near the same pressure as, say, a Taurus Lake, which is located on the other side of the valley. As a result, Williamson Lake offers good fishing for stocked rainbow trout. Rainbow in this lake are readily taken on the fly and can be caught using spinning gear, although success is usually much slower. Trout average about 0.5 kg (1 lb) in size, although can be found much larger. A 2 kg (4.5 lb) fish is rare but not out of the question.

As a high elevation lake, Williamson isn't ice free until a week or two after the lower elevation lakes melt in May. While the water is still cold, the fishing is quite good, as the trout are usually found in closer to shore, cruising the shoals for food. The lake experiences a prolific chironomid hatch about two weeks after ice-off. Fishing a bloodworm or chironomid pattern on a sinking line will usually work well.

The lake also has decent caddis hatches throughout the summer. At times, the big fish in this lake will be quite aggressive towards dry caddis flies and will create quite a splash as they strike your fly as it is stripped across the surface. Often times, the first splash is the fish trying to drag the insect (or, in this case, your fly) under the surface, and patience is needed. Don't try and set the hook if the fish is merely trying to waterlog the insect. Wait until it comes back to take the lure. Dry fly fishers tend to favour Tom Thumbs and Adams, but an Elk Hair Caddis is a popular alternative.

Facilities

Accessed by a short trail, the **Williamson Lake Recreation Site** offers space for about four tenting parties. If the site is full, you can look for other informal campsites in the area. Please ensure you practice no trace camping and keep the area. There is also a hand launch onto the lake for those willing to carry a pontoon boat or small, electric motor only, boat down to the lake.

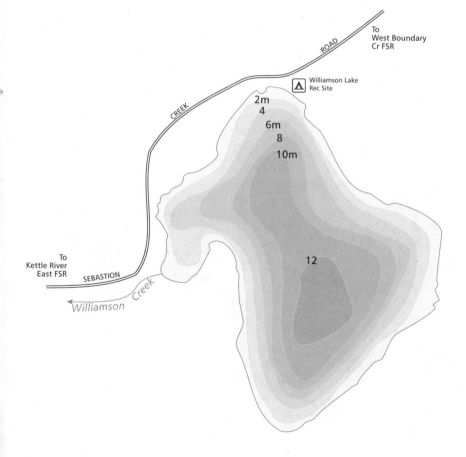

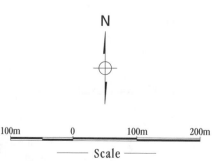

Region 4

Location: 6 km (4 mi) north of Invermere
Elevation: 896 m (2,940 ft)
Surface Area: 12 ha (30 ac)
Mean Depth: 1.6 m (5 ft)
Max Depth: 3.5 m (11 ft)
Way Point: 116° 04' 00" Lon - W   50° 32' 00" Lat - N

Wilmer Lake

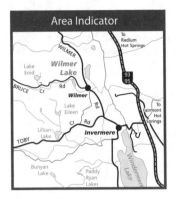

Area Indicator

Species

Rainbow Trout
Brook Trout

Wilbur Lake Fish Stocking Data			
Year	Species	Number	Life Stage
2013	Rainbow Trout	1,000	Yearling
2012	Rainbow Trout	1,000	Yearling
2011	Rainbow Trout	1,000	Yearling

Fishing

Located northwest of Invermere on a good gravel road, Wilmer Lake is quite popular with the locals. The lake is stocked annually with rainbow trout. Until 2001 the lake was also being stocked with brook trout, and, while they are no longer stocking brookies, they have established a self-reproducing population here. Fishing can be good at times for both species.

However, because of the lake's proximity to Invermere and popularity with anglers, the fish caught in this shallow lake are usually quite small. Occasionally, however, the odd big fish can surprise visiting anglers.

Because the lake is so shallow, it can get quite warm in the summer. The best times to fish here are in the spring and fall. Right after ice off, the fish can be found anywhere on the lake, including the extensive shoal areas at the north end of the lake. The fish are quite ravenous at this time, and will take to most anything you offer them that looks like food.

As the water warms up, the fish retreat into the deeper areas of the lake, but before the lake gets too warm, there is a wonderful period of about six weeks when the fishing is outstanding. Fly anglers will have fun matching the many insect hatches. Chironomids or other small nymph flies can produce well. When fishing is slow, try trolling a leech pattern or similar attractor type fly along the drop off zones. During the evenings in late spring, there may even be some dry fly opportunities.

Fishing grinds to a halt over summer, when the water warms up and the fish become quite lethargic. In the fall, the fishing starts to pick up again as the trout are starting to fatten up before the winter. Try using a slightly larger fly in a leech or nymph pattern. Woolly buggers and other attractor patterns can work well, too.

Ice fishing is popular on the lake during the winter months since brook trout are quite active during the winter. Try jigging a small spoon or jig in 1-2 m (3-6.5 ft) of water through the ice for brookies. The odd rainbow trout will hit these presentations as well.

Directions

Travellers can find Wilmer Lake north of Invermere, just outside of the nearby community of Wilmer. From Invermere, follow the Toby Creek Road to the signed road leading to Wilmer. North of Wilmer, the Bruce Creek Forest Service Road travels west passing by the northern end of Wilmer Lake.

Facilities

There are no facilities available at Wilmer Lake, although nearby Invermere has plenty to offer visitors to the area. Accommodations, supplies and helpful advice are only a short drive away.

Other Options

Nearby **Lake Enid** offers a similar fishery to Wilmer Lake. Lake Enid is a popular year round fishing destination that offers stocked rainbow trout and a good population of nice sized brook trout. Both ice fishing and fly-fishing are proven methods on the small lake. There is a good trail system around the lake and a fine picnic area with a small dock for visitors to enjoy.

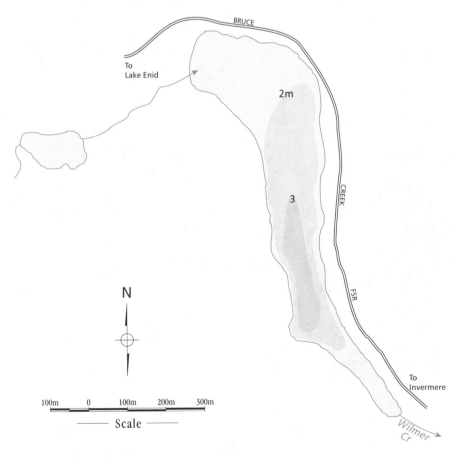

BRUCE

To Lake Enid

2m

3

CREEK

FSR

To Invermere

Wilmer Cr

N

100m   0   100m   200m   300m
— Scale —

Wilson & Little Wilson Lakes

Location: 10 km (6 mi) east of Nakusp

Fishing

Wilson Lake is a long, narrow lake east of Nakusp that is stocked every few years with the Gerrard strain of rainbow trout. Fishing in the lake is generally good for rainbow that average around 0.5 kg (1 lb), although can reach up to 3 kg (6.5 lbs) in size. Kokanee also inhabit the big lake and provide for consistent fishing throughout the season.

Fishing in Wilson Lake is best during the spring, as the heat of summer moves trout to the deeper sections of the lake. Trolling is the main method of angling on the big lake since most of the shoreline is quite steep. Fly-fishing is an effective alternative during the spring and occasionally in the fall.

Nearby Little Wilson Lake is certainly the more scenic of the two lakes as it is set below Mount Fernie. The small lake is also stocked with rainbow trout every few years. Kokanee are found in Little Wilson Lake in good numbers and are best caught on the troll with a small spinner or spoon such as a Wedding Band or Krocodile. Although rainbow can be caught on the fly or by spincasting during the spring from shore, a small boat or floatation device is a definite advantage on this lake.

Some flies that are effective on both Wilson Lakes are the chironomid, leech or bloodworm during the spring. In the summer, attractor type flies such as the Carey Special or Woolly Bugger can produce well with a sinking line. Spincasters can find success with small spinners like the Blue Fox or Panther Marten as well as small spoons such as a Crocodile or Flatfish.

Directions

The Wilson Lakes lie to the east of the town of Nakusp. To find the lakes, follow Highway 6 south to the Wilson Lake Road, which lies just to the north of Box Lake. Wilson Lake Road climbs along Wensley Creek and past the sawmill. At the 7 km mark, take the Wilson Creek Forest Service Road. This 2wd road can be rough in a few sections as it climbs the rocky bluffs south of Wilson Lake before veering north past Little Wilson Lake. Both lakes have recreation sites that provide ample parking for vehicles.

Facilities

The large Wilson Lake is home to two forest recreation sites. The **Wilson Lake West Recreation Site** is a small two table picnic site set on a narrow piece of land below a cliff. A boat launch and small wharf allow anglers to access the lake. **Wilson Lake East Recreation Site** is found on a large open area. This area is well suited for group camping and offers 4 tables, pit toilets and a boat launch for visitors to enjoy. **Little Wilson Lake Recreation Site** is a quiet 3 table site found on a grassy clearing. Hikers will enjoy the old roads and trails around the lake, while anglers and paddlers often take advantage of the boat launch.

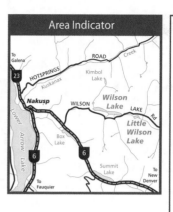

Area Indicator

Species
Rainbow Trout
Kokanee

Elevation: 954 m (3,130 ft)
Surface Area: 140 ha (346 ac)
Mean Depth: 32 m (105 ft)
Max Depth: 85 m (279 ft)
Way Point: 117° 37' 00" Lon - W 50° 14' 00" Lat - N

Little Wilson Lake Fish Stocking Data			
Year	Species	Number	Life Stage
2013	Rainbow Trout	0	Yearling
2012	Rainbow Trout	3,000	Yearling
2011	Rainbow Trout	3,000	Yearling

Elevation: 898 m (2,946 ft)
Surface Area: 27 ha (67 ac)
Mean Depth: 11.9 m (40 ft)
Max Depth: 23.2 m (76 ft)
Way Point: 117° 34' 00" Lon - W 50° 13' 00" Lat - N

Species
Rainbow Trout
Kokanee

Wilson Lake Fish Stocking Data			
Year	Species	Number	Life Stage
2013	Rainbow Trout	2,000	Fry
2012	Rainbow Trout	2,000	Fry

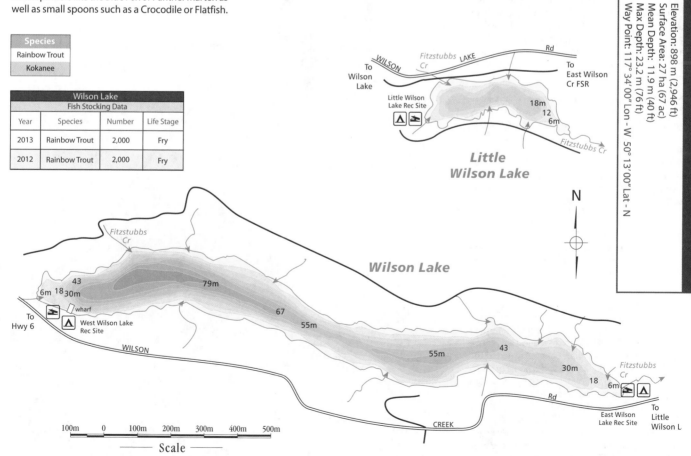

Scale
100m 0 100m 200m 300m 400m 500m

Region 4

Location: South of Invermere
Elevation: 798 m (2,618 ft)
Surface Area: 1,610 ha (3,977 ac)
Mean Depth: 3.5 m (11.5 ft)
Max Depth: 6.5 m (21 ft)
Way Point: 115° 58'00" Lon - W 50° 27'00" Lat - N

Windermere Lake

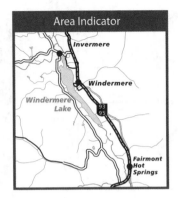

Area Indicator

Species
Bull Trout
Cutthroat Trout
Kokanee
Rainbow Trout

Directions

Found next to Highway 93/95 Windermere Lake is a windy lake that sees most of its recreational activity on the northeast side. Although good access can be found from Invermere or Windermere, the Columbia Lake Indian Reserve and private property limit access to the south of the big lake. To access the lake, boaters should follow the familiar blue boat launching signs from the highway.

Facilities

The city of **Invermere** lies along the northwest shore and the town of **Windermere** is located on the eastern shore. Both communities offer all amenities, such as accommodations, groceries and other supplies. Visitors will find a small marina for boat mooring or launching in Invermere. A paved boat launch can also be found along the northeast side of the lake, just outside of Invermere.

Along with numerous resorts on Windermere Lake, you can find **James Chabot Provincial Park** along the northern shore just outside of the town of Invermere. The park is a popular day-use area that offers a picnic site, sandy beach and playing fields. **Windermere Lake Provincial Park** at the southwest end of the lake is not developed and has no public access.

Fishing

Windermere is about the closest thing to an urban lake as you will find in the Kootenays, with the resort community of Invermere on its northwest shores, and the town of Windermere to the east. As a result, Windermere Lake is a well developed and popular recreation lake. The lake is better known for its water sports rather than fishing but the fishing opportunities should not be overlooked.

The main sportfish species found in Windermere Lake are rainbow trout, cutthroat trout, kokanee and bull trout. Other species that inhabit the lake include bass, perch, char, whitefish and lingcod. Rainbow and cutthroat can reach up to 2.5 kg (5.5 lbs), bull trout to 2.5 kg (5.5 lbs) in size, while kokanee are usually quite small.

Fishing for trout and kokanee in this big lake is best just after ice off when the fish are most active. Trolling is the preferred method of angling in order to cover larger areas of the lake. When trolling try small spoons. During the spring, when water temperatures are uniform, you will have a chance to catch the various species in the upper layer of the lake. Fly-fishing is also possible and can be effective at this time near creek mouths.

For whitefish, the shallows of the lake are best during the spring and fall periods. Whitefish can be caught on spinners and flies. For bass, try jigs, spinners or top water poppers in the shallows during the summer months.

Other Options

Nearby the town of Invermere there are a number of small lakes that would make a good alternative to Windermere Lake. **Lillian Lake** is located to the west via the Toby Creek Road and is home to a day-use recreation site and offers fishing opportunities for stocked rainbow trout and brook trout. Another area lake is **Wilmer Lake** found to the north via the Bruce Creek Road. The small lake is stocked with both rainbow trout and brook trout annually, which provide for plenty of action throughout the year. Both lakes are highlighted in this book.

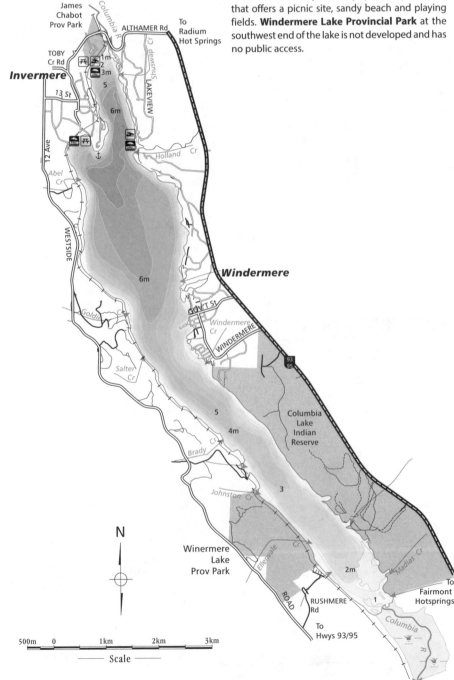

Wolfe & Issitz Lakes

Fishing

The Okanagan is a land of contrasts. Of pocket deserts and giant lakes, of high plateaus and deep valleys, with very little middle ground. And because there isn't a lot of middle ground, there are not a lot of lakes that between the high (at over 1,000 m/3,280 ft) and low (less than 400 m/1,312 ft) elevation levels. But there are some, and these two small lakes located just off highway 3 near Princeton, are representative of the mid-elevation lakes in the area.

Fishing in both lakes can be good on occasion for rainbow trout that can reach up to 1 kg (2 lbs) in size. Wolf Lake also holds a small population of cutthroat. Although there are large baitfish populations in both lakes, rainbow still mainly feed on insect larvae. However, a small streamer pattern or well presented spinner may be the key to hooking into the odd bigger trout looking for larger prey.

As a general rule, though, fly anglers will do better with insect imitations. Early in spring, use a blood-worm or chironomid pattern fished just off the bottom. Leech patterns will also work. As the spring roles on, keep an eye out for other hatches, as trout usually favour the bigger insects. Or maybe they like a little diversity in their menu.

Both lakes are quite shallow, with Issitz Lake being the shallower of the two, and prone to winterkill. Both lakes are shallow enough to be hit quite hard with the summer doldrums. Fishing is fairly uneventful in July and August, and even though the fish will come out to feed in the evenings, they can be very lethargic, offering very little in the way of fight.

In the fall, most of the hatches have ended, and the fish are getting ready for a long cool winter. They will usually chase after slightly larger food, and leeches, nymphs, and attractor patterns like Doc Spratleys are good choices.

Spincasters will do good with small spinners and spoons.

Directions

You can find Wolfe Lake by travelling east along Highway 3 to the Wolfe Lake Indian Reserve. There is a main road off the highway at the reserve that leads to Wolfe Lake. Further to the west of Wolfe Lake lies Issitz Lake, which is accessible via a rough 4wd road that branches off the main access road to Wolfe Lake.

Facilities

There are no facilities available at either of these lakes. For camping accommodations, **Bromley Provincial Park** can be found east of the lakes off Highway 3. The quaint park offers several roadside camping sites in addition to a separate day-use area on the Similkameen River. The town of Princeton is also found to the west and offers several hotels and motels to choose from.

Other Options

West of Issitz Lake, you can find **Lorne Lake** via a rough trail. The lake offers fishing for rainbow trout and success can be quite surprising at times. Between Lorne Lake and Issitz Lake lies **Jackson Lake**. There are also reports of rainbow trout in Jackson Lake, although records are sketchy.

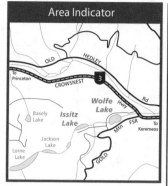

Area Indicator

Species
Rinabow Trout
Cutthroat Trout

Wolfe Lake

Elevation: 595 m (1,952 ft)
Surface Area: 28 ha (69 ac)
Mean Depth: 6 m (20 ft)
Max Depth: 6.5 m (21 ft)
Way Point: 120° 19'00" Lon - W 49° 25'00" Lat - N

Issitz Lake

Elevation: 627 m (2,057 ft)
Surface Area: 16 ha (39 ac)
Mean Depth: 2.5 m (8 ft)
Max Depth: 6 m (20 ft)
Way Point: 120° 21'00" Lon - W 49° 25'00" Lat - N

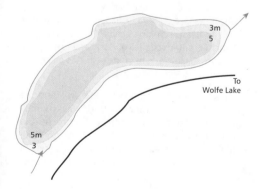

Wolfe Lake Indian Reserve

To Hwy 3

To Issitz Lake

To Issitz Lake

N

100m 0 100m 200m 300m

Scale

Location: 25 km (15.5 mi) north of Kelowna
Elevation: 394 m (1,292 ft)
Surface Area: 916 ha (2,263 ac)
Mean Depth: 16 m (53 ft)
Max Depth: 34 m (112 ft)
Way Point: 119° 23′ 00″ Lon - W 50° 05′ 00″ Lat - N

Wood Lake

Area Indicator

Species
Carp
Kokanee
Perch
Rainbow Trout

Directions

Between Kelowna and Vernon, you will find Wood Lake at the north end of Winfield off the east side of Highway 97. The newly named Pelmewash Parkway (named after the First Nations name for the lake) runs next to the west side of the lake providing good access. There are several launching options including an informal site off the highway and one off Oyama Road at the northeast end of the lake. Be careful when launching larger boats at either site as the shoreline is very shallow.

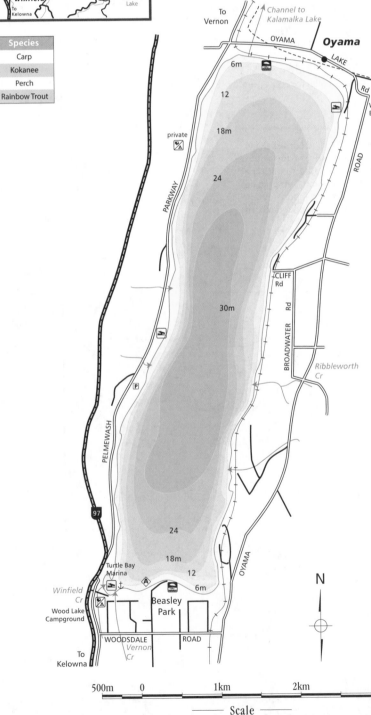

Fishing

Wood Lake lies in the heart of the Okanagan and is a very popular destination throughout the year. During the summer most of the activity is watersport based with skiers, boarders and power boaters ruling the roost. Anglers will find better luck fishing here in early spring (just after ice off), in the fall and again when (and if) the lake ices over in the winter.

Best known for its kokanee, Wood Lake is also home to a few rainbow trout, perch, chub and carp. However, the kokanee fishery has suffered recently due to poor survival rates in 2011 and there is now a limited season along with special restrictions on these prized sportfish. Hopefully the hard work of the Oyama Fish and Game Club to help improve the spawning grounds will help restore this once great fishery.

Trolling for kokanee and rainbow trout along the western shore and southeast corner of the lake can be quite productive. Another decent spot is near the rock outcroppings near the highway boat launch. Shore anglers will find a few parkway pullouts where they can fish from the rocky shore.

Troll slowly at various depths using light gear, such as Willow Leaf and Wedding Band, chartreuse or red spinners or small Lyman lures. Fly-fisherman may target these same areas trolling using a fast sinking line with various coloured Doc Spratleys and weighted leeches. Other areas worth considering are along the eastern shore line, around mid-way across from the western boat launch. Look for ant or mayfly hatches, especially near the eastside creek mouths, during the months of May and June.

Some of the best fishing comes in early winter shortly after the ice forms. Try using a glo hook, or ¼ ounce coloured jig. Often the hook is tipped with powerbait, maggot or mealworm. Most ice fisherman will be concentrated around the middle portions of the lake, fishing at different water depths. Please be careful, since the lake does not always freeze long enough to fish safely throughout the winter. Many years, it doesn't free solid at all.

Check the current regulations before heading out.

Facilities

Visitors can find an informal, but often busy launching site off Pelmewash Parkway about halfway down the lake. A more developed site is found at the northeast end of the lake, off Oyama Lake Road. Regardless of which site you use, parking is limited and the shallow nature of the launches makes it a challenge to launch bigger boats.

Those looking to camp in the area will find the **Wood Lake Campground & Marina** has recently been opened at the south end of the lake next to the **Turtle Bay Marina**. In addition, there are private trailer parks and campgrounds on the west side of the lake. Big public beaches also grace both ends of the lake.

Xenia Lake

Location: 22 km (13.5 mi) northeast of Grand Forks
Elevation: 1,240 m (4,068 ft)
Surface Area: 15 ha (38 ac)
Mean Depth: 10.5 m (34 ft)
Max Depth: 18 m (59 ft)
Way Point: 118° 20' 00" Lon - W 49° 12' 00" Lat - N

Region 8

Fishing

Xenia Lake is a hard to access lake found within the boundaries of Gladstone Provincial Park. The lake is stocked regularly with rainbow trout that provide for some good fishing for trout that can reach up to 1 kg (2 lbs) in size. Spincasters and fly-fishers will find better results fishing from a float tube or a similar device you can carry into the lake.

Due to the high elevation of the lake, fishing can be productive throughout the summer season, making this remote lake a decent angling choice. If you visit the lake in summer and the fishing is relatively slow, try in the evening a few hours before dusk. As the evening approaches, the rainbow in this lake will often start feeding heavily on almost anything at times.

Caddis flies are a good choice throughout the summer, although there are good mayfly hatches well into the summer. A blue dun has often been the fly of choice on Xenia Lake during mayfly hatches. Although the trout in the lake are not usually that fussy, you will definitely improve your success rate with a closely matched fly to the hatch.

Trolling is a popular method of fishing; we've heard of people having good success trolling lime green flies just under the surface, which just goes to show how indiscriminate the fish are. A leech pattern trolled slowly or a streamer pattern like a Muddler Minnow trolled fast can work, too. Anglers with spinning gear can troll a variety of small spoons or spinners. Remember, the lighter the lure, the better the fight.

Other Options

The best alternative to Xenia Lake in the area is the **Granby River**. This beautiful River is easily accessible throughout its length via paved and good gravel forest service roads providing easy access to the river. The river holds both rainbow trout and brook trout and is a real pleasure to fish, especially on the fly. Check the current regulations to ensure the river is open to fishing. Hikers often continue onto the north end of **Christina Lake**. Bring along your fishing road and test your luck for bass and trout near the many creek mouths at this end of the big lake.

Directions

North of Grand Forks, the lake is best accessed off the Granby Road. Follow the paved road for approximately 21 km to the Miller Creek Forest Service Road. Head east along this logging access road to the Xenia Branch logging road. This branch road is quite rough in sections and requires a 4wd vehicle. Depending on current conditions, it may be necessary to hike a portion of the road. It is 6 km (3.6 mi) from the start of the Xenia Branch to the lake, although most people should be able to drive to within 1 km (0.6 mi) of the lake.

Facilities

There is a splendid campsite (formerly a Recreation Site, now a part of **Gladstone Provincial Park** available along the north end of Xenia Lake. There are a few campsites available as well as picnic tables and outhouses. Hikers often utilize the site as a staging area before they climb over the Christina Range and down to Christina Lake. If you can get your vehicle to the lake, there is a rough cartop access area available.

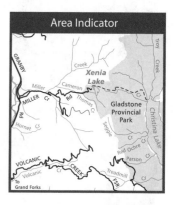
Area Indicator

Species
Rainbow Trout

Xenia Lake Fish Stocking Data			
Year	Species	Number	Life Stage
2013	Rainbow Trout	3,000	Fry
2012	Rainbow Trout	3,000	Fry
2011	Rainbow Trout	3,000	Fry

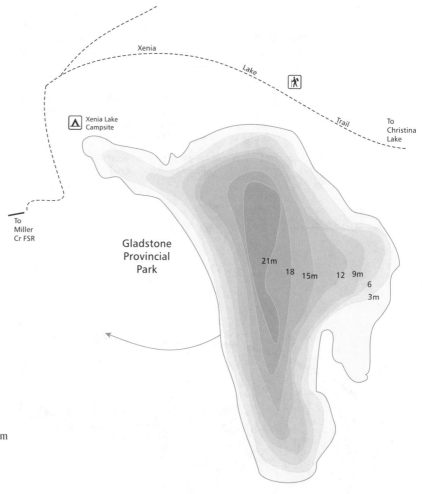

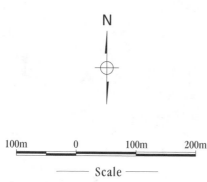

Scale
100m 0 100m 200m

Location: 25 km (15 mi) southwest of Penticton
Elevation: 750 m (2,460 ft)
Surface Area: 35 ha (86 ac)
Mean Depth: 20.1 m (66 ft)
Max Depth: 40 m (130 ft)
Way Point: 119° 45'00" Lon - W   49° 20'00" Lat - N

Yellow Lake

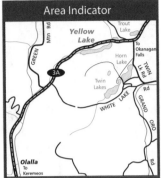

Area Indicator

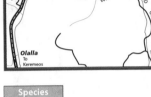

Species	
Rainbow Trout	5
Brook Trout	20
Kokanee	5

Yellow Lake Fish Stocking Data			
Year	Species	Number	Life Stage
2013	Rainbow Trout	15,000	Yearling
2013	Brook Trout	10,000	Fingerling
2012	Rainbow Trout	15,000	Yearling
2012	Brook Trout	15,000	Fingerling
2011	Rainbow Trout	15,000	Yearling
2011	Brook Trout	15,000	Fingerling

Fishing

This popular lake lies alongside Highway 3A between Keremeos and Penticton. With easy access and plenty of trout the lake sees more than its share of anglers. As a result, the Freshwater Fisheries Society of BC stocks the lake heavily with rainbow and brook trout. There are also yellow perch roaming the lake, but it is hoped that these non-native fish will not recover from the major kill off of all fish in 2006.

Trolling is a popular angling method on the lake since the lake is quite narrow and over 1 km (0.6 mi) in length. If the wind is not too strong, fishing from a float tube, canoe or small boat can also be a good way to work the shoals. Trollers can work the drop off area with light tackle in the spring and fall. One area of interest that should be tried near is the small 6 m (19 ft) shoal area that lies near the middle of the lake. This area should be a prime cruising area for trout throughout the year, especially in the spring and fall. As the heat of the summer warms the water, work the deeper areas of the lake.

Fly anglers can try their luck on the ample shoal areas around the lake. Chironomid patterns can be quite productive during the spring but do not rule out the normal nymph patterns, such as the damselfly and dragon fly nymph or variations of those.

Shore fishing can be quite productive from either end of the lake at the rest areas, or off Highway 3A. Light spinning gear with lures like Dick Nite, Panther Martin, wedding bands or even a worm and bobber should serve anglers well.

Fishing in the lake is best in spring and fall since the lake suffers from the summer doldrums and is prone to algae blooms that make the fish muddy tasting. Ice fishing is also popular here, but anglers should be wary of the aerator on the lake.

There is an engine power restriction on Yellow Lake. Be sure to check the regulations for details.

Directions

Yellow Lake stretches along the south side of Highway 3A between Penticton and Keremeos. Parking and access is available at the two small rest areas that are found at either end of the lake.

Facilities

There are no overnight facilities available at Yellow Lake, although the rest areas at either end of the lake. The western site is a bit more developed with picnic tables, washrooms and a better boat launch for cartop boats. The eastern end of the lake is more of a highway pull-out but there is a rustic area to launch small boats as well. For overnight accommodation you can travel south to the town of **Keremeos** or north to the city of **Penticton**. Both have plenty to offer in the way of motels and various other accommodations.

Other Options

The **Twin Lakes** are easily accessible southeast of Yellow Lake off the Twin Lake Road. The lakes are stocked regularly with rainbow trout and brook trout, providing for a decent sport fishery. There is a resort and boat launch at **Nipit Lake**, the eastern most Twin Lake.

N

100m   0   100m   200m   300m
— Scale —

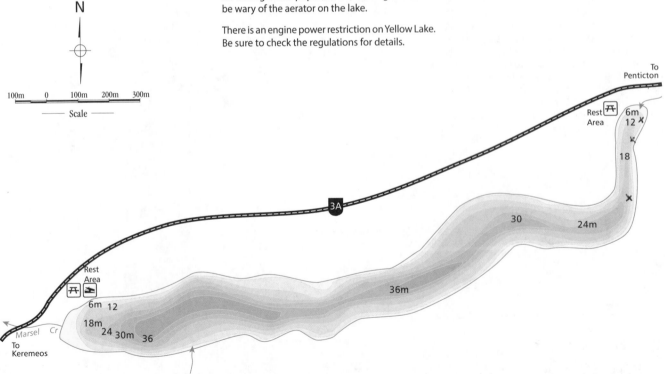

Fishing Tips & Techniques

Bait (Still) Fishing

Probably the simplest way to catch fish and introduce young people or novice anglers to sport fishing is by a technique known as still fishing. When still fishing from the shore or a boat, the angler casts out and waits for a bite. Still fishing can be done with or without the use of float. Floats (bobbers) can be attached to the line so the baited hook stays suspended in the water. The depth can be adjusted by simply sliding the float up or down the line.

Casting just beyond the drop-off or around shoreline structure is very effective. In smaller lakes, a one metre (3-5 ft) leader with a size 8-12 hook is recommended. Weights should be avoided if possible, as they tend to scare off the fish. If you do need a weight, use 1-3 small split shot weights at least 30 cm (12 in) above the hook. Most fish tend to bite on worms and a single egg or roe. Other effective baits include maggots or artificial bait such as powerbait. The trick is to use the lightest line and smallest hook possible.

Ice Fishing

Many of the large, low elevation lakes in Southeastern BC do not ice up, and many high elevation lakes are not accessible. However, there are still quite a few places to try ice fishing in the area. Generally speaking, ice fishing is possible from the end of December through to early March as long as the ice is safe (there will need to be at least 15 cm/6 in of ice to bear weight safely). Jigging a small spoon or other attractant lure up and down has become one of the most popular fishing methods since live bait is not permitted in BC. Also, watch for winter closures.

Rainbow trout tend to slow down in the winter, and ice fishing can be slow, especially later in the winter. Eastern Brook trout, on the other hand, need less oxygen and remain active throughout the winter. If you are looking for a better ice fishing experience, we recommend going to a lake that holds brookies.

Jigging

Jigging can be an effective method of fishing if you can find where the fish are congregating. Jigging is a popular method of fishing though the ice in winter, although it is also widely used for bass fishing throughout the open water season. Jigging is essentially sitting in a prime location, such as near underwater structure and working a jig head and body up and down to entice strikes. Outside of the traditional jig head and (where permitted) bait set up, you will also see anglers jigging spoons and other similar type lures. The great thing about jigging is that when the fish are in the area it can work very well.

Spincasting

Spincasting is another popular and effective fishing method for all types of water. Essentially, spincasting is the process of casting a line from a rod with a spinning reel. The set up is quite simple making it easy for anyone to learn how to fish and have fun at it.

Most tackle shops offer good reel and rod combinations. It is recommended to go with a lightweight rod and 8-pound test or lighter, but this can vary obviously depending on what you are fishing for. The key is to have line light enough to cast and tough enough to withstand trolling and landing some fairly large fish. A good idea is to get an open face reel with removable spools. One spool could have light line (6 lb test or lighter) for small lakes and another have heavier line (8 lb or higher) for rivers and trolling.

Trolling

Trolling is the mainstay of bigger lakes, but also a popular alternative for many smaller lakes. It is a popular fishing method because you are able to cover large areas of water, increasing your chances of success on a lake. Ideally you should use a longer, stiffer rod than traditional spincasting set ups. Eight-pound test is okay for small lakes but you will need heavier line for bigger lakes, especially if using a downrigger.

In addition to the tips under each fish species, we have provided more tips and techniques below. This section is designed to give you a better understanding of the various types of fishing styles as well as a much more elaborate breakdown on fly-fishing. Whether new to the sport of fishing or a wily veteran, we recommend reading through this section to pick a few tricks. We also recommend stopping in at the local tackle shop before heading out. They are the ones that know the local tricks and what has been producing well recently.

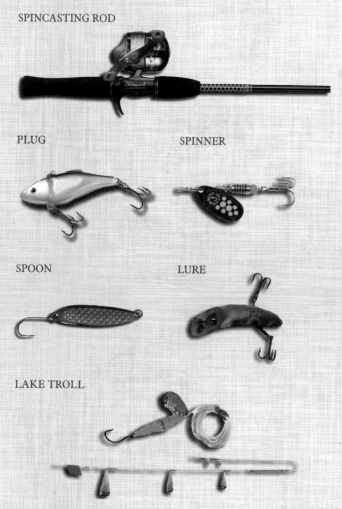

SPINCASTING ROD

PLUG   SPINNER

SPOON   LURE

LAKE TROLL

It is best to troll near structure, along the drop-off or near a mid-lake shallow, such as a sunken island. On larger lakes, trolling for rainbow is very effective. Concentrate on points, inflow creeks or bays. A depth chart or depth finder will help you pinpoint these locations. Lake trolls are popular because of their effectiveness and ease of use on both big and small lakes. These usually consist of a Willow Leaf or Ford Fender with a short leader and a small lure like a Wedding Band or similar along with bait where allowed. There are many shapes, sizes and colours of lures that have proven effective trolling for trout and dollies. Some of the most common trolling lures include Flatfish, Krocodile or Little Cleo spoons. Fly fishers usually troll a leech pattern, particularly in murky water. Other all purpose trolling flies are Carey Specials, Woolly Buggers, and Doc Spratleys. Work the area just off the drop-off in a figure-eight pattern to vary the direction, depth and speed of the fly. When trolling for cutthroat, try a silver Muddler Minnow or other baitfish patterns. In the fall or winter, troll a streamer type fly pattern

Fly-fishing is easily the most popular or at least most talked about fishing method of fishing in BC. It is also the hardest technique to master. Perhaps it is the challenge that attracts so many people to devote so much time. Or maybe it is the fact that once you have caught a fish on fly gear, everything else pales in comparison. Whether it is a small trout or an acrobatic salmon, the shear excitement of landing a fish with fly-fishing gear is exhilarating.

FLY FISHING ROD

BEAD-HEAD NYMPH

CAREY SPECIAL

CHIRONOMID

DOC SPRATELY

like a bucktail quickly behind the boat. As the water warms, try an Apex, Lyman plug or flasher with a hoochie in the 10-30 m (30-90 ft) depth for bigger fish.

Fly-Fishing

Fly-fishing is easily the most popular or at least most talked about fishing method of fishing in BC. It is also the hardest technique to master. Perhaps it is the challenge that attracts so many people to devote so much time. Or maybe it is the fact that once you have caught a fish on fly gear, everything else pales in comparison. Whether it is a small trout or an acrobatic salmon, the shear excitement of landing a fish with fly-fishing gear is exhilarating.

Fly-Fishing Equipment

Basically, there are three parts to a fly-fishing outfit: the rod, the reel and the line. Rods come in a variety of lengths and weights, depending on your size and the size of the species you intend to fish. As an example, a 9 ft, 6-weight rod would be an ideal set up for everything from trout to salmon up to about 5 kg (11 lb) in size. Longer rods are helpful in casting and helping manipulate flies into position on streams, especially on rivers and streams.

To handle bigger fish, fly anglers need a much heavier rod such as an 8 or 9-weight rod. Many fly anglers will have at least two if not three or more rods of different size and weight in order to maximize their fishing experience. Essentially, a smaller size and weight rod would be used for fishing small trout or panfish, while the longer heavier rod would be used on rivers for big salmon.

When picking up a fly reel, the vast majority of reels (or any that are worth buying) will be weighted similar to the way rods are weighted. The reels are actually made to fit the appropriated rod. The difference in the weights of reels is mainly the size of the reel, since larger rods will be loaded with thicker line; therefore, the reel has to be a little larger to hold the increased line size. Also, the reel itself is often physically weighted to suit the rod weight so that the casting motion is balanced properly when casting your fly line.

When fly-fishing lakes, it is necessary to have a floating line in addition to a medium or fast sinking line. The floating line presents dry flies, as well as subsurface wet flies. Dry line can also work well with weighted wet flies. However, a more popular subsurface option is using sink tip line, which is a combination of sinking and floating line where just the end of the fly line sinks. This type of line has a number of advantages, one being the ability to present subsurface flies while retaining the visibility of the fly line on the surface. This helps dramatically in spotting strikes, especially when fishing for trout. One of the best times to surface fish is during the mayfly and caddis hatches, however, trout usually prefer streamers and subsurface flies since they are very reluctant to strike the top of the water.

Medium sinking lines are ideal for fishing wet flies such as nymphs or chironomid pupae near the bottom. The medium sinking line offers the best control when attempting to fish a specific depth. If you do not have a medium sinking line, you can use a longer leader with some weight on your dry line. With a properly weighted fly or leader, this method can produce similar results. This type of presentation is ideal for working a particular depth, such as along a drop-off or along weed beds. Dragonfly, damselfly and even leech patterns can be worked quite effectively this way.

Fast sinking lines are ideal for trolling. If you are not familiar with the lake, trolling a fly is a good way to start. This allows you to cover a lot of distance searching for the ideal spot on the lake. Also, trolling is most effective on lakes with a low population of fish or during the summer doldrums. Woolly Buggers, streamers and leeches are all good all purpose trolling flies. Work the area just off the drop-off in a figure-eight pattern to vary the direction, depth and speed of the fly.

Regardless of which line you run with, you will also need backing and leader. The backing is designed to fill up the spool, as well as to act as reserve for when that fish goes on a 100 metre dash. Most people keep 100–150 metres of backing on their reel. The leader is a thinner monofilament line that attaches to the thick fly line to the fly. Leaders have a thicker butt that tapers to a thin tippet.

Flies

There are numerous books on fly-fishing techniques and how to choose the best fly for the particular season; however, it is really quite simple. Match the hatch! What you want to do is use a fly that most approximates the insect or baitfish on which the sportfish are feeding.

To determine this, spend some time observing the aquatic insects at the lake and try to determine what the fish are rising to and how the insects are moving in the water. If you can not see the adult insect on the water surface then try using a small fine net to scoop up the insects. If you catch a fish, you can also use a throat pump to physically see what the fish are eating. Once you have discovered what type of insect the fish are feeding on, you should try to determine how the insect moves in the water so you can imitate it. For example, is the adult insect sitting motionless on the water or is it rapidly flapping its wings?

Here is a list of recommended flies to include in your fly box. By no means is this exhaustive, but rather a good base to work from:

Bead Head Nymph is a variation of the halfback or pheasant tail nymph patterns, but is often a little more versatile. The fly is already weighted so it can be fished easily in streams and lakes with either sinking or floating line. The bead head also is an attractant that often glistens in the water attracting attention of predatory fish.

Carey Special is versatile enough to be used in both lakes and streams. Try size 4-8 for trout or 6-12 for salmon in red, green or brown. One of the most popular lake patterns in BC, it is a great searching pattern that can simulate many insects, including dragonfly, mayfly and caddis nymphs, as well as leeches. Smaller flies using a simple strip retrieve with sinking line is best in lakes, while moving water requires a bigger fly that is drifted with quicker strips.

Chironomid (Midge) has quickly become one of the most important flies in the fly box of a BC lake angler. Chironomids can be found in every lake in the BC and varies in size and colour depending on the lake and time of year. The fly must always be worked very slowly in the part of the water column that depends on what stage of the main hatch is taking place. The big hatches are mainly in the spring, although they are present all year round.

Doc Spratley is a general-purpose fly that can imitate most insects and a number of leeches. Perhaps the most popular fly in BC, the large sizes can imitate the dragonfly or damselfly nymphs, while smaller versions are like chironomid pupae. Black is the most versatile, but red, green and brown work, too. Depending on what you want to imitate dictates the method of presenting this fly. If you are looking to imitate a dragonfly nymph, stripping the fly in a consistent manner would be appropriate. On the other hand if you are looking to imitate a smaller nymph pattern, a shorter stripping retrieve may be required.

Dragon and Damselfly Nymphs vary in size and colour. Since they are found everywhere, they should certainly be part of every fly box. There are literally dozens of patterns that are used throughout the province and your best bet to know what works is to inquire locally before you head out. These nymphs are often worked deep and even off bottom for cruising trout.

Elk Hair Caddis is a specific caddis imitation fly that revolutionized top water caddis fly fishing. Depending on the time of year your presentations will vary with this type of fly. In the early part of the season, hatching caddis will often flap along the surface attempting to break away. Therefore, your presentation should imitate this. Later in the season when caddis are laying eggs, they will literally smack the water and trout will pounce on them. They key is to be observant of the hatch and what the flies are doing.

Leeches are a definite must in every fly box since they are found in virtually all lakes in BC. Leech patterns are versatile and great for searching lakes. At times, this is all trout are feeding on. Even if they are feeding on something else, they will rarely pass up a well-presented leech.

Mayfly patterns vary dramatically in size and colour. During a hatch, trout can sometimes be so picky that they will literally pass up your mayfly if it is a size or two too small or a wrong colour. However, the mayfly hatch is a big part of the open water season and a good variety of this fly is needed in your box, especially early in the season.

Muddler Minnow imitates a minnow in distress and is the ideal meal for a wide variety of fish. In general, larger fish seem to like bigger presentations of this fly. The fly is mainly worked below the surface although some anglers have been known to put floatant on them and work them on or just below the top of the water for big aggressive fish.

Scud (Shrimp) patterns, similar to chironomids, vary greatly in size and colour depending on the lake. A good rule of thumb is to use whatever colour the lake bottom is. Working the fly needs patience. It should be allowed to sink close to the bottom and retrieved with slow short strips followed by a short pause. Working closer to shore is better, since shrimp are most often found frolicking here.

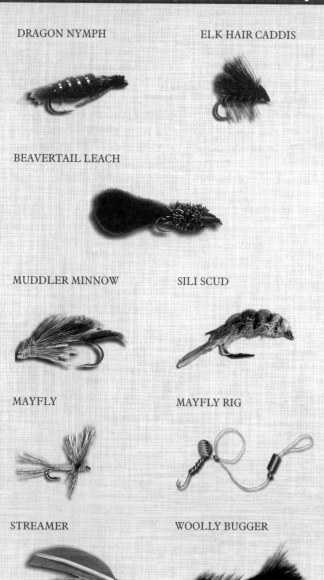

DRAGON NYMPH   ELK HAIR CADDIS

BEAVERTAIL LEACH

MUDDLER MINNOW   SILI SCUD

MAYFLY   MAYFLY RIG

STREAMER   WOOLLY BUGGER

Streamer is a good versatile pattern for all sportfish species as it imitates baitfish or larger meals that most sportfish thrive on. This fly can be of almost any size and colour, but the key is that it should have a long sleek profile in the water and is used to fish subsurface. While you will see bright coloured streamer patterns out there, typically for Ontario lakes you are looking for a pattern that imitates baitfish.

Tom Thumb is one of the more popular dry flies in British Columbia. Size is very important to match the current hatch, especially if surface fishing. While the fly can imitate a number of different insects, it is most commonly used as a caddis imitation.

Woolly Bugger is a good versatile pattern for cutthroat, salmon, steelhead and trout. This fly imitates larger meals such as a baitfish or leeches and can be effective in both streams and lakes. While the most popular colours are olive and black, other colours and variations, such as a bead head, can create a unique fly for that unique situation.

Fishing Tips & Techniques

BC Interior Hatches and Patterns: From ice-on to ice-off, fly patterns of choice should coincide with these major hatches. Chironomid (midge) hatches peak in mid May and continue through June before returning at the end of September. The next insect to hatch is the mayfly, which traditionally runs from May through to mid July. Damselfly patterns are effective in June to August while dragonfly patterns can be used from June to the end of September. Evenings from mid-June to early July can produce some exciting top water action for caddis flies, while terrestrials, such as ants and grasshoppers, hatch in the mid-summer. Water boatman or water bug patterns are best right after ice-off and again in mid-September through October. Finally, shrimp and leech patterns can be productive all year round, as there is not a set hatch period for them.

March- April:	· Dragonfly nymph
All chironomid stages	· Caddisfly/Sedge
· Mayfly nymph	· Shrimp
· Shrimp	· Leeches
· Leeches	· Terrestrials
· Water boatman	
	August:
May:	· Damselfly nymph
·· All chironomid stages	· Dragonfly nymph
· Mayfly nymph	· Caddisfly/Sedge
· Dragonfly nymph	· Shrimp
· Shrimp	· Leeches
· Leeches	· Terrestrials
June:	**September:**
· All chironomid stages	· All chironomid stages
· Mayfly nymph	· Dragonfly nymph
· Damselfly nymph	· Shrimp
· Dragonfly nymph	· Leeches
· Caddisfly/Sedge pupae	· Water boatman
· Shrimp	
· Leeches	**October:**
	· Dragonfly nymph
July:	· Shrimp
· Mayfly nymph	· Leeches
· Damselfly nymph	· Water boatman

Fishing Small Lakes

On smaller lakes, the predominant fish species are rainbow, brook and cutthroat trout. If you are looking for more success and less size on your day out on the water, small lakes are a good bet as there is less water to cover. Fishing near structure such as logs and weeds, shoals or at the edge of a drop-off produces the best results. Food sources also congregate around weeds and inflow or outflow streams and in the thermocline. The thermocline is the area of the lake between the warm surface water and the cold water. Concentrate your efforts in these areas to improve your chances of angling success.

A good way to explore a new lake is to use searching type lures or flies and work them near the subsurface structures. Along with your depth chart map, it is a good bet to invest in a depth finder. Depth finders can give even more detail to the underwater structure that maps simply cannot provide. Another tool that can help when fishing lakes or streams is a good pair of polarized glasses. Polarized lenses will help you spot fish or underwater structure that may not show up on a map or depth finder.

A universal set up that will attract all species is a lake troll with a short leader and a Wedding Band or similar with bait. Flatfish, Krocodile or Little Cleo spoons are trolled, while fly fishers usually troll a leech pattern, particularly in murky water. Other all

purpose trolling flies are Carey Specials, Woolly Buggers, and Doc Spratleys. Work the area just off the drop-off in a figure-eight pattern to vary the direction, depth and speed of the fly. When trolling for cutthroat, try a silver Muddler Minnow or other baitfish patterns.

If you are fishing from shore, try casting along the shore or towards a fallen log, weed bed or drop-off. Use the countdown method to find where the fish are holding. Casting almost any small spinner or spoon with some bait (worms are preferred) can prove successful, but watch for bait restrictions. Favorites are the Panther Martin (silver or black), Mepps Black Fury or Blue Fox. As for lures, a Deadly Dick, small Dick Nite, Flatfish or Kamlooper also work well. The good ol' fashion bait and bobber can be very effective, while fly anglers should pay attention to the current hatch.

As the water warms up and the fishing slows during the late spring, move to a higher elevation lake. By continually moving to higher elevations you can continue to fish the first few weeks of prime time period right until the lakes begin to cool down in the fall. And as the water gets too cold up high, begin moving down to the lower elevations. Most of the high elevation walk-in lakes offer good fly-fishing during their limited season, which lasts from late June until October. Another nice thing about these lakes is the fish are more active when the light penetrates the water. This makes an 11 o'clock arrival a good thing. If the water is murky, you might as well move on, as the lake is experiencing turnover and the fish will rarely bite.

Fishing Bigger Lakes

Big lakes can be intimidating. This is where the map comes in really handy. Study your map for structure and devise a game plan prior to arrival. Once at your spot, use your depth finder to hone in on those really unique structure areas and work them hard before heading on to another area.

On larger lakes, trolling for rainbow is very effective. Concentrate around creek or river mouths. Fish seem to hold around the drop-offs in these areas because of the large amount of feed available. Drop-offs near cliffs or rock walls are also good areas to focus your efforts. In spring, fall or winter, troll a streamer type fly pattern quickly behind the boat so they skim off the surface can produce some big trout. Muddler Minnows, Polar Bear or bucktails are popular choices. As the water warms, try an Apex, Lyman plug or flasher with a hoochie in the 10–30 m (30–90 ft) depth. For deep trolling, downriggers with the aid of a heavy weight will enable you to troll your lure deep enough to find holding areas.

If fishing from shore, working the drop-off around creek mouths is your best bet. Bait balls (a large cluster of worms or eggs and a hook) can be fantastic for Dolly Varden and sometimes rainbow. During the summer a float with a grasshopper can also land you a nice trout.

Fishing Streams & Rivers

Rivers and streams can be a challenge to fish, but at the same time they offer other opportunities that lakes do not. Most notably, hot spots in rivers can be very easy to find as they are often at the bottom of a small waterfall, or the slack water next to the fast water. The main problem with bigger rivers is getting your presentation out far enough from shore to where the fish are holding. The easiest way to overcome this problem is to use a boat if possible. This way you can find seams and pools where fish are holding and get your presentation to where the fish are instead of fighting the current with your cast from shore. You can also access some of the more remote areas that shore anglers are not fishing to find some of the more productive holes.

Of course getting a boat onto smaller streams is often not possible. In these cases, a good set of waiters and river shoes can make a big difference in being able to get to the good holes. To work these streams effectively, you need to sneak up on holes to avoid being detected by trout. Work every pocket, pool or seam no matter the size. Some of the biggest fish are hiding in the most unlikely places. Many of the smaller rivers in the area run quite warm in summer, and wading can be a refreshing break from the heat of the day. Bring along a hat that you can dip in the water, too.

Please Note: There are regulations imposed for many of the lakes and streams in order to preserve the quality of the resource. Always check the regulations before fishing!

Releasing Fish- The Gentle Way

There is a growing trend among anglers to catch and release, unharmed, a part of their allowable catch. As well, more restrictive regulations on specific waters can severly limit the angler's allowable harvest.

A fish that appears unharmed may not survive if carelessly handled, so please abide by the following:

1- Play and release fish as rapidly as possible. A fish played for too long may not recover.

2- **Keep the fish in the water as much as possible.** A fish out of water is suffocating. Internal injuries and scale loss is much more likely to occur when out of water.

3- Rolling fish onto their backs (while still in the water) may reduce the amount they struggle, therefore minimizing stress, etc.

4- Carry needle-nose pliers. Grab the bend or round portion of the hook with your pliers, twist pliers upside down, and the hook will dislodge. Be quick, but gentle. **Single barbless hooks are recommended,** if not already stipulated in the regulations.

5- Any legal fish that is deeply hooked. Hooked around the gills or bleeding should be retained as part of your quota. **If the fish cannot be retained legally, you can improve its chances for survival by cutting the leader and releasing it with the hook left in.**

6- If a net is used for landing your catch, it should have fine mesh and a knotless webbing to protect fish from abrasion and possbile injury.

7- **If you must handle the fish, do so with your bare, wet hands (not with gloves).** Keep your fingers out of the gills, and don't squeeze the fish or cause scales to be lost or damaged. It is best to leave fish in the water for photos. If you must lift a fish then provide support by cradling one hand behind the front fins and your other hand just forward of the tail fin. Minimize the time out of the water, then hold the fish in the water to recover. If fishing in a river, point the fish upstream while reviving it. When the fish begins to struggle and swim normally, let it go.

Go fishing before their childhood becomes the one that got away.

This season, share the joy and relaxation of fishing with your kids. Or introduce a friend to the sport. Before you go, check out the latest stocking reports, pick up tips from the pros and learn how to get your licence at **gofishbc.com**

Freshwater Fisheries Society of BC

IMPORTANT NUMBERS

Fish and Wildlife
BC Fishing Information ....www.BCFishing.com
.... www.sportfishing.bc.ca
Freshwater Fisheries Society of BC .... www.gofishbc.com
Department of Fisheries and Oceans ....www.pac.dfo-mpo.gc.ca
Current salmon and steelhead regulations ....www.env.gov.bc.ca/fw/
............................www.pac.dfo-mpo.gc.ca/recfish/default_e.htm
E-Licensing.................... www.fishing.gov.bc.ca
BC Wildlife Federation.................... www.bcwf.bc.ca
Observe, Record and Report....................1-877-952-7277

General
BC Ferries ....www.bcferries.com
....................................1-800-223-3779
Local Ferry Information
   Galena Bay....................(250) 837-8416
   Kootenay Lake....................(250) 229-4215
   Needles....................(250) 269-7222
Highways Report....................www.drivebc.ca
....................................1-800-550-4997
To Report Forest Fires 1-800-663-5555
....................................*5555 (cellular phones)
Tourism BC ....www.hellobc.com
....................................1-800-435-5622
Updates....................www.backroadmapbooks.com
Weather Conditions............. www.weatheroffice.ec.gc.ca/canada_e.html

Sustainable Resource Development
Ministry of Forests ....www.for.gov.bc.ca
   Arrow Boundary Forest District (Castlegar)............... 250-365-8600
   Kootenay Lake Forest District (Nelson) ....(250) 825-1100
   Columbia Forest District (Revelstoke) 1-866-837-7611
   Okanagan Shuswap Forest District (Salmon Arm)...... 250-558-1700
   Rocky Mountain Forest District (Cranbrook) ....(250) 426-1700
   Southern Interior Forest Region....................(250) 828-4131

Clubs & Organizations
BC Parks/Ministry of Environment....................www.bcparks.ca
Glacier & Revelstoke National Park ....(250) 837-7500
Kootenay National Park....................(250) 347-9615
Okanagan District Office....................250-494-6500
Thompson River District....................250-851-3000
Yoho National Park....................(250) 343-6783
Park Reservations ....www.discovercamping.ca
....................................1-800-689-9025